DRUG ABUSE PREVENTION WITH MULTIETHNIC YOUTH

D1211428

DRUG ABUSE PREVENTION WITH MULTIETHNIC YOUTH

EDITORS
Gilbert J. Botvin
Steven Schinke
Mario A. Orlandi

SAGE Publications
International Educational and Professional Publisher
Thousand Oaks   London   New Delhi

For information address:

SAGE Publications, Inc.
2455 Teller Road
Thousand Oaks, California 91320
E-mail: order@sagepub.com

SAGE Publications Ltd.
6 Bonhill Street
London EC2A 4PU
United Kingdom

SAGE Publications India Pvt. Ltd.
M-32 Market
Greater Kailash I
New Delhi 110 048 India

Printed in the United States of America

Library of Congress Cataloging-in-Publication Data

Main entry under title:

Drug abuse prevention with multiethnic youth / edited by Gilbert J.
  Botvin, Steven P. Schinke, Mario A. Orlandi.
      p. cm.
    Includes bibliographical references and index.
      ISBN 0-8039-5711-4 (alk. paper). — ISBN 0-8039-5712-2 (pbk.,
  alk. paper)
      1. Minority youth—Drug use—United States—Prevention. 2. Youth—
  Drug use—United States—Prevention. 3. Drug abuse—United States—
  Prevention. I. Botvin, Gilbert J. II. Schinke, Steven Paul.
  III. Orlandi, Mario A.
  HV5824.Y68D7713   1995
  362.29'17'08693—dc20   95-13489

This book is printed on acid-free paper.

95 96 97 98 99   10 9 8 7 6 5 4 3 2 1

Sage Production Editor: Diane S. Foster

Contents

PART III: Promising Approaches to Drug Abuse Prevention

Preface

Drug abuse continues to be a major public health problem of huge proportions. Over 430,000 people die each year from cigarette smoking alone. Add to that the mortality caused by alcohol abuse, and the total increases to over 650,000. These are stunning statistics for just two of the many types of drug abuse. The death toll mounts further if mortality related to the use of cocaine and other illicit drugs is included along with that resulting from drug-related homicide and suicide. Although the problem of drug abuse is one that affects all segments of society in this country, nowhere has the ravages of drug abuse been more severe than among racial/ethnic minority groups. Yet relatively little is known about the prevalence, trends, and etiology of drug abuse in these populations. Even less is known about the type of interventions likely to offer the most promise in reducing drug use/abuse.

Adolescent drug use in the United States is the highest in the industrialized world, despite roughly a decade-long downward trend in the use of marijuana and most other illicit drugs during the 1980s and early 1990s. Notwithstanding expenditures of billions of dollars by federal, state, and local agencies to interdict the flow of illicit drugs in this country and discourage youth from getting involved with drugs, recent national survey data indicate that drug use among our nation's youth is once again on the rise. This new upward trend in drug use appears to be relatively broad, including adolescents from different age groups, social classes, geographic regions, and racial/ethnic populations. Concern that these increases in drug use by junior and senior high school students may herald the beginning of a new drug epidemic gives new urgency to the development of effective prevention methods.

Although public information campaigns and school-based drug education programs have been conducted for more than two decades, rigorous
evaluation research is a relatively recent phenomenon. Initial evaluation
studies were methodologically weak, relied on interventions that were
largely atheoretical, and generally failed to include measures of drug use
behavior. Consequently, little credible evidence was available to support the
effectiveness of any approach to drug abuse prevention or to guide the development of new prevention models. Public policy concerning how best to
prevent drug abuse was formulated in a virtual vacuum, and the development
of preventive interventions was based largely on hunches, suppositions, and
informed guesses.

The field of drug abuse prevention research began toward the end of the
1970s with the seminal work of Dr. Richard Evans, a social psychologist
from the University of Houston, who developed a theory-based intervention
founded on what has come to be known as the social influence model. This
new prevention approach was tested in a small but well-designed study that
demonstrated its effectiveness in reducing cigarette smoking among junior
high school students. The success of this study in producing behavioral
effects set off a flurry of prevention research activity. Since then, prevention
research studies have become larger and more methodologically sophisticated. A substantial research literature has emerged over the years that
consists of high-quality studies demonstrating reductions in the incidence
and/or prevalence of tobacco, alcohol, and marijuana use.

Considerable progress has been made over the past 20 years in identifying
effective drug abuse prevention approaches. Although most of these approaches
have been developed and tested in school settings, research has also been
conducted with families and in community settings. Along with an accumulation of empirical evidence concerning the effectiveness of promising drug
abuse prevention methods, considerable information has emerged from high-
quality longitudinal studies concerning the etiology of drug abuse.

Yet despite these exciting advances, a major deficiency in our current
state of knowledge concerns the etiology and prevention of drug abuse
among racial/ethnic populations.

The purpose of this book is to help fill that gap. This book grew out of
a conference held in June 1993 at Cornell University Medical College's
Institute for Prevention Research in New York City. The conference was
sponsored jointly by Cornell University and the National Institute on Drug
Abuse. The conference was designed to be a small "expert" conference that
brought together leading prevention researchers and individuals actively
involved in working with minority youth. In addition to the individuals who
contributed chapters to this book were approximately 30 researchers, community leaders, policy makers, and government employees, who all had

one thing in common—a concern for drug abuse prevention with multi-ethnic youth.

The book begins with a section on ethnicity and ethnic identity. Trimble's chapter (Chapter 1) discusses the important issues of ethnicity and ethnic identity, and their relationship to drug abuse prevention research. In this chapter, he cautions against the use of "ethnic glosses" to group individuals together by virtue of their ethnic group status alone without paying adequate attention to important differences in their ethnic identity and other characteristics. A similar caution is expressed by Collins (Chapter 2). Robert and Mindy Fullilove (Chapter 3) contribute a provocative chapter that focuses on the issue of race and some of the challenges facing researchers who plan to work with minority populations.

The second section of this book focuses on drug use prevalence rates and observed racial/ethnic differences in adolescent drug use. Wallace, Bachman, O'Malley and Johnston (Chapter 4) offer data testing several hypotheses for apparent differences by race/ethnicity, particularly concerning the finding that rates of drug use are *lower* among some racial/ethnic groups than among whites. Kandel (Chapter 5) also explores apparent patterns and paradoxes concerning ethnic group differences in drug use, with a focus on cocaine use. This section also includes several chapters dealing with the etiology of drug use among ethnic minority youth. First, Newcomb (Chapter 6) reviews the literature on risk and protective factors and highlights similarities and dissimilarities among ethnic groups. Rodriguez (Chapter 7) then describes the results of analyses using causal modeling methods to examine drug use among Puerto Rican adolescents and discusses implications for prevention. The final chapter Félix-Ortiz and Newcomb (Chapter 8) in the section, focuses on cultural identity and drug use among Latino and Latina adolescents.

The third and final section of the book focuses on models of drug abuse prevention that either have been demonstrated to be effective with ethnic minority youth or have promise. Botvin (Chapter 9) reviews the school-based drug abuse prevention literature and describes work conducted at Cornell's Institute for Prevention Research with African American and Latino youth. Pentz (Chapter 10) also focuses on developing community support and collaboration when conducting drug abuse prevention research with multiethnic communities, as well as, the need to adapt prevention research methods. Schinke and Cole (Chapter 11) also discuss drug abuse prevention efforts in community settings and present data from their own recent work in New York City. Dusenbury and Diaz (Chapter 12) discuss the process of developing preventive interventions for ethnic minority youth, using their work with homeless youth in New York City. Kumpfer and Alvarado (Chapter 13) summarize the relevant literature concerning family influences on adolescent drug use and describe promising family intervention approaches. Finally, Kim, Coletti, Williams, and Helper (Chapter 14) present information on prevalence rates, prevention models, and cultural factors that need to be understood when working with Asian Americans. Taken together, the material in this book provides important information concerning ethnicity, etiology, and prevention models necessary for conducting high-quality prevention research or identifying promising methods for preventing drug abuse with multiethnic youth.

GILBERT J. BOTVIN

PART

I

Ethnicity and Ethnic Identity

Toward an Understanding of Ethnicity and Ethnic Identity, and Their Relationship With Drug Use Research

Joseph E. Trimble

Omnia mutantur, nos et mutamur in illis.—

As nearly as any chronicler can determine, most cultural groups worldwide have used plants and their derivatives to alter consciousness. Typically classified as psychoactive agents, such substances have been integral components of religious and healing ceremonies, with the most potent often being used by shamans and the high priests of religious sects to place them in contact with a higher power and promote communication with the spirit world. Access and use of psychotomimetic substances have therefore been tightly regulated and controlled.

No one is certain how many psychotomimetic plants have existed in the many millennia of human history. Nonetheless, use of such plants undoubtedly can be traced to our ancestral beginnings. Ethnobotanists estimate there are about 5,000 species containing psychoactive properties that can be found

AUTHOR'S NOTE: I wish to extend my gratitude to the staff at the Tri-Ethnic Center for Prevention Research at Colorado State University for their assistance and support in writing this chapter. Support also was provided through grant support from the National Institute on Drug Abuse (P50 DA07074) and the National Institute on Alcohol Abuse and Alcoholism (AA 08302). I especially thank Scott Bates for his thoughtful and skillful analysis of the data presented in this chapter and Brad Plemons for his assistance in editing and compiling the references.

in most areas of the world. About 20 of the species are very widely used. Ethnobotanists claim that in Central and South America alone, nearly 120 plants can be found that can induce psychotomimetic states—yet only 20 of these species can be found elsewhere in the world. Today four of the more potent species—coca, poppy, cannabis, and tobacco—are cultivated commercially (see Brecher & Editors of Consumer Reports, 1972; Efron, Holmstedt, & Kline, 1967; Inciardi, 1992).

Numerous literary sources and archeological findings suggest that during the early history of humankind, alcoholic-based beverages, where present in a society, were widely used and abused, especially in Old World countries. In contrast, there is little evidence suggesting that psychoactive drugs were flagrantly abused on any large scale. But widespread recreational use of psychoactive drugs in North America and Europe began occurring shortly after the middle of the 19th century. In fact, casual use may have been normative. As Brecher et al. (1972) pointed out, "The United States of America during the nineteenth century could quite properly be described as a 'dope fiend's paradise'" (p. 3). Opiates were the major drug of choice, and were principally taken as elixirs prepared by ersatz physicians. Opium use levels were so high, and use was rampant across so many groups, that several municipal and state governments felt compelled to enact laws prohibiting it. For example, an 1875 San Francisco ordinance was exacted to prohibit opium smoking by Chinese immigrants (Helmer, 1975).

By contemporary standards, late 19th- and early 20th-century drug use in the United States was limited. Indeed, opiates were bottled and cut with herbs, water, flour, and other nontoxic substances to lure the consumer to the drug. Opiate amounts varied. Uncertainties about the contents of over-the-counter medicines and those of the street corner "snake oil salesman" to a large extent prompted the U.S. Congress in 1906 to pass the Pure Food and Drug Act. The act stipulated that medicine claiming to contain amounts of opiates had to state so in precise words. Opiate use seemingly declined somewhat and, for many West Coast immigrant Chinese, went underground. But continuing opiate use following the 1906 legislation apparently was enough of a threat and a nuisance that in 1914 Congress passed the Harrison Narcotic Act making opiate use illegal. The passage of the act relegated opiate use to the criminal realm, thereby adding yet another coin to the underworld. Opiate users and their suppliers were criminals, whereas alcoholics were pitied and tolerated.

The criminalization of opiates and, soon after 1914, other drugs gave the courts and the dominant Euro-American public much fuel for campaigns to rid the streets, if not the country, of undesirables. African Americans, Mexican Americans, Chinese Americans, and American Indians were singled out in one way or another from all other ethnic and nationalistic groups as prime targets for control. Such phrases as *drunken Indian, cocainized Negros, Mexican marijuana menace,* and *dope fiends* emerged from the popular press of the early 20th century to refer to the substance abuse problems of these groups (Banks, 1990; Helmer, 1975; Inciardi, 1992). Exaggerated but nonetheless allegedly documented accounts sensationalized the cocaine use among African Americans, the marijuana "menace" among Mexican Americans, opiate addiction among Chinese, and alcohol abuse among American Indians. Journalistic accounts further fanned public concern and led to more pressure to regulate and control opiates and alcohol. "Control," argued Walker (1981), "offered a means of protecting cherished values for a primarily white and putatively mobile society" (p. 14), and "legislation, whether prescriptive or proscriptive, marked progress against social unrest, class conflict, and moral decay" (p. 14). The general public was becoming increasingly intolerant of crimes committed ostensibly by presumed drug- and alcohol-crazed racial groups.

For the most part, "The conflict over social justice is what the story of narcotics in America is about" (Helmer, 1975, p. 33). African Americans, Chinese Americans, and Mexican Americans were overrepresented in many drug-reporting accounts between about 1900 and the late 1930s. In fact, these groups are still overrepresented in some contemporary drug use reporting systems (Trimble, 1991). The justice meted out against ethnic minority drug offenders created more than the usual outcomes. For the Chinese and Mexicans, the new drug laws actually suppressed participation in the labor force (Helmer, 1975; Morgan, 1990). For African Americans, the laws led to more incarcerations and, for a few, lynchings and violence carried out by vigilante-type white supremacist groups (Banks, 1990). As Morgan (1990) forcefully asserted, "It is vital to understand that the importance of crusades against minorities lies not only in their victimization, but also in the misrepresentation and falsification of their culture" (p. 250). The history of drug use among America's ethnic minorities is understood best by examining the manner in which policy and drug laws were used for oppressive purposes and to further social and class conflict.

Now we are approaching the end of the 20th century: *Omnia mutantur, nos et mutamur in illis;* all things are changing, and we are changing with them. Drug use among ethnic minorities continues to be a point of concern and indeed has generated much more public concern than at any other period in America's short history. Journalists continue to decry the assumed epidemic-like use rates, and the public is calling for more control. Both pleas have stimulated more interest from public agencies at all levels, private foundations, and planners and researchers. Tucker (1985) observed that "there is no lack of commentary on the substance abuse problems faced by ethnic minorities in the United States" (p. 102). Instead of emphasizing that ethnic minority drug use is stimulated by some seemingly elusive endemic character flaw or genetic predisposition, researchers and scholars are searching for sociocultural factors to explain, treat, and/or prevent drug problems. The contents of this book bear testament to their interest.

The fundamental objective of this chapter is to provide a foundation and framework concerning the relationship between ethnicity and drug use behavior. After a short historical prelude, the chapter explores the definitions of ethnicity, selected research findings showing the relationship between ethnic identification and drug use, various procedures for measuring ethnicity, and the role of culture in understanding drug use. A concluding discussion section sets a tone and direction for future research and development in the field.

Ethnic Awareness in America

Social science interest in ethnicity, especially as a potential explanatory variable, began in the late 1950s (see Katz & Taylor, 1988). Interest was fueled by at least two fundamental concerns: (a) the notion that America was a melting pot of different nationalities, ethnic groups, and religious affiliations, and (b) concerns about pluralism and integration. According to Steinberg (1981), the era "witnessed an outbreak of what might be called 'ethnic fever'" in which "the nation's racial and ethnic minorities sought to rediscover their waning ethnicity and to reaffirm their ties to the cultural past" (p. 3). Integration and the melting-pot notion were challenged, if not vilified.

Ethnic pride became a banner to symbolize allegiance, affiliation, and group solidarity. Glazer and Moynihan (1970), in their influential text, *Beyond the Melting Pot,* reinforced "ethnic fever" and the assertions of ethnic minorities. Ethnic identity and pride, however, were well entrenched principally among European descendants—ethnicity, whatever it meant, had not disappeared in the process of settling into a New World life.

The growing interest and seemingly thriving enthusiasm associated with the ethnic construct also brought out the critics. The "new ethnicity," as some preferred to call it, was criticized as divisive, inegalitarian, and racist (Morgan, 1981). Patterson (1977) asserted that ethnicity was an artifact created by hidebound intellectuals who preferred to live in a mythical past. Assimilationists and pluralists also added the argument that true ethnic identities vanished as group after group internalized an elusive American norm; the longer the intergroup contact, the greater the likelihood that all homogeneous ethnics would blend into the mainstream of American society. Moreover, it was argued that as ethnic segregation diminished, so would the saliency of the importance of ethnic identity and group solidarity. Still others maintained that the culture-specific behaviors, values, and lifestyles claimed by ethnic minorities were manufactured contrivances that had no real factual substance.

Interest in the issue of ethnicity has continued to increase in recent years, as demonstrated by the increase in journal articles and books devoted to the subject. However, discussions of ethnicity frequently occur in a highly charged atmosphere. Its very mention, especially in academic circles, sparks discussion about how, without segregation, ethnicity would not survive. Such discussion can and often does turn to the possibility that Americans tend to overemphasize and exaggerate the existence and beneficence of ethnicity (Yinger, 1986). Phrases like *imagined ethnicity* and *pseudoethnicity* are used interchangeably to describe incidents in which some ethnic factor is used to justify an action. In this vein, Gordon (1978) asserted that "students of ethnicity run the risk of finding ethnic practices where they are not, of ascribing an ethnic social and cultural order where they do not in fact influence the person" (p. 151). Consequently, critics may argue about some fanciful line that separates ethnic influences from nonethnic ones. This argument begs the question, When can behavior, personality, values, attitudes, and so forth be attributed to ethnic factors? If an ethnic attribution is not possible or discernible, then what sociocultural and psychological influence can indeed account for the phenomenon?

Greeley (1974) asked an important related question: "Why . . . is ethnic identity important and useful for some Americans?" (p. 298). One relatively benign answer is that ethnicity serves as a convenient form of differentiation: of minorities (from the dominant society and from one another—American Indians from African Americans, Puerto Ricans from Cuban Americans, Japanese Americans from Chinese Americans, etc.); of neighborhoods and communities (Navajo Nation reservation, Chinatown, Japantown, Little Italy, etc.); and of individuals who do not appear to subscribe to a generalized set of norms.

Ethnicity and ethnic identity are not likely to vanish: All countries differentiate their residents on some ethnic factor, and North America may well be a geographic area in which such differentiation is most prevalent. Barth (1969) argued that ethnic boundaries, especially for European immigrants, are more permeable in the United States than in less industrialized societies; however, the "ethnic distinctions are quite . . . often the very foundation on which embracing social systems are built" (p. 10). Ethnic identity is the core of the interpersonal system of many Americans, most notably the major ethnic minority groups, and for that to remain reasonably stable, a social support system must be present.

Interest in counting America's ethnic groups, ancestral origins, and national backgrounds has intensified in recent decades. The U.S. Bureau of the Census has recently expanded its census form to capture more specific information on ethnic identity and ancestral and ethnic origin. On the 1980 census form, ethnic identity was captured with the basic question, "Is this person . . ?" and a list of 14 ethnic groups following the prompt. Three items later was the question, "Is this person of Spanish/Hispanic origin or descent?" (U.S. Bureau of the Census, 1980). In addition, the respondent was asked to indicate the ancestry of each person living in the residence. On the 1990 census form, the question on Hispanic origin was repeated. But in place of the previous question on ethnicity, the Bureau chose to focus on race—respondents were asked to report the race with which they most closely identified (U.S. Bureau of the Census, 1992). Later on in the form was the question, "What is this person's ancestry or ethnic origin?" As a result of these revisions, the Bureau of the Census generated more information on ethnic and racial variables than at any other time in the history of the country.

The results of the 1990 census reveal that the percentages of those identifying with ethnic and racial minority groups increased over the 1980 census percentages. "The rate of increase during the decade for each [of the major ethnic minority groups] exceeded the rate of increase for whites" (U.S. Bureau of the Census, 1992, p. 1). In addition, the proportion of the population marking the "other race" category increased over the 10-period.

Results from the 1990 census-form ancestry item generated interesting findings. German, Irish, English, African American, and Italian were the five most frequently cited ancestral groups, with those of German ancestry accounting for about 58 million of the 1990 U.S. population and those of Italian background accounting for about 15 million. Of specific interest was the finding that some 9 million respondents indicated an American Indian ancestral origin, although only 2 million placed themselves in the "American Indian, Eskimo, and Aleut" ethnic identity category. In contrast, some 24 million indicated that they were of African American ancestry compared to some 30 million who identified themselves as "Black or Negro" on the race item. Taken together, these findings provoke questions about the meaning of self-identification with a racial category and declared ancestry or ethnic origin. For the American Indian category, some 6.2 million more self-identified on the ancestral and ethnic origin item than for the race item (the latter serves as the value from which the actual population count is estimated). Some 6 million more people identified as "Black or Negro" than self-identified as African American on the ancestral origin item. For both ethnic categories, which set of figures more accurately represents the true population count? Did the respondents understand the meaning of the respective ethnic labels? Did some African Americans reject the "Black/Negro" label?

And for American Indians, do the ancestral and ethnic origin findings suggest that there are actually more Indians than reported in the 1990 census? A portion of the problem may rest with the subjective meaning a respondent assigns to an ethnic category, and if that is the case, then the actual estimates may be skewed. Recognize that, with the exception of the "American Indian, Eskimo, and Aleut" label, there are no legal or stringent definitions of America's other ethnic minority groups, and that although the "American Indian, Eskimo, and Aleut" label may have a legal basis, even that category is interpreted and defined differently (see Trimble, 1992; Trimble & Fleming, 1989).

Census counts of ethnic minorities and racial groups belie the importance that each individual places on the behaviors and cognitions of each group. Self-identification is a nominal procedure that at best provides an enumeration. In this procedure, an individual is given a choice that is highly subjective, and for those of mixed racial ancestry, the choice may be more delicate than for those of an exclusive ancestry. Yet enumeration has its value. Without significant information about ethnic and cultural behaviors and cognitions, little can be done with census tallies.

Ethnicity, Ethnic Groups, and Ethnic Identification

The social and behavioral science literature abounds with ethnic terms. Certainly, anthropology contains the most references and uses of the concept, followed by sociology and history. Within the past decade or so, interest in ethnicity and related topics has slowly and maybe even painfully been integrated into psychology. In fact, it now pervades almost all academic disciplines in such forms as ethnobotany, ethnoscience, ethnomedicine, and ethnopsychiatry. Fusing the prefix *ethno-* with the name of an orthodox academic discipline is presumably intended to convey the notion that the discipline attends to something cultural. Yet the terms *cultural* and *ethnic* have different though overlapping meanings.

Adding "ethnic" or "ethno-" to the name of a discipline to broaden its inclusiveness conveys the implication that the amended field in some way previously ignored cultural lifeways and thoughtways. Consider the term *ethnomedicine*—few would argue that all cultures use medicine to heal biological and psychological problems. The recent addition of *ethno* therefore implies that the major field previously ignored or did not view indigenous medical practices as legitimate or worthy of serious study. Nonetheless, ethnomedicine is a subfield, and to set it apart from its parent implies that the researcher and practitioner focus on medicine by emphasizing the knowledge and practices of specific cultural groups. All orthodox disciplines should be inclusive and attend to the knowledge and practices of all humanity—differences indeed exist, and to capture their uniqueness among distinctly different groups by adding *ethno-* or *cultural* does provide a focus.

The term *ethnic* has Latin and Greek origins—*ethnicus* and *ethnikas* both mean "nation." It can be and has been used historically to refer to people as heathens. The related word *ethos,* in Greek, means "custom," "disposition," or "trait." *Ethnikas* and *ethos* taken together can therefore mean a band of people (nation) living together who have common customs.

The linguistic origins of the term *ethnic* convey the import of the rapidly emerging interest in ethnicity, ethnic groups, ethnic identification, and ethnic labeling. Theoretical debates abound about the concepts, how they should be assessed and measured, how groups should be labeled and studied, and how theoretical and research findings should be applied. Unfortunately, much of the research concerning ethnic constructs is devoid of the richness of the debates. Many researchers are almost too casual and carefree about the constructs' use, citing few if any articles concerning controversies and theoretical opinions. A summary of opinions about the concepts may help substantiate their depth and complexity.

ETHNICITY

Several sociologists, anthropologists, and historians have written extensively on ethnicity (for reviews, see Steinberg, 1981; Thompson, 1989; van den Berghe, 1981). The many theoretical positions embraced and advocated range from those that base ethnicity on shared experiences and worldview to those that base it on kinship. Barth's perspective represents the former, in which it is the native's worldview that defines relationships, boundaries, lifeways, and thoughtways (Barth, 1969). The latter, a sociobiological perspective, is most fervently advocated by Pierre van den Berghe (1981), who maintained that "ethnic and racial sentiments are extensions of kinship sentiments" (p. 18) and that "descent . . . is the central feature of ethnicity" (p. 27). To support his argument, he claimed that "there exists a general predisposition, in our species as in many others, to react favorably toward other organisms to the extent that those organisms are biologically related to the actor" (p. 19).

The manifold literature on ethnicity shows how complex the concept is. In its broadest form, the term refers to "any differentiation based on nationality, race, religion, or language" (Greeley, 1974, p. 291). At a slightly more precise level, some theorists prefer to define it as "a collectivity within a larger society having real or putative common ancestry, memories of a shared historical past, and a cultural focus on one or more symbolic elements defined as the epitome of their peoplehood" (Schermmerhorn, 1969, p. 123).

Using this definition, Greeley (1974) maintained that individuals can be classified "into groups on the basis of shared, observable traits to include shared physical characteristics, shared historical experiences, and shared religious identities" (p. 188). Note that Greeley, a sociologist, placed an emphasis on using traits to classify individuals; presumably individuals also use the traits to classify and identify themselves with a distinct ethnic group.

Another sociologist, Milton Yinger (1986), pointed out that

> ethnicity has come to refer to anything from a sub-societal group that clearly shows a common descent and cultural background . . . to persons who share a former citizenship although diverse culturally . . . to pan-cultural groups of persons of widely different cultural and societal backgrounds who . . . can be identified as "similar" on the basis of language, race or religion mixed with broadly similar statuses. (p. 23)

Although the many components of Yinger's conceptualization are inclusive and indeed comprehensive as a starting point, he preferred to distinguish between groups by referring to their unique social and biological characteristics. To form a more concise understanding of the influences of the two characteristics, we must find a shared genetic cohort of descendants who share recognizable and acknowledged geopolitical boundaries.

Geopolitical boundaries change, and consequently, individuals will change their ethnic allegiance and identification as they move from one environment to another. Also, changes in affiliation and corresponding changes in the ethnic core can produce "pseudoethnicity" (or fictional ethnicity). An ethnic core may be exaggerated and contrived to form "imagined ethnicity," in which the relationship between the primordial ethnic core and the emergent form is blended.

ETHNIC GROUP

Ethnic group is yet another elusive concept that increases the complexity of the definitional problem. Yinger (1986) preferred to use the term *ethnie* instead of *ethnic group*. He maintained that for an ethnie (ethnic group) to exist, three conditions must be present: (a) A segment of a larger society must be viewed by others as sharing and demonstrating a distinct language, religious preference, and ancestral homeland; (b) group members must concur with their designation and shared common characteristics; and (c) members, in general, must participate in the events, ceremonies, and activities embedded in their cultural lifeways and thoughtways.

Similar definitions have been offered by others. An ethnic group, maintained Feagin (1978), is one that "is socially distinguished or set apart, by others and/or by itself, primarily on the basis of cultural or nationality characteristics" (p. 9). Thompson (1989) defined an ethnic group as a culturally distinct population that can be set apart from other groups. Such groups, Thompson stated, engage in behaviors "based on cultural or physical criteria in a social context in which these criteria are relevant" (p. 11).

The presence of ethnic groups in any society can vary. In some societies or countries, certain groups are numerically in the minority—hence, such groups have been labeled *ethnic minority groups*. Willemsen and van Oudenhoven (1989) defined ethnic minority groups as those that "differ from the majority of the people in the country or society in which they live. Differences may refer to language, race or religion or a combination of these characteristics" (p. 11). Moreover, these differences may derive from a history of oppression, power imbalances, and a lack of economic opportunities.

In some countries, all ethnic groups are in the minority; some ethnic groups may be numerically in the minority but lack a history of oppression and prejudice, and yet reside in a country with oppressed ethnic groups. Some ethnic groups may be labeled minority but may forcefully reject the category because of its pejorative connotations. To refer to an ethnic group without considering its full range of influences, characteristics, and history would misrepresent and distort its essence.

Smith (1991) proposed a definition in which an ethnic group is viewed as a reference group in which "people who share a common history and culture . . . may be identifiable because they share similar physical features and values, and . . . identify themselves as being a member of that group" (p. 181). Identity development and the texture and disposition of groups constituted the core of Smith's definition. Hence, she preferred to use the term *ethnic reference group,* and in so doing, drew attention to the "individual *in* his or her group and cultural setting . . . and [the] cultural setting relative to its members" (Sherif & Sherif, 1964, pp. 36-37). The reference group serves to set goals and regulate behavior in that individual members gauge their identity and belonging on the basis of responses from like-minded members. Outsiders undoubtedly have their own social and biological benchmarks blended in with stereotypes about ethnic group membership; reference group members, too, have their own standards. Consensual agreement between in-group and out-group members varies and may even be quite discrepant; similarly, agreements will vary within each group. Smith (1991) extended this point to claim that "an ethnic group may be described as a *process* [emphasis added] of self and other ascription" (p. 182).

Reliance on self- and other-attributions in an ethnic context presents further problems. Greeley (1974) suggested that identification may not reflect one's ethnic origins: One may claim ancestry but not identify with the group (recall that more Americans in the 1990 census claimed Native American ancestry than identified as Native Americans). Greeley then posed even more complex questions: "How do those of mixed ethnic origins determine which identification they are going to choose? [And] to what extent does such a choice lead to attitudes and behavior that the chooser defines as being pertinent to the identification he has given himself?" (p. 310).

Ethnic origin, ethnic culture, ethnic identity, and ethnic group membership (ethnic reference group) are common dimensions of ethnicity, yet each is unique. They are also interrelated contextual processes that define components of ethnicity. Simply put, *origin* refers to heritage and ancestral history, *ethnic culture* refers to lifeways and thoughtways passed on from one generation to the next, and *ethnic identity* and *ethnic group membership* are interrelated individual and social categorizations. Ethnic identity has the most relevance and pointed value for social and behavioral scientists, and in recent years, the concept has attracted a good deal of attention in drug and alcohol studies.

ETHNIC IDENTITY

Definitions of *ethnic identity* vary according to the underlying theory embraced by researchers and scholars. Social and behavioral science interest in identity focuses on discovering causal or correlational factors with other variables. To advance the discovery process, measurement scales are developed, tested, refined, and applied to scores of conditions, circumstances, and individuals. Even though ethnic identity is a process, many researchers approach the concept as if it were a static phenomenon. Moreover, without giving much serious thought to the topic, many researchers actually use the term *ethnicity* instead of *ethnic identity,* assuming that they are one and the same. They are not.

Often ethnic identity is associated with one's presumed ethnic personality. In this context, one's personality is inferred from one's identity with an ethnic group. Here again, identifiable cultural factors can influence personality development, but inferring a similarity between identity and personality corrupts both constructs.

Ethnic identity typically is viewed as an affiliative construct: An individual is viewed by others as belonging to a certain group. An individual can also choose to associate with a group, especially if he or she is of mixed heritage. Affiliation can be racial, natal, symbolic, and/or cultural (Cheung, 1993). Racial factors are physiognomic and physical characteristics, and natal factors are "homeland" (or ancestral home) origins of individuals and of their parents and kin. Symbolic affiliation usually implies that individuals choose their ethnic identity by choosing cultural markers that typify or exemplify an ethnic group (e.g., holidays, foods, clothing, artifacts), even though deeply-structured cultural elements of that group may have little influence on their behavior. Cultural factors are the specific lifeways and thoughtways of an ethnic group and are probably the most difficult to assess and measure (see Cheung, 1993, for more details). In conceptualizing ethnic identity, racial, natal, symbolic, and cultural factors must be considered to achieve a full and complete understanding of the construct.

Cheung (1993) defined ethnic identification as "the psychological attachment to an ethnic group or heritage" (p. 1216) and thus placed the construct in the domain of self-perception. Saharso (1989) extended the definition to include social processes that involve one's choice of friends, selection of a future partner, perception of one's life chances, and reactions of others in one's social environment. Both definitions involve boundaries distinguishing "self" and "other," but Saharso's definition includes the component of others' attributions. An individual may strongly identify psychologically with an ethnic group, but the strength and authenticity of the identity is contingent on the acceptance and acknowledgment of "in-group" and "out-group" members.

Ethnic identity is contextual and situational, for it "is a product of social transaction insofar as one assumes an ethnic identity by claiming it and demonstrating the conventional signs of membership. A claimant is always subject to the response of others who may concur with or deny the claim" (Casino, n.d., p. 18). Ethnic actors indeed embody an ethnic consciousness that is closely aligned with the cultural elements of the group with which they affiliate. The ultimate form of the consciousness is "the authentic union of personal identity with communal identity" (Casino, n.d., p. 17). Thus, it is logical to assume that a concordance would exist between personal identity and an outsider's sense of identity based on his or her own categories and intention of self-identification. To promote the union between self and other, individuals often will use ethnological speech patterns and gestures to promote the authenticity of their claim. If outward physical appearances do not mesh with the standard physical criteria or there is the sense that others doubt the identity claim, ethnic actors will tend to exaggerate and give emphasis to mannerisms and speech idiosyncrasies known to be particular and peculiar to the reference group. The ritual or stylistic emphasis frequently occurs when ethnic group members meet or gather in geographic areas that differ from their homelands or communities of common origin; the distinctive ritual is a prime example of situational ethnicity and situated ethnic identity.

Phinney (1990) eloquently summarized the ethnic identity literature that existed for adolescents and adults. Her pointed review focused primarily on measurement and conceptualization of the construct. In prefacing her section on ethnic identity definitions, she stated that there was "no widely agreed on definition of ethnic identity" and that "the definitions that were given reflected quite different understandings or emphasis regarding what is meant by ethnic identity" (p. 500). Undoubtedly social and behavioral scientists believe they have a general sense of the construct; some are indeed rather firm about their positions (van den Berghe, 1981; Weinreich, 1988). Identity as a psychological construct is also the subject of considerable debate; however, the addition of the word *ethnic* pushes the debate into an atheoretical domain. In fact, about a quarter of the studies reviewed by Phinney were not built on a theoretical framework. It is safe to add that almost all of the drug and alcohol studies that assess ethnic identities are not based on a theoretical framework.

Several conceptual approaches to ethnic identity emphasize an individual level of analysis at which notions of identity formation and development are linked to self-concept. Much of the work in this area relies on Tajfel's (1982) theory of social identity. Tajfel basically maintained that one's social identity strongly influences self-perception and consequently should be the central locus of evaluation. The strength or weakness of the self is largely determined by one's status with one's reference groups and how one assesses out-group members. When ethnicity and race form the nexus of an in-group, then self-identity will be correspondingly influenced. One's distinctive ethnic characteristics, however, can be restrictive, for individuals may reject "externally based evaluations of the ingroup" and therefore "may establish their own standards and repudiate those of the dominant outgroup" (Bernal, Saenz, & Knight, 1991, p. 148). Other responses are possible: Individuals may withdraw or choose to dissociate from the referent, thereby creating added psychological complications for themselves. Tajfel's theory has sparked considerable interest in ethnic identity research, but some prefer to carry out the work under the ethnic self-identification rubric (see Phinney, 1990, 1992).

ETHNIC SELF-IDENTIFICATION

Ethnic self-identification and ethnic self-labeling as constructs are typically used interchangeably. Labeling involves the use of tags or markers to refer to and categorize groups and their members. Both in-group and out-group members can use a variety of labels to refer to a specific ethnic group. For example, Buriel (1987) pointed out that numerous labels exist to refer to the Mexican-descent population in the United States, among them, *Mexican, Mexicano, Mexican American, mestizo,* and *Chicano.* Also, over the years, out-group members have coined a few pejorative and offensive labels to refer to those of Mexican descent. In fact, belittling and deprecatory labels exist for all ethnic groups, and all are unequivocally rejected by the members of those groups.

Ethnic labeling has a sociopolitical value and function, especially for census and demographic studies. At a superficial level, at which generalizations about distinct cultural orientations are not used, ethnic labels serve a useful function. Typically, when the labels are used, reference is not made to the deep culture of each group to explain similarities and differences. Data patterns are presented at a gross level to portray findings in the broadest manner possible. However, researchers often use ethnic labels to convey a deeper cultural meaning than the labels will permit.

In eliciting ethnic-specific samples for behavioral and social science research, researchers often rely on ethnic labels to describe and differentiate their respondent groups. In so doing, they assume that the respondents share a common, modal understanding of their ethnic and nationalistic lifeways and thoughtways; it is as if the researcher believes that such groups as American Indians, African Americans, Asian Americans, and others possess commonly held, culturally unique mannerisms, styles, and states. In fact, researchers who rely solely on an "ethnic gloss" to describe ethnic groups actually ignore the richness of cultural variations within these groups and the numerous subgroups characterized by distinct lifeways and thoughtways (Trimble, 1992).

Use of broad "ethnic glosses" to describe an ethnic group in a research venture is poor science. Apart from the fact that "glosses" are gross misrepresentations, their use violates certain tenets concerning external validity and indeed fosters stereotyping. Heath (1978) argued that "categories of people such as those compared under the rubric of 'ethnic groups' are often not really meaningful units in any sociocultural sense" and thus that "it is . . . little wonder that epidemiological and other data collected under such rubrics [i.e., ethnic minorities and other nationalistic groups] are virtually meaningless" (p. 60).

At an individual level, one may rely on labels to describe one's ethnic affiliation and consequently one's identity. Use of the label, however, is a small part of identification, for one is likely to expand the labeling to include other subjective identifiers such as natal background, acculturative status, ego involvement, and attitudes toward own and other groups; behavioral preferences such as language usage, friendship affiliations, music and food preferences, and participation in cultural and religious activities may also be included (Trimble, 1992).

Ethnic self-identification is a distinct psychological variable and "refers to the description of oneself in terms of a critical ethnic attribute; that is, an attribute that defines more than merely describes the ethnic group" (Aboud, 1987, p. 33). In most social settings, use of one attribute may be sufficient; however, other settings may require the use of several related attributes to indicate the strength of one's identity. Vaughn (1987) viewed self-identification as a form of personal identity and differentiated the two from social identity. Personal identity derives from "a sense of self based on interpersonal comparisons" and social identity from "group membership" (p. 74). Rosenthal (1987) and Phinney (1990) viewed subjective identity as a starting point that eventually leads to the development of a social identity based on ethnic group membership. But Rosenthal added that "ethnic identity arises in interaction and is a function not only of the individual and his or her relation to the ethnic group but of the group's place in the wider social setting" (p. 160).

For Weinreich (1986), ethnic self-identification changes according to particular social contexts:

> One's identity as situated in a specific social context is defined as that part of the totality of one's self-construal in which how one construes oneself in the situated present expresses the continuity between how one construes oneself as one was in the past and how one construes oneself as one aspires to be in the future. (p. 307)

Individuals may avoid situations in which their identity is challenged, threatened, humiliated, and castigated, and seek out and preserve, whenever possible, settings that favor the identity state. Self-expression, maintenance of ethnic identity, and situated identities offer promise for understanding the complexities and dynamics of ethnic orientations through Weinreich's theory of identity structure analysis.

Measuring Ethnic Identity

The numerous theoretical perspectives concerning ethnicity, ethnic groups, ethnic identity, and ethnic self-identification mirror the variety of strategies and techniques used to measure the constructs. On this point, Phinney (1990) noted that there are "widely discrepant definitions and measures of ethnic identity, which makes generalizations and comparisons across studies difficult and ambiguous" (p. 500). Measurement approaches range from use of a single item (Richman, Gaveria, Flaherty, Birz, & Wintrob, 1987) to scales containing several dimensions (Phinney, 1992; Weinreich, 1986, 1988). As indicated earlier, some researchers will ask respondents to check their ethnic background and, on the basis of that one item, draw conclusions about ethnic differences (or similarities) that are totally unjustified; still others will select study participants on the basis of surnames or physiognomic appearance and then proceed to generalize results to the total ethnic populations—a procedure as misleading as the use of "ethnic glosses."

Indeed, measuring ethnic identity "is not a simple all or nothing proposition. Researchers have long recognized that a person's level or intensity of identification with a particular ethnicity can vary from a weak-nominal association to a strong-committed association" (Smith, 1980, p. 79).

Perhaps the most widely used procedure is to give respondents a list of ethnic groups and ask them to place a check mark next to the group with which they most identify. Use of the procedure hardly qualifies as a scale, but more than that it is replete with erroneous assumptions. First, it forces a person with a multiethnic background to choose one group. Second, selection of a group does not connote the intensity of identification. Third, the procedure often generates numerous ethnic categories to the point at which stratified and subgroup analyses may not be possible. For example, in a recent survey of 285 faculty at a university in the Pacific Northwest, respondents generated 20 identifiable ethnic groups in response to the open-ended request, "Please indicate your ethnic group orientation." Some of the responses were "Welsh," "Russian Jew," "English," "Asian," "Guatemalan," "Polish/Swede," "Celtic," "Scandinavian," "Native American/Irish," "black," "African American," and "American." Finally, use of the procedure does not permit any comparisons on the basis of deep cultural lifestyle orientations.

Ethnic identity scales assume that one can readily identify with a group and that one prefers to do so. Hence, use of an item that asks one to check or name the group with which one identifies is a good starting point—most multi-item identity scales start off with this question. Phinney's (1992) Multigroup Ethnic Identity Measure (MEIM) actually asks respondents to indicate their ethnic affiliation twice in the 23-item scale: Her scale assesses self-identification through two dimensions, ethnic identity and other group orientation. The ethnic identity dimension also taps affirmation, belonging, ethnic identity achievement, ethnic behaviors, and natural parents' ethnicity.

Weinreich's (1986, 1988) Identity Structure Analysis (ISA) is a complex, highly sophisticated approach to assessing ethnic identity, grounded in psychodynamic, personal construct, and symbolic interactionist theoretical perspectives. ISA can be custom designed to measure identity in an idiographic or nomothetic framework through use of bipolar constructs. Indices can be constructed to measure such constructs as self-image (past, current, and ideal), values, role models, reference groups, empathetic identification, identification conflicts, evaluation of others, and a few other related identity domains. Indeed, as a multi-item measure of identity, Weinreich's ISA sets the standard for comprehensiveness and inclusiveness. If a researcher is interested in exploring identity in great detail, ISA offers wonderful opportunities. However, if one is interested in assessing identity within a survey questionnaire format, use of ISA is not recommended.

Ethnic identity can also be assessed using an interview protocol. Waters (1990) developed an interview schedule containing over 100 questions designed to explore the nature and meaning of ethnicity. Waters maintained that "one constructs an ethnic identification using knowledge about ancestries in one's background" and that "this information is selectively used in the social construction of ethnic identification within the prevailing historical, structural, and personal constraints" (p. 19). Waters's interview schedule moves through a carefully developed set of domains that assists the respondent in constructing an identity. The interview produces a script that requires considerable time and energy to analyze. Although the results undoubtedly yield a rich profile, use of Waters's schedule and research approach has its limitations.

Use of ethnic identity measures in the drug use field thus far has been limited to a reliance on single-line or specifically developed measures that can be included in a lengthy questionnaire (Cheung, 1991a). Caetano (1986), for example, developed a fourfold measure of ethnic identification to assess drinking problems and patterns among a sample of Hispanic households. The scale contained items that assessed (a) ethnicity of family of origin, (b) own or subjective ethnic identity, (c) country of ancestors, and (d) respondent's country of birth. Caetano concluded that "ethnicity of family of origin seems to be the encompassing definition, followed by national group, and there is a good level of agreement between these rubrics" (p. 341).

Oetting and Beauvais (1991) proposed an orthogonal cultural identification theory and a correspondent measurement tool to assess cultural identity. Their approach is built on the assumption that cultural identity is not a linear phenomenon. They argued that cultural dimensions are independent of one another and that an increasing identification with one culture does not produce a decreasing identification with another culture. One could, for example, highly identify with two cultural groups or not identify with any group. Hence, these researchers would argue that an individual could conceivably identify with two, three, or even four cultural groups and be not in the least disoriented or confused about his or her cultural identification.

Oetting and Beauvais (1991) developed a set of items that allows an individual to "*independently* express identification or lack of identification" with several cultural groups (p. 663). They claimed that "in large-scale surveys of adults, only two basic items may be needed to assess identification with any one culture reasonably well: (1) Do you live in the . . . way of life? and (2) Are you a success in the . . . way of life?" (p. 664). Other issues can be added to assess such things as family identification and tradition, participation in cultural events, language preferences, and parental identification to expand the scale's measurement domains and its presumed effectiveness.

The Orthogonal Cultural Identity Scale has been used to determine the relationship between cultural identity and drug use. Results have been mixed. Oetting, Goldstein, Beauvais, and Edwards (1980) found that a moderately strong identification with American Indian culture among fourth to sixth graders predicted less drug use; however, no relationship was found for adolescents. In another study, Oetting and Beauvais (1990) found that Hispanic adolescent females with high cultural identity were less likely to use drugs, particularly marijuana.

Valid and reliable measures of ethnic identification must be grounded in theory or, at a minimum, on several fundamental propositions. Cheung (1991b) reminded us that typically "ethnicity has been treated as no more than a self-evident, *ascriptive* quality, as have been sex and age. Operationally, ethnicity was always measured by one or a combination of a few objective indicators such as color, place of birth, and language, neglecting the subjective aspect of ethnicity" (p. 575). Heath (1991), relying on a deconstructive perspective, forcefully argued that many of the assumptions and usages of ethnicity are "confused in a markedly inconsistent manner [and are] unlikely to yield further insights that are theoretically or conceptually helpful in terms of understanding how alcohol interacts with the human animal" (p. 610). Although both Cheung and Heath were highly critical of the measurement tendencies, they were quick to point out that some positive contributions have been made to the field of ethnicity and drug use, especially in the way the ethnic variable has been viewed in some studies.

Phinney (1990) reminded us that the "most serious need in ethnic identity research is to devise reliable and valid measures of ethnic identity" (p. 508). In the drug abuse field, researchers also must demonstrate that ethnicity is a relevant contribution to understanding and predicting drug use patterns (Heath, 1991). The salience and relevance of ethnicity for drug use research and its corresponding measurement presents a formidable challenge.

We must acknowledge the finding that the measurement of ethnicity is no small task, especially given the debate surrounding its theoretical foundations. Researchers must consider the "various cultural and structural dimensions of ethnicity" (Cheung, 1989, p. 72) and "distinguish between general aspects of ethnic identity that apply across groups and specific aspects that distinguish groups" (Phinney, 1990, p. 508). To accomplish this, we must move away from viewing ethnic groups as homogeneous entities—in fact, there may be more heterogeneity within certain ethnic minority groups than within the dominant groups in American society (Cheung, 1993; Trimble, 1991). Drug use researchers should give more attention to drug use patterns *within* ethnic groups. Tucker (1985) pointed out that "the literature tells us much about heroin addicts . . . but very little about drug addiction within Afro-American or Puerto Rican culture" (p. 1026). Indeed, the popular press and electronic media tend to emphasize inner-city drug problems, and that, in itself, cultivates the notion that ethnic minorities are more likely to be addicts than the general population (Trimble, in press). This notion is an illusion, for there is no definitive evidence available to support it. For this reason and many others, efforts must be taken to appropriately measure ethnicity and identify drug use correlates.

Ethnic Identity as
a Predictor of Drug Use

In his review of the literature on ethnic and racial variations in drug use, Cheung (1991b) concluded that many researchers assume that a direct causal relationship exists between ethnic identification and drug use at the individual level. Most of the studies reviewed in his article, however, did not rely on a scale to assess identity. Also, Trimble, Padilla, and Bell (1987) concluded that although many drug and alcohol studies involve ethnic minorities, few probe the intrinsic depth of ethnicity and its relationship to drug use. Given these conclusions, what is the relationship between ethnic identity and drug and alcohol use? Is ethnic identification mediated by such variables as peer association, family influence, and academic status to predict drug involvement? Although other questions can be generated, emphasis will be given to some research findings that provide partial answers.

In 1991, we implemented a research project to explore the psychosocial correlates of alcohol and drug use among American Indian adolescents. A 52-page multiple-scaled instrument developed by the staff at the Tri-Ethnic Center for Prevention Research at Colorado State University was administered to three groups of 621 (266 male and 355 female) American Indian adolescents from five rural, reservation, and urban environments in the southern central plains and southwestern region of the United States. Three subgroups were identified: high school dropouts, academically at-risk nondropouts, and nondropouts; each dropout was matched to a student of similar academic background who had not dropped out of school and a control respondent.

Four different independent measures were used for analyses: gender, ethnic identification with American Indian culture, peer alcohol association, and family alcohol associations. Using Trimble's (1991) tripartite ethnic identification model (natal, behavioral, and subjective), we assessed seven different identity domains: use of an American Indian language, participation in American Indian traditions and ceremonies, affiliative patterns, self-identification, maternal identification, paternal identification, and acculturative status. The measures were confirmed using confirmatory factor analysis that produced loadings ranging from .517 to .687. Peer and family associations were assessed with two four-item scales (Oetting & Beauvais, 1987). And alcohol involvement, the dependent variable, was measured with two confirmed scales tapping frequency of alcohol use (three items) and drinking style (eight items).

EQS, a program designed for latent variable analysis (Bentler, 1989), was used to generate solutions for the measurement models and to validate the structural equation model (Bates, 1994). Results from the cross-validation analysis appear in Figure 1.1.

The goodness of fit of the model, as measured by the Bentler-Bonet Normed Fit Index (BBNFI), the Bentler-Bonett Non-Normed Fit Index (BBNNFI), and the Comparative Fit Index (CFI), was adequate. The BBNFI was .877, the BBNNFI was .867, and the CFI was .901. The chi-square was significant, revealing a nonexact fit of the model to the data, $\chi^2(58, N = 696) = 255.10$, $p < .001$. However, the large sample size may account for this finding (Cudeck & Browne, 1983).

Although the relationship between each independent variable and alcohol involvement was significantly different from no relationship, only peer alcohol associations accounted for a substantial proportion of the variability (16.7%). The other independent variables combined to account for 4.2%. Ethnic self-identification, gender, and family alcohol associations each accounted for less than 3% of the total variability in alcohol involvement.

The single predictor of membership in an academic status group (i.e., nonattending, attending but with academic problems, or attending) was alcohol involvement. The relationship between them was significant and accounted for 6.6% of the variability. Thus, it was concluded that as alcohol involvement of an Indian adolescent increases, so does the likelihood of having academic problems or dropping out of school.

American Indian identity and gender were found to be unrelated to alcohol involvement. The findings, therefore, suggest that degree of ethnic identity is not a predictor of alcohol use among Indian adolescents. To the contrary, peer alcohol associations and, to a much lesser extent, family alcohol associations predict alcohol use. Both findings are consistent with those of others (see Oetting & Beauvais, 1987; Oetting, Edwards, & Beauvais, 1989).

The results by no means indicate that culture and ethnicity are not useful domains of study in the drug and alcohol field. Indeed, peer associations do influence level of alcohol involvement, as our findings suggest; peers in this study represent other Indian youth with whom a respondent associates.

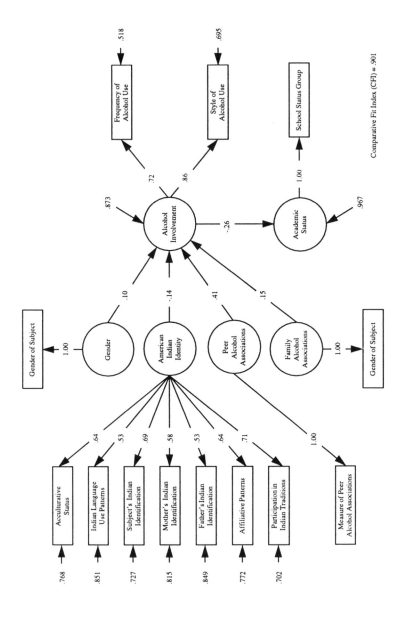

Comparative Fit Index (CFI) = .901

Figure 1.1. Structural or Path Model for Alcohol Involvement, Ethnic Identity, Peer Association, Family Association, and Related Variables

23

The findings merely suggest that one's level of identity does not directly affect a decision to use drugs and alcohol. Given the influence of peer and family associations on alcohol involvement, it is possible that ethnic identity can serve as a mediating variable; that possibility awaits further research and analyses. The findings also warrant further investigation with other ethnic groups with the use of similar or expanded measures.

SUMMARY

Interest in the relationship between ethnicity, ethnic identity, and drug and alcohol use appears to be increasing. The chapters in this book highlight the importance and significance of the field. However, the study and inclusion of ethnicity and ethnic identity in the drug and alcohol use arena are not without controversy. Sociologists were among the first to focus attention on the elusive constructs and were responsible for the development of important theories in the field. They were joined by anthropologists and eventually by psychologists who entered the field to demand more concise operational definitions and appropriate ways to measure the constructs. The debates continue to the present, as does the search for reliable and valid empirical measures.

Public interest in ethnicity is also on the rise, as reflected in responses to census polls and the declaration of one's ancestral origins and identity. The interest also seems to be nudging social and behavioral scientists to identify the cultural factors that evidently contribute to some of the nation's social woes. Drug and alcohol use is one area of concern.

Indeed, dredging for variables and factors lodged in one's *ethos* (lifeways) and *eidos* (thoughtways) is no small undertaking. Dwight Heath (1978) reminded us that "different attitudes toward alcohol and its effects are associated with different patterns of alcohol use and its consequences. These, in turn, are associated with different ideas about what constitutes alcohol-related problems and with the different rates of occurrence of such problems" (p. 4). So if we expect to understand the attitudes and behaviors associated with alcohol and drug use, we must mount an effort that goes beyond superficial cultural explorations. Only through the identification of the attitudes and behavior associated with drug and alcohol use will we be able to design and mount culturally efficacious and resonant intervention programs.

References

Aboud, F. E. (1987). The development of ethnic self-identification and attitudes. In J. S. Phinney & M. J. Rotheram (Eds.), *Children's ethnic socialization: Pluralism and development* (pp. 32-55). Newbury Park, CA: Sage.

Banks, R. (1990). Living the legacy: Historical perspective on African-American drug abuse. In J. Debro & C. Bolek (Eds.), *Drug abuse research issues at historically Black colleges and universities* (pp. 56-110). Atlanta: Clark Atlanta University.

Barth, F. (Ed.). (1969). *Ethnic groups and boundaries.* Boston: Little, Brown.

Bates, S. (1994). *A cross-validated model of the causes and effects of alcohol involvement on American-Indian adolescents.* Unpublished master's thesis, Western Washington University, Bellingham, WA.

Bentler, P. M. (1989). *EQS structural equations program manual.* Los Angeles: BMDP Statistical Software.

Bernal, M. E., Saenz, D. S., & Knight, G. P. (1991). Ethnic identity and adaptation of Mexican-American youths in school settings. *Hispanic Journal of Behavioral Sciences, 13,* 135-154.

Brecher, E. M., & Editors of Consumer Reports. (1972). *Licit and illicit drugs.* Boston: Little, Brown.

Buriel, R. (1987). Ethnic labeling and identity among Mexican-Americans. In J. S. Phinney & M. J. Rotheram (Eds.), *Children's ethnic socialization: Pluralism and development* (pp. 134-152). Newbury Park, CA: Sage.

Caetano, R. (1986). Alternative definitions of Hispanics: Consequences in an alcohol survey. *Hispanic Journal of Behavioral Sciences, 8,* 331-344.

Casino, E. (n.d.). *Introduction to ethnicology: Ways of talking about ethnicity.* Unpublished manuscript.

Cheung, Y. W. (1989). Making sense of ethnicity and drug use: A review and suggestions for future research. *Social Pharmacology, 3,* 55-82.

Cheung, Y. W. (1991a). Ethnicity and alcohol/drug use revisited: A framework for future research. *International Journal of the Addictions, 25,* 581-605.

Cheung, Y. W. (1991b). Overview: Sharpening the focus on ethnicity. *International Journal of the Addictions, 25,* 573-579.

Cheung, Y. W. (1993). Approaches to ethnicity: Clearing roadblocks in the study of ethnicity and substance abuse. *International Journal of the Addictions, 28,* 1209-1226.

Cudeck, R., & Browne, M. W. (1983). Cross-validation of covariance structures. *Multivariate Behavioral Research, 18,* 147-167.

Efron, D. H., Holmstedt, B., & Kline, N. S. (Eds.). (1967). *Ethnopharmacologic search for psychoactive drugs. Proceedings of a symposium held in San Francisco, California* (No. 1645). Washington, DC: Government Printing Office.

Feagin, J. R. (1978). *Racial and ethnic relations.* Englewood Cliffs, NJ: Prentice Hall.

Glazer, N., & Moynihan, D. P. (1970). *Beyond the melting pot.* Cambridge: MIT Press.

Gordon, A. J. (1978). Hispanic drinking after migration: The case of Dominicans. *Medical Anthropology, 2*(4), 61-84.

Greeley, A. M. (1974). *Ethnicity in the United States.* New York: John Wiley.

Heath, D. B. (1978). Foreword. *Medical Anthropology, 2*(4), 3-8.

Heath, D. B. (1991). Uses and misuses of the concept of ethnicity in alcohol studies: An essay on deconstruction. *International Journal of the Addictions, 25,* 607-627.

Helmer, J. (1975). *Drugs and minority oppression.* New York: Seabury.

Inciardi, J. (1992). *The war on drugs II: The continuing epic of heroin, cocaine, crack, crime, AIDS, and public policy.* Mountain View, CA: Mayfield.

Katz, P. A., & Taylor, D. A. (Eds.). (1988). *Eliminating racism: Profiles in controversy.* New York: Plenum.

Morgan, H. W. (1981). *Drugs in America.* Syracuse, NY: Syracuse University Press.

Morgan, P. A. (1990). The making of a public problem: Mexican labor in California and the Marijuana Law of 1937. In R. Glich & J. Moore (Eds.), *Drugs in Hispanic communities* (pp. 233-252). New Brunswick, NJ: Rutgers University Press.

Oetting, E. R., & Beauvais, F. (1987). Common elements in youth drug abuse: Peer clusters and other psychosocial factors. *Journal of Drug Issues, 17,* 133-151.

Oetting, E. R., & Beauvais, F. (1990). Adolescent drug use: Findings of national and local surveys. *Journal of Consulting and Clinical Psychology, 58,* 385-394.

Oetting, E. R., & Beauvais, F. (1991). Orthogonal cultural identification theory: The cultural identification of minority adolescents. *International Journal of the Addictions, 25,* 655-685.

Oetting, E. R., Edwards, R. W., & Beauvais, F. (1989). Drugs and Native-American youth. *Drugs and Society, 3,* 5-38.

Oetting, E. R., Goldstein, G., Beauvais, F., & Edwards, R. W. (1980). *Drug abuse among Indian children.* Fort Collins: Colorado State University, Western Behavioral Studies.

Patterson, O. (1977). *Ethnic chauvinism.* New York: Stein & Day.

Phinney, J. S. (1990). Ethnic identity in adolescents and adults: Review of research. *Psychological Bulletin, 108,* 499-514.

Phinney, J. S. (1992). The multigroup ethnic identity measure: A new scale for use with diverse groups. *Journal of Adolescent Research, 7,* 156-176.

Richman, J., Gaveria, M., Flaherty, J., Birz, S., & Wintrob, R. (1987). The process of acculturation: Theoretical perspectives and an empirical investigation in Peru. *Social Science and Medicine, 25,* 839-847.

Rosenthal, D. A. (1987). Ethnic identity development in adolescents. In J. S. Phinney & M. J. Rotheram (Eds.), *Children's ethnic socialization: Pluralism and development* (pp. 73-91). Newbury Park, CA: Sage.

Saharso, S. (1989). Ethnic identity and the paradox of equality. In J. P. Van Oudenhoven & T. M. Willemsen (Eds.), *Ethnic minorities: Social psychological perspectives* (pp. 97-114). Berwyn, PA: Swets North America.

Schermmerhorn, R. A. (1969). *Comparative ethnic relations: A framework for theory and research.* New York: Random House.

Sherif, M., & Sherif, C. W. (1964). *Reference groups: Exploration into conformity and deviation of adolescents.* New York: Harper & Row.

Smith, E. J. (1991). Ethnic identity development: Toward the development of a theory within the context of majority/minority status. *Journal of Counseling and Development, 70,* 181-188.

Smith, T. W. (1980). Ethnic measurement and identification. *Ethnicity, 7,* 78-95.

Steinberg, S. (1981). *The ethnic myth: Race, ethnicity, and class in America.* New York: Atheneum.

Tajfel, H. (1982). *Social identity and intergroup relations.* Cambridge, UK: Cambridge University Press.

Thompson, R. H. (1989). *Theories of ethnicity: A critical appraisal.* New York: Greenwood.

Trimble, J. E. (1991). Ethnic specification, validation prospects, and the future of drug use research. *International Journal of the Addictions, 25,* 149-170.

Trimble, J. E. (1992). A cognitive-behavioral approach to drug abuse prevention and intervention with American-Indian youth. In L. A. Vargas & J. D. Koss-Chioino (Eds.), *Working* with culture: Psychotherapeutic intervention with ethnic minority children and adolescents (pp. 246-275). San Francisco: Jossey-Bass.

Trimble, J. E. (in press). Ethnic minority substance abuse perspectives: A literature review with commentary. In J. E. Trimble, C. Bolek, & S. Niemcryk (Eds.), *Conducting cross-cultural substance abuse research.* New York: Haworth.

Trimble, J., & Fleming, C. (1989). Providing counseling services for Native American Indians: Client, counselor, and community characteristics. In P. Pedersen, J. Draguns, W. Lonner, & J. Trimble (Eds.), *Counseling across cultures* (3rd ed., pp. 177-204). Honolulu: University Press of Hawaii.

Trimble, J. E., Padilla, A. M., & Bell, C. S. (Eds.). (1987). *Drug abuse among ethnic minorities* (DHHS Publ. No. ADM 87-1474). Washington, DC: Government Printing Office.

Tucker, M. B. (1985). U.S. ethnic minorities and drug abuse: An assessment of the science and practice. *International Journal of the Addictions, 20,* 1021-1047.

U.S. Bureau of the Census. (1980). *Census of the United States* (O.M.B. No. 41-S78006). Washington, DC: Government Printing Office.

U.S. Bureau of the Census. (1992). *Census questionnaire content, 1990 (CQC-4).* Washington, DC: Government Printing Office.

van den Berghe, P. L. (1981). *The ethnic phenomenon.* New York: Elsevier North Holland.

Vaughn, G. M. (1987). A social psychological model of ethnic identity development. In J. S. Phinney & M. J. Rotheram (Eds.), *Children's ethnic socialization: Pluralism and development* (pp. 73-91). Newbury Park, CA: Sage.

Walker, W. O. (1981). *Drug control in the Americas.* Albuquerque: University of New Mexico Press.

Waters, M. C. (1990). *Ethnic options: Choosing identities in America.* Los Angeles: University of California Press.

Weinreich, P. (1986). The operationalisation of identity theory in racial and ethnic relations. In J. Rex & D. Mason (Eds.), *Theories of race and ethnic relations* (pp. 299-320). Cambridge, UK: Cambridge University Press.

Weinreich, P. (1988). The operationalization of ethnic identity. In J. Berry & R. Annis (Eds.), *Ethnic psychology: Research and practice with immigrants, refugees, native peoples, ethnic groups and sojourners* (pp. 149-168). Amsterdam: Swets & Zeitlinger.

Willemsen, T. M., & van Oudenhoven, J. P. (1989). Social psychological perspectives on ethnic minorities: An introduction. In J. P. Van Oudenhoven & T. M. Willemsen (Eds.), *Ethnic minorities: Social psychological perspectives* (pp. 11-24). Berwyn, PA: Swets North America.

Yinger, J. M. (1986). Intersecting strands in the theorisation of race and ethnic relations. In J. Rex & D. Mason (Eds.), *Theories of race and ethnic relations* (pp. 20-41). Cambridge, UK: Cambridge University Press.

Issues of Ethnicity in Research on the Prevention of Substance Abuse

R. Lorraine Collins

Ethnicity and race are typically seen as central to social life in the United States. Social issues, ranging from voter turnout to crime, are couched in ethnic or racial terms. The same can be said for research on substance abuse, in which ethnicity/race is often characterized as a potent sociocultural factor. This emphasis on ethnicity/race serves as a reflection of the broader society from which researchers are drawn and more recently may represent responses to federal mandates for ethnic (and gender) representation in research.

Research on ethnicity and substance use encompasses a wide variety of topics and areas. This chapter is not an exhaustive review of existent research on ethnicity and substance use. Rather it is limited to research on non-European ethnic groups that reside in the United States, and it will highlight issues in the following four areas: (a) ethnicity as a sociocultural factor in substance abuse research, (b) research on the prevention of substance abuse, (c) consideration of socioenvironmental variables in research on the prevention of substance use and abuse, and (d) recommendations for future research. It is hoped that by raising issues in these four areas, research on the prevention of substance use/abuse will better encompass a wide variety of sociocultural and environmental factors.

Ethnicity as a Sociocultural
Factor in Substance Abuse Research

The United States is a multicultural society, and substance use can be found among all of the cultural groups represented in the general population.

In much of the research on substance use and abuse, attention to ethnicity has involved comparative studies in which European Americans (as the numerical and cultural majority) have served as the standard against which other (numerically smaller) non-European ethnic groups have been compared. As described by Jones (1991), "The most common approach is to take an idea, a measurement instrument, or a finding in the literature, and see if blacks differ from whites, if American Indians differ from Anglo-Americans, or if Asians differ from Hispanics and blacks and Anglo-Americans, and so forth" (p. 32). This approach not only can reinforce ethnic stereotypes, but also has added little to theory development and/or the conceptual complexity of notions concerning etiology and effective prevention.

The complexity of the task of conducting research on a variety of ethnic groups begins with conceptualization of the term *ethnicity*. In the United States, researchers and policy makers have sought to simplify the designation of ethnicity, but in so doing have reduced its meaningfulness. We are all familiar with the federal law that defines *minorities* as encompassing four groups: (1) Native American, including American Indian or Alaskan Native; (2) Asian or Pacific Islander, including all areas of Asia and the Indian subcontinent; (3) black, not of Hispanic origin (i.e., persons with an African heritage who are not Caucasian); and (4) Hispanic, having a Spanish cultural heritage, regardless of race. These groupings are clearly based on national origin and race. It is easy to see how quickly such groupings become absurd. Is a Caucasian from Spain a member of the Hispanic minority group or a European American? Is an individual from Central America who has African heritage Hispanic, black, or both? Into what category does an individual with a mix of any of these four categories and a European heritage (or Caucasian race) fall? Who decides the most appropriate grouping for a particular individual? Clearly, in a multicultural society such as the United States, categorizations of this sort can become both useless and ludicrous very quickly. Heath (1991) commented on this state of affairs vis-à-vis alcohol research in his description of five garbled versions of ethnicity. These included ethnicity as race (garbling based on biology) and ethnicity as national heritage (garbling based on politics), each of which was characterized as being "imprecise and unreliable" (p. 607).

Race is a particularly compelling designation in the United States. Possibly as a reflection of the preoccupation with race within the broader society, racial categories often are used in substance abuse research, in which it is common to see references to "white" and "black" subjects, as if these designations had scientific meaning or validity. Race is not an objective, biological category, but rather a social category (Cheung, 1989; Fisher, 1987; Heath, 1991). Physical characteristics that stereotypically determine racial identity (skin color, eye shape, texture of hair) each vary along a continuum and can be combined in an almost infinite number of configurations. In fact, racial categories common in the United States are not homogeneous, but rather encompass variations in physical characteristics, education, social status, cultural background, and much more. Even at the level of genetics (e.g., blood groups, enzymes), within-group differences tend to account for much more of the variance than do between-group differences (Latter, 1980, as cited in Zuckerman, 1990). This variation within racial categories is likely to mean that even when between-group differences are found, they account for less variability than do within-group differences. Even if between-group differences are found, it is important to understand the factors that underlie them. Thus, Betancourt and Lopez (1993) pointed out that even in the case of a biologically based disease such as hypertension, for which "racial" differences are found between groups, "what is of scientific interest is not the race of these individuals but the relationship between the identified biological factors (e.g., plasma renin levels and sodium excretion) and hypertension" (p. 631; see also Anderson, 1989).

Finally, variables other than race (e.g., gender or socioeconomic status [SES]) may be important in determining behavior. These issues have been highlighted in discussions of concerns about science's endorsement and/or contribution to lay notions about the pervasiveness of racial differences (Betancourt & Lopez, 1993; Jones, 1991; Jones, LaVeist, & Lillie-Blanton, 1991; Yee, Fairchild, Weizmann, & Wyatt, 1993). They led Heath (1991) to declare that "the racial model of ethnicity in alcohol studies is bankrupt" (p. 617). It is probably time to declare a similar bankruptcy for racial models of ethnicity in substance abuse research.

Ethnicity has been selected as a more comprehensive and seemingly more representative designation because it involves notions of a shared culture or identity. However, in many cases, ethnic labels have been used interchangeably with racial designations, resulting in a similar set of superficial and simplistic categories. The resulting "ethnic glosses" (Trimble, 1991) are not informative because they, too, are not homogeneous. For most groups, ethnic glosses mask important differences in national origins, cultural traditions, SES, and other variables. For example, Latinos vary in racial origins and are composed of populations from Cuba, Puerto Rico, Mexico, and Central and South America. Each of these populations has a different history and set of traditions in its country of origin as well as within the United States. As a reflection of these factors, Caetano (1986) found differences in drinking patterns and social position on the basis of the specific definition of Latino/Hispanic ethnicity used in a national survey of alcohol use. Asian Americans are composed of populations from various countries in Southeast Asia, China, and Japan, each of which has different cultural traditions, including patterns of substance use. Further, some Asian Americans are new to the United States, and others have lived in the United States for many generations; these differences are likely to affect many aspects of behavior. The designation *American Indian* includes over 500 tribes recognized by the U.S. Bureau of Indian Affairs. Each tribe possesses different traditions, social norms, and patterns of behavior. Persons of African heritage who reside in the United States include both individuals whose families have lived here for hundreds of years and newcomers from a variety of nations. These differences may be manifested in a number of areas, including substance use and other mental health outcomes. For example, among adolescents of African heritage residing in Dade County, Florida, Americans had the highest prevalence of suicide ideation, Haitians had the highest number of suicide attempts, and individuals from the Caribbean had the lowest number of attempts (Vega, Gil, Warheit, Apospori, & Zimmerman, 1993). Similarly, differences in the alcohol use of African American and Afro-Caribbean adolescents residing in New York State have been reported by Welte and Barnes (1987).

As with racial designations, other sources of heterogeneity within ethnic groups include gender, education, acculturation, age, and SES; each of these variables may be independently related to substance use (Caetano, 1986; Collins, 1992). As outlined by Yee et al. (1993), the failure to acknowledge the muddling of race and ethnicity and of nongenetic and quasi-genetic characteristics may be a function of social scientists' lack of knowledge of genetic science, federal policy and practice, lay stereotypes, and/or personal preference. Whatever the case, the ethnic categories currently used in most substance abuse research have little or no scientific meaning.

To further complicate the picture, ethnic/cultural identity may not exist only as a category or on a continuum, as is typical of the approaches used in substance abuse research. Phinney's (1990) review of the research on ethnic identity highlights the complexity of characterizing ethnicity, and presents evidence that ethnicity is not just a label placed on the individual on the basis of external characteristics. Ethnicity must include the identity internalized by the individual. This identity is likely to be the result of an interaction among a variety of elements, including family of origin, cultural traditions, and experiences in society, and may involve a dynamic process that changes developmentally and/or situationally. For example, Oetting and Beauvais (1991) suggested that ethnicity may be best viewed as orthogonal. This means that persons can identify equally strongly (or weakly) with two cultures, adding even more to the misinformation provided by the use of an ethnic gloss. In their data on American Indian adolescents, Oetting and Beauvais found that strong identification with American Indian culture, European American culture, or both cultures had a positive relationship to characteristics such as self-esteem. In fact, the highest self-esteem was found in those adolescents who strongly identified with both cultures (also see LaFromboise, Coleman, & Gerton, 1993). The relationships between cultural identification and substance use were inconsistent and seemed to be related to other factors such as peer influences. However, the orthogonal conceptualization and other multidimensional approaches suggest that some individuals possess a complex sense of cultural identity that cannot easily be categorized. Thus, we again have evidence that the use of ethnic glosses as proxies for ethnic/cultural identity is not likely to be meaningful.

The use of ethnic glosses typically has been designated a methodological issue that affects the replication of studies and/or the external validity of findings (Collins, 1992; Trimble, 1991). In fact, the use of such glosses must be considered more broadly as a conceptual issue that creates core problems in the conduct and interpretation of research. The limited utility of ethnic categories raises some questions about the conceptual maturity of psychosocial research on substance abuse, because research based on ethnic categories typically provides only a context for describing behavior and offers little if anything in terms of consistent explanations of substance use (see Blane, 1993; Collins, 1993a; Lex, 1987; Tucker, 1985).

Research on the
Prevention of Substance Abuse

Prevention of substance use/abuse encompasses a wide variety of theories, strategies, and populations. Because the initial use of alcohol and other substances typically begins during adolescence, many primary prevention efforts are implemented among this age group in the schools. These programs contain interventions designed to change the individual's knowledge, attitudes, and behavior regarding drugs and alcohol and/or reduce risks related to psychological characteristics (e.g., increase self-esteem). In fact, there is accumulating evidence that the components of this type of prevention program may not be very important in the broader sociocultural context in which adolescents function. For example, in a longitudinal (1-year) assessment of a prevention program for a predominantly European American sample of high school students, the variables typically targeted in school-based prevention programs (e.g., knowledge, self-esteem) did not predict drinking-related behavior once social and demographic variables (e.g., gender, parents, friends) had been accounted for (Mauss, Hopkins, Weisheit, & Kearney, 1988). The authors concluded that "the variables targeted by our classroom prevention program turned out to be relatively unimportant, at least net of other variables in students' lives, over which the classroom curriculum could not be expected to exert much (if any) direct influence" (p. 59). Similarly, in research with American Indian youth, cumulative risk factor scores based on variables such as family and peer smoking, family relationships, cultural identification, and religiosity were significantly related to lifetime use of alcohol and other substances (Moncher, Holden, & Trimble, 1990). Findings such as these suggest that sociocultural factors such as SES, peer relations, and poor family relationships are important predictors of substance use among adolescents regardless of their ethnic background (also see Hawkins, Catalano, & Miller, 1992; Oetting & Beauvais, 1987a, 1987b; Rhodes & Jason, 1990).

Possibly because of this tendency to focus on changing individual characteristics, reviews of research on the primary prevention of substance use among adolescents have been uniformly negative in their appraisal of the efficacy of school-based programs (Bangert-Downs, 1988; Moskowitz, 1989; Tobler, 1986). Such reviews find support for changes in knowledge and attitudes regarding alcohol use, but few for changes in behavior. Moskowitz suggested that the most efficacious policies for alcohol prevention are increasing alcohol taxes, enforcing drunk-driving laws, and raising the minimum legal drinking age to 21 years. Pentz et al. (1989) showed that schools with comprehensive antismoking policies and high emphasis on prevention exhibit reduced smoking by adolescents. Policy interventions such as these are likely to affect all members of the society, including members of various ethnic groups.

Many prevention programs for non-European ethnic groups are targeted at adolescents who are characterized as being at "high risk" for substance use/abuse. As previously stated, the designation of risk status can be based on a wide variety of factors, but often includes being from a low SES background, and, in particular, living in economically disadvantaged urban neighborhoods where minorities are concentrated (Coie et al., 1993; Hawkins et al., 1992; National Research Council, 1993). Although the social position of the population is likely to influence risk status (also see Oetting & Beauvais, 1987a; Rhodes & Jason, 1990; Wallace & Bachman, 1991), little if any attention is given to the larger social arena in which the adolescents function. In some cases, programs steeped in the middle-class assumptions and values of the researchers are applied to students from disadvantaged backgrounds. Even "effective" programs that contain the appropriate emphasis on "cultural sensitivity" by incorporating language differences and peer leaders tend to overlook the important role of the broader social environment (e.g., poverty, family disintegration) and instead focus on characteristics of the individual (e.g., skills training). Rhodes and Jason (1990) described this tendency to ignore the impact of economic disadvantage as limiting us to seeing substance use and other deviant behaviors "as resulting from a deficit in the person rather than one possible response that any healthy, adequately functioning individual might have to the disordered or developmentally hazardous environmental circumstances he or she confronts" (p. 396). If substance use represents a response to a maladaptive, disadvantaged environment, then prevention efforts that ignore the factors that create and sustain such environments are likely to fail.

Socioenvironmental Variables in Research on the Prevention of Substance Use and Abuse

Given the consistent message concerning the meaninglessness of ethnic designations, it is difficult to understand the continuing emphasis on ethnicity-based research, particularly when variables other than ethnicity are seen as indicating risk for substance use/ abuse. For example, in their extensive review of risk factors for substance abuse, Hawkins et al. (1992) described some 17 factors within two areas: (a) contextual factors, such as availability of drugs, extreme economic disintegration, and disorganized neighborhoods; and (b) individual and interpersonal factors, such as familial behavior and attitudes regarding substance use, academic failure, and association with drug-using peers. None of these risk factors was specific to a particular ethnic group.

The similarity of risk factors for substance use, regardless of ethnicity, is evident in many studies. Oetting and Beauvais (1987a) reported that peer influences on substance use do not differ for Mexican American, American Indian, and European American adolescents. This finding suggests that peer socialization processes, rather than ethnicity, are an important basis for considering drug-related behavior (see Oetting & Beauvais, 1987b). Brook and colleagues have reported that African American, Puerto Rican, and European American adolescents possess similar risk factors in the areas of drug context, personality, and family (Brook, Brook, Gordon, Whiteman, & Cohen, 1990; Brook, Whiteman, Balka, & Hamburg, 1992). Similarly, in a comparison of Hispanic and non-Hispanic adolescents from the southwest, Schinke et al. (1992) reported that mothers' failure to complete high school and students' low grades were better predictors of the prevalence of substance use than was ethnicity. They concluded that "social and background factors ought to carry greater weight in determining risk and prevention programming than factors associated with ethnic-racial group membership" (p. 123).

Although findings of similarities across groups are helping to underscore the limited utility of reliance on ethnic categories as explanations for substance use, this type of research represents limited progress. Many researchers still cling to ethnic labels and fail to include explanatory variables that could account for findings both within and between groups. This being the state of the current literature, one is left with the dilemma of acknowledging the limitations of ethnic glosses while reviewing research that makes use of such glosses. One can only hope that this state of affairs will change in the future.

One of the sources of heterogeneity both within and between socio-cultural groupings is the group's structural position in the broader society. This typically refers to the group's level of social organization, which allows it to compete with other groups for resources and power within the institutions of the larger society (Cheung, 1989). Generally, a group's structural position is related to its socioeconomic position in society, which in turn is linked to various aspects of substance use. For example, the results from general population surveys typically indicate differences in drinking based on income and education. Thus, Midanik and Room (1992) reported that in a representative national sample, the percentage of drinkers increased from a low of 68% among those with a yearly family income under $9,000 to a high of around 79% for those with a yearly family income of $40,000 or more. However, rates of heavier drinking (5+ drinks/day) were much higher in the low-income sample (19%) than in the high-income sample (6%). Midanik and Room found a similar pattern for education—specifically, a higher proportion of drinkers, but less heavy drinking, among the better educated. These data suggest that drinking varies with social position, with those of lower SES being at higher risk for alcohol-related problems. Drug use (type and context) also varies with SES and/or education. During the late 1970s and early 1980s, powdered cocaine use was often limited to higher SES groups. With the introduction of the much less expensive crack cocaine, levels of use/abuse rose dramatically among lower SES groups (National Institute on Drug Abuse, 1990).

One of the salient structural features on which groups differ is access to economic resources. In the United States, historical and social events have combined to create a situation in which large proportions of members of some non-European ethnic groups are of lower SES. The preponderance of members of non-European groups in the lower classes has resulted in a tendency for behaviors related to their class status to be stereotypically generalized to the entire group. It also has meant that substance-related social problems that reflect the lack of access to economic resources and social power are attributed to enduring psychological (or even biological) characteristics of the group. More generally, this state of affairs is reflected in a tendency to confound ethnicity/race with social class, such that ethnicity is used to explain behaviors that may actually vary on the basis of class (Cheung, 1989; Collins, 1992; Fisher, 1987).

Interestingly, many studies on substance use/abuse still fail to include even a rudimentary description or analysis of characteristics such as SES. Thus, differences are ascribed to ethnicity rather than the impact of the socioeconomic position of the groups being studied. However, there is more and more evidence to suggest the need to move away from focusing on the individual to considering the broader socioeconomic and environmental context. This view was well articulated in a recent report on factors that place adolescents at high risk for a variety of problems, including substance abuse (National Research Council, 1993). Citing the traditional tendency to focus on characteristics of the individual, the panel made the explicit decision to focus on the physical and social environments in which many adolescents must try to function. The panel identified four conditions that created and maintained high-risk environments: (a) poverty and its related stress, (b) increased concentration of the poor in deprived neighborhoods, (c) the failure of service institutions (e.g., health, legal, education, employment) to meet the needs of adolescents, and (d) the impact of racial and ethnic discrimination. Although individual characteristics interact with the social context, it is only with a better understanding of the conditions outlined above, and with interventions to change these conditions, that significant changes in high-risk behaviors are likely to occur.

Socioeconomic position has been shown to play an explanatory role in substance use and abuse. Thus, in Wallace and Bachman's (1991) analysis of sociocultural factors in drug use among a large, multiethnic sample of high school seniors, it was found that drug use among American Indians was linked to socioeconomic status. Wallace and Bachman concluded that

> the higher than average level of drug use reported by Native American youth may be linked to their relatively disadvantaged socioeconomic status. Once the background differences were adjusted, the white versus Native American differences in drug use are virtually eliminated among male seniors and reduced or eliminated among female seniors. (p. 343)

Rhodes and Jason (1990) have made a similar argument with regard to the socioeconomic disadvantages faced by urban African American and Hispanic adolescents. A recent analysis of prevalence data on the smoking of crack cocaine serves as a final illustration of the importance of considering socioeconomic conditions. Lillie-Blanton, Anthony, and Schuster (1993) reanalyzed data from the 1988 National Household Survey that had indicated that crack cocaine smoking was more prevalent among African Americans and Hispanic Americans than among European Americans. When respondents were grouped into neighborhoods reflective of social conditions, the odds ratios for crack smoking did not significantly differ for the three groups. They concluded that "given similar social conditions, crack cocaine smoking does not depend strongly on race per se" (p. 996). They also made the important point that "reporting racial/ethnic differences in illicit drug use without commenting on factors that might account for the observed variations could lead to an erroneous assessment of causal factors and to ineffective preventive interventions" (p. 996). This is an important point because many studies report results based on simplistic ethnic categories and do not mention causal or confounding factors (see Jones et al., 1991), thereby doing a disservice both to the groups being studied and to the advancement of knowledge.

Osborne and Feit's (1992) assessment of the impact of reliance on ethnic categories and the related failure to assess and consider the role of sociocultural factors in medical research is applicable to the state of the art in substance abuse research. They stated, "Ethnic categorization in medical research projects the misleading implication that race is a more important determinant of disease than class, lifestyle, or socioeconomic status" (p. 276). Reliance on ethnic glosses and the failure to adequately assess the role of socioenvironmental factors are likely to leave the erroneous impression that race/ ethnicity is *the* important determinant of substance use. Yet we have just examined evidence that illustrates the importance of socioenvironmental variables. It is true that inclusion of such variables can add to the complexity of conducting research and interpreting findings. However, it is only when such explanatory variables are added that meaningful knowledge will be gained. The alternative is to continue in our well-established ways of thinking and of doing research. This may seem the easier course of action. However, if we take this alternative, we must be aware that maintenance of the status quo can be deleterious for prevention science and for the groups being studied.

Future Research on
the Prevention of Substance Abuse

Before commenting on specific approaches to prevention research, it is important to make some general recommendations about the inclusion of ethnicity as a sociocultural factor in substance abuse research. First, given the conceptual and methodological limitations of much of the comparative research to date, it is important that more of an emphasis be placed on understanding similarities and differences *within* ethnic populations. As stated by Jones (1991), this strategy "would have the twin virtues of reducing the tendency to exaggerate racial differences and of discovering more about the full range of behaviors exemplified by members of racial groups" (p. 16). Such a strategy would not only add to knowledge of sources of within-group variability, but also be likely to undermine many of the stereotypes that contribute to current conceptualizations of substance use among non-European ethnic groups.

When substance abuse research necessitates the inclusion of ethnicity, it may be useful to consider the following recommendations outlined by Jones et al. (1991) in their review of the use of a race variable in epidemiological research. They stated,

> (1) Provide justification when including "race" as a variable. Define the presumed content of the variable in the context of the given study. (2) Describe how "race" is measured. (3) Include explicit measures of socioeconomic status, culture, and genetic endowment as appropriate. . . . (4) Provide an interpretation of observed "race"-associated differences. Discuss ideas for future research that can test hypotheses generated by the findings. (p. 1083)

Betancourt and Lopez (1993) recommended going beyond the specific grouping (whether based on race, ethnicity, culture, or social factor) to consideration of the factors that underlie the grouping. In this way, it would become possible to identify the components that contribute to the effects of the groupings. Rogler (1989) described culturally sensitive research as involving the entire research process, beginning with immersion into the culture(s) being studied (see also Marin, 1993). For prevention researchers, this would include knowledge of the ethnic and socioenvironmental characteristics of the population(s) being studied. These recommendations not only seem highly relevant to research on ethnicity and substance use/abuse, but also provide a minimum set of criteria by which to judge the scientific meaningfulness of ethnicity-based prevention research.

There are many indications that prevention research may be maturing. In a recent article describing a "science of prevention," Coie et al. (1993) outlined 10 major strategies and models for the future of prevention research. Recommendations for future research ranged from developing longitudinal models that emphasize the complex interaction between individual and environmental characteristics, to emphasizing continuous rather than categorical variables (a ban on ethnic glosses would be a nice start). Interestingly, Coie et al.'s listing of "generic risk factors" included individual (e.g., emotional difficulties, developmental delays) as well as social (e.g., neighborhood disorganization, racial injustice) conditions. Once again, there was no mention of ethnicity as related to risk, a clear acknowledgment that it is the individual characteristics and socioenvironmental conditions that can be experienced by members of any group (regardless of ethnicity) that truly contribute to the risk for problem behaviors.

Effective substance use/abuse prevention is likely to result from a multidimensional approach. Such an approach should not only focus on characteristics of the individual but also emphasize interventions related to socioenvironmental conditions. Thus, effective prevention strategies should go beyond substance use per se and include attention to broader social issues—for example, by considering social policies that confront the impact of socioeconomic disadvantage, enhance academic achievement, provide supervised activities for adolescents, and maintain more stable families and neighborhoods (National Research Council, 1993; Wallace & Bachman, 1991). There is a need for research on the effect of community-based preventive education to reduce the levels of substance use as well as the adverse consequences of substance abuse, particularly among high-risk subgroups such as adolescents and pregnant women. Other key issues include (a) developing and testing of theories based on etiological constructs that may explain variations in substance use (Hawkins et al., 1992; Moncher et al., 1990; Tucker, 1985); (b) developing a theoretically based risk assessment model for targeting adolescents at high risk for substance use, as well as for identifying protective and resiliency factors (Coie et al., 1993; Hawkins et al., 1992; Moncher et al., 1990; National Research Council, 1993); (c) addressing issues around bicultural identity (LaFromboise et al., 1993; Oetting & Beauvais, 1991; Phinney, 1990); (d) developing culturally sensitive programs of prevention research (Marin, 1993; Rogler, 1989); and (e) changing social norms regarding drug use, rather than attempting to change individual attitudes and behavior (Hawkins et al., 1992; Moskowitz, 1989).

We have already begun to make progress in research on some of the five areas outlined above. For example, family influences have been cited in numerous studies of the etiology of substance use in different populations, regardless of ethnicity (e.g., Brook et al., 1990, 1992; Moncher et al., 1990; Rhodes & Jason, 1990). Family-based prevention efforts could focus on issues specific to substance use or more generally on maintaining effective family functioning (Coie et al., 1993; Hawkins et al., 1992; National Research Council, 1993; Wallace & Bachman, 1991). Definitions of the family unit are likely to vary based on sociocultural factors. Thus, notions of "the family" should be broad enough to include siblings, parents, and other relatives, as well as others who play a significant role in the individual's life (see Collins, 1990; Marin, 1993). Finally, research on family-based substance abuse prevention could contribute to knowledge of factors related to resiliency in youngsters who do not succumb to social and environmental influences to use/abuse substances.

Cultural sensitivity and the changing of social norms have been highlighted in some approaches to prevention. Even within the multicultural society of the United States, prevention programs developed for the general population are likely to emphasize the values of the numerically larger, European-based culture. Prevention programs that are sensitive to non-European cultural traditions are likely to enhance prevention efforts targeted to ethnic groups (see, e.g., Gilchrist, Schinke, Trimble, & Cvetkovich, 1987). Such programs reflect the norms and traditions of the group(s) being targeted as well as current issues being faced by specific subgroups. Thus, prevention among American Indians might reflect specific tribal traditions as well as the epidemiology of alcohol use for specific groups, so as to better target those at high risk. May (1986) recommended that prevention efforts for American Indians be organized around public health approaches to reducing alcohol-related mortality and morbidity, such as changing alcohol-related laws (e.g., removal of prohibition on alcohol on some reservations). Other approaches of relevance to this community include education, particularly for youth, in which the dissemination of information is combined with skills training to enhance self-esteem and individual empowerment. Prevention among Latinos might reflect issues such as the role of familialism (Marin, 1993) or acculturation. For example, drinking among Mexican American females increases as a function of acculturation (Gilbert, 1991), suggesting that prevention efforts should be targeted at young Latinas who may be caught in a conflict between the norms for moderate alcohol use in the general population of the United States and Mexican cultural norms against women's drinking. These examples highlight the fact that research on the efficacy of culturally sensitive prevention programs must be based on detailed knowledge of the variety of sociocultural and drug-related issues that are encountered by different groups.

Research on strategies for changing social norms for substance use is representative of a broader public policy approach that could be quite effective. This approach acknowledges that some groups (and subgroups) may have norms and/or reasons for substance use that are different from those of the general population. For example, health warnings about the impact of smoking have successfully reduced smoking rates for the general population. However, adolescent females continue to initiate smoking at high rates, possibly as a function of their belief in smoking as a means of controlling weight and the salience of weight control among their cohort (Collins, 1993b). Similarly, during the past decade, changes in social norms regarding the use of illicit substances have led to a general decrease in the prevalence of illicit drug use among high school seniors and college students. However, a comparable change in norms regarding alcohol use has not occurred, and rates of alcohol use have been relatively stable in this population over the same time period (Johnson, O'Malley, & Bachman, 1992). Oetting and Beauvais (1987a, 1987b) also highlighted the role of social norms in their research on the impact of peer associations on drug use. In their view, effective prevention must "eventually influence the choice of peers, the formation of peer clusters, and the development of strong sanctions against drugs in the peer cluster" (Oetting & Beauvais, 1987b, p. 212). More research on the impact of social norms on substance use, particularly as they pertain to peer influences (see Brook et al., 1990), substance use by females (Fillmore, 1987), and the role of acculturation (Gilbert, 1991), is likely to enhance knowledge concerning effective prevention strategies.

Some ethnic communities have attempted to change social norms about substance use by mobilizing prevention efforts to counteract the special targeting of ethnic groups by those who manufacture and sell alcohol and tobacco. Their efforts have included (a) confronting alcohol and tobacco advertising and the marketing of new products targeted to specific ethnic groups and lower SES communities, (b) boycotting liquor stores and cigarette manufacturers, and (c) questioning the impact of civic and sporting events sponsored by alcohol and cigarette manufacturers (Hacker, Collins, & Jacobson, 1987; Maxwell & Jacobson, 1989; McMahon & Taylor, 1990). More research is needed on the impact of these community-generated efforts at prevention and mobilization. Such research would provide not only information on the efficacy of this approach to prevention but also ideas for innovative prevention strategies that could be applied to other groups in other settings. A community prevention approach also suggests that prevention programs may be more effectively mounted in settings where the populations being targeted are likely to congregate, such as the workplace (Nathan, 1984), churches (Prugh, 1986-1987), and child care agencies (Noel & McCrady, 1984).

Although not exhaustive, the research outlined here clearly indicates the variety of issues that need to be included in a broad sociocultural and environmental approach to prevention research. Methodological and conceptually sound research framed within this perspective can offer insights into the development of effective substance abuse prevention for persons of all ages from a variety of backgrounds and social strata. For other recommendations relevant to prevention research, see also recent reviews by Coie et al. (1993), De La Rosa, Adrados, Kennedy, and Milburn (1993), Hawkins et al. (1992), the National Research Council (1993), and Trimble (in press).

SUMMARY

The research reviewed here suggests limited conceptual and methodological progress in research on sociocultural factors as they pertain to ethnicity and the prevention of substance use and abuse. This state of affairs provides tremendous opportunities to advance knowledge on a wide variety of topics. To develop effective strategies, prevention research must begin to face the complexity of ethnicity as well as the interaction of individual and environmental characteristics in determining substance use/abuse. These areas of complexity may demand that prevention researchers become more involved in policy debates and community outreach and organization. We may want to begin our challenge of the status quo by examining our use of ethnic glosses when we label research participants (or ask them to label themselves). We must also be cognizant of our endorsement of the "homogeneity myth" when we conduct studies and analyze data based on ethnic categories that do not represent the variation within groups. We must be careful that comparative research is conducted only when theoretically relevant and that explanatory variables are included in such comparisons. As stated by Lillie-Blanton et al. (1993), "Researchers have the responsibility to go beyond the reporting of racial/ethnic differences, particularly when population groups differ on attributes that can affect the comparison" (p. 997). We must begin to act on this responsibility.

The issues discussed in this chapter become particularly salient given the current mandate to include women and ethnic groups in federally funded research. Although this mandate has the potential to increase progress in our understanding of groups that have been underrepresented in research, it also has the potential to maintain stereotypes and reinforce the status quo. Thus, the potential of the federal mandate and other efforts to broaden the focus of prevention research can only be realized if researchers adopt new approaches to conceptual and methodological issues related to conducting research with ethnic samples and with women. Research that conforms to the words of the federal guidelines by relying on ethnic glosses or gender-based stereotypes will not add to knowledge. It is not sufficient to include a low-income African American sample of adolescents in a prevention study if the strategies being tested are not informed by knowledge of the range of social, environmental, and cultural issues faced by these adolescents. It is not sufficient to discuss the prevalence of substance use among American Indians if the discussion does not include a careful description of tribal affiliation, environmental conditions, level of education, and other sociocultural factors. Prevention researchers do not have to possess the demographic or sociocultural characteristics of the populations they study. However, successful researchers are likely to be those who understand the impact of these characteristics and strive to enhance the communities in which they conduct research. One potential area for making significant contributions is the training and mentoring of researchers who are from non-European backgrounds. The pool of researchers that could be developed as a result of such efforts is likely to ensure future progress in all areas of research on substance use and abuse.

References

Anderson, N. B. (1989). Racial differences in stress-induced cardiovascular reactivity and hypertension. Current status and substantive issues. *Psychological Bulletin, 195,* 89-105.

Bangert-Drowns, R. L. (1988). The effects of school-based substance abuse education: A meta-analysis. *Journal of Drug Education, 18,* 243-264.

Betancourt, H., & Lopez, S. R. (1993). The study of culture, ethnicity, and race in American psychology. *American Psychologist, 48,* 629-637.

Blane, H. T. (1993). Ethnicity. In M. Galanter (Ed.), *Recent developments in alcoholism: Vol. 11. Ten years of progress* (pp. 109-122). New York: Plenum.

Brook, J. S., Brook, D. W., Gordon, A. S., Whiteman, M., & Cohen, P. (1990). The psychosocial etiology of adolescent drug use: A family interactional approach. *Genetic, Social, and General Psychology Monographs, 116,* 111-267.

Brook, J. S., Whiteman, M., Balka, E. B., & Hamburg, B. A. (1992). African-American and Puerto-Rican drug use: Personality, familial, and other environmental risk factors. *Genetic, Social, and General Psychology Monographs, 118,* 417-438.

Caetano, R. (1986). Alternative definitions of Hispanics: Consequences in an alcohol survey. *Hispanic Journal of Behavioral Sciences, 8,* 331-344

Cheung, Y. W. (1989). Making sense of ethnicity and drug use: A review and suggestions for future research. *Social Pharmacology, 3,* 55-82.

Coie, J. D., Watt, N. F., West, S. G., Hawkins, J. D., Asarnow, J. R., Markman, H. J., Ramey, S. L., Shure, M. B., & Long, B. (1993). The science of prevention: A conceptual framework and some directions for a national research program. *American Psychologist, 48,* 1013-1022.

Collins, R. L. (1990). Family treatment of alcohol abuse: Behavioral and systems perspectives. In R. L. Collins, K. E. Leonard, & J. S. Searles (Eds.), *Alcohol and the family: Research and clinical perspectives* (pp. 285-308). New York: Guilford.

Collins, R. L. (1992). Methodological issues in conducting substance abuse research on ethnic minority populations. *Drugs and Society, 6,* 59-77.

Collins, R. L. (1993a). Sociocultural aspects of alcohol abuse: Ethnicity and gender. *Drugs and Society, 8,* 89-116.

Collins, R. L. (1993b). Women's issues in alcohol use and cigarette smoking. In J. S. Baer, G. A. Marlatt, & R. J. McMahon (Eds.), *Addictive behaviors across the lifespan: Prevention, treatment, and policy issues* (pp. 274-306). Newbury Park, CA: Sage.

De La Rosa, M. R., Adrados, J.-L. R., Kennedy, N. J., & Milburn, N. (1993). Current gaps and new directions for studying drug use and abuse behavior in minority youth. In M. R. De La Rosa & J.-L. R. Adrados (Eds.), *Drug abuse among minority youth: Methodological issues and recent research advances* (NIDA Research Monograph No. 130, pp. 321-340). Washington, DC: Government Printing Office.

Fillmore, K. M. (1987). Women's drinking across the adult life course as compared to men. *British Journal of Addiction, 82,* 801-811.

Fisher, A. D. (1987). Alcoholism and race: The misapplication of both concepts to North American Indians. *Canadian Review of Sociology and Anthropology, 24,* 81-98.

Gilbert, M. J. (1991). Acculturation and changes in drinking patterns among Mexican-American women: Implications for prevention. *Alcohol Health and Research World, 15,* 234-238.

Gilchrist, L., Schinke, S., Trimble, J., & Cvetkovich, G. (1987). Skills enhancement to prevent substance abuse among American Indian adolescents. *International Journal of the Addictions, 22,* 869-879.

Hacker, G. A., Collins, R., & Jacobson, M. (1987). *Marketing booze to blacks.* Washington, DC: Center for Science in the Public Interest.

Hawkins, J. D., Catalano, R. F., & Miller, J. Y. (1992). Risk and protective factors for alcohol and other drug problems in adolescence and early adulthood: Implications for substance abuse prevention. *Psychological Bulletin, 112,* 64-105.

Heath, D. B. (1991). Uses and misuses of the concept of ethnicity in alcohol studies: An essay in deconstruction. *International Journal of the Addictions, 25,* 607-628.

Johnson, L. D., O'Malley, P. M., & Bachman, J. G. (1992). *Smoking, drinking, and illicit drug use among American secondary school students, college students, and young adults, 1975-1991.* Rockville, MD: National Institute on Drug Abuse.

Jones, C. P., LaVeist, T. A., & Lillie-Blanton, M. (1991). "Race" in the epidemiologic literature: An examination of the *American Journal of Epidemiology,* 1921-1990. *American Journal of Epidemiology, 134,* 1079-1084.

Jones, J. M. (1991). Psychological models of race: What have they been and what should they be? In J. D. Goodchilds (Ed.), *Psychological perspectives on human diversity in America* (pp. 3-46). Washington, DC: American Psychological Association.

LaFromboise, T., Coleman, H. L. K., & Gerton, J. (1993). Psychological impact of biculturalism: Evidence and theory. *Psychological Bulletin, 114,* 395-412.

Lex, B. W., (1987). Review of alcohol problems in ethnic minority groups. *Journal of Consulting and Clinical Psychology, 55,* 293-300.

Lillie-Blanton, M., Anthony, J. C., & Schuster, C. R. (1993). Probing the meaning of racial/ethnic group comparisons in crack cocaine smoking. *Journal of the American Medical Association, 269,* 993-997.

Marin, G. (1993). Defining culturally appropriate community interventions: Hispanics as a case study. *Journal of Community Psychology, 21,* 149-161.

Mauss, A. L., Hopkins, R. H., Weisheit, R. A., & Kearney, K. A. (1988). The problematic prospects for prevention in the classroom: Should alcohol education programs be expected to reduce drinking by youth? *Journal of Studies on Alcohol, 49,* 51-61.

Maxwell, B., & Jacobson, M. (1989). *Marketing disease to Hispanics: The selling of alcohol, tobacco, and junk foods.* Washington, DC: Center for Science in the Public Interest.

May, P. A. (1986). Alcohol and drug misuse prevention programs for American Indians: Needs and opportunities. *Journal of Studies on Alcohol, 47,* 187-195.

McMahon, E. T., & Taylor, P. A. (1990). *Citizens' action handbook on alcohol and tobacco billboard advertising.* Washington, DC: Center for Science in the Public Interest.

Midanik, L. T., & Room, R. (1992). The epidemiology of alcohol consumption. *Alcohol Health and Research World, 16,* 183-190.

Moncher, M. S., Holden, G. W., & Trimble, J. E. (1990). Substance abuse among Native-American youth. *Journal of Consulting and Clinical Psychology, 58,* 408-415.

Moskowitz, J. M. (1989). The primary prevention of alcohol problems: A critical review of the research literature. *Journal of Studies on Alcohol, 50,* 54-88.

Nathan, P. E. (1984). Alcoholism prevention in the workplace: Three examples. In P. M. Miller & T. D. Nirenberg (Eds.), *Prevention of alcohol abuse* (pp. 387-405). New York: Plenum.

National Institute on Drug Abuse (1990). *National Household Survey on Drug Abuse: Main findings 1988* (DHHS Publication No. ADM 90-1692). Washington, DC: Government Printing Office.

National Research Council. (1993). *Losing generations: Adolescents in high-risk settings.* Washington, DC: National Academy Press.

Noel, N. E., & McCrady, B. S. (1984). Target populations for alcohol abuse prevention. In P. M. Miller & T. D. Nirenberg (Eds.), *Prevention of alcohol abuse* (pp. 55-94). New York: Plenum.

Oetting, E. R., & Beauvais, F. (1987a). Common elements in youth drug abuse: Peer clusters and other psychosocial factors. *Journal of Drug Issues, 17,* 133-151.

Oetting, E. R., & Beauvais, F. (1987b). Peer cluster theory, socialization characteristics, and adolescent drug use: A path analysis. *Journal of Counseling Psychology, 34,* 205-213.

Oetting, E. R., & Beauvais, F. (1991). Orthogonal cultural identification theory: The cultural identification of minority adolescents. *International Journal of the Addictions, 25,* 655-685.

Osborne, N. G., & Feit, M. D. (1992). The use of race in medical research. *Journal of the American Medical Association, 267,* 275-279.

Pentz, M. A., Brannon, B. R., Charlin, V. L., Barrett, E. J., MacKinnon, D. P., & Flay, B. R. (1989). The power of policy: The relationship of smoking policy to adolescent smoking. *American Journal of Public Health, 79,* 857-862.

Phinney, J. S. (1990). Ethnic identity in adolescents and adults: Review of research. *Psychological Bulletin, 108,* 499-514.

Prugh, T. (1986-1987). The black church: A foundation for recovery. *Alcohol Health and Research World, 11,* 52-55.

Rhodes, J. E., & Jason, L. A. (1990). A social stress model of substance abuse. *Journal of Consulting and Clinical Psychology, 58,* 395-401.

Rogler, L. H. (1989). The meaning of culturally sensitive research in mental health. *American Journal of Psychiatry, 146,* 296-303.

Schinke, S., Orlandi, M., Vaccaro, D., Espinoza, R., McAlister, A., & Botvin, G. (1992). Substance use among Hispanic and non-Hispanic adolescents. *Addictive Behaviors, 17,* 117-124.

Tobler, N. S. (1986). Meta-analysis of 143 adolescent drug prevention programs: Quantitative outcome results of program participants compared to a control or comparison group. *Journal of Drug Issues, 16,* 537-567.

Trimble, J. E. (1991). Ethnic specification, validation prospect, and the future of drug use research. *International Journal of the Addictions, 25,* 149-170.

Trimble, J. E. (in press). Drug abuse prevention strategies among ethnic-minority populations. In R. Coombs & D. Ziedonis (Eds.), *Handbook on drug abuse prevention.* Englewood Cliffs, NJ: Prentice Hall.

Tucker, M. B. (1985). U.S. ethnic minorities and drug abuse: An assessment of the science and practice. *International Journal of the Addictions, 20,* 1021-1047.

Vega, W. A., Gil, A., Warheit, G., Apospori, E., & Zimmerman, R. (1993). The relationship of drug use to suicide ideation and attempts among African American, Hispanic, and white Non-Hispanic male adolescents. *Suicide and Life-Threatening Behavior, 23,* 110-119.

Wallace, J. M., & Bachman, J. G. (1991). Explaining racial/ethnic differences in adolescent drug use: The impact of background and lifestyle. *Social Problems, 38,* 333-357.

Welte, J. W., & Barnes, G. M. (1987). Alcohol use among adolescent minority groups. *Journal of Studies on Alcohol, 48,* 329-336.

Yee, A. H., Fairchild, H. H., Weizmann, F., & Wyatt, G. E. (1993). Addressing psychology's problems with race. *American Psychologist, 48,* 1132-1140.

Zuckerman, M. (1990). Some dubious premises in research and theory on racial differences. *American Psychologist, 45,* 1297-1303.

Conducting Research in
Ethnic Minority Communities

Considerations and Challenges

Robert E. Fullilove
Mindy Thompson Fullilove

Race is an important explanatory variable in public health research. In many studies, particularly those that examine drug abuse, sexually transmitted disease, criminal behavior, or a vast array of other social problems, race is one of the most frequently used predictors to "explain" the variation in these variables. Given the frequency with which this type of analysis appears in the literature, it seems reasonable to ask exactly what is being explained (Osborne & Feit, 1992).

Does race, for example, *cause* higher rates of sexually transmitted disease, greater levels of criminal behavior, or higher levels of illicit drug use? Is there some predisposition to deviant behavior that is genetically based? Is, say, risk of exposure to HIV *caused* by larger noses, darker skin, coarser hair, or any of a host of other inherited characteristics that distinguish members of one race from another? If this is, indeed, the model that is being tested, exactly how does the causal process that is being (implicitly) described work?

Causation has always been a problem for researchers (Cook & Campbell, 1979). The search for possible cause-and-effect relationships in data collected via survey research methods, for example, is frequently justified in

AUTHORS' NOTE: This work was supported in part by the Agency for Health Care Policy and Research, Grant No. 1-U01-HS07399.

the hopes that we will find the means to control the phenomena being studied. But how does the use of race as an explanatory variable fit in this scheme? If race is associated with, say, likelihood of using drugs, how is one to make use of this information? Are we to understand that drug abuse can be controlled by changing an individual's race or by finding a race- specific drug use gene and altering it somehow before birth?

We would suggest at this point that the reader actually conduct a "thought experiment" whose object would be to articulate the features of a (statistical) model that attempts to explain how race operates to "cause" drug abuse or sexually transmitted disease or violence. Such thought experiments—considered to be an essential part of the reasoning of no less a thinker than Albert Einstein in the development of the theories of relativity—are suggested here to raise two points. The first is to demonstrate how difficult it is to construct a reasonable explanation of what such analyses tell us. The second is to encourage speculation as to what is being concealed within the race effects that so many studies continue to report.

The reader is no doubt tempted to counter that it is not really "race" that is being examined in such studies but instead—and the choices are vast—socioeconomic status, sociopolitical status, culture, language (not to be confused with culture), region, neighborhood, history, diet, or all of the above. Interestingly enough, however, even a casual examination of articles in some of the more widely circulated public health journals reveals that although race appears in a large number of titles and in a larger number of data tables, justifications and explanations for such an analysis rarely do. If, indeed, race is a proxy for more complex processes and/or social conditions, one might ask why an attempt to specify these processes is so dramatically lacking from much of the literature.

Again, a simple exercise can be proposed. From the 12 issues of the *American Journal of Public Health* published in 1993, we selected the August 1993 issue at random. Table 3.1 lists the titles of the 12 articles that appeared in the "Articles" section of this issue and the manner in which race was or was not reported. As shown, of the 7 articles describing the results of empirical studies conducted in the United States, all 7 used race in the analysis of data. Socioeconomic status variables (education and income) appeared in 2 of the 7 articles.

Readers familiar with this literature will undoubtedly concede the point. A larger sample and a selection of different journals would not produce results that differ dramatically from those reported here. Although a number of these articles were specifically written to demystify the role that race appears to play in complex health behaviors and conditions, none succeeded completely in explaining the apparent variance that is associated with race/ethnicity (see

TABLE 3.1 Race and Other Variables Appearing in "Articles" Section
of the *American Journal of Public Health,* 1993, Vol. 83, No. 8

Author	U.S.?	Race in Title?	Race in Data?	Other Variables?[a]
Population-Based Studies Done in the U.S.				
Keppel & Taffel	yes	no	yes	no
McKenzie & Stephenson	yes	no	yes	yes
Land & Stockbauer	yes	yes	yes	no
Collins & Davis	yes	yes	yes	yes
Booth et al.	yes	no	yes	no
Gfroerer & Brodsky	yes	no	yes	no
Studies Done With Non-U.S. Population				
Goldman et al.[b]	no	no	no	yes
Savitz et al.[c]	no	n/a	n/a	n/a
Campostrini & McQueen[d]	no	n/a	n/a	n/a
Theoretical and/or Non-Population-Based Studies				
Bourgoin et al.[e]	yes	n/a	n/a	n/a
Thijs & Knipschild[f]	no	n/a	n/a	n/a
Pelletier et al.[g]	no	n/a	n/a	n/a

a. Uses other variables that might explain race-based effects.
b. Study conducted in Canada.
c. Study of Vietnamese infant mortality.
d. Study conducted in Scotland.
e. Examined lead content in dietary supplements.
f. Meta-analysis.
g. Theoretical description.

Collins & Davis, 1993). The issue we raise, however, is not an ideological one—we are not proposing that race effects should never be studied. Rather, it is a practical one: How can one make use of these data or these findings to change the conditions that are described?

Typically, such articles conclude by recommending one or more of the following: Race should be used to identify those whom we should treat, advise, provide with resources, educate, train, be concerned about, or submit to further study. Many researchers, aware that they may have raised as many questions as they have answered, conclude with statements to the effect that "the findings reported here are difficult to interpret." Others note that race masks complex relationships that will require further research to disentangle. Suffice it to say, this is a sentiment with which we heartily concur. However, this research is still largely undone.

Considerations in Conducting
Research With Minority Populations

In subsequent sections of this chapter, we argue that two conditions must be considered in research conducted in communities of color. First, the researcher must specify exactly what hypotheses will be tested if and when comparisons are made between respondents or subjects of different races. Specifically, the researcher must describe the features of the model to be tested. How is race being defined, and how is it thought to explain the behaviors or the conditions that are being examined? If criminal behavior or other socially undesirable conditions are being studied, and if race is somehow implicated in explaining the variation that is observed, do the variables that are being used have the potential to be manipulated in some fashion so that the quality of life of the respondents can be improved or so that harmful conditions can be eliminated?

Would policy makers, physicians, politicians, foundation officials, or members of the general public, for example, be able to use results of a proposed study to develop programs, make decisions about how to allocate resources, develop legislation, or vote on proposed legislation that would be relevant to the problem being described? These questions are posed on the assumption that race-based research is more than a simple quest for information for information's sake. Presumably, such research (and the involvement of community respondents) is being pursued with the intent of doing something useful for the respondent as well as for the researcher.

The second consideration in contemplating race-based research is utilitarian. If the desire to be useful and to render some service is, indeed, at the core of our motivation to pursue race-based studies, the concept of "usefulness" certainly deserves further elaboration from the standpoint of the research subject. Is information that is useful for a scientist also, indeed, useful to the respondent who provides it? Will the respondent (or will members of his or her community) benefit as much as the collector from the exercise of collecting and reporting community data? If the answer is "no," has the respondent been compensated in some way for the service he or she has rendered to researchers? If the respondent is to be compensated, how does one establish an equitable "rate of exchange" for the provision of such information in exchange for whatever perquisites accrue to the researcher/ investigator?

The reader may, correctly, protest that such questions are already considered, both implicitly and explicitly, in the process of securing institutional review board approval for a study or in satisfying the requirements that a study conform to the principles and practices of the protection of the rights of human subjects. Again, we concur. However, we ask that the following vignette be considered by the reader before any conclusion is drawn as to the adequacy of such reviews.

The Harlem Household Survey

One of the most thought-provoking studies of the 1990s was published by McCord and Freeman (1990) in the *New England Journal of Medicine.* The article, "Excess Mortality in Harlem," used death certificates and census data to examine the patterns of morbidity and mortality in this well-known African American community. The study's principal conclusion—that black men in Harlem are less likely to live to the age of 65 than men in Bangladesh—was widely reported. The authors' findings were the subject of numerous editorials, the cause for a substantial amount of speculation on the part of members of the public health research community, and the motivation to search for a more precise specification of the causes of such a dismal state of affairs.

In 1991, the Centers for Disease Control agreed to fund the Harlem Hospital Center for Health Promotion and Disease Prevention to conduct a household survey of the health status of Harlem residents. The survey was designed to assess the factors, both behavioral and institutional, that might explain McCord and Freeman's findings. We assumed the direction of this study in the fall of 1992. As African American researchers with a long personal history of contact with Harlem, we never questioned the need to do the study, nor did we question the belief that its results would be useful to the community in general or the study's respondents in particular. When such questions were, in fact, raised, we were taken unaware.

The meeting was held in our offices. Three community "representatives" met with us to discuss "concerns that have been raised about the Household Study." Flyers that had been distributed by survey interviewers had reached their hands, and they were interested in questioning us about our intentions and our motives. "Why did you decide to do this study?" we were asked. We cited the McCord and Freeman (1990) article and explained that such dramatic morbidity and mortality rates demanded further research to understand both the causes and the means of dealing with such a catastrophic public health problem. Our listeners appeared to concede that point, but pressed on.

How much was the study costing? We went through an explanation (specifically tailored for the layperson) of the costs of doing public health research and gave the same general justification for our budget that had been given to the Centers for Disease Control. Our listeners appeared to concede that point, but pressed on.

"Doc. Why do you need another study? You already know that we got some sick people in Harlem? Hell, I coulda saved you all that money. You could have just asked me. I'd have told you. I'd have told you where they live and why they sick.

"Hey. Can't get to a doctor, you get sick. It's simple.

"Wouldn't it have made more sense to spend that money on doctors? Seems to me that if people are sick, you don't study them. You get them a doctor and you pay for their health care. Wouldn't that have been a good idea?

"How come you didn't do that, Doc?"

Indeed.

Next question. "So when you get this information . . . what do you do with it?" We gave a sincere, albeit standard, stock answer. We said, to wit:

"We'll design programs and come up with health promotion campaigns. We'll attempt to secure funding to develop methods for dealing with behaviors and the obstacles that either prevent folks from taking better care of themselves or lead them to increase their risk of getting sick."

"That's good, Doc," came the response, "but what's in it for you? Don't you all get to publish your results and get promoted, and stuff like that?" We allowed as how doing well in research was like any other field, and that there were, indeed, rewards for doing well.

"Well then, would you say that you stood to gain more from doing this project than the people who took part in it? If they had been given a choice between, say, doing the research or buying Harlem some more doctors, do you think they'd have chosen research?

"Just asking, Doc."

Challenges to Conducting
Research in Minority Communities

Although this meeting ended with a pledge on our part to use the results to justify the time, the effort, and the money spent on the study, the questions that were posed have lingered with us. Perhaps we found them so disturbing because the answers were not quite as self-evident as we had presumed.

What does seem evident is that research in communities of color has become increasingly politicized, and that those who conduct such studies may well be asked to justify their efforts to more than just an institutional review board. As we begin the countdown to a new century, African American and Latin leaders are realizing that research dollars are among the very few resources flowing into their communities. Who can say, as a result, that they are not justified in asking to see more of us and to hear more from us before we use their friends and neighbors in surveys and clinical trials?

In many respects we are looking less to politicians and more to public health officials for solutions and answers to public health problems. As Angell (1993) and others have pointed out, society is increasingly attempting to "medicalize" the manner in which a host of social problems are understood and to propose biomedical/public health solutions to them. Violence, drug abuse, and AIDS are prime examples of issues that have both political and public health consequences. When a decision is made to study these problems, however, politicians and community leaders are not necessarily consulted as to the design and execution of a research effort. Nonetheless, if a proposed study expects to spend millions of dollars on the conduct of research in the community, there is every reason to assume that it will eventually come under political scrutiny by community spokespersons.

We would submit that one of the factors that will motivate close community scrutiny of public health studies will be our need and desire to control HIV and TB. Despite the acknowledged need for more effective treatments and for an effective AIDS vaccine, there is tremendous mistrust of the motives of scientists and of the scientific process. With the legacy of the Tuskegee Study still fresh in the minds of many African Americans (see Thomas & Quinn, 1991), there is no doubt that the prospect of "experimenting" with community residents will produce a demand that someone research the researchers.

The heavy burdens imposed by the AIDS epidemic, however, suggest that some attempt to test and evaluate an HIV vaccine in communities that are particularly hard hit by the AIDS epidemic is inevitable, despite the existence of such mistrust. In order to conduct HIV vaccine trials in as ethical a fashion as possible, however, the involvement of as many community members as is feasible in all phases of the development and conduct of such trials will be absolutely essential (Levine, Dubler, & Levine, 1991; Mariner, 1990). In order to ensure that the consequences and benefits of such research are well understood by all of those who will be affected by it, extensive campaigns will be conducted to explain the principles, purposes, benefits, and harms that are associated with such an undertaking.

Suffice it to say, the process of informing the community is very likely to have a different tone and feel than the institutional review board process that university-based researchers understand so well. Moreover, if we create mechanisms in these communities to explain how HIV vaccine trials are to be conducted, it is quite likely that community participants will ask to conduct similar reviews with all research conducted in the community, particularly if such research is supported with public funds. Local leaders might legitimately protest that universities and research institutes do not have the right to go fishing for research subjects anywhere they choose, particularly if the researchers do not reside in the communities or do not have any other involvement in community life other than to do research.

Criteria for Community-Based Minority Research

If community-based review processes for research are created in communities of color, three basic questions are likely to be posed with respect to any given study.[1]

1. *Is race functioning in this study as a risk factor or as a risk marker?*

Does race have biological significance, or is it simply a proxy for other, more complex phenomena? Is race simply a descriptive variable? Communities may question whether a study is likely to stigmatize research participants—and, by extension, the members of the communities from which participants are recruited—by imputing to them higher rates of some socially undesirable behavior (i.e., drug use) or some socially demeaning status (i.e., a criminal record). Will the design of the study provide the means to demystify the role that race ostensibly plays in the phenomena being studied, or is race the only variable being used to examine social, environmental, or economic forces?

The objective in raising this question is not to limit the legitimate pursuit of information, but rather to encourage better planning and better study design. Studies that are conducted simply to collect information not only are a costly waste of resources, but have the potential to do more harm than good. The caveat to "do no harm" should extend to scientific inquiry with the same rigor with which it is used to guide medical judgment and practice. It is reasonable, therefore, to ask for careful thinking and planning for studies that are likely to report racial differences in some important measure of public health or public safety.

2. *Will results of the study produce information and/or recommendations that can be used to improve the conditions that are being examined?*

It will not suffice to show the *potential* that a study has to improve such conditions: Researchers may be asked to specifically outline the process that will be used to go from the collection of data to the use of study findings in the development of programs and/or recommendations for legislators and/or policy makers. The reader may, at this point, protest that no one can foresee, before data are collected, how to use study results in such a fashion. True.

But community leaders may be equally justified in saying, "If you don't know where this thing is going, why should we support it?" They may go so far as to point out, in fact, that researchers do not have—in the name of "science"—an unlimited right to go out and collect information just because it might prove to be "interesting." If such information is, indeed, useful, then they should be able to specify its potential for use before, rather than after, the study has been completed.

3. *Is conducting a study the best use of resources?*

This is, perhaps, the most controversial question to be posed by this process. It is a provocative way of asking if a study is really necessary, and if it is, whether the researchers who have proposed it can convince the people whom they are about to study of its utility. Our experience suggests that scientists believe that they enjoy a special kind of entitlement. They are quite likely, we have discovered, to invoke principles of academic freedom and freedom of inquiry when confronted with the notion that nonscientists might have some say in when, how, and under what circumstances science is to be conducted.

In an earlier draft of this chapter, for example, a colleague became highly agitated by the notion that someone might reject a proposed study on the topic of, say, race and homelessness, on the grounds that the money might be better spent on getting a homeless person of color a home. "Where would communities of color be," he argued, "if scientists refused to conduct any studies in these neighborhoods as a protest against this form of interference?" Our response was that they would pretty much be in the state they are in now. Because the vast majority of the residents of these communities are entirely unaware of how these studies have contributed to an improvement in the quality of their lives, the prospect of not having them done fails to inspire fear and trembling in them.

This is all to suggest that discussions about science change drastically when the discussants are not our peers but are, instead, our subjects. It is also to suggest that many of us would be ill prepared to manage these discussions, and that if we are planning to do community-based research, we had better be prepared to respond to questions and to questioners who have no reason to respect the canons that many of us hold as inviolate and beyond reproach.

SUMMARY

Although we have attempted to be thought provoking in this discussion, a core of pragmatism lies at the heart of our thinking. Our work in communities hard hit by AIDS and drug abuse has made it clear that science is not highly regarded. Residents simply cannot see what science has done *for* them, but many can tell some version of the Tuskegee experiments as an example of what it has done *to* them.

We have tried to suggest that it would be foolish to believe that researchers have unlimited and unchallenged access to the residents of these communities simply because they are doing research. We have tried to suggest that conducting scientific "business as usual" will ultimately result in open hostility and calls for us to justify what we are doing.

Make no mistake about it. Business as usual to many of these community residents is perceived as showing an empirical association between race and evildoing. Business as usual means having scientists insist, on one hand, that race-based research is valid, but being unable to explain, on the other, what it means. Business as usual means spending large sums of money (often supported by their taxes) on studies that do great harm and no apparent "I can see it, touch it, and taste it" good.

In the future, business as usual may well mean going before a community research counsel and planning a study with a team of community representatives. It may mean brushing up on communication skills that are different from those we use to dazzle and awe our graduate students because we will be trying to explain complex issues to groups whose level of education may not extend beyond high school.

We do not mean to suggest that no one in the scientific community is doing this type of community education and negotiation. We want to suggest instead that it ought to be the rule governing our work, rather than the exception.

Note

1. Our thinking here has been greatly influenced by Osborn & Feit (1992). It is their critique of the misuse of race in this body of research that suggested the outlline of the remarks made here.

References

American Journal of Public Health. (1993, August). Vol. ? No.?

Angell, M. (1993). Privilege and health: What is the connection? *New England Journal of Medicine, 329,*126-127.

Booth, R. E., Wattens, J. K., & Chitwood, D. D. (1993). HIV risk-related sexual behaviors among injection drug users, crack smokers, and injection drug users who smoke crack. *American Journal of Public Health, 83,* 1144-1148.

Bourgoin, B. P., Evans, D. R., Cornett, J. R., Lingard, S. M., & Quattrone, A. J. (1993). Lead content in 70 brands of dietary calcium supplements. *American Journal of Public Health, 83,* 1155-1160.

Campostrini, S., & McQueen, D. V. (1993). Sexual behavior and exposure to HIV infection: Estimates from a general population risk survey. *American Journal of Public Health, 83,* 1139-1143.

Collins, J. W., & Davis, R. J. (1993). Race and birthweight in biracial infants. *American Journal of Public Health, 83,* 1125-1129.

Cook, T. D., & Campbell, D. T. (1979). *Quasi-experimentation: Design and analysis issues for field settings.* Boston: Houghton Mifflin.

Gfroerer, J. C., & Brodsky, M. D. (1993). Frequent cocaine users and their use of treatment. *American Journal of Public Health, 83,* 1149-1154.

Goldman, G., Pineault, R., Potvin, L., Blais, R., & Bilodeau, H. (1993). Factors influencing the practice of vaginal birth after cesarian section. *American Journal of Public Health, 83,* 1104-1108.

Keppel, K. G., & Taffel, S. M. (1993). Pregancy-related weight gain and retention: Implications of the 1990 Institute of Medicine Guidelines. *American Journal of Public Health, 83,* 1100-1103.

Land, G. H., & Stockbauer, J. W. (1993). Smoking and pregnancy outcome: Trends among black teenagers mothers in Missouri. *American Journal of Public Health, 83,* 1121-1124.

Levine, C., Dubler, N. N., & Levine, R. J. (1991). Building a new consensus: Ethical principles and policies for clinical research on HIV/AIDS. *Institutional Review Boards, 13,* 1-17.

Mariner, W. K. (1990). The ethical conduct of clinical trials of HIV vaccines. *Evaluation Review, 14,* 538-564.

McCord, C., & Freeman, H.P. (1990). Excess mortality in Harlem. *New England Journal of Medicine, 322,* 173-177.

McKenzie, L., & Stephenson, P. A. (1993). Variation in cesarian section rates among hospitals in Washington State. *American Journal of Public Health, 83,* 1109-1112.

Osborne, N. G., & Feit, M. D. (1992). The use of race in medical research. *Journal of American Medical Association, 267,* 275-279.

Pelletier, D. L., Frongillo, E. A., & Habicht, J. P. (1993). Epidemiologic evidence for a potentiating effect of malnutrition on child mortality. *American Journal of Public Health, 83,* 1130-1133.

Savitz, D. A., Thang, N. M., Swenson, I. E., & Stone, E. M. (1993). Vietnamese infant and childhood mortality in relation to the Vietnam war. *American Journal of Public Health, 83,* 1134-1138.

Thijs, C., & Knipschild, P. (1993). Oral contraceptives and the risk of gall bladder disease: A metanalysis. *American Journal of Public Health, 83,* 1113-1120.

Thomas, S. B., & Quinn, S. C. (1991). Public health then and now. The Tuskegee Syphilis Study, 1932 to 1972: Implications for HIV education and AIDS risk education programs in the black community. *American Journal of Public Health, 81,* 1498-1504.

PART

2

Drug Use Prevalence, Ethnic Differences, and Etiology

Racial/Ethnic Differences in Adolescent Drug Use

Exploring Possible Explanations

John M. Wallace Jr.
Jerald G. Bachman
Patrick M. O'Malley
Lloyd D. Johnston

The use and abuse of licit and illicit drugs has been implicated as a reason for the relatively high number of arrests among black and Hispanic males, as a major factor in the health disparities between whites and America's black and Hispanic populations, and, of course, as a primary cause for the disproportionate share of black and Hispanic adults in drug and alcohol treatment (Secretary's Task Force on Black and Minority Health, 1986). In light of the various "drug-related" problems that disproportionately affect black and Hispanic adults, a relatively high prevalence of drug abuse might be expected among black and Hispanic youth.

Despite this expectation, findings from national, state, and local surveys indicate that, on average, use of licit and illicit drugs is not higher among black and Hispanic youth than among white youth. In fact, the prevalence of drug use among black and Hispanic youth is typically comparable to, if not lower than, that reported by white youth (Austin & Gilbert, 1989; Bachman et al., 1991; Oetting & Beauvais, 1990; Prendergast, Maton, & Baker, 1989; Welte & Barnes, 1987). One possible exception to this general pattern is that

Hispanic youth in general, and Hispanic males in particular, report higher prevalence of cocaine use than other groups (see Table 4.2).

The research literature offers a number of potential explanations for why drug use is not, on average, higher among black and Hispanic youth than among white youth. The primary purpose of this chapter is to examine a number of these explanations. Prior to exploring these explanations, however, national data are presented on racial/ethnic differences in drug use epidemiology and trends.

Monitoring the Future

The data presented and examined in this chapter are drawn from the Monitoring the Future project, which annually surveys large, nationally representative samples of 8th-, 10th-, and 12th-grade students. Data from 12th graders have been collected annually by the University of Michigan's Survey Research Center since 1975. The first collection of data from 8th- and 10th-grade students took place in 1991.

The study uses a stratified cluster sampling procedure that results in samples representative of 8th-, 10th-, and 12th-grade students in the 48 coterminous states. First, particular geographic areas are selected. Next, schools are selected. Finally, students are selected in each school. Approximately 160 schools are selected for 8th graders, 135 for 10th graders, and 135 for seniors. The obtained samples include about 18,000 eighth graders, 16,000 tenth graders, and 16,000 twelfth graders each year.

Students complete machine-readable, self-administered questionnaires during a normal class period. Questionnaire response rates are about 90% for 8th graders, 87% for 10th graders, and 83% for seniors. Absence on the day of data collection is the primary reason that students are missed; in addition, fewer than 1% refuse to complete the questionnaire (see Johnston, O'Malley, & Bachman, 1993, for a more detailed discussion regarding the sampling, data collection, etc.).

The Monitoring the Future study was not explicitly designed to examine racial/ethnic differences in drug use; thus, black and Hispanic youth are not oversampled. In order to increase the number of cases, the analyses presented here combine data from 1991 and 1992. The racial/ethnic distribution of the sample is presented in Table 4.1. The table indicates that approximately 75% of the 8th, 10th, and 12 graders are white, 14% are black, and 10% are Hispanic. Because of their small numbers, young people from other racial/ethnic groups (e.g., Asian Americans, Native Americans) were omitted from the analyses.

TABLE 4.1 Racial/Ethnic Distribution of the Monitoring the Future Project Sample (1991-1992 Data Combined)

	8th		10th		12th	
	N	%	N	%	N	%
White	21,900	74.2	19,600	75.1	21,500	76.8
Black	4,200	14.2	3,900	14.9	3,900	13.9
Hispanic	3,400	11.5	2,600	10.0	26,00	9.3

NOTE: Percentages may not sum 100% due to rounding.

Epidemiology

In an earlier study (Bachman et al., 1991), we documented racial/ethnic differences in the prevalence of drug use among high school seniors (1985-1989 data combined). The data presented in Table 4.2 extend these earlier analyses to cover the classes of 1991-1992. Specifically, the table presents the prevalence of cigarette, alcohol, marijuana, and cocaine use among white, black, and Hispanic high school seniors. The cigarette measure asks, "How frequently have you smoked cigarettes during the past 30 Days?" The wording of the alcohol, marijuana, and cocaine measures is as follows: "On how many occasions (if any) have you used [drug] . . . in your lifetime . . . during the last 12 months . . . during the last 30 days?" The prevalence estimates indicate any use of the specific drug during the specified period. For recent data on racial/ethnic differences on a wider range of drugs, see Johnston et al., 1993).

Are minority youth more likely than white youth to use drugs? Based on data from recent classes of high school seniors, the answer is no. Consistent with findings from earlier research, the data presented in Table 4.2 indicate that drug use is, on average, lowest among black seniors; white seniors have the highest rates of smoking and heavy drinking; Hispanic seniors have the highest rates of cocaine use.

Only 9% of black seniors smoked cigarettes in the last 30 days compared to nearly a third of white seniors and a quarter of Hispanic seniors. More than 20% of white seniors smoked daily compared to 13% of Hispanic seniors and 4% of black seniors. Similar racial/ethnic disparities exist for more frequent use, with 12% of white seniors compared to 5% of Hispanic seniors and 2% of black seniors smoking a half-pack or more of cigarettes per day.

Four out of five white and Hispanic seniors, versus three out of five black seniors, used alcohol in the last year. Further, over half of white and Hispanic seniors used alcohol in the last month compared to less than a third

TABLE 4.2 Prevalence of Cigarette, Alcohol, Marijuana, and Cocaine Use Among American High School Seniors, by Race (1991-1992 Data Combined)

Drug Used	Frequency (%)	Frequency (%)	Prevalence (%)
Cigarettes	30-Day	Daily	Half-Pack
White	31.7	20.5	12.1
Black	8.8	4.3	1.7
Hispanic	25.0	12.5	4.5
Alcohol	Annual	30-Day	5 or More[a]
White	80.2	56.8	31.0
Black	63.6	31.7	10.3
Hispanic	80.3	53.8	21.9
Marijuana	Lifetime	Annual	30-Day
White	36.3	24.9	14.1
Black	23.3	11.5	6.1
Hispanic	40.7	24.7	12.7
Cocaine	Lifetime	Annual	30-Day
White	7.0	3.3	1.3
Black	2.4	1.2	0.7
Hispanic	12.1	5.2	1.9

a. Five or more drinks in a row in a single sitting.

of black seniors. Heavy alcohol use (i.e., five or more drinks in a row) is relatively high among white seniors (31%), somewhat lower among Hispanic seniors (22%), and lowest among black seniors (10%).

With respect to the illicit drugs, lifetime marijuana use is slightly higher among Hispanic seniors (41%) than among white seniors (36%), but there is little difference in their annual prevalences (both 25%) and 30-day prevalences (13% for Hispanic seniors and 14% for white seniors). Black seniors report annual and 30-day prevalences considerably lower than those reported by white and Hispanic seniors; only 12% report use in the last year, and only 6% have used in the last 30 days. As with marijuana, lifetime cocaine use is highest among Hispanic seniors (12% versus 7% for white seniors and 2% for black seniors). Annual cocaine use is also slightly higher among Hispanic youth.

In sum, contrary to media portrayals, and data on "drug-related" problems, prevalence data from high school *seniors* do not substantiate the notion that drug use is higher among black and Hispanic youth than among white youth. In fact, the data indicate that licit and illicit drug use rates among black seniors are substantially lower than rates among either of the other two groups.

Trends

Recent decades have witnessed a number of important changes in drug use among young people. By the late 1970s, nearly two thirds of high school seniors had used an illicit drug in their lifetime, more than half had used drugs in the last year, and almost 40% reported use in the last 30 days (Johnston et al., 1993). Since the peak of the epidemic, illicit drug use has declined significantly; by 1992 only 41% of seniors reported lifetime use, 27% reported annual use, and 14% reported use in the last 30 days. Although there has been a general decline in illicit drug use among American youth between the late 1970s and the mid-1980s, there was a significant increase in the prevalence of cocaine use (Johnston et al., 1993).

Licit drug use (i.e., cigarette and alcohol use) has also declined over time. For example, 41% of seniors in 1979 reported having five or more drinks in a row in the last 2 weeks compared to only 28% by 1992. The decline in cigarette use has been much more modest than that for other drugs. In fact, since 1984, most measures of cigarette use have remained essentially unchanged (Johnston et al., 1993). Figure 4.1 presents trends in the prevalence of cigarette, alcohol, marijuana, and cocaine use for white, black, and Hispanic seniors from 1976 through 1992. With the exception of cigarettes, trends in drug use have been fairly similar for white, black, and Hispanic youth. The figure indicates that whereas there has been relatively little net change in 30-day cigarette use for white and Hispanic seniors since the early 1980s, black seniors' cigarette use has consistently declined. Until around 1990, all three groups showed gradual declines in 30- day alcohol use. Since that time, black and white seniors have continued to experience a slight decline, but among Hispanic youth, there appears to have been a slight increase. Whether the apparent increase in alcohol (and marijuana) use is substantively significant or simply the result of sampling fluctuations can better be answered when another year or two of data are available. With the exception just noted, all three groups have experienced sharp declines in annual marijuana use. Although the increase in annual cocaine prevalence that occurred in the early to mid-1980s was considerably sharper among white and Hispanic seniors than among black seniors, all three groups have experienced the general decline in use that has occurred since that time.

Explanations

The literature on racial/ethnic differences in adolescent drug use offers a number of possible explanations for why self-reported drug use is not higher among black and Hispanic youth and for the apparent discrepancy

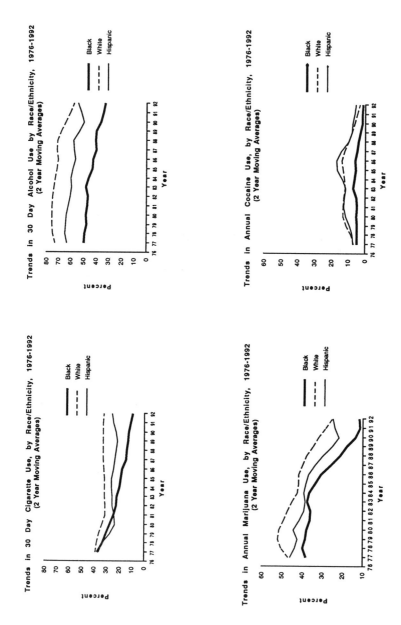

Figure 4.1. Trends in Drug Use Among High School Seniors, by Ethnicity, 1976-1992

64

between minority youths' self-reported drug use and data that suggest that minority group members are disproportionately affected by drug-related problems. A number of these explanations are discussed below and are examined empirically using data from Monitoring the Future's nationally representative samples of 8th-, 10th-, and 12th-grade students.

INVALIDITY HYPOTHESIS

Perhaps the most basic explanation given for the finding of lower levels of self-reported drug use among black and Hispanic youth is that minority youth are simply less likely than white youth to report their drug use truthfully. Mensch and Kandel (1988) suggested that "there may be consistently greater underreporting of deviant activities by black and Hispanic than by white respondents" (p. 120), and according to Kandel (1991), "Self reports of sensitive behaviors, such as drug use, may be subject to reporting bias. . . . In particular, blacks appear to be more likely than other ethnic groups to report their infrequent use of illicit drugs" (p. 371).

There is a growing literature on the validity of self-reported drug use measures (e.g., Johnston & O'Malley, 1985; O'Malley, Bachman, & Johnston, 1983; Rouse, Kozel, & Richards, 1985), but relatively little of this research examines the possibility of racial/ethnic differences in the validity of responses to these measures. In one of the few studies to address this issue, Mensch and Kandel (1988) found that black and Hispanic youth were more likely than white youth to underreport their use of marijuana. It should be noted, however, that this underreporting occurred only at the lowest levels of use, and that no such underreporting was reported for the licit drugs (i.e., alcohol and cigarettes) that show the largest subgroup differences in use. In addition, the data source on which they reported, the National Longitudinal Survey, used face-to-face interviews and required respondents to answer the drug use questions out loud. Given these circumstances, some respondents, particularly minority respondents, might have had some concern about the confidentiality of their responses.

More recently, Wallace and Bachman (1993) used data from Monitoring the Future's high school seniors to investigate the validity of racial/ethnic differences in self-reported drug use. In the absence of objective criteria such as blood or hair samples, racial/ethnic differences in responses to a number of subjective validity measures were examined: specifically, measures concerning the risk level that students perceive is associated with the use of various drugs, their disapproval of someone (18 or older) who would use various drugs, their perceptions of their friends' disapproval of using a particular drug, and the extent to which their friends and other associates use drugs.

Given research that indicates that self-reported drug use is strongly correlated with various attitude and belief measures, it seemed reasonable to expect that students who used drugs least would (a) perceive greater risk in the use of drugs, (b) express greater disapproval of drug use, (c) perceive greater disapproval of their using drugs by their friends, (d) perceive that fewer of their friends use drugs, and (e) report less exposure to people who are using drugs. Table 4.3 presents results of several attitude, belief, and exposure measures. The data presented in the table and elsewhere (Wallace & Bachman, 1993) are consistent with expectations, and roughly parallel self-reported patterns of use. On the basis of patterns of self-reported use, it was expected and generally found that perceived risk and disapproval were highest among black seniors, lower among Hispanic seniors, and even lower among white seniors (see Table 4.3).

Conversely, it was expected, and found, that exposure and friends' use were generally highest among white seniors, somewhat lower among Hispanic seniors, and lowest among black seniors. One exception to this general pattern was that black seniors reported an unexpectedly high proportion of friends who used marijuana (see Wallace & Bachman, 1993). In light of the fact that Hispanic seniors reported higher cocaine prevalences than other groups, it was hypothesized that their responses to cocaine attitudes, beliefs, and exposure items could be correspondingly higher. In general, this hypothesis was also confirmed. For example, Hispanic seniors reported more frequent exposure to cocaine users, consistent with their slightly higher prevalences of cocaine use (see Table 4.3).

In sum, the results for the validity indicators largely parallel the self-reports of drug use. This evidence, coupled with the consistency of the findings across studies that drug use is not higher among black and Hispanic youth, suggests that the self-report data are generally valid. Accordingly, the invalidity hypothesis does not seem sufficient to account for racial/ethnic differences in self-reported use, at least not among high school seniors.

ABSTINENCE/ABUSE HYPOTHESIS

A second explanation given to account for the apparent paradox between the relatively low self-reports of drug use among black and Hispanic youth and their relatively high prevalence of drug-related social problems is the abstinence/abuse hypothesis. This hypothesis highlights the important difference between prevalence (percentage who report any use) and the intensity of use among those who use. The abstinence/abuse hypothesis suggests that although black and, to a lesser extent, Hispanic youth may be more likely than white youth to abstain from the use of most drugs, those who do use are more likely than their white counterparts to use heavily, resulting in a dis-

TABLE 4.3 Racial/Ethnic Differences in High School Seniors' Responses to Selected Validity Indicators (in percentages)

	White	Black	Hispanic
"None" of friends smoke cigarettes	10.7	18.7	14.5
"Disapprove" or "strongly disapprove" of heavy alcohol use	56.1	80.6	70.4
Perceive "great risk" in marijuana use	12.6	26.5	24.8
Exposed to cocaine "often"	6.0	4.5	7.3

proportionate share of drug-related problems. According to Oetting & Beauvais (1990), "Although rates of overall drug use are lower in these minority groups [blacks and Hispanics], those who are using drugs may use them more heavily and a greater proportion, therefore, may end up with drug problems that lead to emergency room treatment" (p. 390).

Are black and Hispanic youth who use drugs more likely to use heavily than are white users? The data presented in Figure 4.2 suggest that the answer is no. The figure presents mean levels of drug use among users, by race/ethnicity (8th-, 10th-, and 12th-grade data combined). In general, racial/ethnic differences in drug use intensity (among users) are consistent with patterns of self-reported prevalence: That is, intensity of use is fairly similar for white and Hispanic students and lower than average for black students. One apparent exception to this general conclusion, however, is the fact that black seniors who use cocaine do not use it less frequently than their white and Hispanic counterparts. Nevertheless, because black users represent only 1% of the total black sample, the abstinence/ abuse hypothesis, in all likelihood, does not account fully for racial/ethnic differences in the experience of drug-related problems.

GENDER DIFFERENCES HYPOTHESIS

A third explanation, the gender differences hypothesis, suggests that the relatively low overall prevalences of drug use among minority youth may result from large within-group gender differences. More specifically, it is hypothesized that the large numbers of females who do not use drugs cause the overall prevalence rates for minority youth to be disproportionately low relative to those for whites. Austin and Gilbert (1989) expressed this hypothesis as follows: "When data are aggregated without gender distinctions, the lower use of drugs by adolescent Latinas tends to 'wash out' the high prevalence of drug use by their male counterparts, thus obscuring the existence of a high-risk population" (p. 2). Given findings of relatively low prevalence of drug use among black females relative to other groups (see

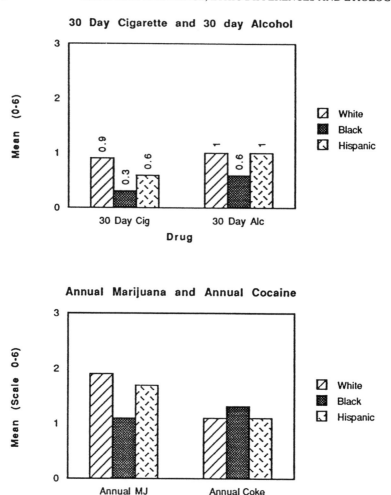

Figure 4.2. Mean Levels of Drug Use, by Race/Ethnicity, 1991-1992 Data Combined

Prendergast et al., 1989), the gender differences hypothesis might be thought to apply to black youth as well.

Data relevant to the hypothesis are presented in Figure 4.3. The figure shows cigarette, alcohol, marijuana, and cocaine prevalence among white, black, and Hispanic youth, separately by gender (8th-, 10th-, and 12th-grade data combined). The general pattern within racial/ethnic groups is the same: Prevalence is typically higher among males than females. The gender gaps within the three groups are generally quite comparable, thus disconfirming the gender differences hypothesis as an explanation for the racial/ethnic differences in self-reported patterns of use.

DROPOUT HYPOTHESIS

Much of our knowledge on racial/ethnic differences in drug use is based on findings from samples of students. The limitation inherent in student samples is that they do not include dropouts, those who are incarcerated, and other young people who are not in school. The extent to which young people are not in school varies considerably by racial/ethnic group. Recent data indicate that 14% of white 20- to 21-year-olds, 18% of black 20- to 21-year-olds, and 43% of Hispanic 20- to 21-year-olds have dropped out (National Center for Educational Statistics, 1989). Given substantial racial/ethnic differences in dropping out of school, one of the most frequent explanations offered to explain racial/ethnic differences in drug use is the dropout hypothesis (Austin & Gilbert, 1989; Bachman et al., 1991; Oetting & Beauvais, 1990; Prendergast et al., 1989).

The dropout hypothesis is derived as follows: (a) Drug use is higher than average among dropouts; (b) there is a disproportionate amount of dropping out among nonwhite youth, particularly Hispanics; therefore, (c) student samples, and senior samples in particular, disproportionately miss nonwhite drug users. Oetting and Beauvais (1990) stated the dropout hypothesis in the following way: School-based surveys consistently underestimate the drug use of some minorities because the minority drug users have high dropout rates; they are not in school to be surveyed.

If the lower levels of drug use reported by black and Hispanic seniors are the result of differential rates of dropping out, the prevalence of drug use might be higher among black and Hispanic 8th graders (when presumably there has been relatively little dropping out). Conversely, by 12th grade, after a disproportionate share of minority youth have dropped out, prevalence would be higher among white youth.

In order to investigate the dropout hypothesis, racial/ethnic differences in drug use are examined by grade level. These analyses are graphically summarized in Figure 4.4 (see Johnston et al., 1993, for a broader range of drugs). Are the patterns of racial/ethnic differences in cigarette, alcohol, marijuana, and cocaine drug use among 8th, 10th, and 12th graders consistent with the dropout hypothesis? For black students the answer is no, but for Hispanic students the data are fairly consistent with the hypothesis. Discussion of the results for individual drugs is presented below.

Because the links between poor school performance (e.g., truancy, low grades, and other correlates of dropping out) and smoking are particularly strong, and because the proportion of Hispanic youth who drop out is

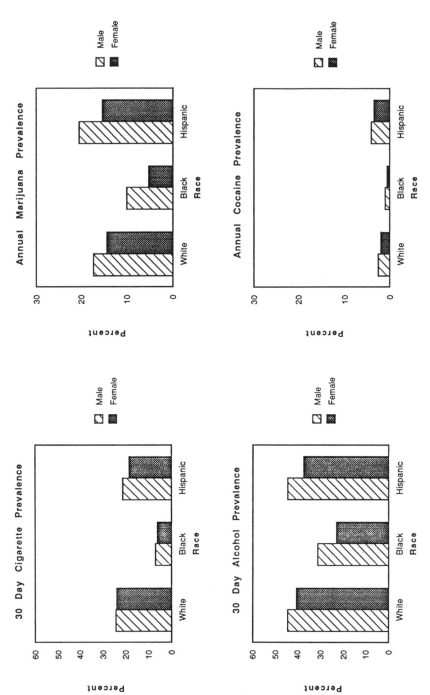

Figure 4.3. Prevalence of Drug Use, by Race/Ethnicity and Gender, 1991-1992 Data Combined.

70

relatively high, one might expect the effect of differential rates of dropping out to be particularly pronounced for Hispanic-white differences in cigarette use. The data tend to confirm this expectation. The percentages of Hispanic and white youth who report that they have smoked in the last 30 days are quite similar among 8th graders; however, among 10th and 12th graders, white youth are more likely than Hispanic youth to have smoked in the last 30 days. The relatively limited use of cigarettes found among black seniors also exists among black 8th and 10th graders. In general, black students are less likely than white or Hispanic students to be past or present smokers at any level of use.

Substantial portions of American youth, regardless of their racial/ethnic identification, have initiated the use of alcohol, and appreciable proportions are current users (i.e., used in the last 30 days). Although the differences are rather small between white and Hispanic 8th, 10th, and 12th graders, the crossover pattern (i.e., higher use at 8th grade but lower use in the later grades) is consistent with that predicted by the dropout hypothesis. Black youth report substantially lower prevalences across all three grade levels. Marijuana is the illicit drug most widely used by American youth. The figure indicates that although there is little difference in annual marijuana use between black and white 8th graders, white 10th and 12th graders are more likely than black 10th and 12th graders to have used marijuana in the past year. Hispanic 8th graders are more likely than white 8th graders to have used marijuana within the last year, but by 12th grade (after many Hispanic youth have probably dropped out) white and Hispanic seniors' marijuana prevalences are virtually identical.

Cocaine use is relatively low among all youth. Nevertheless, Figure 4.4 shows that the pattern of annual use is consistent across grade levels; prevalence is highest among Hispanic youth, intermediate among white youth, and lowest among black youth.

It would be necessary to gather data from the same respondents over time to determine definitively if differential rates of dropping out account for racial/ethnic differences in the prevalence of drug use among 8th graders compared to 12th graders. Such data will become available from the Monitoring the Future project in future years. Meanwhile, the cross-sectional data presented here are quite suggestive: At 8th grade, Hispanic youths' drug use is relatively high, but by 12th grade, when many of the users have probably dropped out, those remaining in school have use levels quite similar to those among white youth. This pattern is clearly consistent with the dropout hypothesis. On the other hand, because differences in dropping out are not particularly large for black and white youth, the dropout hypothesis probably is not sufficient to explain why black youth are less likely than white youth to use drugs.

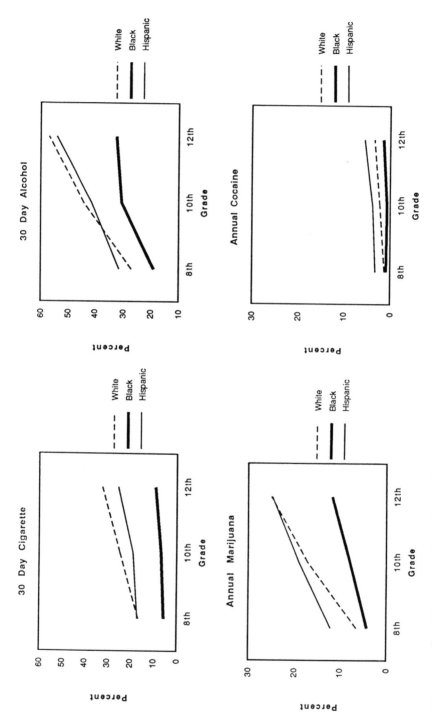

Figure 4.4. Drug Use by Race/Ethnicity and Grade Level, 1991-1992 Data Combined

PRECOCIOUS INITIATION

Although no explanation is offered as to why minority (particularly black) youth may initiate drug use later than white youth, the precocious initiation hypothesis suggests that the race disparity in drug use is a result of later initiation into use among minority youth, relative to white youth. The early initiation hypothesis is one posited by Prendergast et al. (1989) and Harford (1986).

In order to test this hypothesis, retrospective data on the age at which students report they first used a particular substance were compared across racial/ethnic groups. Recognizing that the data for Hispanic youth may be disproportionately affected by dropping out, and in order to minimize recall bias in students' retrospective accounts, we focus now on data from 8th graders only. Figure 4.5 presents cumulative percentages of youth who have initiated use by a given grade level.

The data suggest that comparable proportions of white, black, and Hispanic 8th graders initiate drug use by 4th grade. However, by 5th and 6th grade, more white and Hispanic youth than black youth have initiated cigarette use, and more Hispanic youth than white and black youth have initiated marijuana and cocaine use; initiation of alcohol use is more comparable across racial/ethnic groups. Logistic regressions (not shown) that control for age of first use do not explain away the lower prevalences of drug use reported by black youth.

DISCRETIONARY INCOME

Still another explanation for the race/ethnicity gap in drug use is the "discretionary income" hypothesis. The primary thrust of this argument is economic: Black and Hispanic youth are more likely than white youth to be socioeconomically disadvantaged and thus are less able than white youth to afford either licit or illicit drugs. According to Maddahian, Newcomb, and Bentler (1986), "Perhaps the reason that white students reported greater use of drugs than most other ethnic groups is due to white students having more money and thus able to purchase drugs at their pleasure" (p. 4).

In order to investigate this hypothesis, a series of logistic regressions were estimated that use race/ethnicity and two SES proxies (parental education and a sum of student's employment and given income) as independent variables, and used dichotomous prevalence measures as dependent variables. The resultant log-odds, adjusted for race/ethnicity and SES, were then converted into percentages and compared with the unadjusted prevalences reported by white, black, and Hispanic eighth graders. The results are presented in Figure 4.6.

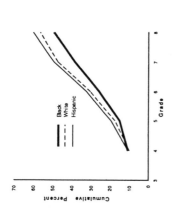

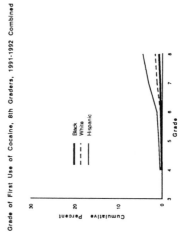

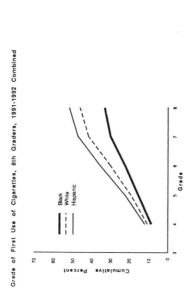

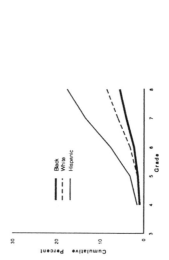

Figure 4.5. Grade of First Drug Use Among Eighth Graders, by Race/Ethnicity, 1991-1992 Data Combined

Figure 4.6 indicates that the unadjusted drug use prevalences are lower among black youth than among white youth and that controlling for SES differences slightly increases the size of this difference. On the other hand, the unadjusted drug use prevalences are higher among Hispanic youth relative to white (and black) youth. Controlling for SES reduces these differences, thus making Hispanic youths' drug use more comparable to that of white youth. This finding suggests that the *higher* prevalence of drug use (cigarette use in particular) among Hispanic youth relative to white youth might be related to Hispanic youths' relatively disadvantaged socioeconomic status.

OTHER EXPLANATIONS

Several other hypotheses have been offered to account for the black-white gap in drug use. One of these explanations is that black youth are less likely than white youth to use drugs because they have less exposure to peer or adult drug users and are less vulnerable to users than are white youth, given equal exposure (Newcomb & Bentler, 1986). According to Oetting and Beauvais (1990), the highest rates of drug use among black and other minority youth might occur in segregated, typically high-crime, and high-poverty areas. Findings from these areas are not well represented in most general population surveys and probably do not generalize to the larger population of minority youth. Another promising but yet to be tested hypothesis concerning the persistent finding of black-white differences in drug use relates to race differences in religion (Harford, 1986; Harper, 1988; Wallace & Bachman, 1991). Given that religiosity is negatively related to drug use, and given that black youth are, on average, more religious than white youth, controlling for religion may help to explain black-white differences in drug use.

Findings from the alcohol literature might provide further insight into the apparent discrepancy between the relatively low self-reports of drug use by black young people and the relatively high prevalence of problems experienced by adults. The alcohol literature suggests that alcohol use begins later among blacks than among whites; however, once initiated, heavy use continues for a longer period of time among blacks (Herd, 1989). This pattern of later initiation with longer periods of heavy use is consistent with both the lower self-reports of use among black youth and with the higher prevalence of drug-related problems among black adults. Thus, data that suggest that black adults experience more drug-related problems than do white adults are not necessarily inconsistent with the self-reports of black youth, and certainly are not sufficient to dismiss the self-reports as invalid. Witnessing the drug-related problems of adults might deter many black youth from using drugs until they are faced with the realities of adulthood (e.g., racism, poverty,

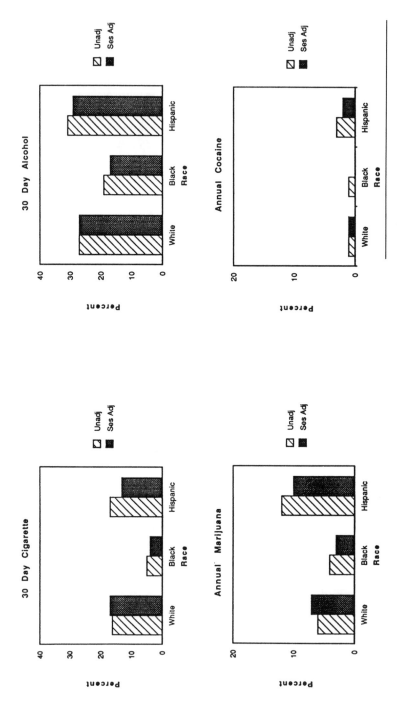

Figure 4.6. Prevalence of Drug Use Among Eighth Graders, by Race/Ethnicity, Unadjusted and Adjusted for Socioeconomic Status, 1991-1992 Data Combined

unemployment, bad relationships) that lead some of the adults around them to use drugs.

Another potential explanation for the apparent discrepancy between self-reports among black people and the number of drug-related problems they experience is the "more bang for the buck" hypothesis. This hypothesis argues that because of their relatively disadvantaged economic status, many black drug users seek the maximum effect for the minimum price. Accordingly, they use the most potent forms of the various drugs (e.g., malt liquor vs. regular beers, menthol cigarettes vs. regular cigarettes, crack vs. cocaine powder, heroin vs. morphine). Because of the increased potency of these drugs, their use is more deleterious to the health of the user and results in relatively high rates of drug-related problems.

To the uncritical observer, self-reports of lower drug use among black and Hispanic youth relative to white youth are inconsistent with several other apparently more "objective" data sources (e.g., Drug Abuse Warning Network [DAWN] data on drug-related emergency room visits, data on juvenile arrests for drug abuse violations, and data on racial/ethnic differences in drug-related mortality and morbidity among adults). The incongruity between these other data sources and self-reports is paradoxical and has been viewed by some as cause to dismiss the self-reports as invalid (see U.S. Office of Technology Assessment [U.S. OTA], 1991). However, a closer examination of these "objective" data is necessary.

For example, DAWN data indicate that minority adults and youth are disproportionately represented in drug-related emergency room incidents. This "fact" ignores the additional fact that until 1990, DAWN data were collected from hospital emergency rooms and medical examiner facilities in metropolitan areas selected specifically *because* those areas were believed to have higher rates of problem drug use (U.S. OTA, 1991). Given that the locations from which the DAWN samples were drawn (e.g., Atlanta, Baltimore, Detroit, Miami) are disproportionately black and Hispanic, the finding that minorities are overrepresented is not at all surprising.

With regard to the arrest data, black youth are disproportionately arrested for (illicit) drug abuse violations (42.2% of arrests). Although arrests for drug abuse violations are disproportionately high (i.e., greater than their 15% representation in the population) among black youth, it is not clear how much of this results from heavy policing of poor, predominantly black neighborhoods, a bias toward the detection and arrest of offenders from certain groups in society (e.g., black male adolescents), and the recent effort to wage a "war" on drugs, and how much actually reflects greater drug-related activity among black youth. For example, a study conducted in Washington, D.C., found that even among black youth (ages 13 to 17) who were arrested, only 25% to 30% tested positive for drugs (McFate, 1990). (It should be noted that this percentage is lower than the 35.4% of high school seniors who reported any annual drug use in 1989 and is not much higher than the 19.7% of seniors who reported any illicit drug use in the last month for that same year; Johnston et al., 1993.) Of course, even though black youth may be less likely than white youth to *use* drugs, a greater proportion of them than white youth may *sell* drugs. However, arrest data may not be a good indicator of adolescent drug use because drug dealers and drug users may be different populations (U.S. OTA, 1991).

In addition to the DAWN data and arrest statistics, aggregate level death statistics, epidemiological data from various government sources, and non-random data from public treatment centers are also cited in raising questions about the validity of drug use self-reports among minority youth. Extrapolating from adult problems to the patterns of use among youth is clearly problematic. For one thing, they are different age cohorts with different historical experiences, and it is not at all clear that the youth of today (of whatever race) will repeat the drug-using experiences of the previous generation. Moreover, much of the data from which information on drug-related mortality and morbidity is determined is also problematic. For example, much data on drug-related problems is drawn from public drug treatment facilities. Because many of these centers are located in inner cities and because many minority group members lack money and insurance coverage to seek private treatment, their overrepresentation in community-based treatment centers is not surprising. In sum, like self-reports, various "objective" data from which conclusions are drawn about the extent of drug abuse among minority youth and adults are not without their problems and are in need of close scrutiny to ascertain their validity and generalizability.

SUMMARY

On the basis of our own research and that of others, it seems reasonable to conclude that the general patterns of racial/ethnic differences are, on the whole, valid. The purpose of this chapter has been to use large nationally representative samples to examine empirically a number of the hypotheses in the research literature that have been offered to account for racial/ethnic differences in drug use. It appears that some of the differences in drug use between white and Hispanic samples of high school seniors can be explained by the fact that Hispanic youth are much more likely than white youth to drop out of school. In fact, the data indicate that some forms of drug use are actually higher among Hispanic youth than among white youth. On the other hand, with regard to black/white differences in drug use, none of the hypotheses examined here seemed to account for the substantial gap.

Clearly, much more research needs to be done to understand racial/ethnic differences in drug use. Perhaps even more important than more research on racial and ethnic differences in drug use, however, is research that focuses on differential patterns of use and abuse within black, Hispanic, and other groups of minority youth. Because of the relatively limited knowledge concerning the correlates and causes of drug use among black and Hispanic youth, the research findings discussed and presented here have probably raised more questions than they have answered. As minority youth become an increasingly large portion of the nation's population, it becomes increasingly important to identify, investigate, and understand factors that influence their drug use, and to broaden efforts to prevent the use and abuse of drugs among all youth.

References

Austin, G. A., & Gilbert, M. J. (1989). Substance abuse among Latino youth. *Prevention Research Update, 3,* 1-26.

Bachman, J. G., Wallace, J. M., Kurth, C. L., Johnston, L. D., O'Malley, P. M., & Neighbors, H. W. (1991). Racial/ethnic differences in smoking, drinking, and illicit drug use among American high school seniors, 1976-1989. *American Journal of Public Health, 81,* 372-377.

Harford, T. C. (1986). Drinking patterns among black and nonblack adolescents: Results of a national survey. *Annals of the New York Academy of Science, 472,* 130-141.

Harper, F. D. (1988). Alcohol and black youth: An overview. *Journal of Drug Issues, 18,* 7-14.

Herd, D. (1989). The epidemiology of drinking patterns and alcohol related problems among U.S. blacks. In D. L. Spiegler, D. A. Tate, S. S. Aitken, & C. M. Christian (Eds.), *Alcohol use among U.S. ethnic minorities* (NIAAA Research Monograph No. 18, pp. 3-50). Washington, DC: Government Printing Office.

Johnston, L. D., & O'Malley, P. M. (1985). Issues of validity and population coverage in student surveys of drug use. In B. A. Rouse, N. J. Kozel, & L. G. Richards (Eds.), *Self-report methods of estimating drug use: Meeting current challenges in validity* (NIDA Research Monograph No. 57, pp. 31-54). Washington, DC: Government Printing Office.

Johnston, L. D., O'Malley, P. M., & Bachman, J. G. (1993). *National survey results on drug use from monitoring the future study, 1975-1992: Vol. 1. Secondary students* (National Institute on Drug Abuse, NIH Pub. No. 93-3597). Washington, DC: Government Printing Office.

Kandel, D. B. (1991). The social demography of drug use. *Milbank Quarterly, 69,* 365-414.

Maddahian, E., Newcomb, M. D., & Bentler, P. M. (1986). Adolescent substance use, impact of ethnicity, income, and availability. *Advances in Alcohol and Substance Abuse, 5,* 63-78.

McFate, K. (1990). Roundtable of experts at Joint Center for Political Studies looks at black males and the drug trade. *Scope Newsletter* (Institute on Black Chemical Abuse), p. 1.

Mensch, B. S., & Kandel, D. B. (1988). Underreporting of substance use in a national longitudinal youth cohort. *Public Opinion Quarterly, 52,* 100-124.

National Center for Educational Statistics. (1989, September). *Dropout rates in the United States: 1988* (NCES Analysis Report, DHHS Pub. No. 248-722/00729). Washington, DC: Government Printing Office.

Newcomb, M. D., & Bentler, P. M. (1986). Substance use and ethnicity: Differential impact of peer and adult models. *Journal of Psychology, 120,* 83-95.

Oetting, E., & Beauvais, F. (1990). Adolescent drug use: Findings of national and local surveys. *Journal of Clinical and Consulting Psychology, 58,* 85-394.

O'Malley, P. M., Bachman, J. G., & Johnston, L. D. (1983). Reliability and consistency in self-reports of drug use. *International Journal of the Addictions, 18,* 805-824.

Prendergast, M. L., Maton, K. I., & Baker, R. (1989). Substance abuse among black youth. *Prevention Research Update, 4,* 1-27.

Rouse, B. A., Kozel, N. J., & Richards, L. G. (Eds.). (1985). *Self-report methods of estimating drug use: Meeting current challenges in validity* (NIDA Research Monograph No. 57). Washington, DC: Government Printing Office.

Secretary's Task Force on Black and Minority Health. (1986). *Chemical dependency and diabetes* (Vol. 7). Washington, DC: Government Printing Office.

U.S. Office of Technology Assessment (U.S. OTA). (1991). *Adolescent health: Vol. 2. Background and the effectiveness of selected prevention and treatment services* (OTA-H-466). Washington, DC: Government Printing Office.

Wallace, J. M., Jr., & Bachman, J. G. (1991). Racial ethnic differences in adolescent drug use: The impact of background and lifestyle. *Social Problems, 38,* 333-357.

Wallace, J. M., Jr., & Bachman, J. G. (1993). Validity of self-reports in student based studies on minority populations: Issues and concerns. In M. R. De La Rosa & J. R. Adrados (Eds.), *Drug abuse among minority youth: Advances in research and methodology* (NIDA Research Monograph 130, pp. 167-200). Rockville, MD: National Institute on Drug Abuse.

Welte, J. W., & Barnes, G. M. (1987). Alcohol use among adolescent minority groups. *Journal of Studies on Alcohol, 48,* 329-336.

Ethnic Differences in Drug Use

Patterns and Paradoxes

Denise B. Kandel

Ethnic differrences in substance use present paradoxes and raise questions taht have yet to be resolved. It is some of these questions that I address in this chapter. I want to stress at the outset that my perspective is that of the epidemiologist, who ignores in most cases the important dimensions of culture, ethnic identification, and acculturation that are crucial to the issues discussed in this chapter.

Over the last two decades, the government has been engaged in an ambitious effort designed to monitor patterns and trends of drug use in the population. In particular, under sponsorship of the National Institute on Drug Abuse, repeated data collections using similar national samples and methods have been implemented so as to monitor trends and changes in patterns of use over time. The two major surveys are Monitoring the Future, the annual school survey of high school seniors initiated in 1975 and expanded as of 1991 to include 8th and 12th graders (Johnston, O'Malley, & Bachman, 1992), and the National Household Survey on Drug Abuse, an annual or biannual house-hold survey of persons 12 years and older (National Institute on Drug Abuse [NIDA], 1992c). Surveys of the general population are supplemented by cen- suses of drug-related casualties that come to the attention of different institutions. These include censuses of morbidity reflected in drug-related emergency room admissions and mortality reflected in drug-use-related

AUTHOR'S NOTE: Work on this chapter has been supported by Research Scientist Award KO5 DA00081 from the National Institute on Drug Abuse.

cases recorded in medical examiner offices, both of which are part of the Drug Abuse Warning Network (DAWN) system (NIDA, 1992a, 1992b), and drug use among arrestees in the Drug Use Forecasting (DUF) system (National Institute of Justice, 1992). The monitoring of drug-related cases in treatment programs has been more episodic due to changes in the way in which pro- grams are funded and in the feasibility of imposing record-keeping requirements as a condition for funding.

Ethnic patterns within a single data set and divergent patterns across data sets are rarely highlighted in the reports issued from these studies. Typically, the press releases attending each new wave of data collection present data for the nation as a whole and for specific age subgroups, but not for different ethnic groups. Ethnic differences are discussed in reports of regional studies carried out in single states or single cities (e.g. Kandel, Single, & Kessler, 1976; Oetting & Beauvais, 1990; Vega, Zimmerman, Warheit, Apospori, & Gil, 1993; Welte & Barnes, 1987). The General Household Survey on Drug Abuse, however, provides in its annual technical reports the data necessary to make ethnic comparisons (NIDA, 1992c). It was only in 1991, 16 years after the initial national survey of high school seniors, that Monitoring the Future published for the first time ethnic-specific rates of drug use (Bachman et al., 1991).

The juxtaposition of epidemiological data from these different sources reveals a major paradox, arising from the divergent ethnic distribution of drug users in general population and in institutional samples.

In this chapter, I describe this paradox in some detail, describe a second one much more briefly, and present some interpretations of the ethnic differences that have been observed. Because in the preceding chapter John Wallace has presented data from Monitoring the Future, for data on general population samples I draw on the National Household Survey on Drug Abuse and the New York State–wide survey of junior and senior high school students that I carried out in 1988 (Kandel & Davies, 1991a). The National Household Survey on Drug Abuse is based on repeated cross-sectional household surveys of national multistage probability samples of household residents 12 years old and over, carried out every 2 or 3 years up to 1988 and annually as of 1990 (NIDA, 1992c). There have been 11 surveys since 1971. The drug questions are self-administered by respondents and the answers placed in a sealed envelope. To provide more precise estimates for certain subgroups in the population, the sample was enlarged in 1991 to over 32,000 respondents (NIDA, 1992c). For the first time, six metropolitan areas were oversampled, and persons living in college dormitories, persons in homeless shelters, and civilians on military installations were included in the sample. The last two surveys included an oversampling of blacks and Hispanics to provide stable race-specific rates, which up to now have not been readily available. Larger sample sizes in these strata give rise to smaller standard errors and more precise parameter estimates. In the New York State survey, over 7,000 students in Grades 7 through 12 were surveyed from 53 schools throughout the state in the spring of 1988. The two-stage random sample represents junior and senior high school students attending New York State public and private schools. A stratified sample of 54 schools and two homerooms from each grade per school was selected. On anonymous, self-administered, structured questionnaires given out in classrooms (84% completion), the students were asked about beer, wine, hard liquor, cigarettes, marijuana, stimulants, inhalants, cocaine (and crack), psychedelics, sedatives, tranquilizers, and heroin. Several other studies present data on ethnic-specific rates of drug use (see Adlaf, Smart, & Tan, 1989; Johnson & Robin, 1992; Kandel et al., 1976; Maddahian, Newcomb, & Bentler, 1986; Newcomb & Bentler, 1986; Oetting & Beauvais, 1990; Vega et al., 1993; Welte & Barnes, 1987).

General Overview
of Epidemiological Trends

The relationships between ethnicity and drug behavior are complex and appear to be changing rapidly. In considering ethnic differences in patterns of use, it is essential to distinguish three parameters: (a) the individual's age; (b) the period of use in the individual's life covered by the estimate, whether lifetime or current use; and (c) the historical period in which the data were obtained.

Whether based on school or general population samples, the age-specific trends from nonclinical samples are identical across studies (e.g., Bachman et al., 1991; Chavez & Swaim, n.d.; De La Rosa, Khalsa, & Rouse, 1990; Gillmore et al., 1990; Harford, 1986; Johnston, O'Malley, & Bachman, 1991; Kandel, Davies, & Davis, 1990; Kandel et al., 1976; Maddahian et al., 1986; NIDA, 1991; Oetting & Beauvais, 1990; Trimble, Padilla, & Bell, 1987; Vega et al., 1993; Welte & Barnes, 1987; Zabin, Hardy, Smith, & Hirsch, 1985). In adolescence and early adulthood, the highest rates of lifetime use of most substances are recorded among Native Americans and the lowest among Asians. Of the three other major groups, the highest rates are observed among whites and the lowest among African Americans. Rates of use among Hispanics are in between those observed among whites and blacks, with the exception of cocaine. Higher rates are observed among Hispanics than among whites or African Americans.

Wallace and his collaborators have presented illustrative data on lifetime, annual, and monthly prevalence of use for a range of drugs for high

TABLE 5.1 Respondents Ever Using Substance During Lifetime by, Ethnicity (New York State Survey—1988)

	Cigarettes %	Marijuana %	Any Cocaine[a] %	Crack %	ILLD[b] %	OID[c] %	Total (N)
White	59.8	29.6	5.9	1.6	34.0	20.3	(5,508)
Black	50.3	25.4	4.6	2.2	26.8	7.3	(715)
Hispanic	57.3	25.1	10.2	2.5	28.5	14.8	(555)
Asian	38.7	6.1	1.9	0.9	11.5	8.2	(288)
American Indian	73.5	45.4	9.5	7.0	51.2	29.6	(71)
Other	55.0	21.1	5.1	3.2	25.0	13.7	(434)

SOURCE: Adapted from Kandel et al., 1990, Table 2.3.
a. Cocaine in any form, including crack.
b. Any illicit drug, including marijuana.
c. Any illicit drug, excluding marijuana.

school seniors from Monitoring the Future for five aggregated surveys for the years 1985-1989. Because of the large size of their sample, Hispanics could be differentiated as Mexican Americans and Puerto Ricans and other Latin Americans, a differentiation that is rarely made. Vega et al. (1993) distinguished between Cubans and other Hispanics. The data for New York State seniors surveyed in 1988 follow identical patterns to those presented for Monitoring the Future (Table 5.1). The inclusion of cigarettes indicates that trends for cigarettes are similar to those for other substances.

There are, however, important changes in ethnic differences involving the relative prevalence of the use of various drugs, in particular cocaine, across the life cycle and across historical time. Indeed, ethnic differences are age graded and vary depending upon the period of use covered by the prevalence estimate and the year when the information was obtained. By 1991, lower rates of use among blacks compared with whites characterized mainly lifetime rates in the population younger than 35 years old. There appear to be differences between data for high school seniors and for adolescents from the General Household Survey.

The General Household Survey on Drug Abuse distinguishes four age groups: adolescence (ages 12-17), early adulthood (ages 18-25), and adulthood (ages 26-34 and 35 and over). Age-specific lifetime use of cocaine among the three major ethnic groups in the general population, from the 1991 NIDA General Household Survey (NIDA, 1992c), is displayed in Table 5.2 for each of the four age groups. The relative position of the groups changes over the life cycle. Hispanics show the most change. At all ages except the oldest (those 35 and older), blacks consistently report lower rates than whites, with the differences the highest in early adulthood at ages 18 to 26. Overall,

TABLE 5.2 Lifetime, Past Year, and Past Month Prevalence Rates of the Use of Cocaine, in the General Population, by Ethnicity 1991

Age/Ethnicity	Ever Used %	Past Year %	Past Month %	Total n
Age 12-17				
White	2.4	1.3	0.3	(3,646)
Black	1.7	1.5	0.5	(2,036)
Hispanic	3.7	2.9	1.3	(2,029)
Age 18-25				
White	20.3	8.2	1.7	(3,689)
Black	10.1	6.0	3.1	(2,032)
Hispanic	15.0	7.1	2.7	(1,917)
Age 26-34				
White	27.8	4.9	1.6	(4,001)
Black	22.1	7.5	2.7	(1,938)
Hispanic	18.6	4.5	2.0	(1,962)
Age 35+				
White	6.4	1.2	0.2	(4,312)
Black	9.7	2.3	1.3	(2,044)
Hispanic	7.8	2.2	1.0	(2,008)
Total white	11.8	2.8	0.7	(15,648)
Total black	11.2	3.9	1.8	(8,050)
Total Hispanic	11.1	3.8	1.6	(7,916)

SOURCE: NIDA, 1992c, Tables 1-B, 4-B, 4-C, 4-D.

among those younger than 35, 35.5% *fewer* blacks than whites reported any *lifetime* experience with cocaine, whereas among those aged 35 and over, 51.5% *more* blacks than whites reported such experiences. Hispanics report the highest rates of cocaine use in adolescence, are in a middle position at ages 18 to 26, drop to the lowest position at ages 26 to 34, and rise above blacks at ages 35 and over.

With regard to use in the last year, lower rates among blacks than whites appear among young adults 18 to 26 years old, but higher rates among those 26 and older. In the national sample, differences have disappeared for those aged 12 to 17. With regard to use in the last month, rates are consistently higher among blacks at every age. This suggests that once they start using cocaine, younger blacks are increasingly likely to persist in their use. This is indeed the case, as will be discussed below.

The relative prevalence of the use of illicit drugs, especially cocaine, among different ethnic groups in the general population appears to be shifting. An analysis of data from successive general population surveys suggests that ethnic patterns of use have evolved over time depending upon individuals' age and recency of use. There seems to be a cascading and

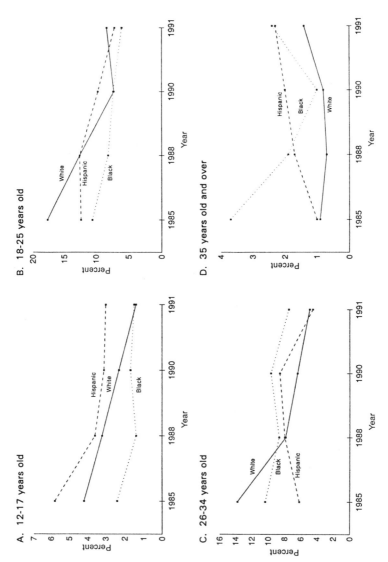

Figure 5.1. Trends in Past-Year Prevalence Rates of Cocaine Use by Race/Ethnicity in Four Age Groups in the General Population (1985, 1988, 1990, 1991)

rippling effect. A differential showing higher rates among blacks appears to be gradually spreading from the older to the younger age groups and to be reflected first in current patterns of use. As I mentioned earlier, up to and including 1985, the higher rates of cocaine use among blacks compared with other groups appeared only among those older than 35 for every prevalence rate, whether lifetime, last year, or last month.

Illustrative and striking data are presented in Figure 5.1 for rates of past-year prevalences for four different years, 1985, 1988, 1990, and 1991, and for each of the four age groups. For the oldest age group, 35 and older, the differences already existed in 1985, were the sharpest in that year, and have persisted throughout the entire period from 1985 to 1991. For the age group 26 to 34, the lines crossed in 1988. The annual rate for blacks was lower than for whites in 1985, only slightly higher in 1988, and almost 50% higher by 1990. The next oldest group, 18 to 25 years old, shows the pattern least consistent with the thesis I am proposing here. Indeed, although the ethnic differences between blacks and whites decreased from 1985 to 1988 and disappeared in 1990 (when the lines crossed 2 years later than they did for the next oldest group), the differences increased again slightly in 1991, rather than decreased, as I would have predicted. For the youngest group, 12 to 17 years old, it is only in 1991 that the rates were the same for both whites and blacks. For each of the prior years, the rates were higher for whites than for blacks. The differences have been decreasing over time.

Data in the National Household Survey are not available broken down simultaneously by sex, ethnicity, and age. In general, stronger ethnic differences characterize patterns of cocaine use among women than men. Black women are especially likely to report lower lifetime experience with cocaine than other women.

These ethnic patterns of use present two paradoxes.

General Population
Versus Treated Cases: A Paradox

One paradox derives from the juxtaposition of data on cocaine use obtained from general population samples and those from cases that come to the attention of various institutions. As I have illustrated, up to age 35, a smaller proportion of blacks than whites, or at most an equal proportion, report having experimented with illicit drugs, whereas Hispanics are generally in an intermediate position. Yet morbidity and mortality cases involving illicit drug users, and especially cocaine users who have come to the attention of various medical, treatment, or criminal institutions, such as drug-related emergency rooms, treatment programs, medical examiner offices, or booking

TABLE 5.3 Race/Ethnicity of All Drug Admissions, Cocaine Admissions, or Cocaine Users in Treated and General Population Samples, 1988 to 1991 (in percentages)

Race/Ethnicity	Drug Abuse Treatment Programs[a] 1989 All Admissions	Emergency Room Episodes[b] 1991 All Drug Admissions	Cocaine Admissions	Deaths in Medical Examiner Offices[c] 1991 All Drug Abuse Deaths	Cocaine Deaths	National Household Sample[d] 1991 Cocaine Users	New York State High School Survey 1988[e] Cocaine Users
White	49.0	56.2	28.9	55.0	38.1	79.1	72.4
Black	26.5	27.1	55.4	30.6	46.1	11.0	6.8
Hispanic	17.5	8.4	8.9	12.2 }	15.8	7.7	12.9
Other/unknown	7.0	8.3	6.8	2.3		2.2	7.9
Total (N)	351,430	400,079	102,727	6,601	2,869	23,396	427

a. From NIDA, 1990a, Table 26.
b. From NIDA, 1992b, Tables 2.02 and 2.08.
c. Based on NIDA, 1992c, Tables 4.01 and 3.01.
d. From NIDA, 1992a, Tables 4-A-D, p. 31. N = population estimate.
e. Based on Kandel et al., 1990, Table 2-10a: 7th-12th graders.

facilities, consistently show an overrepresentation of blacks compared with their distribution in the general population (Table 5.3).

For example, of cocaine-related emergency room episodes recorded in 1991, 28.8% involved whites, 55.4% blacks, and 8.9% Hispanics (Substance Abuse and Mental Health Services Administration [SAMHSA], 1993). In 1989, 49.0% of charts included in the National Drug and Alcohol Treatment Unit Survey (NDATUS) survey of drug treatment facilities covered white clients and 26.5% covered blacks. By contrast, in the 1991 household sample, 79.1% of the self-reported lifetime cocaine users were white, only 11.0% black, and 7.7% Hispanic (NIDA, 1992c, p. 31). The overrepresentation of blacks in clinical samples of drug users compared with their representation in the population or their distribution among drug users in the community seems to be increasing over time. The proportions of blacks in cocaine-related admissions in the DAWN system increased from 41% in 1984 to 54% in 1991; the proportions of whites and Hispanics declined from 36% to 29%, and from 14% to 9%, respectively (NIDA, 1990b; SAMHSA, 1993). Similarly, the proportions of nonwhite admissions recorded in treatment programs by NDATUS increased from 42% in 1987 to 51% in 1989 (NIDA, 1989, 1990b).

Explanations for
Observed Ethnic Patterns

In considering ethnic differences in drug use, two patterns need to be explained: the lower prevalence of drug use among blacks than among whites or Hispanics in noninstitutionalized samples, and the overrepresentation of blacks in institutionalized samples.

ETHNIC DIFFERENCES
WITHIN POPULATION SAMPLES:
METHODOLOGICAL INTERPRETATIONS

Three different explanations can be proposed to explain the differential prevalence rates of drug use in unselected representative population samples. All three explanations are methodological in nature. Two refer to potential methodological weaknesses in the research, in either the quality of the data or the quality of the sample. A third explanation focuses on analytical strategies; it hypothesizes that the association between ethnicity and drug use itself is spurious and explores whether other characteristics associated with these two factors account for the observed associations between them.

Underreporting of Drug Use

One methodological interpretation is that self-reported drug use by blacks may be subject to greater underreporting than self-reports by other ethnic groups. Our group has documented such underreporting by comparing inconsistencies in reported drug use over a 4-year interval in a national longitudinal household sample of young adults (Mensch & Kandel, 1988). The Monitoring the Future team also reported lower quality of data in the answers regarding use of illicit drugs provided by black males than in the answers provided by other high school students (Johnston, Bachman, & O'Malley, 1984). It is not clear to what extent underreporting accounts for ethnic differences in self-reports of drug use.

Exclusion of High-Risk
Individuals and Dropouts

Another methodological explanation is that surveys based on school samples and large national household samples exclude the most deviant adolescents and adults who would exhibit the highest rates of drug use: dropouts, the homeless, persons who are institutionalized or in jail.

Differential dropping out of school of different ethnic groups and, perhaps, differential dropping out of school as a result of drug use among different ethnic groups may in fact partially account for differences in rates by ethnicity observed in samples of high school students, especially 12th graders. In the absence of prospective longitudinal data that would follow students over time, analyses that I carried out on the New York State survey of 7th through 12th graders provide inferential evidence for this interpretation. Three sets of findings are particularly relevant.

First, there are reversals in the ethnic patterns of the use of certain illicit drugs across school grades. In order to assess relative ethnic differences by school grade independent of variations in prevalence levels among the ethnic groups, odds ratios were calculated for the lifetime use of specific classes of drugs for blacks compared with whites for each of three aggregated grade categories (7th-8th, 9th-10th, and 11th-12th graders) (Figure 5.2). Blacks exhibit lower odds than whites (i.e., values lower than 1.0) for the use of every substance in all grades, except for marijuana, cocaine, crack, and heroin in the lower grades. There is a consistent pattern of change in the odds ratios between blacks and whites across grade categories. For every substance except cocaine, the ratio decreases across all three categories; for cocaine, the ratio decreases between the 9th-10th grades and the 11th-12th grades. As students progress through junior and senior high school, the

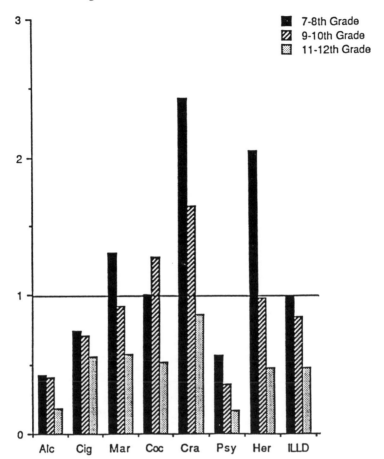

Figure 5.2. Odds Ratios for the Use of Substances by Grade in School for Black Compared to White Students

relative position of blacks and whites diverges over time, and the differential in prevalence levels in favor of whites becomes greater.[1]

Second, the proportions of heavily involved drug users increase with grade in senior high school among white and Hispanic students but decline among blacks. Two indicators of degree of involvement are available: use of a substance more than 40 times and daily use. The latter has too low a frequency to permit a grade-specific analysis. The proportions of users who have used a substance more than forty times increase with school grade among white and Hispanic students but decline among black students (Table 5.4). For instance, among whites, 12% of cocaine users among 9th and 10th graders report having used the drug 40 or more times compared with 18%

TABLE 5.4 Proportions of Cocaine Users Who Ever Used Cocaine More Than Forty Times by Ethnicity and Grade in School (New York State Survey—1988)

	%	n
White		
9th-10th	12	(78)
11th-12th	18	(201)
Black		
9th-10th	44	(12)
11th-12th	34	(16)
Hispanic		
9th-10th	12	(20)
11th-12th	19	(30)

SOURCE: Kandel et al., 1990, Appendix Table 2-6.

TABLE 5.5 Mean Age of Onset Into the Use of Cocaine and Crack by Grade and Ethnicity (New York State Survey—1988)

	Cocaine		Crack	
	M	n	M	n
7th-8th grades				
White	12.2	(27)	12.4	(11)
Black	12.0	(2)	10.8	(4)
Hispanic	12.3	(3)	—	(0)
9th-10th grades				
White	14.4	(78)	13.9	(26)
Black	15.0	(12)	16.4	(5)
Hispanic	14.6	(20)	14.5	(8)
11th-12th grades				
White	15.7	(201)	15.4	(39)
Black	15.7	(16)	17.1	(4)
Hispanic	15.5	(30)	16.0	(5)

SOURCE: Kandel et al., 1990, Table 3-6.

among 11th and 12th graders. Similar trends are observed for Hispanics. Among blacks, by contrast, the proportions of frequent cocaine users decline from the lower to the upper grades of high school, from 44% to 34%. However, caution must be exercised in the interpretation of the data because of the small number of users in the lower grades, especially among minorities.

Finally, there are important reversals over grades in the relative ages of onset reported for cocaine, and especially crack, by the three ethnic groups (Table 5.5). The mean ages of onset reported for crack are lower for blacks than whites in earlier grades but higher in higher grades. Thus, in the 7th and 8th grades, blacks report ages of onset into crack that are 1.5 years lower on the average than among whites (10.8 years versus 12.4 years). (No crack users are recorded for Hispanics.) The pattern is completely reversed by the 11th and 12th grades. In those grades, the average age of onset into crack is higher by over 1.5 years among blacks than among whites, and higher by about a year among blacks than among Hispanics. Similar differences appear for cocaine, although the differences are very much attenuated in the 7th and 8th grades. There are very small variations with respect to marijuana, although black students report slightly younger ages of onset at every grade level. Because of the relatively small numbers of crack users, especially in the lower grades, the estimated ages of onset are statistically unreliable. However, the data tentatively suggest that crack may be an important factor in dropping out of school by minority adolescents, especially black adolescents.

Other supporting evidence for this interpretation is provided by the standard deviations of the ages of onset. These indicate the dispersion of the ages at which students start to use drugs. By inference, the restriction in the dispersion of age of onset into cocaine and crack suggests that the cocaine and crack users who are in the upper grades of high school exclude those who experimented with these drugs at an early age. The restriction is greater for blacks than for whites. The standard deviation is 1.0 for blacks in the last two grades of high school compared to 3.5 in the middle two grades. For whites, the comparable standard deviations are 1.8 in the middle two grades and 1.8 in the upper two grades. However, the small cell sizes for minorities affect the standard deviations and the robustness of the results. Thus, these ethnic comparisons can only be made very tentatively.

These patterns suggest that black adolescents who use certain types of drugs drop out of school more frequently than white or Hispanic drug users. Not only do a lower proportion of crack and cocaine users appear to remain in school among blacks than among whites, but, not unexpectedly, those who are in school appear to be, by inference, the lighter users and those who initiated drug use at a later age. Black students who become heavily involved in illicit substances, especially cocaine, may have disproportionately dropped out of school by the highest grade levels. The substantial increases in the average age of onset for cocaine and crack between the older two grade levels suggest that a proportion of those who began using these substances in junior high school no longer appear in the senior high school sample. We can only speculate that the students' use of cocaine and crack contributed to their leaving school.

Potential Spuriousness of Observed Associations

Another class of interpretation to account for ethnic variations within general population samples explores the hypothesis that race and ethnicity

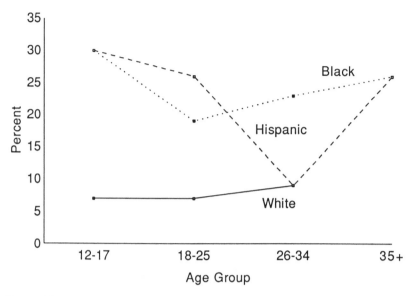

Figure 5.3. Proportions Using Cocaine Once a Week or More Among Those in the General Population Who Used Cocaine in the Last Year, by Age Group and Ethnicity (1991)

are markers for other variables and that the observed associations between ethnicity and rates of drug use are due to other factors. It is only within the last 2 years that three publications have systematically tested this hypothesis. The studies reached opposite conclusions.

The basic question is this: Are there characteristics of the different ethnic groups that, if controlled, could account for variations in observed rates of use and would eliminate these differences? The characteristics could be at different levels of explanation. They could be attributes of the individual or attributes of the individual's social context. Within the former, a distinction can be made between sociodemographic characteristics and lifestyle characteristics.

Controlling for individual characteristics does not appear to reduce observed ethnic differences in drug use, as documented by two of the three studies. The Monitoring the Future group carried out an analysis in five aggregated surveys (1979-1984), controlling successively for sociodemographic characteristics and for lifestyle variables (Bachman et al., 1991; Wallace & Bachman, 1991). The ethnic differences in prevalence of drug use (i.e., cigarettes, alcohol, marijuana, and cocaine) persisted with controls for sociodemographic characteristics, including parental education and urban/rural location. Controlling for lifestyle variables, especially religious participation, truancy, and level of peer activity, reduced the differences somewhat. These factors accounted least for the differences between blacks and whites (Wallace & Bachman, 1991).

Similarly, Vega et al. (1993) reported for a sample of male 6th and 7th graders, drawn from the greater Miami area, that controlling for the number of risk factors experienced by these preadolescents did not reduce ethnic differences in rates of alcohol use among white non-Hispanics, Cuban Hispanics, other Hispanics, and blacks (Figure 5.3). The risks included such factors as depression, delinquency, perceived peer use, and family substance problems. At the lowest level of risks, there were few differences among the four ethnic groups. The differences were strongest at the highest level of risks, at which rates were the lowest for blacks: 12% reported having ever used illicit drugs, compared with 36 to 40% among the other three groups.

However, a contrasting conclusion was reached with respect to neighborhood effects by James Anthony and his colleagues at Johns Hopkins University. An innovative analysis of crack/cocaine use designed to control for community residence was carried out on the 1988 National Household Survey on Drug Abuse (Lillie-Blanton, Anthony, & Schuster, 1993). The authors examined 1,532 separate area segments sampled within the primary sampling units from which the survey respondents were drawn and selected the 128 neighborhoods in which at least one cocaine/crack user and one nonuser resided. They obtained a sample of 138 crack/cocaine users and 801 nonusers, among whom they examined rates of reported use by each of four ethnic groups. Controlling for neighborhood effects accounted completely for observed ethnic differences in prevalence of drug use. The odds of smoking crack were identical among African Americans, Hispanics, and whites. The authors' conclusion was that neighborhood characteristics account for observed rates of drug use among different ethnic groups.

Of the neighborhood characteristics that Anthony and his colleagues controlled, the percentages of minorities, the percentages of young and middle-aged people, residence in large metropolitan areas, and location in the western part of the United States were the important variables. Education and income did not distinguish the neighborhoods. The authors assumed that contextual variables (which they did not measure), such as drug availability and unspecified "social conditions," would account for the neighborhood effects.

These are provocative conclusions that need further replication. The difficulties of carrying out such analyses are highlighted by the fact that although the investigators started with a sample of over 8,000 respondents drawn from 1,532 census tracts, they identified only 138 cocaine/crack users.

In summary, three interpretations—underreporting, exclusion of dropouts and other high-risk groups, and spuriousness of the associations—

attempt to account for the differential prevalences of drug use among different ethnic groups observed within population samples.

ETHNIC DIFFERENCES BETWEEN
POPULATION AND INSTITUTIONAL SAMPLES

Again, three explanations can be proposed to explain the overrepresentation of blacks in samples of persons who have had contacts with institutions compared with representative population samples. Two explanations deal with differences in samples captured by population surveys and institutions. A third points to ethnic variations in severity of drug involvement among those who ever have experimented with a particular class of drugs.

National Versus Community Samples

An argument is made that national samples are not the best source of data with which to compare the ethnic distribution of treated cases, which tend to come disproportionately from ghetto areas and large urban centers (Brunswick, 1988). The only population surveys to report very high rates of illicit drug use for blacks are community surveys of urban low-income blacks (Brunswick, Merzel, & Messeri, 1985). Such surveys, however, typically do not have matched comparison groups of poor urban whites.

Bias in Institutional Contacts

Another explanation advanced to account for the contrasting ethnic distributions among users in epidemiological surveys and those drawn from institutions is that there is a bias involved in access to treatment and contact with institutions. Individuals who appear in the federal statistics—such as those who seek medical care in emergency rooms, are apprehended by the police, or are treated in a drug treatment program, especially in public programs funded by states or the federal government—are not a representative sample of the population. The bias may be related to social class, sex, ethnicity, or other demographics. A larger proportion of whites than blacks may seek care from private physicians and may be underrepresented in government-financed programs.

Extent of Involvement in Drugs

I believe that another important factor may explain the overrepresentation of blacks in institutional or clinical samples. Although fewer blacks than whites experiment with various illicit drugs, following initial experimenta-

TABLE 5.6 Degree of Drug Involvement Among Cocaine Users and Cigarette Smokers, by Ethnicity (New York State Survey—1988)

	Proportion of Cigarette Smokers Who Used			Proportion of Cocaine Users Who Used		
	Daily	40+ times		Daily	40+ times	
	%	%	(n)	%	%	(n)
White	21.3	36.0	(3,279)	2.6	16.0	(309)
Black	12.8	19.0	(358)	12.1	46.3	(29)
Hispanic	14.5	24.4	(318)	1.3	16.8	(55)

SOURCE: Kandel et al., 1990, Tables 2-9 and 2-10.

tion a higher proportion of blacks than whites become heavily involved in using these drugs, use more potent forms of drugs, persist in their use, and develop problems with their drug use, although not necessarily to the extent of meeting criteria for drug abuse or drug dependence disorders.

Higher Involvement. Of those who ever used cocaine, blacks (and Hispanics) report heavier involvement than whites. In the 1991 National Household Survey, those who reported to have used cocaine at least once a week within the last year represented 7.1% of the last-year users among whites, but 21.1% among Hispanics and 23.1% among blacks (NIDA, 1992c, Table 21-B-D).

I have observed parallel differences in two other samples that I have analyzed. In a national sample of young men and women aged 19 to 27 surveyed in 1984 in the National Longitudinal Survey of the Labor Force Experiences of Youth (NLSY), 22% of black men who had used cocaine within the last 30 days reported using it 20 or more times compared with 14% of white men (Kandel & Davies, 1991b, Table 8). Among the junior and senior high school students that I surveyed in 1988, more than twice as many black as white (or Hispanic) cocaine users reported having used the drug more than 40 times (see Table 5.6). The proportion of daily users among cocaine users was at least five times higher among blacks than among whites or Hispanics. These patterns hold for cocaine and other illicit drugs, except marijuana, but not for cigarettes and alcoholic beverages.

Greater Persistence of Use. The greater persistence of drug use among blacks and Hispanics compared with whites appears especially with respect to cocaine. For instance, in the National Household Survey on Drug Abuse, it is reflected in the proportions, among those who ever experimented with cocaine, of those who reported using the drug within the last 30 days preceding the 1991 survey: 16% among blacks and 14% among Hispanics did so compared with 6% among whites. Similarly, if one uses another

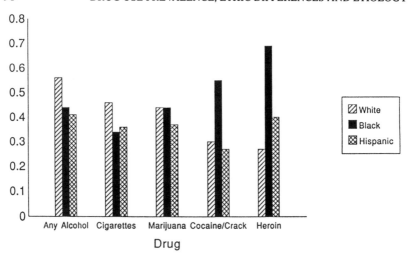

Figure 5.4. Persistence of Drug Use by Ethnicity: Ratio of Last-Month Use Over Lifetime Use in the New York State High School Survey—1988

measure of persistence, the ratio of those who used cocaine at least once a week among those who used cocaine within the last year, at every age throughout the life span, blacks show much higher persistence than whites (Figure 5.3).

Similar ethnic differences appear among the students in the New York State high school survey (Figure 5.4). However, these ethnic differences in persistence appeared for cocaine and heroin, although not for marijuana, cigarettes, or alcoholic beverages.

Ethnic differences in persistence of use have become accentuated over time. The differentials between blacks and whites in persistence rates in the use of cocaine have increased over the last 6 years. The ratios of proportions persisting among blacks over whites were calculated for each of the four national population surveys carried out since 1985. The proportions persisting were 1.3 times higher for blacks than for whites in 1985, over 1.8 times higher in 1988, but 3.4 times higher in 1990 and 2.1 times higher in 1991 (based on data reported in NIDA, 1988, 1990a, 1991, 1992c).

Use of More Potent Drugs. In addition, what little evidence is available suggests that blacks are more likely than whites to use more potent forms of a particular drug class. Thus, more blacks report using crack than any other group. In 1991, the proportion of crack users among blacks in the general population (4.3%) was almost three times that observed among whites (1.5%) and twice that observed among Hispanics (2.1%) (NIDA, 1992c,

Table 5-B, 5-C, 5-D). The ethnic differences are greater among those aged 26 to 34 than among those aged 18 to 25.

Blacks are somewhat more likely than any other group to use drugs intravenously. In 1991, twice as many blacks as whites (2.4% vs. 1.7%) reported lifetime needle use of cocaine, heroin, or amphetamines (NIDA, 1992c, Table 19). (The confidence intervals of these two estimates do not overlap.)

Furthermore, blind seroprevalence surveys indicate much higher rates of HIV-positive childbearing women and HIV-positive newborns among blacks than any other group. In New York State, for the period November 1987 to March 1990, the rate of HIV-positive newborns was 2.19 for blacks compared with 0.34 for whites and 1.43 for Hispanic babies (Novick et al., 1991). These results are free of any self-reported or sampling biases. Because of the known association between intravenous drug use and AIDS (DesJarlais, Friedman, & Novick, 1989), the seroprevalence results provide strong supporting evidence for ethnic differences in problematic drug use.

One set of data, however, is not consistent with the argument that I am developing. We would assume that persistence in use and degree of involvement would increase the risk of meeting criteria for drug abuse and/or dependence. The data from the Epidemiological Catchment Area (ECA), a study of the epidemiology of psychiatric disorders sponsored by the National Institute on Drug Abuse in the early 1980s (Robins & Regier, 1991), however, are not consistent with this hypothesis. In fact, slightly lower rates of cases of drug abuse/dependence meeting diagnostic criteria were observed among minorities than among whites in the general population in 1980-1984. The overall lifetime prevalence for drug disorders was 6.4 among whites, 5.5 among blacks, and 4.4 among Hispanics; 1-year prevalence was 2.7, 2.7, and 2.0, respectively (Anthony & Helzer, 1991, Table 6-6). Furthermore, in a prospective 1-year follow-up of incidence of new cases in the ECA sample that controlled for census track location, race/ethnicity was not a risk factor for developing drug abuse/dependence in adulthood (Anthony, 1991). This contradiction remains to be explained.

Reflections on
a Further Paradox

Ethnic patterns in substance use among adolescents raise a second paradox. This paradox leads us to take a somewhat broader perspective that moves us from an exclusive concern with drug use to a concern with the participation in and meaning of deviant behaviors in the lives of young people from different ethnic backgrounds.

Numerous studies have established that substance use is related to other deviant activities, such as early sexual activity, delinquency, truancy, and dropping out of school (Dryfoos, 1990; Elliott, 1993; Jessor & Jessor, 1977). This covariation is found equally among African Americans and other minorities (Farrell, Danish, & Howard, 1992; Watts & Wright, 1990). The sizes of the correlation coefficients among African Americans reported by Farrell et al. (1992) are very similar to those observed in white samples (e.g., Donovan & Jessor, 1985), with the exception of lower correlations of drug use with church attendance among the blacks compared with the whites.

The second paradox is this: Although the prevalence of substance use is lower among minority youths than whites, the prevalences of behaviors other than drug use are higher. For instance, black youths, especially males, initiate sexual activity and childbearing at an earlier age than whites (MMWR, 1993; Hayes, 1987). Dropout rates are higher among blacks, and especially Hispanic youths, than whites (Kaufman & McMillen, 1992). Thus, although there is covariation among various problem behaviors, the causal connection among them in different ethnic groups remains to be clarified. Such connections may vary in strength, and perhaps even in direction, among different groups. For instance, I and my colleagues documented that drug use was a risk factor for early sex and premarital pregnancy among whites (Mensch & Kandel, 1992; Rosenbaum & Kandel, 1990). The effect for premarital pregnancy did not hold for blacks. This nonfinding never appeared in print, however. Because the model did not fit blacks as well as whites, the editors asked us to omit these data and that part of the discussion from our manuscript. The relative fit of different causal models across different ethnic groups is a very underdeveloped area of research.

These divergent trends, within a certain commonality, lead us to consider that youths of different ethnic groups may take different paths toward deviance (Hagan, 1991). Different causes may give rise to the same behavior across different groups. Conversely, the same behavior may arise in response to different conditions and have quite a different meaning for young people and different consequences for their psychosocial adjustment depending upon their ethnic background.

Much remains to be understood regarding ethnic variations in patterns of drug use. It is to be hoped that the data presented in this volume, the juxtaposition of different perspectives, and the work stimulated by these discussions will help us move toward a better understanding of the paradoxes and the issues raised by epidemio-logical data on patterns of drug use among young people of different backgrounds.

Summary

Ethnic patterns in drug use in the general population are reviewed, and differences according to age, period prevalence, and historical time are highlighted. In adolescence and young adulthood, blacks report lower lifetime rates of drug use than whites or Hispanics. At older ages (35 and over), blacks report consistently higher rates than whites. This latter pattern appears to be gradually spreading into younger age groups and for recent point prevalence. Ethnic-specific rates of drug use observed in general population samples raise at least two paradoxes. One paradox derives form the contrast with the ethnic distributions of drug-related cases recorded in medical, legal, and treatment institutions, where blacks are overrepresented. Another paradox is that the lower rates of drug use reported by black youths compared with whites contrast with black youth's higher participation in problem behaviors other than drug use. Interpretations of the ethnic distributions of drug users within representative population samples and of the contrast between these distributions and those of drug users in institutions are presented and discussed. Interpretations of within-population differences are methodological and include underreporting of drug use, exclusion of at-risk groups from representative samples, and spuriousness of the associations between ethnicity and drug use. Interpretations of the overrepresentation of blacks in institutional compared with general population samples include lack of sample comparability, bias in who comes into contact with institutions, and differential severity of drug involvement among users from different ethnic groups. Implications of the data for understanding deviant participation among adolescents from different ethnic groups are discussed.

Note

1. The statistical significance of these across-grade reversals between white and black students was confirmed by a logit analysis performed through a log-linear procedure. The race-by-grade interaction was tested for several substances, namely beer, marijuana, cocaine, use of any illicit drugs (ILLD), and use of illicit drugs other than marijuana (OID), and found to be significant (data not presented). This would be the expected pattern if black drug users dropped out of school more frequently than white users.

References

Adlaf, E. M., Smart, R. G., & Tan, S. H. (1989). Ethnicity and drug use: A critical look. *International Journal of the Addictions, 24,* 1-18.

Anthony, J. C. (1991). The epidemiologic study of drug addiction and related syndromes. In N. S. Miller (Ed.), *Comprehensive Handbook of drug and alcohol addiction* (pp. 55-86). New York: Marcel Dekker.

Anthony, J. C., & Helzer, J. E. (1991). Syndromes of drug abuse and dependence. In L. Robins & D. Regier (Eds.), *Psychiatric disorders in America* (pp. 116-154). New York: Free Press.

Bachman, J. G., Wallace, Jr., J.M ., O'Malley, P. M., Johnston, L. D., Kurth, C. L., & Neighbors, H. W. (1991). Racial/ethnic differences in smoking, drinking, and illicit drug use among American high school seniors, 1976-89. *American Journal of Public Health, 81,* 372-377.

Brunswick, A. F. (1988). Black males and substance use. In J. T. Gibbs, A. F. Brunswick, & M. E. Connor (Eds.), *Young, black, and male in America* (pp. 166-187). Dover, MA: Auburn House.

Brunswick, A. F., Merzel, C. R., & Messeri, P. A. (1985). Drug use intitation among urban black youth: A seven year follow-up of developmental and secular influences. *Youth & Society, 17,* 189-216.

Brunswick, A. F., & Messeri, P. (1986). Drugs, lifestyle and health. *American Journal of Public Health, 76,* 52-57.

Chavez, E. L., & Swaim, R. C. (n.d.). *Epidemiology of Mexican-American adolescent substance use: A comparison of Mexican-American and white non-Hispanic 8th and 12th grade students.* Fort Collins: Colorado State University, Tri-Ethnic Center for Study of Drug Abuse Prevention.

Childbearing patterns among selected racial/ethnic minority groups—United States, 1990. (1993, May 28). *Morbidity and Mortality Weekly Report, 42*(20), 398-403.

De La Rosa, M. R., Khalsa, J. H., & Rouse, B. A. (1990). Hispanics and illicit drug use: A review of recent findings. *International Journal of the Addictions, 25,* 665-691.

DesJarlais, D. C., Friedman, S. R., & Novick, D. M. (1989). HIV-1 infection among intravenous drug users in Manhattan. *Journal of the American Medical Association, 261,* 1008-1012.

Donovan, J. E., & Jessor, R. (1985). Structure of problem behavior in adolescence and young adulthood. *Journal of Consulting and Clinical Psychology, 53,* 890-904.

Dryfoos, J. G. (1990). *Adolescents at risk.* New York: Oxford University Press.

Elliott, D. S. (in press). *Health enhancing and health compromising lifestyles.* In S. G. Millstein, A. C. Petersen, & E. O. Nightingale (Eds.), *Promoting the health of adolescents: New directions for the twenty-first century* (pp.   ). New York: Oxford University Press.

Farrell, A. D., Danish, S. J., & Howard, C. W. (1992). Relationship between drug use and other problem behaviors in urban adolescents. *Journal of Consulting and Clinical Psychology, 60,* 705-712.

Gillmore, M. R., Catalano, R. F., Morrison, D. M., Wells, E. A., Iritani, B., & Hawkins, J. D. (1990). Racial differences in acceptability and availability of drugs and early initiation of substance use. *American Journal of Drug and Alcohol Abuse, 16,* 185-206.

Hagan, J. (1991). Destiny and drift: Subcultural preferences, status attainments, and the risks and rewards of youth. *American Sociological Review, 56,* 567-582.

Harford, T. C. (1986). Drinking patterns among black and nonblack adolescents: Results of a national survey. *Annals of the New York Academy of Sciences, 472,* 130-141.

Hayes, C. D. (Ed.). (1987). *Risking the future.* Washington, DC: National Academy Press.

Jessor, R., & Jessor, S. L. (1977). *Problem behavior and psychosocial development: A longitudinal study.* New York: Academic Press.

Johnson, E. O., & Robin, S. S. (1992, August). *Epidemiology and behavior: The case of race, ethnicity and adolescent drug use.* Paper presented at the annual meeting of the Society for the Study of Social Problems.

Johnston, L. D., Bachman, J. G., & O'Malley, P. M. (1984). *Monitoring the future: Questionnaire responses from the nation's high school seniors, 1983.* Ann Arbor, MI: Institute for Social Research.

Johnston, L. D., O'Malley, P. M., & Bachman, J. G. (1991). *Drug use among American high school seniors, college students and young adults, 1975-1990: Vol. 1. High school seniors.* Rockville, MD: National Institute on Drug Abuse.

Johnston, L. D., O'Malley, P. M., & Bachman, J. G. (1992). *Smoking, drinking, and illicit drug use among American secondary school students, college students, and young adults, 1975-1991.* Rockville, MD: National Institute on Drug Abuse.

Kandel, D. B., & Davies, M. (1991a). Cocaine use in a national sample of U.S. youth (NLSY): Epidemiology, predictors and ethnic patterns. In C. Schade & S. Schober (Eds.), *The epidemiology of cocaine use and abuse* (NIDA Research Monograph 110, pp. 151-188). Rockville, MD: National Institute on Drug Abuse.

Kandel, D. B., & Davies, M. (1991b). Decline in the use of illicit drugs by high school students in New York State: Comparison with national data. *American Journal of Public Health, 81,* 1064-1067.

Kandel, D. B., Davies, M., & Davis, M. (1990). *New York State Youth Survey.* Albany: New York State Office of Mental Health.

Kandel, D. B., Single, E., & Kessler, R. (1976). The epidemiology of drug use among New York State high school students: Distribution, trends and change in rates of use. *American Journal of Public Health, 66,* 43-53.

Kaufman, P., & McMillan, M. M. (1992). *Dropout rates in the United States: 1991.* Washington, DC: National Center for Education Statistics.

Lillie-Blanton, M., Anthony, J. C., & Schuster, C. R. (1993). Probing the meaning of racial/ethnic group comparisons in crack cocaine smoking. *Journal of the American Medical Association, 269,* 993-997.

Maddahian, E., Newcomb, M. D., & Bentler, P. M. (1986). Adolescents' substance use: Impact of ethnicity, income, and availability. *Advances in Alcohol and Substance Abuse, 5*(3), 63-78.

Mensch, B. S., & Kandel, D. B. (1988). Underreporting of substance use in a national longitudinal youth cohort. *Public Opinion Quarterly, 52,* 100-124.

Mensch, B. S., & Kandel, D. B. (1992). Drug use as a risk factor for premarital teen pregnancy and pregnancy outcome in a national sample of young women. *Demography, 29,* 409-429.

National Institute of Justice. (1992). *Drug use forecasting 1991 annual report.* Washington, DC: National Institute of Justice, Office of Justice Programs.

National Institute on Drug Abuse. (NIDA) (1988). *Demographic characteristics and patterns of drug use of clients admitted to drug abuse treatment programs in selected states: Trend data 1979-1984.* Rockville, MD: Author.

National Institute on Drug Abuse. (NIDA) (1989). *National Drug and Alcoholism Treatment Unit Survey (NDATUS) 1987 final report.* Rockville, MD: Author.

National Institute on Drug Abuse. (NIDA) (1990a). *National Drug and Alcoholism Treatment Unit Survey (NDATUS) 1989: Main findings report.* Rockville, MD: Author.

National Institute on Drug Abuse. (NIDA) (1990b). *National Household Survey on Drug Abuse: Population estimates 1988.* Rockville, MD: Author.

National Institute on Drug Abuse. (NIDA) (1991). *National Household Survey on Drug Abuse: Population estimates 1990.* Rockville, MD: Author.

National Institute on Drug Abuse. (NIDA) (1992a). *Annual emergency room data 1991.* Rockville, MD: Author.

National Institute on Drug Abuse. (NIDA) (1992b). *Annual medical examiner data 1991.* Rockville, MD: Author.

National Institute on Drug Abuse. (NIDA) (1992c). *National Household Survey on Drug Abuse: Population estimates 1991* (Revised November 20, 1992). Rockville, MD: Author.

Newcomb, M. D., & Bentler, P. M. (1986). Substance use and ethnicity: Differential impact of peer and adult models. *Journal of Psychology, 120,* 83-95.

Novick, L. F., Glebatis, D. M., Stricof, R. L., MacCubbin, P. A., Lessner, L., & Berns, D. S. (1991). II. Newborn seroprevalence study: Methods and results. *American Journal of Public Health, 81*(Suppl.), 15-21.

Oetting, E. R., & Beauvais, F. (1990). Adolescent drug use: Findings of national and local surveys. *Journal of Consulting and Clinical Psychology, 58,* 385-394.

Robins, L. N., & Regier, D. A. (Eds.). (1991). *Psychiatric disorders in America.* New York: Free Press.

Rosenbaum, E., & Kandel, D. B. (1990). Early onset of adolescent sexual behavior and drug involvement. *Journal of Marriage and the Family, 52,* 783-798.

Substance Abuse and Mental Health Services Administration. (SAMHSA) (1993). *Preliminary estimates from the Drug Abuse Warning Network.* Rockville, MD: SAMHSA, Office of Applied Studies.

Trimble, J. E., Padilla, A. M., & Bell, C. S. (1987). *Drug abuse among minorities.* Rockville, MD: National Institute on Drug Abuse.

Vega, W. A., Zimmerman, R. S., Warheit, G. J., Apospori, E., & Gil, A. G. (1993). Risk factors for early adolescent drug use in four ethnic and racial groups. *American Journal of Public Health, 83,* 185-189.

Wallace, J. M., Jr., & Bachman, J. G. (1991). Explaining racial/ethnic differences in adolescent drug use: The impact of background and lifestyle. *Social Problems, 38,* 333-357.

Watts, W. D., & Wright, L. S. (1990). The relationship of alcohol, tobacco, marijuana, and other illegal drug use to delinquency among Mexican-American, black, and white adolescent males. *Adolescence, 25,* 171-181.

Welte, J. W., & Barnes, G. M. (1987). Alcohol use among adolescent minority groups. *Journal of Studies on Alcohol, 48,* 329-336.

Zabin, L. S., Hardy, J. B., Smith, E. A., & Hirsch, M. B. (1985, March). *Substance use and its relation to sexual activity among inner-city adolescents.* Paper presented at NIDA Technical Review on Drug Abuse and Adolescent Sexual Activity, Pregnancy and Parenthood.

Drug Use Etiology Among Ethnic Minority Adolescents

Risk and Protective Factors

Michael D. Newcomb

The influences that generate drug use and abuse among children and teenagers are many, varied, and far from clearly understood. Some may be similar across ethnic groups, whereas others may be unique or different for various ethnic populations. In general, most drug use initiation occurs with friends or peers who are themselves using drugs. However, the stage for this event has been established much earlier by their parents, cultural upbringing, neighborhood and community, and society at large (Newcomb & Bentler, 1989).

This chapter begins with a general review of the domains and variables that have been related to or predictive of drug use. This is followed by a description of multiple risk and protective factor approaches, with an empirical example of multiple risk and protective factors for drug use among Latino adolescents. Next, differential exposure to risk or protective conditions across various ethnic groups is reviewed, and differences in response or associations to these etiological factors in the form of drug involvement for different ethnic groups are considered. Finally, problem behavior theory is reviewed to emphasize the importance of considering interrelated behaviors when developing drug prevention programs.

TABLE 6.1 Summary of Risk Factors for Drug Use

Domain	Risk Factor
Culture and society	Laws favorable to drug use
	Social norms favorable to drug use
	Availability of drugs
	Extreme economic deprivations
	Neighborhood disorganization
Interpersonal	Parent and family drug use
	Positive family attitudes toward drug use
	Poor/inconsistent family management practices
	Family conflict and disruption
	Peer rejection
	Association with drug-using peers
Psychobehavioral	Early/persistent problem behavior
	Academic failure
	Low commitment to school
	Alienation
	Rebelliousness
	Favorable attitudes toward drug use
	Early onset of drug use
Biogenetics	Inherited susceptibility to drug abuse
	Psychophysiological vulnerability to drug effects

Etiological Domains and Variables

A number of variables have been studied for their ability to predict drug involvement. All of these various factors fall within four distinct domains (e.g., Lettieri, 1985): (a) biogenetic influences, (b) psychobehavioral factors (these may take several forms including personality, attitudes, and activities), (c) interpersonal forces (i.e., school, peers, and family), and (d) cultural and social environment. A child or teenager can be considered "at risk" or protected from drug use due to forces or conditions within each of these four areas.

In a recent review, Hawkins, Catalano, and Miller (1992) summarized the possible risk and protective factors for youthful drug use and identified 17 potential causes. These 17 factors reflect the four general domains cited above and are summarized in Table 6.1. Biogenetic factors include potential heritability of drug abuse vulnerability and psychophysiological susceptibility to the effects of drugs. Psychobehavioral influences include early and persistent problem behaviors, academic failure, low degree of commitment to school, alienation and rebelliousness, attitudes favorable to drug use, and early onset of drug use. Interpersonal forces include family alcohol and drug behavior and attitudes, poor and inconsistent family management practices, family conflict, peer rejection in elementary grades, and association with drug-using peers. Finally, included among cultural/societal factors are laws and norms favorable toward drug use, availability of drugs, extreme economic deprivation, and neighborhood disorganization.

Some types of alcohol and other drug abuse may have a genetic contribution. However, for initiation of drug use and progression to drug abuse, environmental, social, and psychological factors have received the most attention. Although biogenetic influences certainly affect the potential emergence of drug abuse, they are clearly shaped and modified by other personal attributes, interpersonal relationships, and environmental conditions (e.g., Marlatt, Baer, Donovan, & Kivlahan, 1988).

Several influences were not directly addressed in the review by Hawkins et al. (1992). These include psychoemotional factors, such as anxiety, need for excitement, depression, or antisocial personality, and contextual factors, such as physical or sexual abuse or other stressful life events (e.g, Harrison, Hoffmann, & Edwall, 1989; Newcomb & Harlow, 1986; Newcomb & McGee, 1991; Zucker & Gomberg, 1986).

Although not specifically mentioned by Hawkins et al. (1992), certainly the *best* predictor of future behavior is past behavior. Therefore, the strongest predictor of present drug involvement is past drug use. Peer influences, such as modeling of drug use behavior, provision of drugs, and attitudes and behavior that encourage drug use, are generally viewed as secondary only to prior experience with drugs.

Another obvious factor related to drug use initiation is age. The risk for initiating drug use increases for most drugs to a peak during mid- to late adolescence and decreases thereafter (Kandel & Logan, 1984). Typically tobacco has the youngest age of peak vulnerability. Increased likelihood of beginning use of alcohol, marijuana, and psychedelics occurs next. Initial cocaine use has typically occurred in young adulthood, although this pattern may be changing due to the rise in crack cocaine use among certain groups. Because crack is an inexpensive, smokable, and highly addictive form of cocaine, it may be more alluring and available to teenagers. Although Kandel and Yamaguchi (1993) recently showed that crack use typically occurs subsequent to licit drugs and marijuana, this does not preclude the possibility that the age of crack initiation may be younger than age of initiation for regular cocaine or that these findings may not apply to more homogeneous groups of inner-city minority youth.

Kandel (1975) suggested and demonstrated that stages in types of drug use involvement occur in a relatively fixed sequence beginning with no use, progressing to initial drug involvement with tobacco, beer, or wine, then hard liquor, then marijuana, and then other illicit drugs, including cocaine, inhalants, and hallucinogens. This is a probabilistic model rather than a deterministic one: Being at one stage in the sequence does not guarantee advancing to the next, but rather means that all previous stages have already been traversed (Newcomb & Bentler, 1989). Some qualifications of this sequence have been established, particularly with prospective data (e.g., Newcomb & Bentler, 1986) and suggestions that smokable substances may cluster (i.e., cigarettes and marijuana), licit drugs may influence each other (i.e., alcohol and nonprescription medications), and heavy alcohol use occurs subsequent to marijuana use (Donovan & Jessor, 1983). Nevertheless, it provides an important conceptual model with which to approach drug prevention because gateway drugs can be identified and targeted.

Unfortunately, most of the research on stages or sequencing of drug involvement has been conducted on white or combined samples of white and other ethnic groups. However, Brook, Hamburg, Balka, and Wynn (1992) demonstrated that the sequence of drug use from no use to alcohol or cigarettes, marijuana, and finally other illicit drugs occurred for both African American and Puerto Rican adolescents. Further, Ellickson, Hays, and Bell (1992) found that weekly drinking occurred subsequent to marijuana use for Hispanic, black, and white youth, but followed use of hard drugs for Asians.

Despite the compelling notion that the causes of drug use may be different from the causes of drug abuse and dependence, until quite recently little systematic research has addressed this important issue (e.g., Glantz & Pickens, 1992). This vital research agenda was directly thwarted by political demands to make no distinctions between teenage use and abuse of drugs. Nevertheless, several investigators have found that most drug use occurs due to social influences, whereas the abuse of drugs is more strongly tied to psychological factors and processes, such as self-medication against emotional distress (Carman, 1979; Newcomb & Bentler, 1990; Paton, Kessler, & Kandel, 1977).

Multiple Risk and Protective Factors

Many and certainly more of these various influences have been related to involvement with drug use or abuse, but none has ever been found to be the primary factor that causes drug use or abuse. Because the range of variables leading to initial drug involvement is so large, recent views of this phenomenon have emphasized the risk factor notion, often used in medical epidemiology (Bry, McKeon, & Pandina, 1982; Moncher, Holden, & Trimble, 1990; Newcomb, Maddahian, & Bentler, 1986; Newcomb, Maddahian, Skager, & Bentler, 1987; Scheier & Newcomb, 1991). As might be expected, these risk factors include the very same environmental, behavioral, psychological, and social attributes discussed above. It seems highly unlikely that any one factor or even a few factors will ever be found that account fully and totally for all variations of drug involvement.

Rather, child and adolescent drug involvement is multiply determined and can be reached via multiple pathways. The more risk factors a youngster is exposed to that encourage drug use, the more likely it is that he or she will use or abuse drugs. For instance, Moncher et al. (1990) showed that a multiple risk factor index was linearly related to reported prevalence of using beer/wine, inhalants, marijuana, and cocaine among a sample of Native American youth. Exposure to more risk factors not only is a reliable correlate of drug use, but increases drug use over time, implying a true etiological role (Newcomb & Félix-Ortiz, 1992; Newcomb et al., 1986; Scheier & Newcomb, 1991). Theoretically, this perspective implies that drug use is but one of many coping responses for a teenager who is exposed to an increasing number of vulnerability or risk conditions. The particular factors are not as important as the simple accumulation of vulnerability conditions in the person's life.

However, some risk conditions may be unique to particular minority groups, whereas other forces may operate across ethnic groups. For instance, acculturation (e.g., Black & Markides, 1993; Caetano & Mora, 1988), cultural competence (i.e., Szapocznik & Kurtines, 1993), or cultural identity (Félix-Ortiz & Newcomb, Chapter 8 of this volume) are all important considerations for understanding drug involvement among Latinos, whereas these constructs may be irrelevant for whites or Euro-Americans who have lived in one country for many generations.

The converse of risk factors for drug use is protective factors that reduce the likelihood and level of drug use and abuse. Protective factors are those psychosocial influences that have a direct effect on limiting or reducing drug involvement (Newcomb, 1992). Very recently, the risk factors approach to drug use and abuse has been expanded to test for multiple protective factors as well (Newcomb, 1992; Newcomb & Félix-Ortiz, 1992). As with risk conditions, there may be forces within a particular ethnic group that are uniquely protective for them and are not relevant for other ethnic groups.

Protective factors may also operate in a different manner than simply having a direct effect on reducing drug involvement. They may, in fact, buffer or moderate the association between risk factors and drug use and abuse (Brook, Cohen, Whiteman, & Gordon, 1992; Newcomb & Félix-Ortiz, 1992; Stacy, Newcomb, & Bentler, 1992). Protective factors that moderate the relationship between risk for drug use or abuse can involve aspects of the environment (e.g., maternal affection), culture, or the individual (e.g., introversion or self-acceptance). For instance, Stacy et al. (1992) found that a high degree of self-acceptance moderated the relationship between peer use of hard drugs and self-use of hard drugs; a strong relationship between these variables existed for those low in self-acceptance, but little association was found between these variables for those with high self-acceptance. Newcomb and Félix-Ortiz (1992) also tested the buffering effects of multiple protective factors on the relationship between multiple risk factors and drug use and abuse. Several significant effects were noted, primarily for illicit drugs.

An Example of Multiple Risk and
Protective Factors Among Latino Adolescents

A concrete example of these multiple influences is contained in findings from a study by Félix-Ortiz and Newcomb (1992). This paper was based on data from a long-term prospective study of drug use beginning in early adolescence (Newcomb & Bentler, 1988). Analyses presented here are from the fourth wave of data collected during mid- to late adolescence. At that time, data were gathered from 117 Latino teenagers in Los Angeles County high schools.

Fourteen items or scales were selected from this database as possible risk or protective factors for drug use. Very few teenagers should have many risk or protective factors (Newcomb & Félix-Ortiz, 1992), so the upper and lower 20% of the distribution of each factor were specified as either risk or protection. In this way, two variables were created from each factor, one capturing the 20% at risk and the other the 20% protected. These 28 variables (two for each factor) were correlated with five frequency of drug use scales (for cigarettes, alcohol, cannabis, cocaine, and other hard drugs). The average correlation (AC) was calculated across the five drugs for each of the 28 variables. A factor was assigned to the risk index if the AC was greater for the risk version of that factor when compared to the AC for the protected version of that factor. If the AC of protected version of a factor was larger than the risk version, the factor was assigned to the protective index.

In this manner, seven factors were assigned to the risk index and seven factors to the protective index (Newcomb & Félix-Ortiz, 1992). These assignments revealed a conceptual distinction between the risk and protective factors. The protective factors were more psychological, attitudinal, and home related (i.e., grade point average, law abidance, religiosity, self-acceptance, good home relationships), whereas the risk factors appeared more environmentally embedded (i.e., perceived peer and adult drug use, availability of drugs, important people/community support for drug use, low perceived opportunity in life). In other words, in terms of these factors examined, risk emerges from the outside or (perceived) external conditions of the teenager, whereas protective forces are those within the adolescent.

The seven risk factors (each scored "0" for *no risk* and "1" for *at risk*) were summed into a multiple risk factor index. Similarly, the protection

TABLE 6.2 Correlations Between Risk and Protective Factor indexes and Drug Use for Latino Adolescents ($N = 117$)

	Risk Factor Index	Protective Factor Index	Z-Difference Between Correlations
Cigarettes			
Frequency	.31***	−.13	2.98**
Quantity	.33***	−.13	3.13**
Alcohol			
Frequency	.47***	−.35***	5.79***
Quantity	.53***	−.32***	6.09***
Cannabis			
Frequency	.68***	−.31***	7.57***
Quantity	.67***	−.30***	7.38***
Cocaine			
Frequency	.40***	−.26**	4.56***
Other Hard Drugs			
Frequency	.54***	−.27**	5.82***

NOTE: Risk and protective factor index correlated −.30 ($p < .001$)
**$p < .01$; ***$p < .001$.

factors (each scored "0" for *no protection* and "1" for *protected*) were summed into a multiple protective factor index. As expected, most teenagers (over 60%) received a score of 0 or 1 on each of these indexes. Very few received a score of 6 or 7 and therefore were collapsed into the grouping of 5 or more.

One very important question concerns whether risk and protection are simply the opposite ends of a single continuum. This notion would predict that the risk and protective factor indexes should be highly negatively correlated. In fact, the correlation between these two indexes for the Latino adolescents was significant but modest, $r = −.31$. Therefore, on the basis of this empirical determination of risk and protection, the two indexes, though sharing some degree of association (less than 10% of common variance), capture conceptually distinct domains and are moderately independent.

Next, these indexes were correlated with each of the five frequency of drug use scales and three quantity of use scales (for cigarettes, alcohol, and cannabis). All correlations were significant (except for the protective factor index with the two cigarette scales) and in the expected directions (positive for the risk factor index and negative for the protective factor index). These are presented in Table 6.2.

In addition, the Duncan-Clark test was used to compare the magnitude of the absolute value of the correlations for each index. These tests revealed that the apparently higher correlations with the risk index were, in fact, significantly larger when compared to the analogous correlation with the protection index; the finding indicates that this group of risk factors is significantly

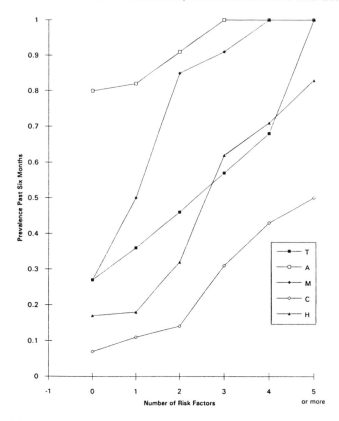

Figure 6.1. Association Between Latino Adolescents' Number of Risk Factors and 6-Month Prevalence of Using Tobacco (T), Alcohol (A), Marijuana (M), Cocaine (C), and Other Hard Drugs (H)

more associated with drug use than is this group of protective factors. Nevertheless, when both indexes were allowed to predict drug use in multiple regression analyses (Félix-Ortiz & Newcomb, 1992), each index contributed significant and unique variance to explaining the drug use scores, with the exception of the protective factor index for Latino males on the two cigarette scales.

The associations between number of risk factors and 6-month prevalence of using the five drugs are depicted in Figure 6.1. Similarly, the associations between number of protective factors and the prevalence of using the five drugs are depicted in Figure 6.2. These document the positive correlations between the risk factor index and drug use scales (Figure 6.1) and the negative correlations between the protective factor index and the drug use scales (Figure 6.2).

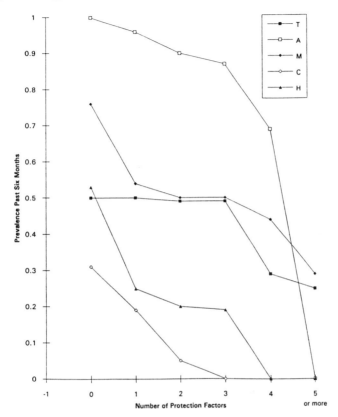

Figure 6.2. Association Between Latino Adolescents' Number of Protective Factors and 6-Month Prevalence of Using Tobacco (T), Alcohol (A), Marijuana (M), Cocaine (C), and Other Hard Drugs (H)

A final issue involves the buffering role of multiple protective factors in a person exposed to multiple risk conditions: Does high protection moderate the relationship between risk and drug use? There were three significant interaction effects between multiple risk and protection indexes in the Félix-Ortiz and Newcomb (1992) analyses of these data. Figure 6.3 plots the significant interaction effect for quantity of cocaine use among Latinas, Figure 6.4 presents the significant interaction effect for hard drug frequency among Latinas, and Figure 6.5 presents the interaction for hard drug frequency among Latino males. In all three figures, those at low risk had a lower level of drug use regardless of protection (capturing the main effects) and a much flatter slope than the high-risk group. Those at high risk for drug use reported much greater drug involvement if they had low protection than those

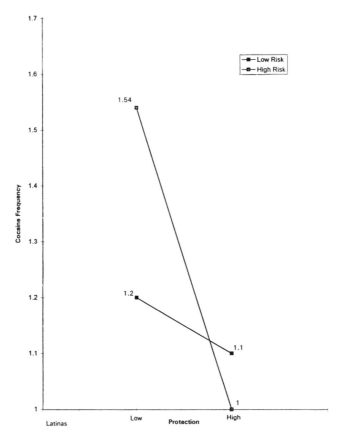

Figure 6.3. Interaction Effect Between Multiple Risk and Protection Indexes for Quantity of Cocaine Use Among Latina Adolescents

with high protection. In other words, protective factors for these drugs are most important among those at high risk for drug use. These are quite dramatic results and emphasize the critical buffering role of protective factors, especially for those at high risk.

Ethnic Variations in Exposure to
Risk or Protective Conditions for Drug Use

There are at least two ways to examine ethnic differences for etiological factors related to drug involvement. The first approach involves consideration of differences in exposure to recognized risk or protective conditions

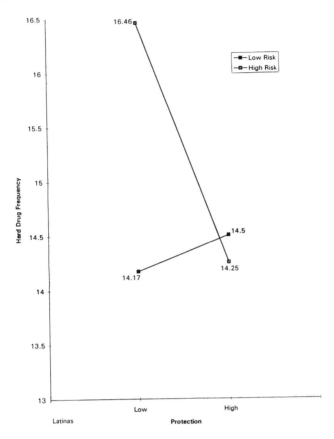

Figure 6.4. Interaction Effect Between Multiple Risk and Protection Indexes for Hard Drug Frequency Among Latina Adolescents

related to drug use. The second approach considers the degree of association between exposure to etiological factors and drug involvement and how these associations may also differ across ethnic groups.

An alternate approach assumes that varying patterns of etiological conditions among ethnic groups may explain the differential levels of drug involvement across the groups; if differences in these etiological factors are controlled, then there should be no ethnic differences in drug use. This approach has been used by several researchers, although most investigators using this method do not explicitly describe the variations in etiological factors across ethnic groups, nor the differential associations between these and drug use among the groups. For instance, Bachman et al. (1991) concluded that drug use differences among six ethnic groups (white, black, Mexican Ameri-

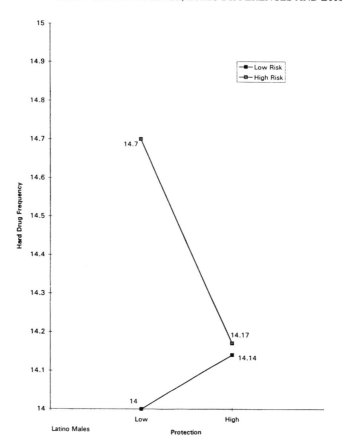

Figure 6.5. Interaction Effect Between Multiple Risk and Protection Indexes for Hard Drug Frequency Among Latino Adolescent Males

can, Puerto Rican/Latino American, Asian American, and Native American) were not primarily attributable to family composition, parent education, region of the country, or urban/rural place of residence. Similarly, Wallace and Bachman (1991) attempted to explain drug use differences among these six groups in terms of background and lifestyle variables. Background variables (i.e., parent education, number of parents in home) could not account for these differences, whereas lifestyle variables (i.e., grades, truancy, job involvement, religiosity) substantially reduced but did not eliminate differences among these ethnic groups on drug use. Further, Newcomb and Bentler (1986) found that significant ethnic differences remained in use of beer/wine/hard liquor, cannabis, and pills among blacks, Hispanics, Asians, and whites after controlling for exposure to both adult and peer models for using these drugs.

The remainder of this section selectively reviews the literature on differential exposure to risk or protective conditions across ethnic minority groups. This review is restricted to studies that involve differences in factors specifically related to drug use and does not reflect the literature on ethnic differences on general deviance. Therefore, studies such as Furstenberg, Morgan, Moore, and Peterson (1987), which examined racial differences in the timing of adolescent intercourse, are not included, even though age of sexual involvement is certainly strongly associated with teenage drug use (e.g., McGee & Newcomb, 1992).

Due to space limitations, this is not an exhaustive or comprehensive review, but reflects some of the recent attempts to identify ethnic differences in risk and protective factors for drug use. Eleven studies are used to describe differential exposure to risk and protective conditions across ethnic groups. All of these ethnic differences address established risk or protective factors for drug use.

Kaestner, Rosen, and Appel (1977) compared white, black, and Hispanic subjects in regard to state and trait anxiety and the sensation-seeking scales. No differences among these groups were found for the anxiety scales. However, significant differences were found on all subscales and the total sensation-seeking scale. White subjects had significantly higher scores than blacks and Hispanics on all sensation-seeking scales. Blacks scored higher than Hispanics on only the thrill and adventure seeking scale. No other significant differences among groups were found.

Kleinman and Lukoff (1978) compared white and black subjects on factors related to drug use. They found only two significant differences between groups. Whites had more friends involved with drug use, and blacks reported greater involvement with stolen goods.

Maddahian, Newcomb, and Bentler (1986) compared the number of friends who provided drugs; perceived ease of acquiring cigarettes, alcohol, marijuana, and other drugs; and amount of earned and given income among Hispanics, blacks, Asians, and whites. Significant differences among ethnic groups were found on nearly all of these comparisons. In general, perceived provision of drugs by friends was highest for Hispanics and whites (with the exception that blacks reported the highest peer provision of cigarettes), followed by blacks, and was generally lowest among Asians. A similar pattern was found for the perceived ease for acquiring drugs, although for these comparisons, the blacks and Asians were very similar. Finally, Asians and whites reported higher earned income than the other two groups, whereas Hispanics and blacks reported more given income (i.e., allowance) than Asians or whites.

Maddahian, Newcomb, and Bentler (1988a) compared the intentions to use five types of drugs among Hispanics, blacks, Asians, and whites. Significant differences were found for only cigarettes and hard drugs. Blacks and Hispanics reported much greater intentions to use cigarettes than did whites and Asians. Hispanics, blacks, and whites reported similar levels of intentions to use hard drugs, compared to much lower intentions for Asians.

Newcomb and Bentler (1986) compared black, Hispanic, Asian, and white adolescents with regard to their perceptions of the number of peers and adults who used beer/wine/hard liquor, cannabis, and pills. Significant ethnic differences were found on all four types of drugs. Blacks and whites reported more peer models of beer/wine use than Hispanics and Asians did. Whites reported more peer models of hard liquor use than blacks and Asians. Blacks reported more cannabis-using peers than all other groups, Hispanics and whites reported similar levels of peer cannabis use, and Asians reported the fewest peers who used cannabis. Finally, blacks, Hispanics, and whites reported similar exposure to pill-using peers, which was far greater than for Asian teenagers. Whites and Hispanics reported similar numbers of adults using beer/wine, and the white group reported significantly more than either blacks or Asians did. Blacks and whites reported significantly more adult models of liquor use than Asians did. Blacks reported significantly more adult models of cannabis use than all other groups, Hispanics and whites reported similar exposure, and Asians reported the least. Finally, blacks reported the most adult models of pill use, followed by Hispanics, whites, and Asians.

Russell, Cooper, and Frone (1990) compared black and white subjects in regard to a positive family history of alcoholism. They found no significant difference between blacks (27%) and whites (23%) on the prevalence of familial alcoholism.

Wallace and Bachman (1993) examined differences among six ethnic groups on perceived risk, disapproval, friends' disapproval, friends's use, and exposure to several types of drugs (use and frequent use of cigarettes, alcohol, marijuana, and cocaine). They found that American Indian and white high school seniors reported the least perceived risk for drug use, whereas Puerto Rican/Latino and Asian American seniors reported the greatest perceived risk for drug use. Greatest disapproval for numerous patterns of drug involvement was reported most often by Asian Americans and least by American Indians and whites. A similar pattern was found for friends' disapproval for various patterns of drug use. Friends' perceived drug use was highest among Mexican American, Puerto Rican/Latino, and American Indian seniors and lowest among African American and Asian American seniors. Finally, exposure to drug-using environments was highest among American Indians and white seniors, and lowest among Asian Americans and blacks. Some exceptions to these general patterns were evident in regard to specific drugs.

The several remaining studies examined an even wider variety of putative risk and protective factors for drug use, three incorporating the multiple risk factor methodology. Because even more detailed findings are reported in these papers, only a brief summary of results is provided.

Castro, Maddahian, Newcomb, and Bentler (1987) compared white, black, Hispanic, and Asian Pacific adolescents on 11 variables reflecting disruptive life events, perceived stressfulness of family life changes, social conformity, and peer influences. Significant ethnic differences were found on five of these. Blacks reported the greatest number of relocation events, although they also reported the least stressfulness arising from relocation changes. Blacks also reported the most religious commitment, the most friends who gave them cigarettes, and the most friends who used cigarettes.

Maddahian, Newcomb, and Bentler (1988b) compared the same four groups for the percentage at risk on 10 risk factors for drug use. Significant ethnic differences were found on 7 of these: low religiosity (lowest risk for blacks), early alcohol use (highest risk for whites), poor self-esteem (lowest risk for blacks), deviance (greatest risk for Hispanics), sensation seeking (lowest risk for blacks), and peer and adult drug use (lowest risk for Asians).

Vega, Zimmerman, Warheit, Apospori, and Gil (1993) compared four ethnic groups (whites, Cubans, "other Hispanics," and blacks) on prevalence of risk on 10 factors reflecting family, psychosocial, peer, and deviance influence. Significant ethnic differences were found on all 10 factors. Low family pride was a more prevalent risk factor for whites, family substance use was least among Cubans, parent smoking was highest for whites and Cubans, whites were at least risk for poor self-esteem, blacks were at greatest risk due to depression, whites were at least risk due to a suicide attempt, blacks perceived least peer substance use but the greatest peer approval for using drugs, and whites were at least risk due to willingness to engage and actual involvement in non-normative behavior.

Three studies compared the actual number of risk factors across different ethnic groups. All three reported significant differences. Vega et al. (1993) reported that blacks had significantly more risk factors than whites, Cubans, and other Hispanics. Maddahian et al. (1988b) found that whites and Hispanics had a similarly high number of risk factors compared to Asians, who had fewer, and blacks, who had the least. Finally, Newcomb et al. (1987) found that "other" ethnicities and American Indians had the greatest number of risk factors, followed by Hispanics and whites, and then by blacks and Asians.

The dissimilarity in conclusions among these three studies is striking, considering that they all used a similar methodology. However, the samples were drawn from distinct geographical locations: Florida for Vega et al. (1993) and Southern California for the other two. It is quite likely that ethnic groups with similar labels are in fact quite different. This emphasizes the importance of carefully understanding the particular ethnic group being studied and recognizing that within-group differences in general categorical groups may be as great or greater than apparent between-group differences. Certainly the Hispanics (mostly Mexican American) on the West Coast may be quite different than the Cubans and other Hispanics on the southeast border of the United States. Similarly, African American populations may be quite distinct based on geographical location (as whites may be as well). The very high risk of the "other" ethnic category noted by Newcomb et al. (1987) is quite interesting. This may reflect greater vulnerability arising from ethnic ambiguity or inadequate identification with any ethnic group.

Ethnic Variations in Associations Between Etiological Factors and Drug Use

The previous section revealed several differences in exposure to risk or protective conditions among ethnic groups. However, this does not mean that greater exposure necessarily leads to greater drug involvement to the same extent for all populations. It is also possible that variations in the degree of association between exposure to risk factors and drug use may occur across ethnic groups. Although there is less research on this issue, several studies have addressed it, and a selected group of these is reviewed below.

Akutsu, Sue, Zane, and Nakamura (1989) compared Asian and Caucasian students in regard to sociocultural and physiological correlates of alcohol consumption. In both groups, neither demographics nor acculturation was significantly associated with alcohol use, whereas attitudes toward drinking was a reliable correlate in each group. However, physiological reactivity was significantly related to alcohol use only among the Asians.

Brook, Whiteman, Balka, and Hamburg (1992) examined many variables as possible correlates of drug use among separate samples of African American and Puerto Rican teenagers living in New York City. Many of the variables were significantly related to drug use in both groups, and they covered five domains, including personality/ behavior/attitudes, family, peers, drug context, and ecology. Variables reflecting a sixth area of acculturation were not significantly related to drug use for either group. In analyses that I conducted, the analogous correlations for each group were statistically compared to determine whether the magnitude of association for each variable with drug use differed by ethnic group. On no variable were the correlations significantly different for African Americans compared to Puerto Ricans. This may reflect a greater impact of inner-city up- bringing compared to ethnic background.

Castro et al. (1987) compared white, black, Hispanic, and Asian Pacific teenagers regarding correlates of cigarette smoking. They found that perceived stressfulness of life events was not significantly correlated with cigarette smoking in any of these groups. On the other hand, peer smoking behaviors were significantly correlated quite highly with cigarette smoking in all four groups. Disruptive family events were significantly correlated with cigarette smoking in white and Asian Pacific groups, but unrelated in the other two. Finally, social conformity was significantly associated with less cigarette smoking among white, black, and Asian Pacific teenagers, but was reliably correlated with *more* cigarette smoking among Hispanics.

Kaestner et al. (1977) correlated the number of drugs used with state and trait anxiety and the sensation-seeking scales among groups of whites, blacks, and Hispanics. They found that the two anxiety measures were significantly correlated with fewer drugs used for the whites, but there were positive (nonsignificant) associations between these variables for the blacks and Hispanics. Although all of the sensation-seeking scales were significantly related with use of more drugs in the total, combined sample, there were various differences in correlations among the ethnic groups. For instance, disinhibition was significantly correlated with use of more drugs for whites and blacks, but had a slight negative correlation for the Hispanics. On the other hand, thrill and adventure seeking was significantly correlated with using more drugs among the whites, was positive but not significant for the Hispanics, and was slightly negative for the blacks. These patterns may be somewhat unstable due to the relatively small sample sizes (30 in each group).

Kleinman and Lukoff (1978) compared American blacks, West Indian blacks, and whites on factors related to drug use. They found "significant differences between the three ethnic groups with respect to factors which are related to drug use" (p. 195). In further analyses, however, they showed that most predictive factors were similar across the groups (including attachment to conventional or deviant patterns) and that the primary differential association among the groups was related to friends' drug use. Friends' drug use had no effect on the drug use of West Indian blacks, but was a highly significant predictor among each of the other two groups.

Maddahian et al. (1988a) contrasted the correlations between intentions to use a drug and actual drug use across Hispanic, black, Asian, and white teenagers. These comparisons were conducted on five different drugs (cigarettes, alcohol, cannabis, nonprescription medications, and hard drugs) both cross-sectionally and over time. There were no significant differences among ethnic groups for the correlations related to use of hard drugs. There were significant differences in cross-sectional correlations for all four other drugs. For cigarettes, Hispanics had a significantly higher correlation than the blacks. For alcohol, blacks had a significantly lower correlation than both

Hispanics and whites. In regard to cannabis, blacks had a significantly lower correlation than all three other groups. Turning to nonprescription medications, Asians had a significantly higher correlation than all other groups, and blacks had a significantly lower correlation than all other groups. There were fewer significant differences across groups on the partial correlations across time. These were found for only alcohol and cannabis, for which Asians and blacks had higher correlations than Hispanics or whites. In other words, when prior drug use was considered, intentions had less effect for whites and Hispanics than for blacks and Asians.

Neff, Prihoda, and Hoppe (1991) compared machismo, self-esteem, and education as predictors of maximum drinking among white, black, and Mexican American male drinkers. Among whites, machismo was significantly related to maximum drinking regardless of self-esteem or education status, but had somewhat greater effects in low-self-esteem/low-education and high-self-esteem/high- education groups. For the Mexican Americans, machismo only affected maximum drinking in low-self-esteem/low-education and high-self-esteem/high-education subgroups. Among blacks, machismo was not significantly related to maximum drinking, but the trend was for machismo to be related to *less* maximum drinking.

Newcomb and Bentler (1986) compared the correlations between self-use of beer/wine, liquor, cannabis, and pills and perceived peer and adult use of these same drugs across black, Hispanic, white, and Asian teenagers. For peer drug use, there were significant differences across groups for beer/wine and liquor: There was a significantly positive correlation for beer/wine among whites compared to a significantly negative correlation for the blacks, whereas whites had a significantly larger correlation for liquor compared to the blacks. For adult drug use, there were significant differences in correlations across groups for cannabis and pills: Hispanics and whites had significantly larger correlations for cannabis than blacks, whereas for pill use whites had a significantly higher correlation than Asians or blacks (who had a significantly negative correlation).

Russell et al. (1990) compared the differential effects of a positive family history for alcohol abuse on alcohol abuse/dependence among black and white men and women. In regard to age, they reported that the risk for alcohol problems related to a positive family history increased with age for whites, but decreased with increasing age for blacks. Turning to sex, they found that "the excess of alcohol abuse/dependence associated with a positive family history for alcoholism/problem drinking is approximately twice as high among white females and black males as it is among white males and black females" (p. 223).

Vega et al. (1993) examined 10 predictors of lifetime alcohol use in separate regression analyses for whites, blacks, Cubans, and other Hispanics. Although they did not directly compare these groups on the regression equations, some interesting patterns can be noted. For instance, low family pride and willingness to engage in non-normative behavior were significant predictors in all ethnic groups. Delinquency, low self-esteem, and suicide attempts were significant predictors only in the other Hispanic group. Depression was a significant predictor only among the whites. Perceived peer use, peer approval, parent substance use problems, and parent smoking were significant predictors in all ethnic groups except whites.

Watts and Wright (1990) reported correlations between four types of drug use (alcohol, tobacco, marijuana, and other illegal drugs) and minor delinquency and violent delinquency for groups of Mexican Americans, whites, and blacks. Although the authors did not directly compare these correlations across ethnic groups, I conducted these statistical contrasts. The correlation between minor delinquency and other illegal drugs was significantly higher for the Mexican Americans than for the whites. No other differences in correlations were found for minor delinquency. Two significant differences in correlations were found for violent delinquency: Mexican Americans had significantly higher correlations between violent delinquency and both alcohol and other illegal drugs than did the white group.

Two studies report correlations between a risk factor index and drug use across ethnic groups. Newcomb et al. (1987) found that whites had a significantly higher correlation between a risk factor index and a composite substance use score than did Asian or Hispanic teenagers. Finally, Maddahian et al. (1988b) reported cross-sectional and across-time (partial) correlations between a risk factor index and five types of drug use (cigarettes, alcohol, cannabis, non- prescription medications, and hard drugs). Among the cross-sectional correlations, there were significant differences across ethnic groups for cannabis (whites significantly higher than blacks) and hard drugs (blacks significantly lower than all three other groups). There were no significant differences among the four ethnic groups on the longitudinal partial correlations, corroborating the findings from Maddahian et al.'s earlier article on intentions to use drugs (Maddahian et al., 1988a).

Overall, it appears that many of the predictors of drug use are similar across ethnic groups. However, this review suggests both that exposure to these differs across different ethnic groups and that the reaction or response to these in the form of drug use may vary across ethnicities. Such information is particularly valuable for fine-tuning interventions for specific ethnic groups.

Drug Use and Other Problem Behaviors

Drug use and abuse do not occur as isolated events, nor as distinct aspects of an individual's behavior. They are typically only aspects or symptoms of a cluster of behaviors and attitudes that form a syndrome or lifestyle of problem behavior or general deviance (McGee & Newcomb, 1992; Newcomb & McGee, 1991). Problem behavior theory (Jessor & Jessor, 1977) provides a valuable conceptualization within which to understand how teenage drug use reflects but one aspect of a deviance-prone lifestyle. Adolescent substance use is considered only one facet of a constellation of attitudes and behavior that are considered problematic, unconventional, or nontraditional for a specific developmental stage. More generally, this syndrome involves "behavior that is socially defined as a problem, a source of concern, or as undesirable by the norms of conventional society, . . . [the] occurrence [of which] usually elicits some kind of social control response" (Jessor & Jessor, 1977, p. 33). For adolescents, these deviant behaviors include alcohol abuse, illicit drug use, precocious sexual involvement, academic problems, frequency of various sexual activities, deviant attitudes, and delinquent behavior.

Several studies have confirmed a syndrome of problem behaviors among adolescents and young adults by revealing either that one common latent factor accounts for the correlations among several indicators of problem behavior or that all of these constructs are highly correlated (Donovan & Jessor, 1985; McGee & Newcomb, 1992; Newcomb & Bentler, 1988; Newcomb & McGee, 1991). For instance, Newcomb and Bentler (1988) found that teenage polydrug use was highly correlated with low social conformity, criminal activities, deviant friendship network, early sexual involvement, and low academic potential. McGee and Newcomb (1992) used higher-order confirmatory factor analyses to examine the construct of general deviance at four ages from early adolescence to adulthood and found that the construct was highly reliable at early and late adolescence. In short, the concept of problem behavior appears to describe adequately a set of factors that encourage and coexist with adolescent drug use.

An example of this syndrome is depicted in Figure 6.6 as a latent-factor model and represents late adolescence (from McGee & Newcomb, 1992). A second-order construct of General Deviance accounted for significant and substantial portions of variance among five first-order constructs. General Deviance was most represented by the constructs of Drug Use (90%) and Sexual Involvement (84%). The attitudinal construct of (low) Social Conformity contributed the third largest amount of variance to General Deviance (58%), followed by Criminal Behavior (35%) and Academic Orientation (18%).

In terms of drug abuse prevention, the implications of this syndrome are clear. Adolescent drug use cannot be most efficiently prevented without consideration and attention directed toward the other types of deviance and problems of adolescence. These deviant characteristics form an interwoven net of attitudes and behavior that must be addressed not by focusing on single strands but by considering the entire fabric.

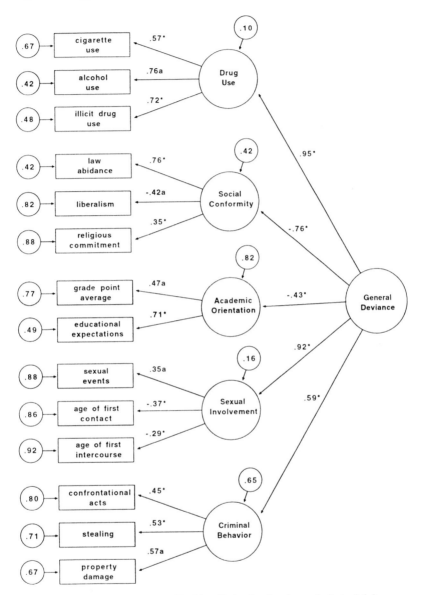

Figure 6.6. Latent Factor Model of Problem Behavior Syndrome in Late Adolescence

Unfortunately, these findings have not been replicated in different ethnic groups. On the basis of the differential association observed between drug use and other types of delinquency or problem behavior reviewed above (e.g.,

Vega et al., 1993; Watts & Wright, 1990), it seems possible that this syndrome may have different patterns for various ethnic groups. Some information is vital for attempts to apply problem behavior implications to interventions with ethnic minority teenagers.

SUMMARY

Clearly, there are many etiological influences for drug use and abuse that reflect many aspects of a biopsychosocial model; no one factor or even a small group of factors can be considered the sole or determining risk or protective condition. Furthermore, many of these risk and protective influences change as a function of developmental period (Newcomb, in press). Therefore, all intervention programs must be multifaceted and specialized to the particular developmental age of the population of concern.

To construct relevant, appropriate, and effective drug prevention programs for diverse populations, it is essential to target such interventions at the most salient risk and protective conditions for each group. As evident from this review, some factors are important for many groups and others are relevant only for specific populations. Most important, this area of cross-cultural comparative research is not well developed, and the present conclusions are only cursory and preliminary. We need to know much more about which risk and protective factors are most prevalent and influential in regard to drug use for various ethnic groups. Although there will certainly be common components among prevention programs for different ethnic populations, a generic program cannot be used with all groups. Important and vital differences characterize these various populations that must be incorporated into any intervention efforts.

Finally, drug use and abuse do not occur in isolation, but are often strongly associated with other deviant attitudes, activities, and other forms of non-normative behavior. Therefore, all prevention efforts must be broad based, with multiple targets for change, because a limited focus on a single problem behavior or aspect of general deviance may lack sufficient power and generalization to affect the underlying structure and predilection toward deviance. However, this construct of general deviance has not been established among very many nonwhite populations, suggesting caution when generalizing this syndrome to diverse ethnic groups. Clearly, more research is also required in this area.

References

Akutsu, P. D., Sue, S., Zane, N. W. S., & Nakamura, C. Y. (1989). Ethnic differences in alcohol consumption among Asians and Caucasians in the United States: An investigation of cultural and physiological factors. *Journal of Studies on Alcohol, 50,* 261-267.

Bachman, J. G., Wallace, J. M., Jr., O'Malley, P. M., Johnston, L. D., Kurth, C. L., & Neighbors, H. W. (1991). Racial/ethnic differences in smoking, drinking, and illicit drug use among American high school seniors, 1976-89. *American Journal of Public Health, 81,* 372-377.

Black, S. A., & Markides, K. S. (1993). Acculturation and alcohol consumption in Puerto Rican, Cuban-American, and Mexican-American women in the United States. *American Journal of Public Health, 83,* 890-893.

Brook, J. S., Cohen, P., Whiteman, M., & Gordon, A. S. (1992). Psychosocial risk factors in the transition from moderate to heavy use or abuse of drugs. In M. D. Glantz & R. Pickens (Eds.), *Vulnerability to drug abuse* (pp. 359-388). Washington, DC: American Psychological Association.

Brook, J. S., Hamburg, B. A., Balka, E. B., & Wynn, P. S. (1992). Sequences of drug involvement in African-American and Puerto Rican adolescents. *Psychological Reports, 71,* 179-182.

Brook, J. S., Whiteman, M., Balka, E. B., & Hamburg, B. A. (1992). African-American and Puerto Rican drug use: Personality, familial, and other environmental risk factors. *Genetic, Social, and General Psychology Monographs, 118,* 417-438.

Bry, B. H., McKeon, P., & Pandina, R. (1982). Extent of drug use as a function of number of risk factors. *Journal of Abnormal Psychology, 91,* 273-279.

Caetano, R., & Mora, M. E. M. (1988). Acculturation and drinking among people of Mexican descent in Mexico and the United States. *Journal of Studies on Alcohol, 49,* 462-471.

Carman, R. S. (1979). Motivations for drug use and problematic outcomes among rural junior high school students. *Addictive Behaviors, 4,* 91-93.

Castro, F. G., Maddahian, E., Newcomb, M. D., & Bentler, P. M. (1987). A multivariate model of the determinants of cigarette smoking among adolescents. *Journal of Health and Social Behavior, 28,* 273-289.

Donovan, J. E., & Jessor, R. (1983). Problem drinking and the dimensions of involvement with drugs: A Guttman scalogram analysis of adolescent drug use. *American Journal of Public Health, 73,* 543-552.

Donovan, J. E., & Jessor, R. (1985). Structure of problem behavior in adolescence and young adulthood. *Journal of Consulting and Clinical Psychology, 53,* 890-904.

Ellickson, P. L., Hays, R. D., & Bell, R. M. (1992). Stepping through the drug use sequence: Longitudinal scalogram analysis of initiation and regular use. *Journal of Abnormal Psychology, 101,* 441-451.

Félix-Ortiz, M., & Newcomb, M. D. (1992). Risk and protective factors for drug use among Latino and white adolescents. *Hispanic Journal of Behavioral Sciences, 14,* 291-309.

Furstenberg, F. F., Morgan, S. P., Moore, K. A., & Peterson. J. L. (1987). Race differences in the timing of adolescent intercourse. *American Sociological Review, 52,* 511-518.

Glantz, M., & Pickens, R. (Eds.). (1992). *Vulnerability to drug abuse.* Washington, DC: American Psychological Association.

Harrison, P., Hoffmann, N. G., & Edwall, G. E. (1989). Sexual abuse correlates: Similarities between male and female adolescents in chemical dependency treatment. *Journal of Adolescent Research, 4,* 385-399.

Hawkins, J. D., Catalano, R. F., & Miller, J. Y. (1992). Risk and protective factors for alcohol and other drug problems in adolescence and early adulthood: Implications for substance abuse problems. *Psychological Bulletin, 112,* 64-105.

Jessor, R., & Jessor, S. L. (1977). *Problem behavior and psychosocial development.* New York: Academic Press.

Kaestner, E., Rosen, L., & Appel, P. (1977). Patterns of drug abuse: Relationships with ethnicity, sensation-seeking and anxiety. *Journal of Consulting and Clinical Psychology, 45,* 462-468.

Kandel, D. B. (1975). Stages in adolescent involvement in drug use. *Science, 190,* 912-914.

Kandel, D. B., & Logan, J. A. (1984). Patterns of drug use from adolescence to young adulthood: I: Periods of risk for initiation, continued use, and discontinuation. *American Journal of Public Health, 74,* 660-666.

Kandel, D. B., & Yamaguchi, K. (1993). From beer to crack: Developmental patterns of drug involvement. *American Journal of Public Health, 83,* 851-855.

Kleinman, P. H., & Lukoff, I. F. (1978). Ethnic differences in factors related to drug use. *Journal of Health and Social Behavior, 19,* 190-199.

Lettieri, D. J. (1985). Drug abuse: A review of explanations and models of explanations. *Advances in Alcohol and Substance Abuse, 4,* 9-40.

Maddahian, E., Newcomb, M. D., & Bentler, P. M. (1986). Adolescent's substance use: Impact of ethnicity, income, and availability. *Advances in Alcohol and Substance Abuse, 5,* 63-78.

Maddahian, E., Newcomb, M. D., & Bentler, P. M. (1988a). Adolescent drug use and intention to use drugs: Concurrent and longitudinal analyses of four ethnic groups. *Addictive Behaviors, 13,* 191-195.

Maddahian, E., Newcomb, M. D., & Bentler, P. M. (1988b). Risk factors for substance use: Ethnic differences among adolescents. *Journal of Substance Abuse, 1,* 11-23.

Marlatt, G. A., Baer, J. S., Donovan, D. M., & Kivlahan, D. R. (1988). Addictive behaviors: Etiology and treatment. *Annual Review of Psychology, 39,* 223-252.

McGee, L., & Newcomb, M. D. (1992). General deviance syndrome: Expanded hierarchical evaluations at four ages from early adolescence to adulthood. *Journal of Consulting and Clinical Psychology, 60,* 766-776.

Moncher, M. S., Holden G. W., & Trimble, J. E. (1990). Substance abuse among Native-American youth. *Journal of Consulting and Clinical Psychology, 58,* 408-415.

Neff, J. A., Prihoda, T. J., & Hoppe, S. K. (1991). "Machismo," self-esteem, education and high maximum drinking among Anglo, black and Mexican-American male drinkers. *Journal of Studies on Alcohol, 52,* 458-463.

Newcomb, M. D. (in press). Predictors and consequences of drug use: A developmental perspective within a prospective study. *Journal of Addictive Diseases.*

Newcomb, M. D. (1992). Understanding the multidimensional nature of drug use and abuse: The role of consumption, risk factors, and protective factors. In M. D. Glantz & R. Pickens (Eds.), *Vulnerability to drug abuse* (pp. 255-297). Washington, DC: American Psychological Association.

Newcomb, M. D., & Bentler, P. M. (1986). Substance use and ethnicity: Differential impact of peer and adult models. *Journal of Psychology, 120,* 83-95.

Newcomb, M. D., & Bentler, P. M. (1988). *Consequences of adolescent drug use: Impact on the lives of young adults.* Newbury Park, CA: Sage.

Newcomb, M. D., & Bentler, P. M. (1989). Substance use and abuse among children and teenagers. *American Psychologist, 44,* 242-248.

Newcomb, M. D., & Bentler, P. M. (1990). Antecedents and consequences of cocaine use: An eight-year study from early adolescence to young adulthood. In L. Robins (Ed.),

Straight and devious pathways from childhood to adulthood (pp. 158-181). Cambridge, UK: Cambridge University Press.

Newcomb, M. D., & Félix-Ortiz, M. (1992). Multiple protective and risk factors for drug use and abuse: Cross-sectional and prospective findings. *Journal of Personality and Social Psychology, 63,* 280-296.

Newcomb, M. D., & Harlow, L. L. (1986). Life events and substance use among adolescents: Mediating effects of perceived loss of control and meaninglessness in life. *Journal of Personality and Social Psychology, 51,* 564-577.

Newcomb, M. D., Maddahian, E., & Bentler, P. M. (1986). Risk factors for drug use among adolescents: Concurrent and longitudinal analyses. *American Journal of Public Health, 76,* 525-531.

Newcomb, M. D., Maddahian, E., Skager, R., & Bentler, P. M. (1987). Substance abuse and psychosocial risk factors among teenagers: Associations with sex, age, ethnicity, and type of school. *American Journal of Drug and Alcohol Abuse, 13,* 413-433.

Newcomb, M. D., & McGee, L. (1991). The influence of sensation-seeking on general deviance and specific problem behaviors from adolescence to young adulthood. *Journal of Personality and Social Psychology, 61,* 614-628.

Paton, S., Kessler, R. C., & Kandel, D. B. (1977). Depressive mood and illegal drug use: A longitudinal analysis. *Journal of Genetic Psychology, 131,* 267-289.

Russell, M., Cooper, M. L., & Frone, M. R. (1990). The influence of sociodemographic characteristics on familial alcohol problems: Data from a community sample. *Alcoholism: Clinical and Experimental Research, 14,* 221-226.

Scheier, L. M., & Newcomb, M. D. (1991). Psychosocial predictors of drug use initiation and escalation: An expansion of the multiple risk factors hypothesis using longitudinal data. *Contemporary Drug Problems, 18,* 31-73.

Stacy, A. W., Newcomb, M. D., & Bentler, P. M. (1992). Interactive and higher-order effects of social influences no drug use. *Journal of Health and Social Behavior, 33,* 226-241.

Szapocznik, J., & Kurtines, W. M. (1993). Family psychology and cultural diversity. *American Psychologist, 48,* 400-407.

Vega, W. A., Zimmerman, R. S., Warheit, G. J., Apospori, E., & Gil, A. G. (1993). Risk factors for early adolescent drug use in four ethnic and racial groups. *American Journal of Public Health, 83,* 185-189.

Wallace, J. M., Jr., & Bachman, J. G. (1991). Explaining racial/ethic differences in adolescent drug use: The impact of background and lifestyle. *Social Problems, 38,* 333-357.

Wallace, J. M., Jr., & Bachman, J. G. (1993). Validity of self-reports in student based studies on minority populations: Issues and concerns. In M. R. De La Rosa & J.-L. R. Adrados (Eds.), *Drug abuse among minority youth: Advances in research and methodology* (Research Monograph No. 130, pp. 167-200). Rockville, MD: National Institute on Drug Abuse.

Watts, W. D., & Wright, L. S. (1990). The relationship of alcohol, tobacco, marijuana, and other illegal drug use to delinquency among Mexican-American, black, and white adolescent males. *Adolescence, 25,* 171-181.

Zucker, R. A., & Gomberg, E. S. L. (1986). Etiology of alcoholism reconsidered: The case for a biopsychosocial approach. *American Psychologist, 41,* 783-793.

Causal Models of Substance Abuse Among Puerto Rican Adolescents

Implications for Prevention

Orlando Rodriguez

Barriers to Developing
Effective Prevention Programs

Advancing our state of knowledge about effective substance abuse prevention among minority youth faces several barriers. First, we do not know about what has worked in prevention programs for minority youth because by and large, the programs are ad hoc, undocumented, and not empirically tested. Second, we do not know to what extent existing findings from experimental interventions are applicable to the sociocultural context of minority youth. Third, social science findings about the etiology of adolescent substance abuse for the most part have not been translated into interventions that address the impact of socially significant institutions in the adolescent's world, such as the family and neighborhood peers. Finally, social science findings themselves follow assumptions about youth's lives based on the sociocultural experiences of white middle-class youth from small-city and suburban settings; thus, it is not clear to what extent the findings are applicable to inner-city youth with different sociocultural experiences.

The Nature of Prevention Research

Our state of knowledge regarding prevention of substance abuse by minority youth has been in large part determined by the nature of prevention research. Two styles of prevention research may be discerned. One type, constituting the bulk of prevention programs, has been guided by assumptions derived from conservative or liberal ideologies rather than by social science theory and research. Although such programs are aimed at all sectors of the population, a considerable number of them have been implemented in inner-city minority youth settings. A positive feature of these programs is that they often build in interventions with family members, neighborhood peers, community programs, and work settings. But they generally lack systematic attention to documentation, replicability, and experimental testing. Consequently, after decades of programs, little is known about what strategies truly reduce substance abuse among these youth.

The ad hoc nature of most prevention programs may be contrasted with that of a relatively small number of programs, funded by the national health research institutes or foundations, that address well-developed theories of what motivates youth to use drugs or alcohol and are implemented on the basis of established methodologies, with detailed manuals for replicability and results tested through experiment. These programs have yielded considerable knowledge of what types of interventions are likely to be effective, but from the point of view of minority inner-city situations, they have some limitations.

Limitations of Past Prevention Research

Minority youth, especially those from the inner city, are seldom the subjects of such interventions, and when they are included, the prevailing assumption is that the interventions are culture-free, universally applicable to youth regardless of their class and ethnic cultures. Experimental interventions have been developed, consciously or unconsciously, with the sociocultural experiences of white middle-class adolescents, experiences that are congruent with the sociocultural background of most designers of prevention programs. The existing methodology may indeed be universally applicable, but because minority youth have not received separate analytical scrutiny in experimental prevention programs, and because studies generally have not examined ethnic or class differences in responses to interventions, the question remains whether such programs suit the sociocultural background of minority youth.

Another limitation of experimental interventions is that they take place within a fairly narrow range of adolescent experience, mainly the social relations of the classroom. With some exceptions, interventions have not been developed to reach out to other significant aspects of the adolescent experience that are likely to affect youth's decisions to use substances: the family, the neighborhood peer group, and other adult institutions such as the work world. Yet we know from several decades of theory and research on adolescent problem behavior that out-of-school social contexts exert strong influences on youth's decisions to become involved in substance use.

To improve our understanding about effective prevention for minority youth, it is necessary to extend current modalities to inner-city minority youth, modifying them on the basis of theoretical notions about how sociocultural context makes a difference in the perceptions and beliefs of minority youth and their social institutions. Toward this aim, it is also necessary to increase our knowledge of the etiology of substance abuse among minority youth.

Beliefs and Social Factors

In line with these aims, this chapter examines data from a survey of South Bronx Puerto Rican adolescents to explore the interrelations among beliefs about substance use and social factors that influence substance use. The beliefs focused on in this chapter correspond to those addressed in some types of prevention programs. They concern antiuse reasons often promoted by prevention programs, centered on health and psychological consequences of substance use, social sanctions, and moral values. Although change in beliefs does not constitute the whole universe of prevention efforts, it is an important component, along with the desirable motivational state that all interventions aim to instill in their subjects.

The social predictors, on the other hand, are important behavioral and psychological aspects of youths' relations with their families, peer groups, and other institutions of the world of inner-city Puerto Rican adolescents. These are the small-group and institutional components of youth life identified in etiological research as central influences on youth problem behavior. Although prevention programs often address these influences, they usually do so only through the youth themselves, not through direct action on family members and other important social groups.

Social science models of substance abuse are limited insofar as they ignore the types of perceptions about substance use that are the focus of prevention programs. Prevention programs are likewise limited in that they do not encompass direct interventions aimed at the powerful family and peer worlds. A useful question, therefore, is to determine whether these two influences, beliefs about substance use and the broader social factors, can be integrated into a causal model. This integration should have two useful results: It will inform prevention programs by determining to what extent intervention efforts can be improved by developing approaches to the broader social groups implicated in the adolescent's decision to use substances; and it will shed light on how current etiological models can be improved by including within them youths' beliefs about the consequences of using substances. The magnitude of influence of the two types of factors is a clue to the results that one type should produce in a prevention program. For example, if beliefs about substance use have a large and significant effect on that behavior, and if consideration of social factors does not reduce the effect of substance use beliefs nor increase the explanatory power of the model, this would provide grounds for prevention programs to focus on the motivations underlying substance use. On the other hand, if the introduction of social factors reduces the effects of such beliefs, this would imply that prevention programs must broaden their efforts to the larger social world of the adolescent.

Sociocultural Issues

Another important objective of this chapter is to incorporate sociocultural issues into the discourse in etiological research on prevention and problem behaviors. Research on minorities, at least with respect to Hispanics, is rich in cultural content, but mainly without reference to mainstream social science conceptualizations. Delinquency and drug use research on minority populations has often relied on explanations that link such behaviors to subcultural characteristics—for example, ethnically based norms and values. Although subcultural theories have had an important influence in deviance research, they have not been integrated into mainstream drug use and delinquency research, and have seldom been empirically tested through large-scale sample surveys. On the other hand, mainstream models have generally not been informed by the insights from studies of minority group problem behavior, nor have they been tested among these subpopulations. Therefore, it is important to consider how explanations derived from the sociocultural experiences of minority groups provide additional insights not encountered within mainstream approaches.

Subcultural theories of problem behavior have also been applied to prevention issues for minority youth. For example, research at the Hispanic Research Center has examined how the use of Puerto Rican folktales improves children's self-esteem and prevents the development of problem behaviors (Costantino, Malgady, & Rogler, 1985). The concept was then applied to interventions with adolescents, utilizing the notion of Puerto Rican folk heroes and heroines as role models (Costantino, Malgady, & Rogler, 1988).

Another example is the work first developed by Szapocznik, Scopetta, Kurtines, and Aranalde (1978) utilizing the concept of acculturation as a critical issue in the development of problem behavior among Hispanic youth. *Acculturation* refers to the social psychological process whereby immigrants and their offspring change their behavior and attitudes toward those of the host society as a result of contact and exposure to the new dominant culture (Berry, 1980; Padilla, 1980). The concept of acculturation has been linked to negative life experiences, such as the emergence of mental illness, and to problem behaviors, such as delinquency and drug use. Its link to problem behavior has been conceptualized in terms of the stresses associated with adapting to conflicts between the host culture and that of the country of origin. It is argued that acculturation stresses create a risk of dysfunctional behaviors such as substance use and delinquency (Anderson & Rodriguez, 1984; Oetting & Beauvais, 1991; Rogler, Cortes, & Malgady, 1991; Szapocznik, Kurtines, & Fernandez, 1980). Evidence is provided for this hypothesis by studies finding higher rates of substance use, suicide, eating disorders, and other problem behaviors among acculturated and/or second-generation Hispanics (Buriel, Calzada, & Vazquez, 1982; Burnam, Hough, Karno, Escobar, & Telles, 1987; Caetano, 1987; Gilbert, 1987; Graves, 1967; Rodriguez, Recio, & De La Rosa, 1993; Sommers, Fagan, & Baskin, 1993; Sorenson & Golding, 1988). However, some studies provide contradictory evidence (Fernandez-Pol, Bluestone, Morales, & Mizruchi, 1985; Neff, 1986), and with few exceptions (Rodriguez et al., 1993), the effect of acculturation has not been examined in conjunction with other variables from the mainstream social science literature.

The clinical work of Szapocznik and colleagues shows how the concept of acculturation can be utilized for prevention purposes. They have advanced two family-focused treatment models specifically for Hispanics. Operating from the conviction that acculturation presents the immigrant Hispanic family with disruptions in its closely knit structure, Bicultural Effectiveness Training (Szapocznik, Santisteban, Kurtines, Perez-Vidal, & Hervis, 1984; Szapocznik, Santisteban, Rio, Perez-Vidal, Kurtines, & Hervis, 1986) is targeted at intergenerational and intercultural family-adolescent conflicts. Bicultural Effectiveness Training encourages the development of more harmonious family relations by appreciation of both original Hispanic cultural values and behaviors and those of the adopted mainstream American culture. The other approach, Family Effectiveness Training, has been employed with families of preadolescents at risk for future conduct disorders (Szapocznik, Santisteban, Rios, Perez-Vidal, & Kurtines, 1986). It is intended to reestablish family structural properties that have become dysfunctional.

Testing Competing Models

Two arguments have been advanced for examining how causal models of minority youth substance use can enhance prevention programs for such populations. Models integrating substance use beliefs and social factors should help to determine to what extent programs should focus on the broader social world of the adolescent. Models expanding mainstream conceptualizations by integrating sociocultural factors should provide clues as to how current approaches should be modified to reach minority youth. In the service of these objectives, the analysis here examines how South Bronx Puerto Rican adolescents' beliefs about the consequences of using different types of substances influence their substance use behavior. Analysis then turns to the interrelations among beliefs and social factors in the production of substance use.

Methodology

SAMPLE

Data are drawn from the Puerto Rican Adolescent Survey, a two-wave panel survey (1986 and 1987) of a probability sample of the South Bronx's Puerto Rican male adolescent population aged 12 to 19 (Rodriguez, 1991). Sampling yielded 1,170 eligible males, 1,077 of whom (92%) agreed to participate in the study. Respondent loss in the second wave was less than 17%, resulting in an overall response rate of 76%. Information was self-reported in confidential face-to-face interviews. Respondents were guaranteed anonymity and confidentiality, and all data collected were protected by a Certificate of Confidentiality from the U.S. Department of Health and Human Services.

MEASURES

The dependent variables are five substance use indexes based on frequency of use at the time of the second wave of the following: (a) cigarettes; (b) alcohol; (c) any or all use of marijuana, PCP, tranquilizers, or inhalants; and (d) any or all use of hardcore drugs (heroin, cocaine, cocaine in crack form, methadone, and opium). The fifth index ranked use according to the most serious substance reported, following the ordering of seriousness described above, with "none" as the lowest rank, and with amphetamines and/or barbiturates (not examined separately because of low numbers) as the next-to-highest rank. Table 7.1 shows how these variables and other measures used in the analysis are defined and constructed. Table 7.2 presents summary statistics for these variables. The numbers after the variables indicate the time order (i.e., Wave 1 or Wave 2).

Substance Use Beliefs

The substance use beliefs measures were constructed from 17 questions asked of respondents about reasons for not using drugs or alcohol. All but one of these questions were taken from a battery utilized in the University of Michigan Survey Research Center's annual survey of high school seniors (Johnston, O'Malley, & Bachman, 1992). Three indexes were constructed from these: physical health and psychological consequences beliefs, such as believing that using substances would result in becoming addicted (nine items); beliefs about social sanctions, such as fear of arrest (six items); and moral beliefs (two items). Two items ("too expensive" and "not available") were discarded because they did not imply perceived negative consequences for using substances.

Social Factors

Included among the social predictors are family-related measures (a Family Involvement and a Socialization Index), peer group measures (Peer Involvement, Exposure to Drug-Using Peers), School Involvement, Educational-Occupational Strain, and Acculturation. Age was also included as a control variable. The Family, School, and Peer Involvement indexes are based on questions that ask about the respondent's involvement in each of these groups at different days and times of the week. The Socialization Index combines the Parent Involvement Index and the Parent Efficacy Index. The former is based on Time 1 questions about respondents' perceptions of their parents' involvement in their supervision. The latter is based on Time 1 questions asked of parents about their perceived efficacy in supervising their children. The Exposure to Drug-Using Peers Index is constructed from questions asking about the respondent's friends' use of marijuana, hashish, amphetamines, or barbiturates. Educational Occupational *Strain* is constructed from four questions about respondents' aspirations and expectations about school and job prospects. Strain was defined as the extent of discrepancy between aspirations and expectations. With the exception of the Acculturation Scale (see Table 7.1) and of the questions constituting the Socialization Index, which were created for the Puerto Rican Adolescent Survey, all of the social indexes replicate those found in Elliott and associates' National Youth Survey (Elliott, Huizinga, & Ageton, 1985). Szapocznik's scale (Szapocznik et al., 1978) was included as a measure of acculturation. The scale is based on questions from Wave 2 concerning language preferences,

TABLE 7.1 Definitions of Variables and Measures Used in Analysis

Variable	Definition
Substance Use	Separate measures were constructed for frequency of use of cigarettes, alcohol, marijuana, and hardcore drug use at T2. In the latter, the following substances were included: heroin, cocaine, crack cocaine, methadone, and opium. For cigarettes, alcohol, and marijuana, responses range from 0 (*none*) to 8 (*twice a day*). The Hardcore Drug Index adds individual scores for the substances referred to above. The Substance Use Seriousness Index ranks respondents in terms of the most serious substance used. Scores are 0 (*none*), 1 (*cigarettes*), 2 (*alcohol*), 3 (*marijuana, PCP, tranquilizers, or inhalants*), 4 (*amphetamines or barbiturates*) and 5 (*hardcore drugs*).
Substance Use Beliefs	Three indexes were created from a battery of T2 questions asking about respondents' reasons for not using substances. For each reason, respondents answered *true* (assigned a value of 1) or *not true* (assigned a value of 0). The Physical and Psychological Health Beliefs Index combines responses to nine items representing reasons such as "concern about psychological damage." The Social Sanctions Index combines responses to six items representing reasons such as "fear of getting arrested." The Moral Beliefs Index combines responses to two items representing reasons such as "It is against your beliefs."
Family, School, and Peer Involvement	Amount of time spent with the family, in academic activities at school, and with friends (T2). For each scale, three questions ask the respondent to report the number of afternoons and evenings in an average week, Monday through Friday, and the time spent on weekends, in each setting. Responses ranged from 1 (*none*) to 6 (*six*) for weekdays, and from 1 (*none at all*) to 6 (*a great deal*) for weekends. A score was obtained by summing over the three items for each scale, with a high score reflecting a high level of involvement.
Socialization Index	Combines the Parent Involvement and Parent Efficacy indexes. The first index is constructed from two T1 questions asked of parents about their perceived ability to control their children. The second index is constructed from six T1 questions asked of respondents concerning their parents' ability to supervise them: for example, "Your parents know where you are all the time."
Exposure to Drug-Using Peers	How many of the respondent's friends (a) used marijuana or hashish and (b) used prescription drugs such as amphetamines or barbiturates when there was no medical need for them during the past year (T2). Response categories ranged from *all of them* (5) to *none of them* (1). A summary score was obtained by summing the two responses.
Acculturation Scale	Questions are taken from Szapocznik and associates' scale (Szapocznik et al., 1978), included as a measure of acculturation and biculturalism. At T2, five items concerning language

(continued)

TABLE 7.1 Continued

Variable	Definition
	preferences, cultural ways of relating to girlfriends, ethnicity of friends, and ethnic self-identification are combined with two items concerning preference for American music and dance. The first set of questions allows for five responses, ranging from *all Spanish* or *all Puerto Rican* to *all American* or *all English.* The middle responses denoted acceptance of both U.S. and Hispanic cultural traits. In the music and dance preference questions, five responses for each question ranged from *do not at all like* to *like very much,* with the middle response being *neither like nor dislike.*
Educational and Occupational Strain	Extent of reported discrepancy between aspirations and expectations in occupation and school life. Aspirations questions ask how important it is to have a good job or career after finishing school and to go to college. Responses range from 1 *not important at all* to 3 *very important.* Expectations questions ask how good are the respondent's chances for these two goals, and they have three responses: *poor* (1), *fair* (2), and *good* (3). Responses to the two questions were cross-classified to construct a 6-point discrepancy scale, with 1 indicating the lowest strain (*very important—good*) and 6 indicating the highest strain (*Very important—poor*). A score was obtained by summing over the two items for each question.

cultural ways of relating to girlfriends, ethnicity of friends, and ethnic self-identification, and questions about the respondent's preference for American dance and music.

Results

BELIEFS AND SUBSTANCE USE

Table 7.3 shows the relationships between beliefs about the consequences of using substances and substance use. The table shows moderate relationships between individual beliefs and use of each substance. The influence of beliefs is stronger with respect to seriousness of substance use. With respect to cigarette smoking, the strongest reasons for not smoking are not enjoying substances, not liking to associate with users, and friends' dislike of substances. With respect to avoiding alcohol, the strongest reasons are perceived loss of self-control, fear of getting arrested, not liking to associate with users, and friends' dislike of substances. Moral beliefs also have moderate correlations with not using alcohol. For marijuana, several physical health and

TABLE 7.2 Means and Standard Deviations of Variables Used in Analysis

Variable	M	SD	N
Frequency cigarette use	1.10	2.59	894
Frequency alcohol use	0.99	1.70	891
Frequency marijuana use	0.39	1.39	895
Frequency hardcore substance use	0.18	1.15	890
Seriousness of Drug Use Index	0.86	1.32	1,077
Health Beliefs Against Drugs Index	7.97	1.83	893
Social Sanctions Beliefs Index	5.49	1.46	885
Moral Beliefs Against Drugs Index	1.54	0.68	897
T2 family involvement	13.16	3.96	898
T1 parental efficacy and involvement	36.00	5.55	1,072
T2 school involvement	7.68	4.65	898
T2 peer involvement	11.82	4.13	898
T2 exposure to drug-using peers	2.74	1.32	893
T2 education-occupation strain	4.30	2.28	897
T2 Acculturation Index	125.71	36.50	898
Age	15.66	2.24	1,071

psychological beliefs, especially not enjoying drugs, are important reasons. Also important are friend-related reasons and fear of arrest; moral beliefs also play a role. With respect to avoiding hardcore drugs, the strongest reasons are not enjoying substances and friend-related reasons. The same reasons enumerated above play strong roles in determining the seriousness of substance use, and friend-related reasons are particularly pronounced. When the reasons are aggregated into health beliefs, sanctions, and moral indexes, health beliefs and sanctions have the strongest correlations with respect to all substances. Both types of beliefs have the same magnitude of correlation, and moral beliefs have a weaker effect.

BELIEFS AND SOCIAL FACTORS
AS PREDICTORS OF SUBSTANCE USE

Analysis now turns to the interrelationships among substance use beliefs and social factors with respect to substance use. Social factors considered are family involvement and parental socialization, involvement with peers and exposure to substance-using peers, involvement in school,

TABLE 7.3 Pearson Correlations of Beliefs About Substance Use With Specific Types of Substance Use

Beliefs	Cigarettes	Alcohol	Marijuana	Hardcore Drugs	Use Seriousness Index
Possible psych. damage	-.1267***	-.1399***	-.2039***	-.1392***	-.1983***
Possible phys. damage	-.1024**	-.1550***	-.2033***	-.0858**	-.1528***
Becoming addicted	-.1066***	-.1597***	-.1657***	-.1044***	-.1831***
Loss of energy or ambition	-.0954**	-.1587***	-.2223***	-.0936***	-.2090***
Possible loss of self-control	-.1740***	-.2332***	-.2975***	-.1748**	-.2549***
Might use stronger or hard drugs	-.1690***	-.1686***	-.2098***	-.1259***	-.2098***
Don't enjoy using drugs	-.2096***	-.2002***	-.4439***	-.3028***	-.3627***
Might have a bad trip	-.0760	-.2143***	-.2936***	-.1135***	-.2083***
Don't feel like getting high	-.1618***	-.1612***	-.2585***	-.1441***	-.2412***
Index of Health and Psych. Beliefs	-.2132***	-.2653***	-.3943***	-.2187***	-.3454***
Getting arrested	-.0743	-.2267***	-.1610***	-.0435	-.1969***
What adults in neighborhood might think	-.0455	-.1143***	-.1613***	-.0773	-.1755***
Parents would disapprove	-.0395	-.0188	-.0567	-.0361	-.0495
Girlfriend would disapprove	-.0830**	-.0753	-.0822**	-.0371	-.1194***
Don't like being with drug users	-.2972***	-.3338***	-.5028***	-.3007***	-.4557***
Friends don't do drugs	-.2750***	-.2990***	-.4273***	-.2531***	-.4212***
Index of Beliefs About Social Sanctions	-.2289***	-.2848***	-.3663***	-.1944***	-.3911***
Against beliefs	-.0668	-.2196***	-.2598***	-.1664***	-.2494***
Puerto Rican should not do	-.1227***	-.2134***	-.2161***	-.0657	-.2260***
Moral Beliefs Index	-.1175***	-.2672***	-.2932***	-.1423***	-.2933***
Drugs too expensive	-.0465	-.0211	.0179	.0442	-.0370
Drugs not available	-.0544	-.0695	-.0138	-.0253	-.0218

$**p < .01; ***p < .001.$

occupational-educational strain, acculturation, and age as a control variable. Table 7.4 shows the results of hierarchical regressions on the specific substance use types of the beliefs and social factors. For each substance, the first regression shows the effects of the beliefs alone, and the second regression shows the effects of all variables combined.

Cigarette Use

For cigarette use, the regression in Column 1 shows social sanctions beliefs to have the key effect on reducing use. Health beliefs have a smaller effect, and moral beliefs are nil. The regression's R^2 shows weak effects for these beliefs. When the social structural predictors are added (Column 2), the effect of social sanctions beliefs is considerably reduced but remains significant, whereas health beliefs retain almost the same magnitude. Among the social predictors, age, school involvement, and use of substances by peers have the strongest and most significant effects.

Alcohol Use

In contrast to cigarette use, moral and sanctions beliefs have important effects with respect to alcohol use, whereas health effects have less influence. The regression R^2 is stronger than that of cigarette use but still less than moderate. Family factors, peers' substance use, school involvement, and age have significant effects. The introduction of these factors into the regression reduces the effect of social sanctions but has less effect on the other beliefs' role.

Marijuana Use

Marijuana use is influenced by social sanctions and health beliefs, and to a lesser extent by moral beliefs. The moderate magnitude of the regressions' R^2 indicates that the influence of these is stronger than with respect to alcohol or cigarettes. The introduction of the social factors reduces the effects of social sanctions but has minimal effects on the other beliefs. Peers' substance use, school involvement, and age have the only significant effects on marijuana use. The effect of age is weaker with respect to this substance than to cigarettes or alcohol.

Hardcore Drug Use

Social sanctions and health beliefs have the strongest influence in reducing use of hardcore drugs. The effect of moral beliefs is not significant,

TABLE 7.4 Hierarchical Regressions of Substance Use Types on Substance Use Beliefs and Social Structural Factors

Variable	Cigarettes (1)	Cigarettes (2)	Alcohol (1)	Alcohol (2)	Marijuana (1)	Marijuana (2)	Hardcore Drugs (1)	Hardcore Drugs (2)	Seriousness Index (1)	Seriousness Index (2)
MORAL	.00	-.02	-.15***	-.14***	-.12***	-.10**	-.03	-.03	-.13***	-.11***
SOCSANCT	-.18***	-.07	-.19***	-.07*	-.22***	-.12***	-.12**	-.02	-.26***	-.14***
PHYSPSYC	-.11***	-.08*	-.09*	-.08*	-.22***	-.19***	-.14***	-.12**	-.13***	-.11***
FINVOL2		.02	-.07*		.01		-.00		-.06*	
SOCIALIZ		-.02		-.08**	-.04		-.11***		-.08**	
PINVOL2		.05		.03		.02		.04		.07*
PALDRUG2		.18***		.13***		.27***		.19***		.24***
SINVOL2		-.14***		-.02		-.11***		-.08*		-.00
EDOCDSP2		.05		.06		.00		-.02		.08**
ACCULT2		.02		.05		.03		-.01		.06**
AGE		.18***		.24***		.07*		.03		.23***
R–Square[a]	.06	.08	.12	.24	.20	.31	.06	.12	.19	.37

NOTE Key:
MORAL=Beliefs about morality of using substances; PINVOL2 = Involvement with peers; SOCSANCT = Beliefs about social sanctions of using substances; PALDRUG2 = Exposure to substance-using peers; SINVOL2 = School involvement; PHYSPSYC = Beliefs about consequences to physical or psychological health; EDOCDSP2 = Educational and occupational discrepancy between aspirations and expectations; FINVOL2 = Family involvement; ACCULT2 = Acculturation Index SOCIALIZ = Family Socialization Index; AGE = Age of respondent. All changes in magnitude R^2 are significant at .001 level.
*$p < .05$; **$p < .01$; ***$p < .001$.

and the regression R^2 is weak. The introduction of social factors reduces the effects of social sanctions but has little effect on the other beliefs. Socialization, peers' use of substances, and school involvement are the only significant predictors. Although age has significant effects on the use of other substances, it has no effect on hardcore drug use.

Seriousness of Substance Use

The final regression examined the effects of beliefs and social factors on the seriousness of substance use. Social sanctions play a strong role, and moral and health beliefs play a weaker but significant role. However, the effect of social sanction beliefs is halved when the social factors are introduced. All social variables, except school involvement, have significant effects. Peers' substance use and age have the strongest effect, but it is notable that the family variables, strain, and acculturation also have significant effects, whereas school involvement has no effect.

SUMMARY OF RESULTS

Moral beliefs have the strongest effect with respect to marijuana, but they have a weak effect overall. Social sanctions beliefs have the strongest effects with respect to all the other substances. Health beliefs have the strongest effect with respect to marijuana, and the second strongest effect with respect to all substances. Social factors consistently reduce the effects of social sanctions beliefs, generally reducing them by about half. The social factors have a minimal effect on health and moral beliefs. Peers' substance use has the strongest effect on use of all substances. Age also has similarly strong effects on use of substances, with the exception of hardcore drugs. School has consistently significant effects on all substances except seriousness of use. Family variables are significant with respect to alcohol use, hardcore drug use, and seriousness of use. Strain and acculturation have significant effects only on seriousness of use. Notably, although involvement with peers has a significant effect only with respect to seriousness of use, in all cases it is associated with substance use rather than reduction.

Conclusions and
Implications for Prevention

The effects on substance use of substance use beliefs should provide clues as to the effectiveness of a program's focusing on one versus another type of belief as part of its prevention approach. Health-related beliefs and beliefs about the social consequences of using substances have moderate effects on youth's decisions to use substances. These are stronger than moral beliefs, whose effects are stronger than health belief effects only with respect to alcohol use. The effects on substance use of health-related and moral beliefs are independent of social factors such as parental socialization and peers' substance use. In contrast, beliefs about social sanctions are considerably attenuated by the insertion of social factors into the model. Peers who use substances, inadequate socialization, lack of involvement in schooling, and other social factors of the adolescent world are likely to prevent the emergence of or to attenuate beliefs about the social consequences of using substances, or to produce counterbeliefs.

The data suggest that programs focusing on health and moral beliefs as part of their prevention approach will not encounter social forces that attenuate such beliefs. They will encounter such forces, however, if they focus on social sanctions beliefs. Prevention efforts focused upon the latter will be less effective without addressing the beliefs of peers, family members, and other significant elements of the adolescents' social world.

The results of these analyses provide some information about the potential benefit of expanding interventions to social groups in the adolescent's lives. They suggest that outreach to the family is not as important as outreach to the peer group. Nevertheless, the results with respect to seriousness of drug use and hardcore drug use suggest that interventions that reach out to the family are likely to increase their effectiveness in instilling beliefs in youths. Focusing on occupational and educational issues (e.g., improving school attendance) would also have some direct benefits in terms of substance use.

The analysis results with respect to age also have implications for prevention programs. They suggest the limitations that programs face as adolescents age into young adulthood, and thus reinforce the necessity of focusing prevention programs upon younger adolescents.

In terms of magnitudes of coefficients, the peer group is the key group involved in the decision to use substances. Program interventions that include members of the adolescent's peer group would increase the probability of influencing the adolescent's beliefs about negative consequences of substance use, especially those relating to social sanctions. Such interventions would seem particularly important among inner-city groups like the one included in this sample, because in an inner-city context, the neighborhood and the school are often socially separate, and peers from the neighborhood, a powerful social world in itself—are not necessarily seen in a school setting.

The role of acculturation in drug abuse prevention also requires some comments. Although the regression findings show effects for acculturation only for seriousness of use—and these are of the same magnitude as those found for family, school, and strain factors—the role of acculturation in prevention should be further explored and developed. The mainstream explanatory concepts and measures used in this analysis reflect decades of thought about the social sources of youth problem behavior. In contrast, the theory of acculturation and problem behavior is recent, and the development of appropriate measures has not received the methodological attention that the other social concepts have over time. Thus, the modest results for the acculturation variable are encouraging and should be taken as evidence of the potential importance of designing prevention interventions, such as those of Szapocznik and his colleagues, that focus on acculturation as an important psychological issue to be addressed.

References

Anderson, E., & Rodriguez, O. (1984). Conceptual issues in the study of Hispanic delinquency. *Research Bulletin* (Fordham University, Hispanic Research Center, NY), 7, 1-2.

Berry, J. (1980). Acculturation as adaptation. In A. M. Padilla (Ed.), *Acculturation: Theory, models, and some new findings* (pp. 9-25). Boulder, CO: Westview.

Buriel, R., Calzada, S., & Vazquez, R. (1982). Relationship of traditional Mexican American culture to adjustment and delinquency among three generations of Mexican American male adolescents. *Hispanic Journal of Behavior Sciences, 1,* 41-55.

Burnam, M., Hough, R., Karno, M., Escobar, J., & Telles, C. (1987). Acculturation and lifetime prevalence of psychiatric disorders among Mexican Americans in Los Angeles. *Journal of Health and Social Behavior, 28,* 89-102.

Caetano, R. (1987). Acculturation and drinking patterns among U.S. Hispanics. *British Journal of Addiction, 82,* 789-799.

Costantino, G., Malgady, R. G., & Rogler, L. H. (1985). *Cuento therapy: Folktales as a culturally sensitive psychotherapy for Puerto Rican children.* Maplewood, NJ: Waterfront.

Costantino, G., Malgady, R. G., & Rogler, L. H. (1988). Folk hero modeling therapy for Puerto Rican adolescents. *Journal of Adolescence, 11,* 155-165.

Elliott, D. S., Huizinga, D., & Ageton, S. S. (1985). Risk and protective factors for alcohol and other drug problems in adolescence and early adulthood: Implications for substance abuse prevention. *Psychological Bulletin, 112,* 64-105.

Fernandez-Pol, B., Bluestone, H., Morales, G., & Mizruchi, M. (1985). Cultural influences and alcoholism: A study of Puerto Ricans. *Alcoholism: Clinical and Experimental Research, 9,* 443-446.

Gilbert, M. J. (1987). Alcohol consumption patterns in immigrant and later generation Mexican American women. *Hispanic Journal of Behavioral Sciences, 9,* 299-314.

Graves, T. (1967). Acculturation, access, and alcohol in a tri-ethnic community. *American Anthropologist, 69,* 306-321.

Johnston, L. D., O'Malley, P. M., & Bachman, J. G. (1992). *Smoking, drinking, and illicit drug use among American secondary school students, college students, and young adults, 1975-1991.* Rockville, MD: National Institute on Drug Abuse.

Neff, J. (1986). Alcohol consumption and psychological distress among Anglos, Hispanics, and blacks. *Alcohol and Alcoholism, 21,* 111-119.

Oetting, E. R., & Beauvais, F. (1991). Orthogonal cultural identification theory: The cultural identification of minority adolescents. *International Journal of the Addictions, 25,* 655-685.

Padilla, A. M. (1980). The role of cultural awareness and ethnic loyalty in acculturation. In A. M. Padilla (Ed.), *Acculturation: Theory, models and some new findings* (pp. 47-84). Boulder, CO: Westview.

Rodriguez, O. (1991). *The Puerto Rican adolescents survey* [Machine-readable datafile]. Bronx, NY: Fordham University, Hispanic Research Center.

Rodriguez, O., Recio, J. L., & De La Rosa, M. (1993). Integrating mainstream and subcultural explanations of drug use among Puerto Rican youth. In M. De La Rosa & J. L. Recio (Eds.), *Drug use among minority youth: Advances in research and methodology* (NIDA Research Monograph No. 130, pp. 8-31). Washington, DC: U.S. Department of Health and Human Services.

Rogler, L., Cortes, D. E., & Malgady, R. (1991). Acculturation and mental health status among Hispanics: Convergence and new directions for research. *American Psychologist, 46,* 585-597.

Sommers, I., Fagan, J., & Baskin, D. (1993). Sociocultural influences on the explanation of delinquency for Puerto Rican youths. *Hispanic Journal of Behavioral Sciences, 15,* 36-62.

Sorenson, S. B., & Golding, J. M. (1988). Prevalence of suicide attempts in a Mexican-American population: Prevention implications of immigration and cultural issues. *Suicide and Life Threatening Behavior, 18,* 322-333.

Szapocznik, J., Kurtines, W. M., & Fernandez, T. (1980). Bicultural involvement and adjustment in Hispanic-American youth. *International Journal of Intercultural Relations, 4,* 353-365.

Szapocznik, J., Santisteban, D., Kurtines, W., Perez-Vidal, A., & Hervis, O. (1984). Bicultural effectiveness training: A treatment intervention for enhancing intercultural adjustment in Cuban-American families. *Hispanic Journal of Behavioral Sciences, 6,* 317-344.

Szapocznik, J., Santisteban, D., Rio, A., Perez-Vidal, A., & Kurtines, W. (1986). Family effectiveness training for Hispanic families: Strategic structural systems intervention for the prevention of drug abuse. In H. P. Lefley & P. B. Pedersen (Eds.), *Cross cultural training for mental health professionals* (pp. 245-261). Springfield, IL: Charles C Thomas.

Szapocznik, J., Santisteban, D., Rio, A., Perez-Vidal, A., Kurtines, W., & Hervis, O. (1986). Bicultural effectiveness training (BET): An intervention modality for families experiencing intergenerational/intercultural conflict. *Hispanic Journal of Behavioral Sciences, 8,* 303-330.

Szapocznik, J., Scopetta, M. A., Kurtines, W., & Aranalde, M. A. (1978). Theory and measurement of acculturation. *Interamerican Journal of Psychology/Revista Interamericana de Psicologia, 12,* 113-130.

Cultural Identity and Drug Use Among Latino and Latina Adolescents

María Félix-Ortiz
Michael D. Newcomb

A common assumption made when studying drug use among Latino[1] adolescents is that the group is homogeneous, and possible within-group differences are often ignored (see Trimble, Chapter 1 of this volume). There is some evidence that recent immigrants differ in their drug use patterns from members of their ethnic group who have already settled in the United States (e.g., Holck, Warren, Smith, & Rochat, 1984). However, the impact of cultural identity on adolescent drug use has not been given much attention. In this chapter, we examine the relationship between cultural identity and drug use among Latino adolescents. Cultural identity is measured multidimensionally (along continua of Latino and American identity) and across several domains (e.g., language, values, behavior). Various types of drug use (both licit and illicit, including inhalants) are also examined, as well as patterns of drug use (quantity and frequency).

Many previous studies have attempted to confront acculturation issues using between-group designs, thereby inferring cultural effects when differences are found. Researchers have applied this approach to the Latino population by drawing random samples of Mexican American and Anglo adolescents and then comparing group means to draw conclusions about the effects of culture on drug use. However, this approach can be misleading. Given potentially large within-group differences, it is inappropriate to draw conclusions about the effects of culture from studies that do not carefully and directly assess important cultural variables.

Dimensions of Cultural Identity

Although many have acknowledged the complexity of cultural identity as a phenomenon (e.g., Trimble, Chapter 1 of this volume), attempts to measure it have relied on unidimensional and reductionistic measures (e.g., Cuellar, Harris, & Jasso, 1980) rather than profile-type measures that capture and describe multiple dimensions of cultural identity.

Cultural change among Latinos is most commonly described with quantitative models. Most define this change as a unidimensional process along one domain, although some prefer to conceptualize it as occurring along two or more domains. Cultural change is typically treated as unidirectional, with *change* defined as the degree to which a member of the minority cultural group incorporates the attributes of the dominant majority. However, this view cannot easily account for changes in different domains that occur at varying rates, because information is typically collapsed into one global score. Most important, a unidimensional conceptualization cannot capture strong concurrent identification with more than one culture.

The phenomenon of cultural change is recognized as an important process for the individual, but this process is more poorly understood than its common descriptor, *acculturation,* implies. This descriptor is biased in that it implies a unidimensional process. With the emergence of new, complex models of cultural change, new descriptors of the process should be considered. In our work, the term *cultural identity* is used to distinguish new conceptualizations of this process from older conceptualizations referred to as *acculturation. Cultural identity* is a descriptor that (a) allows for a multi- dimensional conceptualization along various domains and (b) recognizes a distinct process that occurs as part of personality formation versus a process that occurs between groups.

Multidimensional models of cultural change and identity are gaining in acceptance because they can describe the complex process more thoroughly and precisely. From this perspective, *cultural change* is defined as a dynamic process involving personal background, contextual factors, and the degree of exposure to an alternate culture (Szapocznik & Kurtines, 1980). In their study of Miami's Cuban population, Szapocznik and Kurtines (1980) found evidence of a unidimensional process of acculturation (i.e., assimilation) among the first wave of immigrants, who had no Hispanic community support in their new home. However, those who came later were more likely to experience a biculturation process (i.e., both American and Cuban). The later immigrants were able to maintain their cultural traditions through the established Miami Cuban community, while simultaneously adopting traditions of the dominant Euro-American culture. The most powerful of these multidimensional models allow for strong identification with more than one culture (Oetting & Beauvais, 1991).

In attempting to define *cultural identity*, many investigators have identified various domains such as knowledge about the culture, ethnic traditions, behavior, and, most commonly used, preferred language and language proficiency (e.g., Clark, Kaufman, & Pierce, 1976; Keefe & Padilla, 1987). Ethnic pride, preferred ethnic affiliation, and ethnic identity are other common domains. Because behavior is often influenced by values and attitudes, one could argue that cultural identity could be best captured by measures of values orientation. However, most instruments do not incorporate adequate measures of an underlying value system. Attempts at defining attitudinal acculturation as a distinct construct have met with mixed success. Most of these studies include only a small number of items to assess values and typically tap broad values of human nature and time orientation, rather than specific values unique to a specific culture.

The Role of "Acculturation" in Drug Use

These limitations in the assessment of cultural identity have contributed to the confusing picture of cultural identity and drug use. Some have found cultural identity to be associated with decreased drug use (e.g., Burnam, Hough, Karno, Escobar, & Telles, 1987), whereas others have found a positive relationship (e.g., Markides, Krause, & Mendes de Leon, 1988). In studies of bicultural students, some have found positive relationships with drug use (e.g., Amaro, Whitaker, Coffman, & Heeren, 1990), and others have not (e.g., Szapocznik & Kurtines, 1980).

In most studies of cultural influences and drug use, single scores representing cultural identity are correlated with one type of drug use. In some instances, preferred language is used to measure cultural identity and correlated with drug use. As a result, cultural identity is found to be either completely risk inducing or completely protective. A profile-type measure of cultural identity would allow one to see the relationship between specific components of cultural identity and drug use (e.g., Keefe & Padilla, 1987).

Several hypotheses about how acculturation or cultural identity is related to drug use among Latinos have been advanced. Most models are linear and expect that the level of acculturation is either positively or negatively associated with drug use. Other models are interactive and suggest that drug use is most related to lack of identity with either culture, and that low or high levels of drug use are related to biculturalism. The conceptualizations are summarized in the following four hypotheses linking drug use to cultural identity.

1. *Cultural identity may be risk inducing.* Individuals who are strongly identified with their cultural heritage may be at risk for drug use because their values and behavior may conflict with those of the dominant culture. These individuals may lack essential skills and attitudes that might ensure success in the dominant culture.

2. *Cultural identity may be protective.* A strong cultural identity may be associated with better adjustment. However, acceptance of Anglo norms with concomitant detachment from an individual's cultural heritage may place individuals at high risk for drug use because they may be alienated from their family and peer support groups.

3. *Bicultural identity may be risk inducing.* This hypothesis maintains that the stress of negotiating two cultures increases the likelihood of psychological disorders. This stress may be particularly severe and problematic among immigrant families, in which rapidly acculturating adolescents are in conflict with their more traditional parents and turn to drug use.

4. *Bicultural identity may be protective.* This hypothesis suggests that a Mexican American who is integrated into the dominant culture but maintains ties and personal identification with his or her traditional culture may be at less risk for drug use than the completely assimilated individual. This person may draw on support and resources from either culture.

Method

RECRUITMENT OF PARTICIPANTS

Survey data were collected from 516 9th- and 10th-grade students of Latino descent in the Los Angeles area. Fifty-seven percent of the sample was female and 43% was male. Most participants were 15 to 16 years old, first generation of Mexican descent, and raised by parents without a high school diploma.

MEASURES OF SUBSTANCE USE

Because quantity of drug use is more predictive of problem or disruptive drug use than frequency of drug use (Stein, Newcomb, & Bentler, 1988), both frequency and quantity measures of drug use were used. Use of multiple drugs was captured as a latent construct of polydrug use that reflected the extent of involvement (frequency and quantity) with all five types of drug use.

More specifically, frequency of cigarette, alcohol, marijuana, inhalant, and other hard drug use was assessed for the past 6 months on 7-point anchored scales ranging from *never* (1) to *more than once a day* (7). Quantity of cigarette, alcohol, and marijuana use was rated on 7-point anchored scales ranging from *no ingestion* (1) to *heavy use* (7) (i.e., two packs of cigarettes a day or more, six or more alcoholic beverages, and six or more marijuana cigarettes).

CULTURAL IDENTITY SCALES

A multidimensional measure of cultural identity was used to assess cultural identity across several domains, including value and attitude domains. Three domains were assessed along both American and Latino dimensions: (a) cultural familiarity, (b) language proficiency, and (c) traditional family role expectations (feminism, conceptualized as a more American philosophy, and *respeto,* conceptualized as more Latino). Language and behavior were also assessed. The 10 multi-item scales were Spanish Proficiency, English Proficiency, Spanish Language Preference, Familiarity With American Culture, Familiarity With Latino Culture, Preferred Latino Affiliation, Latino Activism, Perceived Discrimination, *Respeto,* and Feminism (Félix-Ortiz, Newcomb, & Myers, 1994; Félix-Ortiz et al., 1992).

Results

MEAN COMPARISONS
OF CULTURAL IDENTITY GROUPS

Cultural Familiarity

A multivariate analysis of variance (MANOVA) was conducted using Familiarity With American Culture and Familiarity With Latino Culture as independent variables, each with two levels (high and low as determined by a median split). The eight drug use measures were used as dependent variables. Because sex had no main effects on drug use or interaction with cultural identity, males and females were collapsed into a single group. Results of the separate ANOVAs are presented in Table 8.1.

There were no significant main effects for Familiarity With American Culture and no significant effects for Familiarity With Latino Culture. Those who reported greater familiarity with Latino culture reported significantly less frequent marijuana use during the past 6 months than those Latino adolescents unfamiliar with Latino culture.

One significant and two marginal ($p < .10$) interactions were obtained. These three interactions are plotted in Figures 8.1a, 8.1b, and 8.1c. Marginal students (those unfamiliar with both Latino and American cultures) used alcohol most frequently and in largest amounts, followed by biculturals (high familiarity with both cultures; see Figures 8.1a and 8.1b). Those students with high Latino familiarity but low American familiarity drank least frequently

TABLE 8.1 Mean Comparisons of Cultural Identity Groups on Drug Use

Familiarity With Latino Culture	Familiarity With American Culture			F Values		
	Low	High	Total	Am.	Lt.	Am. × Lt.
Frequency of Cigarette Use Over the Last 6 Months						
Low	1.89	1.55	1.76	1.80	0.01	1.60
High	1.71	1.70	1.70			
Total	1.82	1.64				
Frequency of Alcohol Use Over the Last 6 Months						
Low	5.21	4.82	5.07	0.00	1.01	2.93*
High	4.57	4.99	4.84			
Total	4.98	4.93				
Frequency of Marijuana Use Over the Last 6 Months						
Low	1.55	1.46	1.51	0.35	4.70**	0.08
High	1.30	1.27	1.28			
Total	1.46	1.34				
Frequency of Inhalants Use Over the Last 6 Months						
Low	1.82	1.65	1.76	0.10	0.56	3.22*
High	1.53	1.77	1.68			
Total	1.72	1.73				
Frequency of Other Hard Drug Use Over the Last 6 Months						
Low	4.41	4.31	4.38	1.43	0.59	0.27
High	4.38	4.12	4.22			
Total	4.40	4.38				
Quantity of Cigarette Use Over the Last 6 Months						
Low	0.42	0.23	0.35	1.08	0.29	1.72
High	0.36	0.38	0.37			
Total	0.40	0.33				
Quantity of Alcohol Use Over the Last 6 Months						
Low	1.85	1.59	1.75	0.44	0.21	4.46**
High	1.20	1.70	1.52			
Total	1.61	1.66				
Quantity of Marijuana Use Over the Last 6 Months						
Low	0.45	0.32	0.40	0.26	0.88	0.95
High	0.28	0.32	0.30			
Total	0.39	0.32				

$*p \le .10$; $**p \le .05$. Am. = American; Lt. = Latino

and in the lowest amounts. Those students only familiar with American culture drank somewhat more often and in greater amounts than those only familiar with Latino culture, but less than biculturals. This pattern of use also emerged for frequency of inhalant use (see Figure 8.1c).

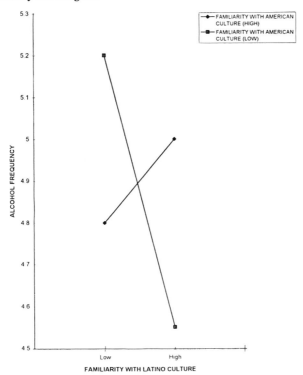

Figure 8.1a. Interactions of Familiarity With Latino Culture and Familiarity With American Culture on Frequency of Alcohol Use. Note that the scales along the *y* axis are different across figures 8.1a, 8.1b, and 8.1c.

Language Proficiency

A MANOVA was conducted using English Language Proficiency and Spanish Language Proficiency as independent variables, each with two levels (high and low as determined by a median split). As in the previous analyses, males and females were collapsed into a single group, and the eight drug use scales were used as dependent measures. Results of the separate ANOVAs are presented in Table 8.2.

There were no significant main effects for English Language Proficiency, whereas there were significant main effects for Spanish Language Proficiency on all eight drug use scales. Those who had high Spanish language proficiency reported significantly less frequent use of all substances during the past 6 months and in lower quantities than those students with poor Spanish language skills.

There were no significant interactions, but one was marginal ($p < .10$) on cigarette frequency, as plotted in Figure 8.2. As evident in the figure,

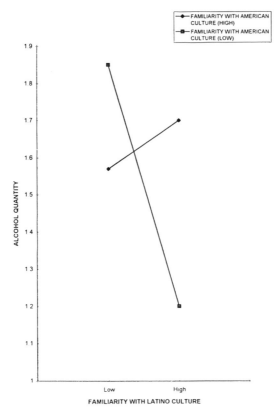

Figure 8.1b. Interactions of Familiarity With Latino Culture and Familiarity With American Culture on Frequency of Inhalant Use. Note that the scales along the *y* axis are different across Figures 8.1a, 8.1b, and 8.1c.

Spanish proficiency had little effect on cigarette frequency when English proficiency was high. However, when English proficiency was low, level of Spanish proficiency had a profound effect on cigarette frequency. For those students with poor English skills, also having poor Spanish skills was extremely risk inducing, as evidenced by the highest frequency of cigarette use, whereas having good Spanish language skills was extremely protective, as apparent in the lowest frequency of cigarette use.

STRUCTURAL EQUATION MODELS

Two structural equation models (SEM) were constructed to test for influences of cultural identity on drug use among Latino boys and Latinas (Newcomb, 1990). First, confirmatory factor analyses (CFAs) were conducted

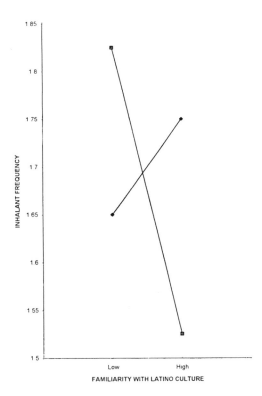

Figure 8.1c. Interactions of Familiarity With Latino Culture and Familiarity With American Culture on Quantity of Alcohol Use. Note that the scales along the *y* axis are different across Figures 8.1a, 8.1b, and 8.1c.

to verify that measured variables were captured reliably by latent constructs, to determine the degree of model fit, and to examine latent construct inter-correlations. Two latent constructs were hypothesized to reflect five of the culture identity scales (Defensive Latino Activism,[2] with indicators of Latino activism, preferred Latino affiliation, and perceived discrimination; and Traditional Family Role Expectations, with indicators of *respeto* and [low] feminism), whereas the other five cultural identity scales were retained as measured variables and not expected to reflect any latent construct. Six drug use scales were hypothesized to reflect three first-order latent constructs (Cigarette Use, with indicators of cigarette frequency and quantity; Alcohol Use, with indicators of alcohol frequency and quantity; and Marijuana Use,

TABLE 8.2 Mean Comparisons of Language Proficiency Groups on Drug Use

| Spanish Proficiency | English Proficiency | | | F Values | | |
	Low	High	Total	Eng.	Sp.	Eng. × Sp.
Frequency of Cigarette Use Over the Last 6 Months						
Low	2.02	1.86	1.92	0.26	7.73***	3.07*
High	1.44	1.72	1.57			
Total	1.66	1.79				
Frequency of Alcohol Use Over the Last 6 Months						
Low	5.32	5.20	5.25	1.22	5.37**	2.62
High	4.42	5.04	4.70			
Total	4.77	5.12				
Frequency of Marijuana Use Over the Last 6 Months						
Low	1.59	1.63	1.61	1.42	15.43****	0.51
High	1.13	1.32	1.22			
Total	1.31	1.48				
Frequency of Inhalants Use Over the Last 6 Months						
Low	1.90	1.82	1.86	0.39	4.50**	1.74
High	1.51	1.73	1.61			
Total	1.66	1.78				
Frequency of Other Hard Drug Use Over the Last 6 Months						
Low	4.62	4.41	4.49	0.07	6.87***	1.43
High	4.07	4.20	4.13			
Total	4.28	4.31				
Quantity of Cigarette Use Over the Last 6 Months						
Low	0.56	0.48	0.52	0.00	13.99****	1.03
High	0.20	0.27	0.23			
Total	0.33	0.38				
Quantity of Alcohol Use Over the Last 6 Months						
Low	2.01	1.92	1.96	0.13	11.12****	0.80
High	1.27	1.49	1.37			
Total	1.56	1.71				
Quantity of Marijuana Use Over the Last 6 Months						
Low	0.52	0.57	0.55	0.76	16.26****	0.12
High	0.14	0.24	0.19			
Total	0.29	0.41				

$*p \leq .10$; $**p \leq .05$; $***p \leq .01$; $****p \leq .001$. Eng. = English; Sp. = Spanish

with indicators of marijuana frequency and quantity), and these three constructs as well as frequency of inhalant and hard drug use were used as indicators of a second-order construct of Polydrug Use.

If these models were satisfactory, then initial structural models were tested with unidirectional paths substituted into the CFA model to represent

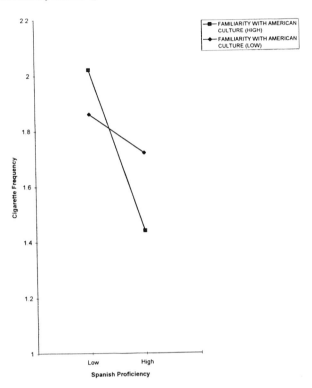

Figure 8.2. Interaction of Spanish Proficiency and English Proficiency on Frequency of Cigarette Use

the relationships of cultural identity constructs and measured variables to drug use variables. At this point, final SEMs were created by adding significant nonstandard or specific paths (Newcomb, 1994) using the multivariate Lagrange multiplier test and subsequently deleting nonsignificant paths using the Wald test (Chou & Bentler, 1990).

CFA Model

For Latino boys, the CFA model fit well, $\chi^2(103, N = 221) = 211$, $p <$ .001, CFI (Comparative Fit Index; Bentler, 1990) = .94. Factor loadings for the Polydrug Use construct ranged in magnitude from .46 to .94; first-order factor loadings ranged in magnitude from .74 to .96. Latent construct factor loadings for the Cultural Identity factors ranged in magnitude from .41 to .68. Polydrug use was significantly correlated with more defensive Latino activism, more traditional family role expectations, and less Spanish proficiency, and marginally associated ($p < .10$) with higher English proficiency and less familiarity with Latino culture.

For Latinas, the CFA model also fit well, $\chi^2(103, N = 295) = 186, p < .001$, CFI = .96. Factor loadings for the Polydrug Use construct ranged in magnitude from .31 to .97; first-order factor loadings ranged in magnitude from .71 to .99. Latent construct factor loadings for the Cultural Identity factors ranged in magnitude from .32 to −.96. Polydrug use was significantly correlated with more defensive Latino activism, less Spanish proficiency, and more English proficiency, and marginally related ($p < .10$) to fewer traditional family role expectations.

SEMs

The initial SEM for Latino males fit well, $\chi^2(103, N = 221) = 211, p < .001$, CFI = .94. After significant paths were added and nonsignificant paths deleted, the final SEM for Latino boys fit the data well, $\chi^2(111, N = 221) = 198, p < .001$, CFI = .95. In this final model, seven nonstandard or specific effects were added that reflect two types of relationships: paths from the residuals of cultural identity variables to drug use constructs or drug use measured variables. Figure 8.3 presents the factor structure and significant paths for the Latino boys' final SEM.

Polydrug use was significantly influenced by greater English proficiency, less familiarity with Latino culture, and more defensive Latino activism. Polydrug use was also influenced specifically by more perceived discrimination and less feminism. Cigarette use was predicted by less *respeto*. Alcohol use was predicted by more defensive Latino activism. Inhalant frequency was predicted by more Latino activism and more perceived discrimination. Finally, frequency of other hard drug use was influenced by more defensive Latino activism.

For Latinas, the initial SEM fit well, $\chi^2(103, N = 295) = 186, p < .001$, CFI = .96. After significant specific or nonstandard paths were added and nonsignificant paths deleted, the final SEM for Latinas fit the data quite well, $\chi^2(107, N = 295) = 176, p < .001$, CFI = .96. In this final model, six nonstandard or specific effects were added. This final model is presented in Figure 8.4.

Polydrug use was significantly predicted from less traditional family role expectations and more perceived discrimination. Cigarette use was influenced by greater defensive Latino activism. Alcohol use was predicted from low Spanish proficiency, greater English proficiency, and lack of Spanish language preference. Finally, frequency of inhalant use was increased by greater defensive Latino activism.

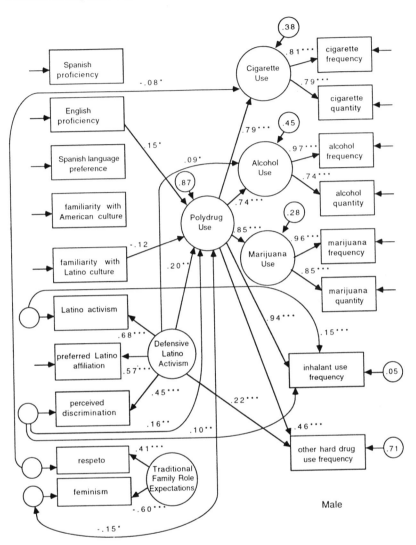

Figure 8.3. Final Structural Model for Males. Circles represent latent constructs, rectangles represent measured variables, and one-headed arrows represent factor loadings or paths between variables. Parameter estimates are standardized, and significant (*$p < .05$; **$p < .01$; ***$p < .001$) and residual variances are shown in small circles.

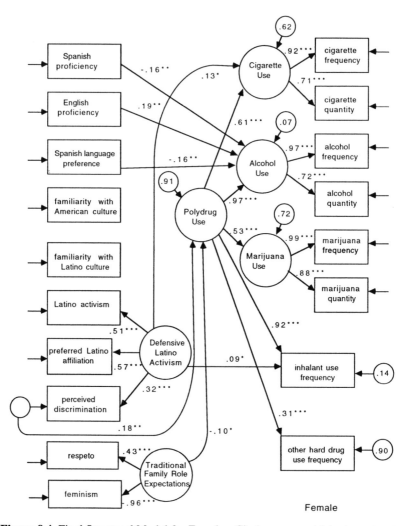

Figure 8.4. Final Structural Model for Females. Circles represent latent constructs, rectangles represent measured variables, and one-headed arrows represent factor loadings or paths between variables. Parameter estimates are standardized, and significant (*$p < .05$; **$p < .01$; ***$p < .001$) and residual variances are shown in small circles.

Discussion

Drug use among Latino adolescents is a complex, multiply-determined behavior. Cultural identity does affect drug use, but the relationship depends on the type of drug use, gender, and particular aspects of cultural identity. Assessing frequency and quantity of drug use can capture differences in drug use (experimental vs. recreational vs. problem use), and each individual has his or her own pattern of use, which may be influenced by a number of variables, including cultural identity. Cultural identity consists of multidimensional domains, each of which may have unique effects on drug use. For certain types of drug use, these multiple dimensions interact and are differentially related to drug use. A unidimensional measure of cultural identity that is distilled into a single score cannot capture the complexity of these relationships. This reductionist approach may also account for the often conflicting results found in this literature. The approach taken in this study illustrates how certain components of cultural identity are associated with increased drug use (e.g., defensive Latino activism), whereas others are associated with decreased drug use (e.g., traditional family role expectations for Latinas).

Furthermore, external sociopolitical influences, such as discrimination, are part of Latino cultural identity, and hostile or defensive reactions to these inequalities appear to increase drug use among Latinos in the United States. This illustrates the often neglected, dynamic aspect of cultural identity development that involves both intrapsychic influences and perceived environmental receptivity and response. The implication of this conceptualization is that intervention must occur at higher systems levels as well as at the level of the individual. Government policy, education as an institution, and the media could be examined for their role in shaping societal response to individuals who opt to develop or retain a strong cultural identity. A hostile societal response (e.g., racist policies, ethnocentric curricula, and negative portrayals of ethnic characters) appears to have a role in drug use among Latinos. On the other hand, empowerment and political change efforts within the Latino community may help channel defensive reactions to discrimination (and resulting drug use) toward more creative and effective solutions.

BICULTURALITY

It was important to measure cultural identity multidimensionally. For example, biculturals (as indicated by their familiarity with both cultures) used certain drugs less often than marginals, but used them more frequently than either Latino-identified or American-identified students. Why? It may be that the stress of negotiating two cultural systems (and perhaps not feeling that they fit in with either or are ruling out one or the other) is associated with greater drug use. An alternative explanation is that biculturals may have assumed two different patterns of drug use. Mexicans have been described as low-frequency, high-quantity alcohol users: relative to U.S. national samples, alcohol use is infrequent but often to intoxication (Gilbert & Cervantes,

1986). If the two patterns of alcohol consumption are combined, you may find American-type high-frequency drinking combined with Mexican-type high-quantity drinking, a pattern that is similar to that seen among biculturals in this sample. However, this pattern may not persist into second or third generations as dominant culture influences become more entrenched.

CULTURAL IDENTITY
BEHAVIORS AND VALUES

Among Latinas, it appears that feminism (through traditional family role expectations) is associated with increased drug use. Feminism may contribute to increased drug use among Latinas in at least two ways. First, it may be stress inducing to adopt attitudes that will conflict with more traditional values encouraged by family or community. Second, pressures to conform to traditional sex roles may be strong in a large, cohesive Latino system. This may generate resentment and trigger rebellious behavior in some Latinas. It may be that drug use among Latina youth is a way in which stress resulting from conflicting belief systems is relieved and a way in which Latinas rebel. It may be important that efforts to familiarize and socialize Latino students to American ideals extend beyond school to the student's Latino community. This might decrease any conflict between the student's developing belief/value system and his or her family's more traditional beliefs/values.

A similar explanation may apply to the relationship between defensive Latino activism and increased drug use among both boys and girls. The Latino who perceives discrimination may withdraw from both the mainstream European American group (through affiliation with other like-minded Latino peers) and the mainstream Latino group (through militant activism). By adopting an "antiwhite" attitude rather than a pro-Latino attitude in his activism, he marginalizes himself from those with more traditional belief systems (e.g., America as benevolent) and becomes more susceptible to stress and less likely to cope effectively. This isolation from the larger mainstream communities may be compounded by isolation from early adolescent peers, who may not tolerate anyone who refuses to conform. Activism does not usually emerge until later adolescence, as evidenced on college campuses across the country.

Attachment to the community may be a critical defense against drug use among Latino adolescents. Reactive and defensive activism may serve to alienate Latino youth and place them at risk for drug use. Perceived discrimination may lead a youth to believe there are few opportunities for community involvement. This may also threaten self-worth, thus increasing vulnerability for drug use. On the other hand, respect for others may enhance a Latino boy's sense of attachment to the conventional order, thus decreasing his vulnerability for drug use. Clearly, research is needed to test these hypothesized mediators of the relationships found here.

LANGUAGE VERSUS FAMILIARITY VARIABLES AND DRUG USE

Language variables were more powerfully and consistently associated with drug use for girls than for boys. Across both sexes, Spanish proficiency was associated with decreased drug use. Among Latino boys, familiarity with Latino culture was associated with less drug use. In addition, for alcohol and inhalant use, familiarity with Latino culture and American culture interacted to predict these types of drug use distinctly from language variables. Familiarity with Latino culture may indicate a fundamental connection with a community that passes along cultural information. Spanish proficiency does not necessarily ensure this connection, and it may be this connection to community that decreases risk for *certain* types of drug use. However, language proficiency may be more important than familiarity with cultures for Latina teens as the basis of important dyadic relationships. Whereas, Latino boys may be more concerned with belonging to a group or community that requires familiarity with the culture as well as some language proficiency. This is evident in the importance many young men place on affiliation with a "gang," "crew," or "posse." Language, often used as a proxy for cultural identity, is limited in its utility as a pure indicator of cultural identity. Language proficiency and cultural familiarity may be indicators of attachment to community, and this sense of belonging may be a critical factor in understanding what may drive drug use in Latino adolescents.

LIMITATIONS

Although this study has its strengths, it also has its limitations. However, these limitations can inform future research in this area. These shortcomings include the use of self-report. Self-report is subject to influences of social desirability, particularly when the questions are about potentially stigmatizing behavior or attitudes such as drug use. There may be a tendency for youth to underreport drug use for fear of reprisals if their individual responses are identified and disclosed to parents and teachers. However, there may also be a tendency to overreport drug use to appear more rebellious and unique as an individual.

Furthermore, the cultural identity scales require additional development, and exploration of intervening factors in the relationship between cultural identity and drug use among Latino youth is needed. Measurement of distinctive Latino values and attitudes requires further exploration. Finally, cultural identity may have indirect effects on drug use through risk and protective factors for drug use. Factors such as self-acceptance and conventionality may be affected by cultural identity. These factors may then place an individual at risk for drug use. For example, low self-acceptance resulting from problems in cultural identity may then increase the likelihood of drug involvement.

IMPLICATIONS

Despite the limitations of this study, the data suggest the need for programs that foster cultural identity among Latino youth, positive Latina and Latino role models for Latino youth, and cohesive, positive activism and feminism within Latino communities. Programs that foster cultural identity may be important curriculum components for Latinos. These programs might include basic (and positive) education about Latino history and heritage that can serve to (a) inspire pride and self-acceptance, (b) convey a sense of how Latinos have contributed to and "fit" into the conventional order, and (c) dispel beliefs that Latinos are an ineffectual people. It would also be important to provide Latino role models, contemporary as well as legendary, who can inspire pride and teach important skills. Finally, these data suggest the importance of a cohesive Latino community with its own cultural traditions, celebrations, and positive activism that fully involve every youth, male and female, and reward each one for his or her contributions to the community. However, this focus on encouraging cultural identity is not "the" solution for the drug problem and should be balanced with the building of basic coping skills and the enhancement of protective factors in the environment.

Notes

1. *Latinos* refers to all Spanish-speaking groups or people of Latin American descent (e.g., Mexicans, Cubans, Puerto Ricans, South and Central Americans). Although the convention of *Latina/os* is often used to include females as well as males, *Latinos* will be used to refer to both.

2. Some may bristle at the suggestion that all political activism among Latinos may be associated with drug use. We would like to emphasize that activism is a complex behavior that may, across individuals, express a variety of attitudes and motivations. Activism that emerges principally from hostility or a need for revenge is probably different from activism that emerges principally from a desire to educate others and prevent further discrimination. It is the former to which we refer as *defensive* Latino activism.

References

Amaro, H., Whitaker, R., Coffman, G., & Heeren, T. (1990). Acculturation and marijuana and cocaine use: Finding from HHANES 1982-1984. *American Journal of Public Health, 80*(Suppl.), 54-60.

Bentler, P. M. (1990). Comparative fit indexes in structural models. *Psychological Bulletin, 107,* 238-246.

Burnam, M. A., Hough, R. L., Karno, M., Escobar, J. I., & Telles, C. A. (1987). Acculturation and lifetime prevalence of psychiatric disorders among Mexican Americans in Los Angeles. *Journal of Health and Social Behavior, 28,* 89-102.

Chou, C. P., & Bentler, P. M. (1990). Model modification in covariance structure modeling: A comparison among likelihood ratio, Lagrange multiplier, and Wald tests. *Multivariate Behavioral Research, 25,* 115-136.

Clark, M., Kaufman, S., & Pierce, R. C. (1976). Explorations of acculturation: Toward a model of ethnic identity. *Human Organization, 35,* 231-238.

Cuellar, I., Harris, L. C., & Jasso, R. (1980). An acculturation scale for Mexican American normal and clinical populations. *Hispanic Journal of Behavioral Sciences, 2,* 199-217.

Félix-Ortiz, M., Newcomb, M. D., & Myers, H. (1994). A multidimensional scale of cultural identity for Latino and Latina adolescents. Hispanic Journal of Behavioral Sciences, 16, 99-115.

Félix-Ortiz, M., Newcomb, M. D., Myers, H., Lengua, A., Torres, M. E., & Villagra, B. (1992, August). *A multidimensional measure of cultural identity for Latino/a adolescents.* Paper presented at the annual meeting of the American Psychological Association, Washington, DC.

Gilbert, J., & Cervantes, R. C. (1986). Patterns and practices of alcohol use among Mexican Americans: A comprehensive review. *Hispanic Journal of Behavioral Sciences, 8,* 1-60.

Holck, S. E., Warren, C. W., Smith, J. C., & Rochat, R. W. (1984). Alcohol consumption among Mexican American and Anglo women: Results of a survey along the U.S.-Mexico border. *Journal of Studies on Alcohol, 45,* 149-154.

Keefe, S. E., & Padilla, A. M. (1987). *Chicano ethnicity.* Albuquerque: University of New Mexico Press.

Markides, K. S., Krause, N., & Mendes de Leon, C. F. (1988). Acculturation and alcohol consumption among Mexican Americans. *American Journal of Public Health, 78,* 1178-1181.

Newcomb, M. D. (1990). Social support by many other names: Toward a unified conceptualization. *Journal of Social and Personal Relationships, 7,* 479-494.

Newcomb, M. D. (1994). Drug use and intimate relationships among women and men: Separating specific from general effects in prospective data using structural equations models. *Journal of Consulting and Clinical Psychology, 62,* 463-476.

Oetting, E. R., & Beauvais, F. (1991). Orthogonal cultural identification theory: The cultural identification of minority adolescents. *International Journal of the Addictions, 25,* 655-685.

Stein, J. A., Newcomb, M. D., & Bentler, P. M. (1988). Structure of drug use behaviors and consequences among young adults: Multitrait-multimethod assessment of frequency, quantity, work site, and problem substance use. *Journal of Applied Psychology, 73,* 595-605.

Szapocznik, J., & Kurtines, W. (1980). Acculturation, biculturalism, and adjustment among Cuban Americans. In A. M. Padilla (Ed.), *Acculturation: Theory, models, and some new findings* (pp. 139-157). Boulder, CO: Westview.

PART

3

Promising Approaches to Drug Abuse Prevention

Drug Abuse
Prevention in School Settings

Gilbert J. Botvin

The development and testing of approaches for preventing adolescent drug abuse have largely focused on school populations and have, until recently, been limited to white, middle-class students. This chapter contains a summary of the school-based prevention research literature, with an emphasis on what is currently known about effective prevention approaches from existing empirical evidence. Although most of the extant drug abuse prevention research literature consists of studies conducted with predominantly white populations, this literature is important because it provides a starting point for the development and testing of approaches that may be effective with other populations or may lead to the identification of approaches that are particularly effective with specific racial/ethnic minority populations. Also included in this chapter is a summary of the research conducted over the past few years with African American and Hispanic adolescents at Cornell's Institute for Prevention Research.

Schools as the Locus
of Prevention Efforts

Schools have served as the primary locus of drug abuse prevention efforts for several decades. Despite their traditional educational mission, schools have been asked to assume responsibility for a variety of social and health problems. Many states mandate schools to provide their students with programs in health education and/or tobacco, alcohol, and drug education as well as teenage pregnancy and AIDS education. Although there has been considerable debate about whether schools should provide programs dealing with health and social problems, particularly at a time when there is renewed concern about academic standards, the simple truth is that schools offer the most efficient access to large numbers of children or adolescents. Moreover, many educators are gradually recognizing that problems such as drug abuse are a significant barrier to the achievement of educational objectives. The U.S. Department of Education, for example, has included "drug-free schools" as one of its goals for improving the quality of education in this country.

Over the past couple of decades, several different types of prevention approaches have been conducted in school settings. Some of these were grounded in theory; most, however, were not. These approaches can be divided into four general prevention strategies: (a) cognitive/information dissemination approaches, (b) affective education, (c) social resistance skills training, and (d) personal and social skills training.

These approaches typically involve classroom activities either alone or in combination with school-wide activities such as poster contests and assembly programs. Programs using these approaches have been conducted largely by school staff (e.g., teachers, health educators, drug counselors), peer leaders, or outside professionals (e.g., doctors or police).

Cognitive and Affective
Prevention Approaches

INFORMATION DISSEMINATION

The most common prevention approach utilized by schools relies on teaching students factual information about drugs and drug abuse. Typically, students are taught about the dangers of tobacco, alcohol, or drug use in terms of the adverse health, social, and legal consequences. Informational programs also define various patterns of drug use, the pharmacology of drugs, and the process of becoming a drug abuser.

Some programs have police officers come into the classroom and discuss law enforcement issues, including drug-related crime and penalties for buying or possessing illegal drugs. Other programs have used doctors or other health professionals to talk about the adverse health effects of using drugs. Still others invite former drug addicts into the classroom to discuss the problems that they have encountered as the result of drug abuse.

Programs that rely exclusively on providing students with facts about drugs and drug abuse are conceptually based on a cognitive model of drug use/abuse. Such a model assumes that individuals make a more or less rational decision to use drugs or not use drugs. Individuals who use drugs are believed to do so, according to this model, because they are unaware of the adverse consequences of drug abuse. The solution to the problem of drug abuse, when framed in this way, is to educate students about the negative consequences of drug abuse—to increase their knowledge of factual information about drugs and drug abuse. This model of drug abuse assumes that once armed with the necessary facts, students will make a rational and informed decision not to use drugs.

Despite the widespread use of this type of drug abuse prevention approach, the evaluation literature indicates quite clearly that these approaches are not effective (Dryfoos, 1993). Evaluation studies have shown that most prevention programs are able to demonstrate an impact on knowledge or factual information. Some studies have also demonstrated an impact on attitudes. However, these studies have consistently indicated that cognitive approaches do not affect behavior: They do not reduce or prevent tobacco, alcohol, or drug use. They also indicate quite clearly that increased knowledge of drugs and the dangers of drug use has no impact on either drug use behavior or intentions to use drugs. Consequently, the existing literature calls into question the basic assumption of the cognitive model—that increased knowledge will result in attitude and behavior change. Some studies have even suggested that informational approaches may lead to increased usage because they may serve to stimulate curiosity (Swisher, Crawford, Goldstein, & Yura, 1971).

Because it may seem counterintuitive that knowledge would not help reduce or prevent drug use, this may need some additional elaboration. It is likely that an awareness of the hazards of using drugs does play some role in deterring drug use among many individuals. Thus, it would not be appropriate to conclude from the prevention evidence that factual information is entirely superfluous. The important point to keep in mind, however, is that the etiology of drug abuse is complex and multifactorial (see Newcomb, Chapter 6 of this volume). Although it is difficult to argue that knowledge is of no value, it is only one of many factors involved in the initiation of drug use among adolescents.

AFFECTIVE EDUCATION

Another common approach to drug abuse prevention has been referred to as *affective education*. This prevention strategy was based on the belief that the risk of using drugs could be reduced through programs designed to promote affective development. This prevention approach is based on a different set of assumptions than information dissemination, which has a cognitive orientation. Instead of focusing on cognitive factors, affective education emphasizes the personal and social development of students.

Affective education takes a somewhat broader approach to the problem of drug abuse than information dissemination by implicitly recognizing the role of psychosocial factors. In some respects, this approach has foreshadowed some of the more comprehensive competence enhancement drug abuse prevention approaches currently being used by several research groups. For example, components of affective education approaches that are used in some prevention programs include decision making, effective communication, and assertiveness. Studies evaluating the effectiveness of affective education have produced disappointing results. Although affective education approaches have been able to demonstrate an impact on one or more of the correlates of drug use, they have not been able to demonstrate an impact on drug use itself (Kearney & Hines, 1980; Kim, 1988).

Though more comprehensive than information dissemination approaches, the affective education approach to drug abuse prevention has several major weaknesses. These include a focus on a narrow and incomplete set of etiologic determinants, the use of ineffective methods to achieve stated program goals (such as the use of experiential games and classroom activities rather than skills-training methods), a lack of domain-specific information related to drug abuse, and the inclusion of "responsible use" norm-setting messages that may be counterproductive.

Social Influence Approaches

Toward the end of the 1970s, a major shift in drug abuse prevention research began. This shift occurred in part out of a growing disappointment with traditional prevention approaches and a recognition of the importance that psychosocial factors played in promoting the initiation of drug use. Unlike previous prevention approaches, the intervention strategies that have been the focus of prevention research during the 1980s and early 1990s have a stronger grounding in psychological theories of human behavior.

THE SOCIAL INFLUENCE MODEL

Richard Evans and his colleagues at the University of Houston are credited with launching this new line of prevention research (Evans, 1976; Evans et al., 1978). Evans's work emphasized the importance of social and psychological factors in promoting the onset of cigarette smoking and utilized a prevention approach based on McGuire's persuasive communications theory (McGuire, 1964, 1968). From this perspective, adolescent cigarette smoking is conceptualized as being the result of social influences (persuasive messages) from peers and the media in the form of offers from peers to smoke cigarettes, advertising appeals, or exposure to smokers who may serve as role models for these students.

PSYCHOLOGICAL INOCULATION

The prevention approach developed by Evans and his coworkers is based on a concept in McGuire's work (McGuire, 1964, 1968) called *psychological inoculation,* which, as applied by Evans to cigarette smoking, was designed to "inoculate" adolescent nonsmokers against the type of prosmoking persuasive messages they would be likely to encounter by exposing them to these messages, first in a relatively weak form and then in progressively stronger forms.

In addition to preparing adolescents for eventual exposure to prosmoking persuasive influences from peers and/or the media, the prevention approach developed by Evans also attempted to teach tactics for dealing with such influences. A common situation for adolescents is that they will be offered a cigarette by a peer and called "chicken" if they refuse to smoke. They are taught to handle this type of a peer pressure situation by having responses ready, such as "If I smoke to prove to you that I'm not chicken, all I'll really be showing is that I'm afraid not to do what you want me to. I don't want to smoke; therefore, I'm not going to." Or, because adolescents are likely to see peers posturing and acting "tough" by smoking, they can be taught to think to themselves, "If they were really tough, they wouldn't have to smoke to prove it."

The prevention approach developed by Evans and his associates was initially presented as a series of films. In addition to films including material designed to increase awareness of the social influences to smoke cigarettes and techniques for resisting them, this prevention approach also included periodic surveys of smoking, with feedback to students concerning actual smoking rates and information about the immediate physiological effects of smoking. Surveys were conducted biweekly, and saliva samples were collected as an objective measure of smoking status. The smoking rates in each classroom (which were lower than what most adolescents thought) were announced to all of the students in order to help correct the common misperception that cigarette smoking is a highly normative behavior engaged in by nearly everyone.

In a seminal paper for the prevention field, students receiving (a) assessment and feedback concerning classroom smoking rates were compared with other students receiving (b) assessment and feedback along with the inoculation intervention and (c) a control group (Evans et al., 1978). The results of this study produced the first evidence in over two decades that prevention could work—that individuals receiving a prevention program would have significantly lower rates of tobacco, alcohol, or other drug use than those not receiving the program. In the case of this study, the students in the two prevention conditions had smoking onset rates that were about half the rate observed in the control group.

An interesting aspect of this study that has assumed more prominence over the years is that the inoculation intervention did not produce any incremental reduction in smoking onset over that produced by the assessment/feedback procedures. In fact, in retrospect, it is evident that the inoculation intervention had little or no effect on the students receiving it with respect to reducing smoking onset. Rather, the prevention effect that was observed and generally attributed to the inoculation component of the intervention was the result of providing students with feedback concerning the actual levels of smoking in their classroom. Because this feedback showed smoking rates to be considerably lower than students actually believed them to be, the feedback provided information that "corrected" the widely held misconception that nearly everybody smoked cigarettes. Although correcting normative expectations was incorporated into the prevention approaches tested by other researchers throughout the 1980s, the importance of this intervention component has largely been underestimated. Still, the dramatic success of the smoking prevention study published by Evans and his associates in 1978 led to an explosion of prevention research—initially targeting cigarette smoking and later targeting alcohol and other drugs—that has transformed the entire prevention field.

SOCIAL RESISTANCE SKILLS

Over the years several variations on the prevention strategy described above have been developed and tested. In general, these approaches placed less emphasis on psychological inoculation, which was the cornerstone of the approach developed by Evans. The approaches that followed were all designed to target the psychosocial factors believed to promote the use of tobacco, alcohol, and other drugs. Emphasis was placed on dealing with social influences from peers and the media to use drugs. However, an important difference in these approaches was the focus on teaching students the skills needed to resist these influences.

These approaches have been referred to in the literature as *social influence* approaches (because they target the social influences promoting drug use), *refusal skills* approaches (because a central feature of these approaches is that they teach students how to refuse drug use offers), and either *social resistance skills* or simply *resistance skills* approaches (because they teach students skills for resisting social influences to engage in drug use). These terms are used interchangeably in the literature, and any one of them is an appropriate descriptor for this class of prevention approaches. The term *resistance skills* is used in this chapter because it nicely captures two distinctive aspects of these prevention approaches: (a) the focus on increasing students' resistance to negative social influences to engage in drug use and (b) the focus on *skills* training.

As a class of preventive interventions, these approaches are similar in that they are based on social learning theory (Bandura, 1977) and a conceptual model that stresses the fundamental importance of social factors in promoting the initiation of adolescent drug use. Although this model includes social influences coming from the family, peers, and the media, the focus of most preventive interventions is on the last two of these, with the primary emphasis being placed on peer influences.

Students are taught how to recognize situations in which they are likely to experience peer pressure to smoke, drink, or use drugs so that they can avoid these high-risk situations. They are also taught how to resist direct or subtle peer pressure to engage in drug use. This generally involves teaching students both what to say and how to say it in the most effective way possible. Many adolescents do not want to smoke, drink, or use drugs, but they lack the confidence or skills to refuse offers to engage in these behaviors. These prevention programs are particularly helpful to these students, who have the opportunity to acquire the knowledge and skills needed to recognize and avoid these situations or, if they should find themselves in a peer pressure situation, the confidence and skills to handle these pressures. In addition, these programs send a clear message that it is at the very least acceptable, if not outright desirable, to resist peer pressure to use drugs.

Following the original model developed by Evans, these approaches also typically include a component designed to correct the perception that the majority of adolescents smoke, drink, or use drugs. Research has shown that adolescents have a general tendency to overestimate the prevalence of tobacco, alcohol, and drug use (Fishbein, 1977). This has been accomplished in various ways. One method is first to ask students to estimate how many teenagers and how many adults smoke, drink, or use drugs and then to provide them with the correct statistical information from national or regional survey data. A second method is to conduct a survey of the school or class and then provide them with the results. A third method is to have students conduct their own surveys and provide the results to the class. These programs also frequently have a component that is intended to make students aware of the influences from the media to which they will be exposed, with a particular emphasis on the techniques used by advertisers to influence consumer behavior. Students are taught how to recognize advertising appeals designed to sell tobacco products or alcoholic beverages, as well as how to formulate counterarguments to those appeals.

The target population for most of the research conducted with resistance skills training approaches has been junior high school students. Some studies have targeted younger or older populations, such as fifth and sixth graders or high school students. The length of prevention approaches based on the resistance skills training model has ranged from as few as 3 or 4 sessions to as many as 11 or 12 sessions conducted over a 2-year period. Different types of program providers have also been used in various research studies. Some programs have been implemented by research staff members, others by regular classroom teachers.

Many prevention programs teaching resistance skills have done so with the assistance of peer leaders serving as program providers. These students are either older (e.g., 7th graders may be taught by 9th or 10th graders) or the same age as the students participating in the prevention program. A common argument for using peer leaders as program providers is that they have greater credibility with junior high school age students than adults with respect to lifestyle issues because adolescence is a time characterized by some degree of rebellion against parents and other adult authority figures. In addition to providing students with information concerning rates of drug use and skills for resisting offers to use drugs, a potentially powerful benefit of peer leader programs is that they may help alter school norms regarding drug use and its social acceptability. To the extent that peer leaders are viewed by students as credible sources of information and influential role models who do not regard drug use as being socially acceptable, peer leader prevention programs may have an important impact on normative beliefs supportive of nondrug use.

A growing number of studies testing interventions based on the social influence approach have documented its effectiveness (Arkin, Roemhild, Johnson, Luepker, & Murray, 1981; Hurd et al., 1980; Luepker, Johnson, Murray, & Pechacek, 1983; Perry, Killen, Slinkard, & McAlister, 1983; Telch, Killen, McAlister, Perry, & Maccoby, 1982). The focus of most of these studies has been on smoking prevention, with some studies reporting results in terms of smoking onset (preventing the transition from nonsmoking to smoking), others reporting results in terms of overall smoking prevalence, and still others reporting results with respect to an index measure or scale of smoking involvement.

For the most part, these studies have indicated that this type of prevention approach is capable of reducing drug use by 30% to 50% after the initial intervention (based on a comparison of the proportion of smokers in the experimental group to the proportion of smokers in the control group). Studies reporting results in terms of smoking incidence have shown reductions ranging from approximately 30% to 40% (comparing the proportion of new smokers in the experimental group to the proportion of new smokers in the control group). Several studies have demonstrated reductions in the overall prevalence of cigarette smoking in terms of both occasional smoking (one or more cigarettes per month) and/or for regular smoking (one or more cigarettes per week). Reductions in smoking prevalence have ranged from approximately 40% to 50%. Although there are fewer studies assessing the impact on resistance skills training approaches to substances other than tobacco, such as alcohol or marijuana, the magnitude of the reductions reported has generally been similar to that found for smoking (e.g., McAlister, Perry, Killen, Slinkard, & Maccoby, 1980).

Over the years, several follow-up studies have been published that report positive behavior effects lasting for up to 3 years (Luepker et al., 1983; McAlister et al., 1980; Telch et al., 1982). However, data from several longer term follow-up studies have shown that these effects gradually decay over time (Flay et al., 1989; Murray, Davis-Hearn, Goldman, Pirie, & Luepker, 1988), suggesting the need for ongoing intervention or booster sessions. Because little is known about the nature and timing of booster interventions, additional research is needed. Also, because relatively little research has been conducted with substances other than tobacco, data concerning the durability of prevention effects on other substances are not available.

The studies testing resistance skills training approaches have been similar in most respects. There are, nonetheless, some differences. In order to gain a better understanding of the underlying mechanism of these programs and to develop more effective interventions, the various intervention components of these programs deserve closer scrutiny. A common component of several resistance skills training approaches has been a procedure through which individuals make a public commitment not to smoke, drink, or use drugs. However, a study by Hurd and his colleagues (Hurd et al., 1980) suggests that this component may not contribute to any observed prevention effects. Another common component is the use of videotaped or filmed prevention materials similar to those utilized by Evans and his colleagues (Evans et al., 1978). Still, it is not yet clear what type of media material is the most effective or the extent to which it is a necessary component of these prevention programs. Little is also known about the optimal time of intervention (age or grade level), program length, program structure, type of provider, type of booster intervention and its timing, or characteristics of the individuals who are the most affected by these interventions.

Finally, nearly all of the studies testing resistance skills training approaches have used peer leaders. Moreover, some studies have attempted to determine the effectiveness of peer leaders relative to other program providers. By and large, the existing evidence supports the use of peer leaders for this type of prevention approach (Arkin et al., 1981; Perry et al., 1983). Yet it is not altogether clear from the available evidence that peer leaders are either necessary or better than other providers. In fact, a point that is often overlooked in discussing peer leaders is that although resistance skills training programs using peer leaders have been successful, the peer leaders have nearly always functioned as assistants to adult program providers who had primary responsibility for implementing the prevention program. The adult providers generally have been either teachers or members of the project staff. The peer leaders in these studies have typically had well-defined but rather limited roles in these programs. Also, using peer leaders may not necessarily be beneficial to all students. For example, the results of one study suggested that although boys and girls may be equally affected by resistance skills training programs when conducted by teachers, girls may be more influenced by peer-led interventions than boys (Fisher, Armstrong, & deKler, 1983). Thus, more work is necessary to determine the most appropriate type of program provider and the optimal mix of responsibilities between adult and peer providers.

Personal and Social Skills Training

Psychological inoculation and resistance skills training approaches are both based on the assumption that adolescents do not want to smoke, drink, or use drugs. The underlying conceptual framework for these approaches is that adolescents begin to smoke, drink, or use drugs either because they succumb to the persuasive messages targeted at them or because they lack the necessary skills to resist social influences to use drugs. However, the extant literature indicates that drug use/abuse has a complex etiology and that some adolescents may actually want to use drugs. In other words, rather than wanting to say "no" to drug use offers, they may actually want to say "yes." For some adolescents, using drugs is not a matter of yielding to peer pressure, but has instrumental value. It may, for example, help them deal with anxiety, low self-esteem, or a lack of comfort in social situations. To the extent that this is correct, prevention approaches will need to go beyond the social influences model to interventions that are broader based and more comprehensive.

Studies concerning the etiology of tobacco, alcohol, and drug use indicate that a variety of cognitive, attitudinal, social, personality, pharmacological, and developmental factors promote and help maintain substance use (Blum & Richards, 1979; Jessor & Jessor, 1977; Jones & Battjes, 1985; Kandel, 1978; Meyer & Mirin, 1979; Newcomb, Chapter 6 of this volume; Newcomb & Bentler, 1988; Wechsler, 1976). It therefore seems logical to conclude that the most effective prevention strategy would be one that is comprehensive, targeting a broad array of etiologic determinants.

Research has been conducted over more than a decade with broader based prevention approaches that emphasize the teaching of generic personal and social skills (Botvin, Baker, Botvin, Filazzola, & Millman, 1984; Botvin, Baker, Filazzola, & Botvin, 1990; Botvin, Baker, Renick, Filazzola, & Botvin, 1984; Botvin, Eng, & Williams, 1980; Botvin, Renick, & Baker, 1983; Gilchrist & Schinke, 1983; Pentz, 1983; Schinke, 1984; Schinke & Gilchrist, 1983, 1984). The type of prevention strategy is more comprehensive than traditional cognitive/affective approaches or resistance skills training approaches. Moreover, unlike affective education approaches, which rely on experiential classroom activities, these approaches emphasize the use of proven cognitive-behavioral skills training methods.

The theoretical foundation for these approaches is Bandura's social learning theory (Bandura, 1977) and Jessor's problem behavior theory (Jessor & Jessor, 1977). Drug abuse is conceptualized as a socially learned and functional behavior that is the result of the interplay between social (interpersonal) and personal (intrapersonal) factors. Drug use behavior is learned through a process of modeling/ imitation and reinforcement and is influenced by an adolescent's cognitions, attitudes, and beliefs.

Although these approaches have several features that they share with resistance skills training approaches, a distinctive feature is their emphasis on the teaching of generic personal self-management skills and social skills. These skills are taught using a combination of instruction and demonstration, feedback, reinforcement, behavioral rehearsal (in-class practice) and extended (out-of-class) practice through behavioral homework assignments.

Examples of the type of personal and social skills typically included in this prevention approach are decision-making and problem-solving skills, cognitive skills for resisting interpersonal and media influences, skills for enhancing self-esteem (goal-setting and self-directed behavior change techniques), adaptive coping strategies for dealing with stress and anxiety, general social skills (complimenting, conversational skills, and skills for forming new friendships), and general assertive skills (requests and refusals). This prevention approach teaches both these general skills and their application to situations related directly to tobacco, alcohol, or drug use. Thus, an added benefit of this type of program is that it teaches students a repertoire of skills that they can use to deal with many of the challenges confronting adolescents in their everyday lives, including but not limited to drug use.

The purpose of programs based on this model is to provide students with the type of generic skills for coping with life that will have broad application. This contrasts markedly with resistance skills training approaches that are designed to teach students information and skills relating to the domain or problem of drug use. Although the domain-specific or problem-specific resistance skills training model is most easily contrasted with the generic skills training model, the most effective approaches appear to be ones that integrate features of both. In fact, there is some evidence suggesting that generic skills training or competence enhancement approaches are only effective if they also contain domain-specific material.

The target population for most of the studies conducted with the personal and social skills training approach has been middle/ junior high school students. The vast majority of published studies have involved students who were in the 7th grade during the first year of intervention. Multiyear studies and follow-up studies have involved students during the 8th and 9th grades, and some more recent studies have followed students up to the 10th and, in one case, 12th grade (Botvin, Baker, Dusenbury, Botvin, & Diaz, 1995), although, for the most part, studies including follow-up data on these older populations have yet to be published. On the other end of the age spectrum, very little work has been done with younger populations, although some studies have been conducted with 6th graders. The reason for this quite clearly is that because the base rates of drug use are typically low even during the beginning of the adolescent years, researchers have generally avoided younger populations because of the difficulty in demonstrating statistically significant behavioral effects.

Research with generic skills training approaches has utilized interventions having program lengths that range from as few as 7 sessions to as many as 20 sessions during the primary year of intervention. However, most interventions have consisted of between 10 and 15 class sessions. Some of these prevention programs have been conducted at a rate of one class session per week; others have been conducted at a rate of two or more sessions per week. Generic skills training interventions have been implemented through a variety of subject areas. Although the most logical academic area for programming and conducting these interventions is health or drug education, they have been scheduled through science, social studies, and physical education. Both school administrators and researchers have used a great deal of creativity and flexibility in scheduling these prevention programs during the academic year. Although certain subject areas appear to be a more natural venue for drug abuse prevention programs, these programs have been successfully implemented in many different subject areas and several different points during the school year. No clear evidence exists at this point regarding which subject area is most conducive to implementing these programs.

Consistent with the research conducted with social resistance skills training approaches, most of the studies conducted with approaches that emphasize the teaching of personal self-management skills and generic social skills have been implemented with adults as the primary program providers. In many cases, these adults were regular classroom teachers, but in some cases, they were outside health professionals (i.e., members of the research project staff). Some studies used college students as program providers, whereas others used either same-age or older peer leaders. Although peer leaders, when used, frequently had clearly delineated responsibilities and worked under the direction and supervision of an adult primary provider, some studies actually used peer leaders who had sole responsibility for conducting these interventions and who did so on their own, without the help of adult providers. Studies testing this prevention strategy have shown that it can be successfully implemented by peer leaders, outside health professionals, and teachers.

Over the years, a number of evaluation studies have been conducted testing the efficacy of generic, personal, and social skills training approaches to drug abuse prevention. These studies have consistently demonstrated behavioral effects as well as effects on hypothesized mediating variables. Importantly, the magnitude of reported effects of these approaches has typically been relatively large. These studies have generally produced reductions 40% to 80% in drug use behavior. One criticism of contemporary prevention programs is that even though they have been able to demonstrate impressive reductions in the incidence and prevalence of drug use behavior, these reductions have generally occurred with respect to experimental or occasional use. Although it is important to demonstrate reductions in the early stages of drug use, critics argue that what matters most is demonstrating reductions in more frequent levels of use—the type of regular use that results in addictive or compulsive patterns of use. Data from two studies with a prevention program called Life Skills Training deal directly with this issue by demonstrating reductions of 56% to 67% in the proportion of pretest nonsmokers becoming regular smokers 1 year after the conclusion of the prevention program without any additional booster sessions (Botvin & Eng, 1982; Botvin et al., 1983). For those students receiving booster sessions, these reductions have been as high as 87% (Botvin et al., 1983).

Results of studies utilizing generic skills training approaches, such as the Life Skills Training (LST) Program, have also demonstrated an impact on other forms of drug use. Several studies have demonstrated an impact on the use of alcohol (Botvin, Baker, Botvin, et al., 1984; Botvin, Baker, Dusenbury, Tortu, & Botvin, 1990; Botvin, Baker, Renick, et al., 1984; Pentz, 1983) and marijuana (Botvin, Baker, Botvin, et al., 1984). These reductions have generally been of a magnitude equal to that found with cigarette smoking. However, the prevention effects found for alcohol use have been more variable than those found for tobacco and marijuana.

Testing the Limits of
Current Prevention Models

Considerable progress has been made in developing effective prevention approaches. Both social resistance skills training approaches and more comprehensive school-based approaches that focus on resistance skills as well as personal and social skills have produced impressive short- and intermediate-term reductions in cigarette smoking. Significant prevention effects have also been reported in several studies for alcohol and marijuana use. However, little is known about the long-term durability of these approaches or the extent to which they can prevent more severe forms of drug involvement such as polydrug use or the use of illicit substances other than marijuana.

DURABILITY OF PREVENTION EFFECTS

Although considerable progress has been made in the field of drug abuse prevention over the past 15 years, the results of some longer term follow-up studies have raised serious questions about the utility of existing prevention approaches for producing permanent reductions in drug use. Studies have consistently demonstrated short-term effects. Several studies have demonstrated reductions in drug use (relative to controls) for up to 3 or 4 years (e.g., Botvin, Baker, Dusenbury, et al., 1990; Murray, Pirie, Luepker, & Pallonen, 1989). However, considerable variability seems to exist in both the magnitude of initial program effects and their durability. Different studies testing essentially the same intervention strategy have produced different results. For example, researchers at RAND (Ellickson & Bell, 1990) tested a social influence approach including the teaching of resistance skills that was similar to that used by researchers at the University of Minnesota (Murray et al., 1989). Although the study by Murray and his colleagues produced prevention effects that were present for 4 years, the RAND study produced effects that totally eroded by the time of the 3-year follow-up, which took place at the end of the ninth grade.

The results of several longer term follow-up studies have overshadowed many of the advances of the past few years. These studies (Ellickson, Bell, & McGuigan, 1993; Flay et al., 1989; Murray et al., 1989) have all indicated that prevention effects produced during junior high school totally erode by the end of high school. Dryfoos (1993) recently suggested that the results of these follow-up studies indicate that school-based interventions are not powerful enough to produce lasting prevention effects. She argued for the use of multicomponent prevention approaches similar to that employed by Pentz and her colleagues (see Pentz, Chapter 10 of this volume), which includes components targeting the family and the larger community.

However, before we sound the death knell of school-based interventions or conclude that they are not capable of producing lasting effects, it is worth considering possible explanations for the fact that prevention effects have deteriorated in these studies. Several factors have been suggested as possible explanations for the apparent erosion of prevention effects (Resnicow & Botvin, 1993). The intervention approaches tested in these studies may not have produced durable effects lasting until the end of high school because (a) the length of the intervention may have been inadequate, (b) booster sessions either were not included or were inadequate, (c) the intervention was not implemented with sufficient fidelity to the intervention model, and/ or (d) the intervention model was based on faulty assumptions, was incomplete, or was otherwise deficient.

Long-term follow-up data from a large-scale prevention trial conducted by Botvin and his colleagues (Botvin, Baker, et al., 1995) demonstrate that school-based prevention programs can produce long-term reductions in drug use. These data also suggest that previous follow-up studies may have failed to show results for one or more of the reasons suggested above. Students (N = 3,597) from 56 schools in New York State who participated in a drug abuse prevention trial starting in the fall of 1985 (when they were in the 7th grade) were located, and data were collected at the end of the 12th grade in school, by telephone, and/or by mail. The average length of follow-up was 6 years after the initial baseline assessment. Follow-up results indicated that there were significantly fewer smokers, "heavy" drinkers, or marijuana users among students who received the LST prevention program during the 7th grade and had booster sessions during the 8th and 9th grades.

PREVENTING POLYDRUG USE

In order to assess the impact of the prevention program on more serious levels of drug involvement, treatment and control students in the Botvin, Baker, et al. (1995) follow-up study were also compared in terms of polydrug use (defined in this study as the monthly or weekly use of multiple gateway substances). At the end of the 12th grade, there were 44% fewer LST students than controls who used all three gateway drugs (tobacco, alcohol, and marijuana) one or more times per month and 66% fewer LST students who reported using all three substances one or more times per week. Prevention effects were also found for 12 hypothesized mediating variables in the direction of decreased drug abuse risk. The strongest prevention effects were produced for the students who received the most complete implementation of the prevention program. Finally, although prevention effects were produced regardless of whether providers were trained at a formal training workshop with periodic feedback and consultation or merely viewed a provider training videotape and received no feedback or support from project staff, the strongest effects were produced by the teachers who attended annual training workshops and received ongoing support. Prevention effects were found using both the individual and school as the unit of analysis. Moreover, attrition rates were equivalent for treatment and control conditions, as were pretest levels of drug use for the final analysis sample. This supports the argument that prevention effects were not the result of differential attrition or the nonequivalence of the conditions.

PREVENTING ILLICIT DRUG USE

An underlying assumption of primary prevention efforts is that if they prevent or reduce the use of tobacco, alcohol, and/or marijuana, they will have a corresponding impact on the use of other substances further along the developmental progression. In other words, preventing gateway drug use will also translate into later reductions in the use of illicit drugs such as cocaine or heroin. However, although this rationale is commonly used to justify targeting gateway drug use, it has never been tested. This issue was addressed in the Botvin, Baker, et al. (1995) study by analyzing data collected from an anonymous subsample of students involved in the long-term follow-up study described above. Data were collected by mail from 454 individuals (mean age = 18.86) who were contacted after the end of the 12th grade. The length of follow-up was 6.5 years from the initial baseline. The survey assessed the use of 13 illicit drug categories following those used by the University of Michigan Monitoring the Future study (e.g., Johnston, O'Malley, & Bachman, 1994). Significantly lower levels of drug involvement (relative to controls) were found for the LST students on two composite measures of illicit drug use as well as for specific drug categories. There were lower levels of illicit drug use by the composite measure for illicit drug use overall and by the measure of illicit drug use other than marijuana. By individual drug category, significantly lower levels of use were found for LSD/other psychedelics, PCP, heroin, and inhalants.

Prevention With Minority Youth

A gap in the drug abuse prevention field that has only begun to be addressed recently concerns the lack of high-quality research with racial/ethnic minority populations. In developing preventive interventions for minority populations, two strategies have been followed. One strategy, based on the assumption that the etiology of drug abuse is different for different populations, involves the development of interventions designed to be population-specific. The other strategy, based on the assumption that the etiology of drug abuse is more similar than different across populations, involves the development of interventions designed to be generalizable to a broad range of individuals from different populations.

Our own research at Cornell with the combined resistance skills and generic life skills approach called Life Skills Training (LST) has followed the second course—making modifications where warranted to maximize generalizability, cultural sensitivity, relevance, and acceptability to varied populations. Although there is only limited data concerning the etiology of drug abuse among minority populations, existing evidence suggests that there is substantial overlap in the factors promoting and maintaining drug use/abuse among different racial/ethnic groups (Bettes, Dusenbury, Kerner, James-Ortiz, & Botvin, 1990; Botvin, Baker, et al., 1993; Botvin, Epstein, Schinke, & Diaz, 1994; Botvin, Goldberg, Botvin, & Dusenbury, 1993; Dusenbury et al., 1992; Epstein, Botvin, Diaz, & Schinke, 1995; Newcomb, Chapter 6 of this volume).

A second reason for pursuing this course is that most urban schools contain individuals from multiple racial/ethnic groups. Therefore, even if there were differences across populations warranting different interventions, it would be extremely difficult to implement separate interventions for different racial/ethnic groups for both logistical and political reasons. Thus, given the choice of two or more effective interventions, it would be important to give consideration to issues of feasibility as well as effectiveness.

Although some Asians have been included in the studies conducted in our research, the major racial/ethnic groups involved in the most recent research studies with minority populations are African American and Hispanic youth. As was the case with previous research with white, middle-class youth, the initial focus of this research was on cigarette smoking, followed by a focus on other gateway substances. Research has been conducted over the past 8 years to test the generalizability of the LST approach. This research has progressed through the following sequence: (a) exploratory (qualitative) research consisting of focus group testing and key informant interviews, (b) expert review of intervention methods and materials, (c) consumer-based review of intervention materials and methods, (d) small-scale pilot studies, and (e) large-scale randomized field trials. Modifications in intervention materials and methods were made as necessary throughout the process of development and testing. None of the modifications deriving from the etiologic literature concerning minority youth or the review process delineated above involved changes to the underlying prevention strategy. Rather, these changes related to the reading level of intervention materials, the inclusion of appropriate graphics (e.g., illustrations or pictures of minority youth), language, role-play scenarios, and examples appropriate to the target population.

HISPANIC YOUTH

The first study testing the effectiveness of the LST approach with a minority population involved predominantly Hispanic youth (Botvin, Dusenbury,

Baker, James-Ortiz, & Kerner, 1989). The study included 471 7th graders (46% male) attending eight public schools in the New York metropolitan area. The sample consisted of predominantly lower income Hispanic students (74%), as well as a small percentage of African American (11%) and white (4%) students. Schools were randomly assigned to conditions. Significant posttest differences between the experimental and the control group were found, controlling for pretest smoking status, gender, social risk for becoming a smoker, and acculturation. Intervention effects were also found for knowledge concerning the immediate consequences of smoking, smoking prevalence, the social acceptability of smoking, decision making, normative expectations concerning adult smoking, and normative expectations concerning peer smoking.

Data from a large-scale randomized trial (Botvin et al., 1992) also demonstrated significant program effects when implemented with predominantly Hispanic urban minority students. This study involved 3,501 students from 47 public and parochial schools in the greater New York City area. Intervention materials were modified (based on the results of our pilot study and input from consultants, teachers, and students) to increase their relevance to Hispanic youth as well as to ensure a high degree of cultural sensitivity. Schools were randomly assigned to experimental and control conditions. Using school means as the unit of analysis, significant reductions in cigarette smoking were found for the adolescents who received the LST program when compared to controls at the end of the 7th grade. Follow-up data demonstrated the continued presence of prevention effects through to the end of the 10th grade (Botvin, 1994).

AFRICAN AMERICAN YOUTH

Before testing the LST approach on African American youth, we once again subjected the intervention materials and methods to an extensive review to determine their cultural appropriateness for this population. Following this, a small-scale study was conducted with nine urban junior high schools in northern New Jersey (Botvin, Batson, et al., 1989). The pretest involved 608 seventh-grade students. Of these, 221 were in the treatment group and 387 in the control group. The sample was 87% African American, 10% Hispanic, 1% white, and 2% other. Schools were randomly assigned to treatment and control conditions within each of the three participating communities. Students in the treatment schools received the LST program; students in the control schools received the smoking education curriculum normally provided by their school. Throughout the prevention program, classroom observation data and teacher feedback were collected.

Results indicated that there were significantly fewer posttest smokers in the treatment group than in the control group based on moking status in the past month. Significant treatment effects were also found for knowledge of smoking consequences, normative expectations regarding adult smoking prevalence, and normative expectations regarding peer smoking prevalence.

A large-scale prevention trial involving predominantly African American youth from 46 inner-city schools in northern New Jersey provided additional empirical support for the effectiveness of this prevention approach with this population (Botvin & Cardwell, 1992). Schools were randomly assigned to treatment ($n = 21$) and control ($n = 25$) conditions after first blocking on school-wide smoking rates. Students ($N = 2,512$) were pretested in the spring of 1990 while they were in the seventh grade, posttested in the early winter of 1991 and posttested again in the spring of 1991 at the end of the eighth grade. In the treatment condition, all eligible classes in participating schools received the LST intervention; in the control group all classes received the health (smoking) education normally provided to the students. The final analysis sample was 97% minority and 3% white; of the total sample, 78% were African American, 13% were Hispanic, 1% were Native American, 1% were Asian, and 3% classified themselves as "other." Initial posttest results showed significantly less smoking for students in the treatment group who received the intervention in the seventh grade and booster sessions in the fall of the eighth grade when compared with both the non-booster-treatment group and the controls. At the final follow-up, students who received booster sessions and the original intervention had significantly lower rates of smoking than the controls.

GENERIC VERSUS CULTURALLY FOCUSED APPROACHES

A recently completed study tested the relative effectiveness of the LST approach, which had been previously found to be effective with a broad range of students, and a prevention approach specifically tailored to African American and Hispanic youth (Botvin, Schinke, Epstein, & Diaz, 1994). Both prevention approaches were similar in that they taught students a combination of generic "life skills" and skills specific to resisting offers to use drugs. However, the tailored or culturally focused approach was designed to embed the skills-training material in myths and legends derived from the African American and Hispanic cultures. Six junior high schools containing predominantly (95%) minority students were assigned to (a) receive the LST program, (b) receive the culturally focused prevention approach, or (c) serve as an information-only control group. The sample was 48% African American, 37% Hispanic, 5% white, 3% Asian, and 8% other. Students were pretested and posttested during the seventh grade. Results indicated that students in both skills-training prevention conditions had lower intentions to drink beer or wine relative to the information-only controls, and that the students in the LST condition had lower intentions to drink hard liquor and use illicit drugs. Both skills-training conditions also influenced several mediating variables in a direction consistent with nondrug use. According to these results, both prevention approaches were equally effective, producing significant reductions in behavioral intentions to drink and use illicit drugs, and suggesting that a generic drug abuse prevention approach with high generalizability may be as effective as one that is tailored to individual ethnic populations. These data, therefore, provide support for the hypothesis that a single drug abuse prevention strategy can be used effectively with multiethnic populations.

Follow-up data ($N = 456$) collected 2 years later at the end of the ninth grade found significant prevention effects for both prevention approaches (Botvin, Schinke, Epstein, & Diaz, in press). Students in both skills-training prevention conditions drank alcohol less often, became drunk less often, drank less alcohol per drinking occasion, and had lower intentions to use alcohol in the future relative to the controls. However, these data also showed that the culturally focused intervention produced significantly stronger effects on these variables than the generic LST approach. The findings of the follow-up study are particularly interesting because although they suggest that it may be possible to develop a preventive intervention that is effective for a relatively broad range of students, they also indicate that tailoring interventions to specific populations can increase their effectiveness with inner-city minority populations.

SUMMARY

Substantial progress has been made in drug abuse prevention over the past 15 years. It has become clear that some of the most widely used prevention approaches are either ineffective or of unproven effectiveness. Notable among these are traditional prevention approaches that rely on the provision of information concerning the adverse consequences of drug abuse, affective education, and alternatives to drug use. More recent research has demonstrated the efficacy of prevention approaches that focus on psychosocial factors associated with drug use initiation and/or drug abuse. These approaches emphasize the teaching of social resistance skills either alone or in combination with generic personal and social skills. Studies testing the efficacy of these approaches have shown that they are capable of reducing drug use for up to 6 years. Although most of this research has been conducted with cigarette smoking, prevention effects have also been demonstrated for alcohol and marijuana use. Limited evidence also exists showing that school-based drug abuse prevention programs can produce reductions in more serious levels of drug involvement beyond the occasional use of a single gateway drug. Prevention effects have been produced for weekly gateway polydrug use as well as for the use of illicit drugs other than marijuana such as LSD, PCP, heroin, and inhalants.

Research with these prevention approaches has been tested with predominantly white, middle-class populations. A few studies, however, have also provided preliminary evidence of the utility of these approaches with inner-city minority populations consisting mainly of African American and Hispanic youth. These data provide empirical support for the thesis that the same type of prevention approach may be effective with multiple populations. Moreover, the evidence from one recently conducted 3-year study indicates that tailoring interventions to the target populations can further increase their effectiveness. Thus, prevention approaches such as the LST approach can be used effectively with a broad range of individuals from different ethnic backgrounds when students from different populations are mixed together in the same schools. On the other hand, when schools consist of a single ethnic minority group, adapting a proven prevention program to that particular population can further enhance its effectiveness. If these findings hold up after additional research is conducted, this would greatly simplify the process of disseminating and implementing effective school-based drug abuse prevention programs throughout the United States.

Although considerable progress has been made in school-based drug abuse prevention, more research is necessary with ethnic minority populations either to extend the work conducted so far with the current generation of psychosocial prevention approaches or to identify new prevention approaches. Nonetheless, the available evidence provides important information about effective prevention models and a useful foundation on which to develop, test, and refine future drug abuse prevention approaches suitable to a broad range of individuals from a diversity of racial/ethnic backgrounds.

References

Arkin, R. M., Roemhild, H. J., Johnson, C. A., Luepker, R. V., & Murray, D. M. (1981). The Minnesota smoking prevention program: A seventh grade health curriculum supplement. *Journal of School Health, 51,* 616-661.

Bandura, A. (1977). *Social learning theory.* Englewood Cliffs, NJ: Prentice Hall.

Bettes, B. A., Dusenbury, L., Kerner, J., James-Ortiz, S., & Botvin, G. J. (1990). Ethnicity and psychosocial factors in alcohol and tobacco use in adolescence. *Child Development, 61,* 557-565.

Blum, R., & Richards, L. (1979). Youthful drug use. In R. I. Dupont, A. Goldstein, & J. O'Donnell (Eds.), *Handbook on drug abuse* (pp. 257-267). Washington, DC: Government Printing Office.

Botvin, G. J. (1994). *Smoking prevention among New York Hispanic youth: Results of a four-year evaluation study.* Unpublished manuscript.

Botvin, G. J., Baker, E., Botvin, E. M., Dusenbury, L., Cardwell, J., & Diaz, T. (1993). Factors promoting cigarette smoking among black youth: A causal modeling approach. *Addictive Behaviors, 18,* 397-405.

Botvin, G. J., Baker, E., Botvin, E. M., Filazzola, A. D., & Millman, R. B. (1984). Alcohol abuse prevention through the development of personal and social competence: A pilot study. *Journal of Studies on Alcohol, 45,* 550-552.

Botvin, G. J., Baker, E., Dusenbury, L., Botvin, E. M., & Diàz, T. (1995). Long-term follow-up results of a randomized drug abuse prevention trial in a white middle-class population. *Journal of the American Medical Association, 273,* 1106-1112.

Botvin, G. J., Baker, E., Dusenbury, L., Tortu, S., & Botvin, E. M. (1990). Preventing adolescent drug abuse through a multimodal cognitive-behavioral approach: Results of a three-year study. *Journal of Consulting and Clinical Psychology, 58,* 437-446.

Botvin, G. J., Baker, E., Filazzola, A., & Botvin, E. M. (1990). A cognitive-behavioral approach to substance abuse prevention: A one-year follow-up. *Addictive Behaviors, 15,* 47-63.

Botvin, G. J., Baker, E., Renick, N., Filazzola, A. D., & Botvin, E. M. (1984). A cognitive-behavioral approach to substance abuse prevention. *Addictive Behaviors, 9,* 137-147.

Botvin, G. J., Batson, H., Witts-Vitale, S., Bess, V., Baker, E., & Dusenbury, L. (1989). A psychosocial approach to smoking prevention for urban black youth. *Public Health Reports, 104,* 573-582.

Botvin, G. J., & Cardwell, J. (1992). *Primary prevention (smoking) of cancer in black populations.* (Final Report to National Cancer Institute [NIH], Grant No. N01-CN-6508). New York: Cornell University Medical College.

Botvin, G. J., Dusenbury, L., Baker, E., James-Ortiz, S., Botvin, E. M., & Kerner, J. (1992). Smoking prevention among urban minority youth: Assessing effects on outcome and mediating variables. *Health Psychology, 11*(5), 290-299.

Botvin, G. J., Dusenbury, L., Baker, E., James-Ortiz, S., & Kerner, J. (1989). A skills training approach to smoking prevention among Hispanic youth. *Journal of Behavioral Medicine, 12,* 279-296.

Botvin, G. J., & Eng, A. (1982). The efficacy of a multicomponent approach to the prevention of cigarette smoking. *Preventive Medicine, 11,* 199-211.

Botvin, G. J., Eng, A., & Williams, C. L. (1980). Preventing the onset of cigarette smoking through life skills training. *Preventive Medicine, 9,* 135-143.

Botvin, G. J., Epstein, J. A., Schinke, S. P., & Diaz, T. (1994). Correlates and predictors of smoking among inner city youth. *Developmental and Behavioral Pediatrics, 15,* 67-73.

Botvin, G. J., Goldberg, C. J., Botvin, E. M., & Dusenbury, L. (1993). Smoking behavior of adolescents exposed to cigarette advertising. *Public Health Reports, 108,* 217-224.

Botvin, G. J., Renick, N., & Baker, E. (1983). The effects of scheduling format and booster sessions on a broad-spectrum psychosocial approach to smoking prevention. *Journal of Behavioral Medicine, 6,* 359-379.

Botvin, G. J., Schinke, S. P., Epstein, J. A., & Diaz, T. (1994). The effectiveness of culturally focused and generic skills training approaches to alcohol and drug abuse prevention among minority youth. *Psychology of Addictive Behaviors, 8,* 116-127.

Botvin, G. J., Schinke, S. P., Epstein, J. A., & Diaz, T. (in press). The effectiveness of culturally-focused and generic skills training approaches to alcohol and drug abuse prevention among minority youth: Two-year follow-up results. *Psychology of Addictive Behaviors.*

Dusenbury, L., Kerner, J. F., Baker, E., Botvin, G. J., James-Ortiz, S., & Zauber, A. (1992). Predictors of smoking prevalence among New York Latino youth. *American Journal of Public Health, 82,* 55-58.

Dryfoos, J. G. (1993). Preventing substance use: Rethinking strategies. *American Journal of Public Health, 83,* 793-795.

Ellickson, P. L., & Bell, R. M. (1990). Drug prevention in junior high: A multi-site longitudinal test. *Science, 247,* 1299-1305.

Ellickson, P. L., Bell, R. M., & McGuigan, K. (1993). Preventing adolescent drug use: Long term results of a junior high program. *American Journal of Public Health, 83,* 856-861.

Epstein, J. A., Botvin, G. J., Diaz, T., & Schinke, S. P. (1995). The role of social factors and individual characteristics in promoting alcohol among inner-city minority youth. *Journal of Studies on Alcohol, 56,* 39-46.

Evans, R. I. (1976). Smoking in children: Developing a social psychological strategy of deterrence. *Preventive Medicine, 5,* 122-127.

Evans, R. I., Rozelle, R. M., Mittlemark, M. B., Hansen, W. B., Bane, A. L., & Havis, J. (1978). Deterring the onset of smoking in children: Knowledge of immediate physiological effects and coping with peer pressure, media pressure, and parent modeling. *Journal of Applied Social Psychology, 8,* 126-135.

Fishbein, M. (1977). Consumer beliefs and behavior with respect to cigarette smoking: A critical analysis of the public literature. In *Federal Trade Commission report to Congress pursuant to the Public Health Cigarette Smoking Act of 1976.* Washington, DC: Government Printing Office.

Fisher, D. A., Armstrong, B. K., & deKler, N. H. (1983). A randomized-controlled trial of education for prevention of smoking in 12 year-old children. Paper presented at the 5th World Conference on Smoking and Health, Winnipeg, Canada.

Flay, B. R., Koepke, D., Thomson, S. J., Santi, S., Best, J. A., & Brown, K. S. (1989). Six-year follow up of the first Waterloo school smoking prevention trial. *American Journal of Public Health, 79,* 1371-1376.

Gilchrist, L. D., & Schinke, S. P. (1983). Self-control skills for smoking prevention. In P. F. Engstrom, P. N. Anderson, & L. E. Mortenson (Eds.), *Advances in cancer control* (pp. 125-130). New York: Alan R. Liss.

Hurd, P., Johnson, C. A., Pechacek, T., Bast, C. P., Jacobs, D., & Luepker, R. (1980). Prevention of cigarette smoking in 7th grade students. *Journal of Behavioral Medicine, 3,* 15-28.

Jessor, R., & Jessor, S. L. (1977). *Problem behavior and psychosocial development: A longitudinal study of youth.* New York: Academic Press.

Johnston, L. D., O'Malley, P. M., & Bachman, J. G. (1994). *National survey results of drug use from Monitoring the Future study, 1975-1993: Vol. 1. Secondary school students.* Rockville, MD: U.S. Department of Health and Human Services.

Jones, C. L. & Battjes, R. J. (Eds.). (1985). *Etiology of drug abuse: Implications for prevention* (NIDA Research Monograph No. 56). Washington, DC: Government Printing Office.

Kandel, D. B. (1978). Convergences in prospective longitudinal surveys of drug use in normal populations. In D. B. Kandel (Ed.), *Longitudinal research on drug use: Empirical findings and methodological issues* (pp. 3-38). Washington, DC: Hemisphere.

Kearney, A. L., & Hines, M. H. (1980). Evaluation of the effectiveness of a drug prevention education program. *Journal of Drug Education, 10,* 127-134.

Kim, S. (1988). A short- and long-term evaluation of "Here's Looking at You." II. *Journal of Drug Education, 18,* 235-242.

Luepker, R. V., Johnson, C. A., Murray, D. M., & Pechacek, T. F. (1983). Prevention of cigarette smoking: Three year follow-up of educational programs for youth. *Journal of Behavioral Medicine, 6,* 53-61.

McAlister, A., Perry, C. L., Killen, J., Slinkard, L. A., & Maccoby, N. (1980). Pilot study of smoking, alcohol, and drug abuse prevention. *American Journal of Public Health, 70,* 719-721.

McGuire, W. J. (1964). Inducing resistance to persuasion: Some contemporary approaches. In L. Berkowitz (Ed.), *Advances in experimental social psychology* (pp. 192-227). New York: Academic Press.

McGuire, W. J. (1968). The nature of attitudes and attitude change. In G. Lindzey & E. Aronson (Eds.), *Handbook of social psychology* (pp. 136-314). Reading, MA: Addison-Wesley.

Meyer, R. E., & Mirin, S. M. (1979). *The heroin stimulus: Implications for a theory of addiction.* New York: Plenum.

Murray, D. M., Davis-Hearn, M., Goldman, A. I., Pirie, P., & Luepker, R. V. (1988). Four and five year follow-up results from four seventh-grade smoking prevention strategies. *Journal of Behavioral Medicine, 11,* 395-405.

Murray, D. M., Pirie, P., Luepker, R. V., & Pallonen, U. (1989). Five and six-year follow-up results from four seventh-grade smoking prevention strategies. *Journal of Behavioral Medicine, 12,* 207-218.

Newcomb, M. D., & Bentler, P. M. (1988). *Consequences of adolescent drug use: Impact on the lives of young adults.* Newbury Park: Sage.

Pentz, M. A. (1983). Prevention of adolescent substance abuse through social skill development. In T. J. Glynn, C. G. Leukefeld, & J. B. Ludford (Eds.), *Preventing adolescent drug abuse: Intervention strategies* (NIDA Research Monograph No. 47, pp. 195-232). Washington, DC: Government Printing Office.

Perry, C., Killen, J., Slinkard, L. A., & McAlister, A. L. (1983). Peer teaching and smoking prevention among junior high students. *Adolescence, 9,* 277-281.

Resnicow, K., & Botvin, G. J. (1993). School-based substance use prevention programs: Why do effects decay? *Preventive Medicine, 22,* 484-490.

Schinke, S. P. (1984). Preventing teenage pregnancy. In M. Hersen, R. M. Eisler, & P. M. Miller (Eds.), *Progress in behavior modification* (16th ed., pp. 31-63). New York: Academic Press.

Schinke, S. P., & Gilchrist, L. D. (1983). Primary prevention of tobacco smoking. *Journal of School Health, 53,* 416-419.

Schinke, S. P., & Gilchrist, L. D. (1984). Preventing cigarette smoking with youth. *Journal of Primary Prevention, 5,* 48-56.

Swisher, J. D., Crawford, J. L., Goldstein, R., & Yura, M. (1971). Drug education: Pushing or preventing? *Peabody Journal of Education, 49,* 68-75.

Telch, M. J., Killen, J. D., McAlister, A. L., Perry, C. L., & Maccoby, N. (1982). Long- term follow-up of a pilot project on smoking prevention with adolescents. *Journal of Behavioral Medicine, 5,* 1-8.

Wechsler, H. (1976). Alcohol intoxication and drug use among teenagers. *Journal of Studies on Alcohol, 37,* 1672-1677.

Prevention Research in Multiethnic Communities

Developing Community Support and Collaboration, and Adapting Research Methods

Mary Ann Pentz

Increasingly, research indicates that preventive interventions aimed at changing social influences on drug use have shown the most significant effects on delaying the onset of tobacco, alcohol, and marijuana use in adolescents, with some programs also slowing the progression of drug use (Hansen, 1992). Social influences include modeling of drug use by peers, family members, and significant adults; overt or covert sanction of drug use by these individuals; consequences of drug use; availability of and access to drugs; and, perhaps most prominently, perceived social norms for drug use in a community. Social influences prevention programs heavily emphasize social learning theory principles of behavior change, including cognitive (self-efficacy) and behavioral (skills mastery) change at the individual or personal (p) level as well as cognitive (vicarious modeling and perceived peer norms) and behavioral (skills application in interpersonal situations) change at the situational (s) level (Bandura, 1977). An underlying assumption of these programs is that the cognitive-behavior change principles of skills modeling, rehearsal, feedback, and practice are adaptable to any ethnic population or culture because participants generate their own skills situations. Based on these principles, social influences programs appear to be effective, whether they teach counteractive skills specific to drug use or broader social skills that can be applied

193

to counteracting drug use influences (Botvin & Botvin, 1992; Hansen, 1992; Tobler, 1992).

Most of the published prevention research has focused on effects of social influences programs delivered in public schools, with school-attending youth, the majority of whom are white (Botvin & Botvin, 1992; Tobler, 1992). Recently, several of these programs have been adapted for use with different ethnic groups in and out of school settings, including African American, Hispanic, and American Indian youth (e.g., Botvin et al., 1989; Johnson et al., 1990; Oetting & Beauvais, 1991; Schilling, Schinke, Nichols, & Botvin, 1989). Results thus far suggest that social influences approaches can be successfully adapted to different racial/ethnic groups without sacrificing social learning theory principles of person- and situation-level change. Although limitations in research designs have prohibited determining whether the magnitude of prevention program effects is the same for different ethnic groups as for white populations, significant program effects that have been found suggest that social influences approaches to prevention are effective with, as well as adaptable to, multiethnic groups. These results are consistent with epidemiological studies, which have shown similar patterns of social influences as risk factors for drug use among white and several different ethnic groups of adolescents (e.g., Bachman, Johnston, & O'Malley, 1991; Johnson et al., 1990).

It appears, then, that person-level (p) and situation-level (s) factors that constitute social influences on adolescent drug use development and prevention may be generalizable across multiethnic groups in and out of school settings. It is logical to assume that these same principles should apply to broader, community-based drug prevention efforts developed in multiethnic communities. However, community-based prevention requires that one pay attention to environmental (e) as well as p and s factors in drug use epidemiology and prevention, particularly when organizing community leaders (Sarason, 1974).

Several examples of effective community organization have been reported in the research literature, most of which have developed behavioral preventive interventions based on p and s factors and have used environmental-level risk factors to predict a community's interpretation of a health problem and likely motivation to support and participate in a preventive intervention (Altman, 1986; Bracht, 1990). The community heart health studies (e.g., Stanford, Minnesota, Pawtucket, North Karelia) have developed direct patient-client, interpersonal skills, and mass media interventions for heart disease prevention based on p and s levels of behavior change (Altman, 1986; Bracht, 1990; Farquhar, Fortmann, & Maccoby, 1984; Perry, Klepp, & Shultz, 1988; Puska et al., 1989). Interventions are delivered by professionals (e.g., physicians, nurses), paraprofessionals (health educators), and volunteers based on s-level factors of trainer-trainee compatibility. Community leaders are prompted to organize by highly credible medical professionals, with some attention to e-level factors of community resources, and perceived importance of heart disease prevention. Most of these studies have involved primarily white communities. Other community prevention studies have focused more on e level factors to develop interventions and organize community leaders (e.g., Brown, 1984; Chavis & Wandersman, 1990). On this level, interventions tend to consist of events and policy changes rather than program delivery. Leaders are typically prompted to organize at the grassroots level in response to a critical community incident involving alcohol or other drug abuse. Most of these studies have also involved primarily white communities. Community action studies on changing adverse physical or social conditions have focused almost entirely on e-level factors to mobilize the community and organize leaders (Brown, 1984; Chavis & Wandersman, 1990; Feighery & Rogers, 1990; Florin, Chavis, Wandersman, & Rich, in press; Florin & Wandersman, 1990). With few exceptions (e.g., Florin et al., in press), interventions tend to consist of lobbying for resources and improvements in existing service delivery systems rather than program delivery. Leaders are prompted to organize at the grassroots or neighborhood level in response to the adverse condition. Unlike other community prevention studies, community action projects have involved multiethnic communities, particularly African American and Jewish communities. Finally, several recent drug abuse prevention demonstration studies have used research agency guidelines to develop community coalitions for drug abuse prevention; development of interventions and organization of community leaders is essentially theory-free and iterative, and community driven rather than research driven (e.g., Fighting Back, 1993; Wandersman & Goodman, 1992). Leaders are prompted to organize to be eligible for receipt of research agency funds. Ethnicity of communities varies widely.

Almost none of these community prevention studies have attempted to integrate p, s, and e factors in organizing the community. Certainly none have addressed acculturation and other issues that could affect the conduct of prevention research in multiethnic communities. The next sections summarize issues in the conduct of prevention research in multiethnic communities and outline an integrated $p \times s \times e$ theoretical perspective that attempts to reinterpret some p, s, and e factors for multiethnic communities.

Issues in the Conduct of Prevention
Research With Multiethnic Communities

The range and interdependent nature of the issues and needs of multiethnic communities are complex, and beyond the scope of this chapter. For a more in-depth discussion, the reader is referred to several reviews of the literature (e.g., Landrine & Klonoff, 1992; Oetting & Beauvais, 1991; Pentz, 1994, in press-a). In summary, however, at least four major issues should be considered in planning prevention research in multiethnic communities: (a) the stereotype of equating ethnicity with risk; (b) cultural themes of health, disease, and prevention; (c) the stereotype of researcher as adversary; and (d) acculturation stress. As the remainder of this chapter demonstrates, each of these should be acknowledged by researchers and used as a point of discussion and feedback with community leaders when assessing community readiness for prevention and subsequently gaining support for community organization.

EQUATING ETHNICITY WITH RISK

Two disturbing trends have emerged in recent federal research announcements for prevention with minority populations: the uncritical and growing acceptance of the notions that (a) preventive interventions that have already been developed on white populations will not generalize to different ethnic groups and that (b) minority (ethnic) groups are at higher risk for drug use and other diseases than whites. Three sources are responsible. First, the announcements themselves perpetuate the notion that these trends must be accurate. Researchers, in order to secure funding, produce or reinterpret research information to support these notions, and over time, minority or ethnic status *becomes* a risk factor for drug use. Second, national archival databases, such as Drug Use Forecasting (DUF) and the Drug Abuse Warning Network (DAWN), show an overrepresentation of minority drug abusers in public prisons and hospitals. The same trends were found for representation of minorities in the mental health system in the 1950s and 1960s. Reexamination of those data indicated that the reason minorities are overrepresented is primarily an economic one, and secondarily—and less easily demonstrated—a prejudicial labeling one. Historically, ethnic groups lack the resources and finances to avoid prosecution and to obtain private care. In our own data on adolescent and parent drug use, minority status and socioeconomic status are very highly correlated ($r = .75 - .78$), and moderately to highly intercorrelated with drug use ($r > .45$). However, when each is controlled for the other factor as well as other demographic covariates, SES retains the relationship to drug use, and the minority status relationship almost disappears. These results, as well as the results of the epidemiological and prevention studies mentioned earlier, would suggest that minority/ethnicity as a risk factor is a proxy for SES. Ironically, the third source of the perpetuated stereotype may be minority interest groups, which note the lack of available preventive services and fiscal resources as an argument for needing more or different resources than other populations. An increase in drug abuse risk resulting from a lack of preventive services, again, is an economic rather than an ethnic issue. The same economic argument can be applied to predicting poor implementation and diffusion of prevention programs (see the ethnic validity model, Javier, 1992). This is particularly apparent in inner-city urban areas where minority groups tend to reside and where services of all types tend to be inadequate or overburdened. Given the confounding of ethnicity and SES with drug use risk, let us examine the relatively sparse literature on the special cultural needs of ethnic groups that appear to be independent of SES.

CULTURAL THEMES OF HEALTH, DISEASE, AND PREVENTION

Results of anthropologic research, using primarily ethnographic methods of observation, have yielded several cultural themes pertinent to the conduct of prevention research in multiethnic communities. Health is regarded in some cultures as a slow process of environmental and personal accommodation and a sense of well-being, self- esteem, and personal wholeness rather than a set of observable physical indicators (Landrine & Klonoff, 1992). Thus, for example, physiological differences found between Native Americans, Asians, and whites in alcohol assimilation and flush response, and between African Americans and whites in smoking uptake and low birthweight, may have little meaning to ethnic cultures outside of the medical profession (Landrine & Klonoff, 1992; Pentz, 1994). Disease is perceived as a lack of accommodation and wholeness, with symptoms in some cultures described in terms of good versus bad blood or hot versus cold, rather than prevalence rates of drug use or other disease-risk behavior (Landrine & Klonoff, 1992). In the specific case of drug use, use is at times a part of ritual, and quantitative indexes of abuse are not as meaningful as indexes of cultural rejection (Caetano & Medina-Mora, 1988; Legge & Sherlock, 1991). Principles of prevention may not be as meaningful as concepts of a slow evolution of well-being and healing. Western societal preventive intervention tools of education, social support seeking, resources, and independence may not be relevant or may require reinterpretation in terms of self-value growth, confidant and family support, and interdependency (Fisher, Auslander, Sussman, Owens, & Jackson-Thompson, 1992). Skills-related prevention concepts of verbal communication, peer groups, and group peer pressure situations may not be as important as nonverbal communication, identification of what constitutes a peer group, and covert (internalized) situations for behavior (Schilling et al., 1989). Finally, identifying a population or community as at risk on the basis of an epidemiologically defined set of risk criteria may not be as meaningful or as motivating as redefining *risk* in terms of a general population or community "anomie" (see Landrine & Klonoff, 1992; Hawkins, Catalano, & Miller, 1992).

RESEARCHER AS ADVERSARY

Several overviews of prevention research suggest a bipolar tendency of communities to organize for prevention either as a result of grassroots, "bottom-up" pressure in response to a critical negative event or chronic condition, or as part of a researcher/expert, "top-down" plan prompted by a funding opportunity (e.g., Giachello, 1992; Goodman & Steckler, 1990; Pentz, Alexander, Cormack, & Light, 1990; Pentz, Cormack, Flay, Hansen, & Johnson, 1986; Rothman, 1979). The published literature suggests that ethnic and multiethnic communities tend to organize at the grassroots level and that if the project is initially prompted by research, they may reject what is perceived as white or majority tenets of research (see Chavis & Wandersman, 1990; Oetting & Beauvais, 1991; Pentz, 1994). Little is known about whether rejection of research-driven community organization by multiethnic communities is due to lack of access to prevention researchers, distrust of researchers, or failure of researchers to recognize and "package" prevention in terms of the community's *perceived* needs, norms, and solutions (Pentz et al., 1986). In approaching multiethnic communities, the prevention researcher might assume that all three possibilities are operating, and make changes accordingly. The changes include, but are not limited to, linking with local colleges and academicians and acting as a process consultant to reframe the utility of research as needs assessment or accountability to the community, and intervention as a trial solution to the community's stated needs.

Conclusions drawn from recent conferences on prevention research in minority communities, as well as reexamination of the process of existing community-based prevention programs, suggest that the most effective strategy for organizing communities for prevention may be a combined top-down/ bottom-up, community/research partnership (Altman, 1986; Pentz, 1994). Characteristics of and research predictions about past bipolar tendencies of communities, as well as characteristics and predictions about prevention based on a balanced community/research partnership, are shown in Table 10.1.

ACCULTURATION STRESS

A final consideration is that communities populated by one dominant minority group, populated by mixed minority groups, or experiencing a rapid in-migration of one or more minority groups, may be subject to several stressors on the community's capacity to organize effectively for prevention,

TABLE 10.1 Continuum of Community/Versus Research-Driven Perspectives on Effective Community Prevention, Adapted to Multiethnic Communities

	Community-Driven	Community-Research Partnership	Research-Driven
Theory	Atheoretical	Integrated $p \times s \times e$ theory, with attention to acculturation	Integrated
Model	None	Structural + process	Structural + process
Organization	Grassroots, bottom-up	Interdependent top-down, bottom-up	Top-down
Process	Iterative	Flexible sequential	Fixed sequential
Accountability	Anecdotal information, number served, or none	Anecdotal + number served + program evaluation	Research
Experimental control	None	Moderate	High
Projected effects	Unknown	High	Weak to moderate
Generalizability	None	High, with cultural adaptation	Low, no cultural adaptation

including attributions of helplessness, which tend to depress community resident feelings of empowerment; attributions by others that minority status is equated with high risk for drug abuse; and difficulty of acculturation to majority social norms for behavior (Landrine & Klonoff, 1992; Pentz, 1994, in press-a). Attempting to accommodate to majority norms, minority communities may show an unusually high tolerance for conditions that would be considered unacceptable to other communities. Thus, by the time a critical incident or initiating event to community organization for drug abuse prevention does occur, it may serve as a flashpoint for aggressive or destructive behavior before positive organization can be realized (Oetting & Beauvais, 1991; Pentz, 1994). The prevention researcher should anticipate that a multiethnic community undergoing acculturation stress is likely to react quickly, and often negatively, to proposals for prevention research that have few, or delayed timelines for, tangible products.

An Integrated Theoretical Perspective

Community organization for prevention can be expressed as the interaction of person-, situation-, and environment-level factors that are bounded by a community (Pentz, 1993). Person-level factors are intraindividual variables that predict which community leaders will organize and whether they will organize effectively. In the case of alcohol and drug abuse prevention, nonsmoking status and previous civic service involvement of community leaders are associated with active participation in community organization for drug abuse prevention (see Pentz, 1986; Pentz & Montgomery, in press). Situation-level factors involve interindividual variables. Regular communication among leaders of different community agencies and centrality of these communications are associated with increased community organization and decreased drug use among community leaders (Freeman, 1978; Galaskiewicz, 1979; Valente & Pentz, 1990). Finally, environment-level factors involve organizational and system-level variables. Active representation of businesses, reallocation of existing resources, and concise, well-disseminated prevention-oriented policies are associated with greater initial and sustained community organization for drug abuse prevention (Green, Kreuter, Deeds, & Partridge, 1980; Pentz, 1989, in press-b).

Central to developing an understanding of the complexities involved in applying an integrated $p \times s \times e$ perspective to community prevention research is identifying what constitutes a "community." Sarason and others have emphasized that a community can be identified on the basis of geographic, social/sociocultural, and psychological boundaries; all three boundaries should be considered in developing and tailoring preventive interventions to the specific needs and resources of the community (Sarason, 1974).

In the multiethnic community, as in other communities, community organization should be devoted to developing a comprehensive prevention strategy that frames the target individual or group within the $p \times s \times e$ perspective. In the special case of the multiethnic community, however, the individual or group must be considered as being in constant movement or tension within the successive environments that contribute to, confound, or even eliminate cultural differences hypothesized by anthropological research and assumed by the prevention researcher. For the adolescent, at a minimum, these successive environments would include the family, immediate peer group, neighborhood, and school. Furthermore, given the possibility of culture/environment interaction effects, planning and evaluating the aggregate effects of multiple, fluid prevention strategies may be a more realistic goal than the effect of a single, structured program in a multiethnic community (Fisher et al., 1992).

Several researchers have proposed adaptations of the $p \times s \times e$ perspective to multiethnic communities. Some, like Fisher et al. (1992) and Baranowski (1992), propose that a traditional behavior change model be applied, with ethnic and community-specific applications of modeling, natural contingencies, cues, self-attribution, and self-efficacy as p-level factors, skills and social support as *s* factors, and empowerment as an *e* factor. For example, social support for adolescents in a multiethnic community would be interpreted as the use of a confidant and high-density, informal social networks rather than use of a trusted, credible adult or professional. Empowerment would be sought through locality or neighborhood development, volunteer partnerships, and use of an initial lead or host agency rather than through large-scale community organization for drug abuse prevention, professional partnerships, or initial establishment of an independent community organization. Sussman, among others, proposes that the $p \times s \times e$ perspective be tailored further to the multiethnic community by including perceptions of the majority culture or other communities and attention to physical space, crime, and housing at the neighborhood level (Sussman, 1992). This perspective requires that community organization address deficits in basic care and the physical environment as a major, and perhaps first, component of a prevention strategy (Fisher et al., 1992).

A General Model of
Community Prevention Research

To be useful to community leaders as well as to researchers, a model of community prevention research should specify the structure, process, implementation, maintenance, and outcomes of community organization. Each can be expressed as a phase in community organization. A simple version of this model was developed for a large multicommunity trial for adolescent drug abuse prevention, the Midwestern Prevention Project (Pentz, 1986; Pentz et al., 1989). This 10-step model to community organization begins with identification of the target community and population and ends with a continuous-loop mechanism for maintaining community organization and prevention program implementation. Each step is evaluated for its completion; the model presupposes that effective community organization cannot occur until all steps are completed.

An expanded model of the preparation phase, particularly useful in multiethnic communities, posits that researchers and community leaders prepare for formal organization in four steps: (a) obtaining an informal consensual assessment of background conditions in the community, and having previous experience with prevention and research; (b) promoting readiness of the community for organization; (c) building support and collaboration for organization; and (d) formally developing the community organization (Pentz, 1994). Two studies of neighborhood block organizations in racially mixed metropolitan areas, the Neighborhood Participation Project in Nashville and the Block Booster Project in New York City, showed that blocks receiving professionally provided training and feedback in organization development and materials for suggested programs were significantly less likely to decline in participation after 10-month follow-up (Florin et al., in press). Pentz and colleagues reported a similar finding from Public Broadcasting System stations to organize community leaders for drug abuse prevention after the viewing of the Chemical People series starting in 1983 (see Pentz & Valente, 1993). Task forces that included a professional in drug abuse prevention as a member and trainer of other members were significantly more likely to be operating after 15-month follow-up. These studies suggest that informational training and feedback are important for preparing any community to organize for prevention.

The varying roles of the researcher at each stage of preparation are summarized in Table 10.2, along with general strategies for promoting progress through each stage, and underlying theoretical and research assumptions. Specific stages are discussed below.

ASSESSING BACKGROUND CONDITIONS

Through informal discussions with contacts in the proposed community and review of archival records and local print media coverage, the prevention researcher should determine the most culturally familiar and acceptable methods of approaching the community for prevention. Methods may include, but are not limited to, the following forms of approach:

- *Word of mouth*—a grassroots, lateral communication strategy characterized by a credible resident or leader from within the community who seeks informal communication with the outside researcher or who is informally referred to the outside researcher, and who subsequently returns and spreads information to other residents or leaders
- *Designated information seeking*—characterized by a community pressure group that sends a designate to an outside researcher to gather and return with information that will support the pressure group's cause
- *Support/resource seeking*—characterized by one or several residents or leaders who know what they want for prevention and seek appropriate outside research support

In almost all cases, these communication models assume self-recognition or a strong sense of identity by the multiethnic community. Note that all three of these models assume that the first approach for prevention is from inside the community out toward the researcher. Unfortunately, almost all approaches for prevention research thus far have come from the outside in. The prevention researcher should determine, then, not only the best method

TABLE 10.2 General Stages of Community Prevention Research, With Strategies Adapted to Multiethnic Communities

Stage of Research	Strategy	Role of Researcher	Underlying Assumption
Acknowledging need for prevention	Reframe etiology and epidemiology as per needs stated by community; seek convergence of opinion about etiology and epidemiology of drug use and importance of drug use problem.	Process consultant	Drug use etiology and epidemiology are the same across communities.
Selecting/planning preventive intervention	Exchange research information about effective and generalizable behavioral interventions, with community preventions and anecdotal information about effective strategies and resilient populations; translate latter to research findings.	Information sharer	Behavioral interventions are culturally adaptable.
Adopting, implementing intervention	Exchange research information about effective adoption and implementation, with community perceptions and interpretation of intervention meaningfulness (ecological validity), and provide support.	Information sharer, resource/service provider	Principles of adoption and implementation are generalizable.
Disseminating intervention	Assess dissemination needs and preferences for packaging intervention.	Advisor	Principles of dissemination are generalizable; packaging is culture-specific.

of communication approach but also a means for the community to initiate the approach.

ASSESSING AND PROMOTING
COMMUNITY READINESS

Research from education, mass communications, school and community psychology, and social work suggests several criterion indicators of community readiness for prevention (Boruch & Shadish, 1983; Brown, 1984; Chavis & Wandersman, 1990; Fisher et al., 1992; Goodman & Steckler, 1990; Pentz, 1986; Pentz & Valente, 1993; Perkins, Florin, Rich, Wandersman, & Chavis, 1990; Prestby & Wandersman, 1985; Sarason, 1974; Wandersman & Giamartino, 1980; Zimmerman & Rappaport, 1988). These are organized in Figure 10.1, in sequence. Proposed strategies for promoting readiness through expediting the achievement of each criterion are also shown, as well as general predictors of each criterion. According to this figure, community self-recognition or identity presupposes all other criteria, followed by perceived awareness of the importance of the prevention problem and the need for prevention research, and perceived opportunity for intervention, which will vary according to whether the community's typical modus operandi is passive, active, or reactive to related community problems. The proposed figure assumes that a reluctant or lagging community can be *made* ready for community organization for prevention and prevention research, under limited circumstances. The circumstances include the availability of credible community leaders who want and are willing to champion preventive intervention, the availability of local credible media, and the judicial use of social marketing techniques to set the public agenda for prevention and to target community leaders and consumers for prevention interest and participation.

GAINING SUPPORT
AND COLLABORATION

Most multiethnic communities will have had little, no, or negative past experiences with researchers from outside of the community. The prevention researcher can modify perceptions and clarify and expedite the process of research by negotiating his or her role with community leaders as soon as it is determined that the community is ready for intervention. Because the field of community prevention research is small and minority researchers are lacking, it is likely that the prevention researcher will be from outside the multiethnic community or be perceived as an outsider. Thus, it is doubtful that the researcher will be accepted as a community partner early on unless there is already grounds for an interdependent relationship (e.g., a researcher

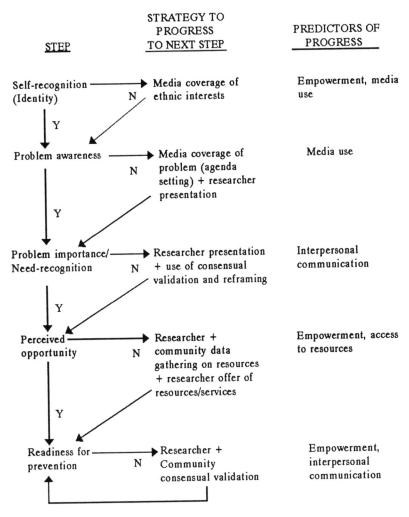

Figure 10.1. Model of Community Readiness

from a major hospital that serves as the major provider for an inner-city African American community). In that case, an early partnership can be sought and developed on the basis of improving the existing interdependent relationship. If the researcher is perceived as an insider to the multiethnic community and seeks an early partnership role, he or she must be prepared for the possibility of being pressured into an ethnic advocacy role over time. If the pressure is likely, the researcher may want to consider negotiating a

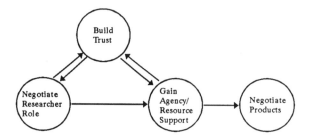

Figure 10.2. A Model for Gaining Support and Collaboration

more neutral advisor role rather than a partnership role. Other roles also have their disadvantages: A controller role is not feasible in most circumstances, and a consultant role has no experimental control. An advisor role, must allow the inclusion of other expertise, although it facilitates the maintenance of some experimental control through constructive critical feedback to community leaders.

After negotiating his or her role, the researcher should aim to build community and community leader trust by modeling personal behaviors that are culturally acceptable and by acknowledging and using community norms for communication and intervention. Building trust is reciprocally affected by the researcher's attempts to gain support and collaboration for research from local businesses, service groups such as churches, credible host or lead agencies for community organization such as the United Way, and credible ethnic support groups in the community. With the community's trust and support, the researcher may then delineate and negotiate tangible research products that are valued by the community. For example, the feedback or accountability derived from evaluating behavioral outcomes of a preventive intervention may not be as important to the community as improving net-working across previously contentious interest groups, gaining the support of local mass media, or enrolling community residents in local health and social services. A simple process model of gaining support and collaboration is shown in Figure 10.2.

ORGANIZING THE COMMUNITY

Following preparation is the actual development of the community organization. Organizing communities effectively to address a particular problem or goal requires initial resources, a structure recognized by leaders and residents, specific production activities, and outputs or outcomes (Goodman, & Steckler, 1990; Pentz & Montgomery, in press). In any community, organization will vary as a function of individual community differences in baseline characteristics, initiating events or conditions, and community leader factors, particularly community readiness and community and leader perceptions of empowerment. The particular form of organization—for example, organization of a coalition versus a nonprofit agency for prevention—will vary systematically according to several parameters: resource networks, incentive systems, and problem acuteness (Prestby & Wandersman, 1985). Resource networks include but are not limited to financial support, information/communication, and physical and social support and transportation. Leaders will tend to centralize their communications and new organizational efforts around the sources of these networks. In a disaffected, isolated minority community with no indigenous business leaders and a distrust of local government run by whites, new community organization might mobilize around neighbors who represent an active communication or transportation network. Incentive systems may be *material, solidary,* or *purposive* (Perkins et al., 1990; Prestby & Wandersman, 1985). If community leaders and residents perceive increased goods, services, and facilities as the major means to improve the community, then organizations will focus on acquiring and reinforcing participants with materials. Organization will be oriented toward solidary incentive systems if community residents and leaders experience a low sense of affiliation combined with a need to address the threatening community problem collectively. If the drug abuse problem in a community is acute, community leaders may decide to organize an initial task force to investigate the problem's size and origins before deciding on a course of intervention. A task force is usually mobilized quickly, gives rapid feedback to community leaders and residents about the scope of the problem, and then is disbanded and/or replaced with other, more permanent structures to plan, deliver, and monitor interventions to address the problem. An alternative is development of a coalition that is structured to represent a formal "united front" and has local policy change as an explicit or implicit goal. The Center for Substance Abuse Prevention (CSAP) Community Partnership grants require the development of this type of community organization to address local problems of drug abuse control and prevention.

An abbreviated community organization model is shown in Figure 10.3. A detailed description and examples of application of this model are provided elsewhere (Pentz, 1994).

An Illustration of Community Organization in a Large Metropolitan Area With Mixed Minority Representation

The Midwestern Prevention Project (MPP) is a multicommunity, multicomponent drug abuse prevention program for adolescents being conducted in the 26 communities that make up the Kansas City (Kansas), Kansas City

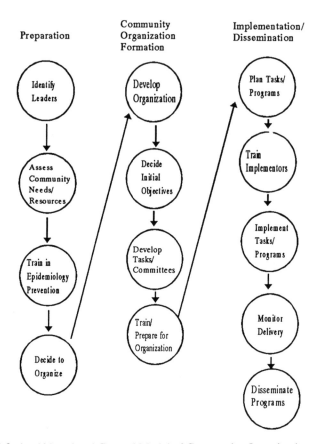

Figure 10.3. An Abbreviated General Model of Community Organization

(Missouri), and Indianapolis (Indiana) metropolitan areas (Pentz, 1986; Pentz et al., 1989). The predominant minority group in both cities is African American (approximately 19%), although Hispanic representation has grown to over 5% between the 1980 and 1990 U.S. censuses.

The MPP is conducted as a research trial; as such, the design and implementation of all program components are based on theory and results of past prevention research. The program components are introduced sequentially into schools and communities to maintain community interest in long-term drug abuse prevention intervention. The components, in order, are (a) mass media programming (an average of 31 events and programs per year); (b) a school program (11-13 sessions in Grade 6 or 7, followed by a 5-session booster in Grade 7 or 8 and a multicomponent high school environmental change program that is currently under development); (c) a parent program that includes parent education and organization throughout middle school; (d) community organization that includes initial and continuing training of community leaders in drug abuse etiology, epidemiology, and prevention; (e) a series of short- and long-term programs, campaigns, and policy change initiatives that complement other program components; and (f) local health policy change at the town and city levels, including the promotion of beer taxes and smoking ordinances. Unlike CSAP Community Partnership demonstrations and the community heart health studies, community organization in the MPP was delayed until the effects of other program components could be fed back to the community as a "success" to motivate long-term commitment to organization.

The community organization in each MPP site is a formal organization for drug abuse prevention that is organized at the city level, with formal and informal leaders who represent the interests of each community within the metropolitan area. Eleven committees serve as substructures within each organization to implement prevention programs, campaigns, and events. The committees are organized according to research and community service function (e.g., research, medical, and recreational youth committees).

Minority interests are given special attention in each community organization via a separate committee, the Minority Issues Committee, that is structured to conduct additional needs/resources assessments for minority groups, adapt program content and campaigns to special cultural needs (e.g., reinterpreting reinforcement of implementers and participants in the form of a youth rap contest), and planning effective strategies to maximize participation of minority groups in programs (e.g., relocating parent group meetings to churches rather than schools). The community organization in Kansas City, the Kansas City Drug Abuse Task Force, has been in operation since 1987; the organization in Indianapolis, the I-STAR Community Council, has been in operation since late 1988. Both community organizations have reported positive outcomes in adolescent drug use behavior, changes in community social norms for drug use, increased interleader and interagency communications and cooperation regarding delivery of drug abuse prevention and treatment services, dissemination of the school program component throughout their respective states, and initiatives that are expected to result in prevention policy change.

Adapting Research
Methods for Formative Evaluation

Formative evaluation is a crucial step in adapting existing theories and community organization models to multiethnic communities. At a minimum, formative evaluation should include the early use of focus groups to generate or validate cultural themes, procedures, and content; measures, intervention, and design development; piloting; and early revision.

On the basis of the discussion in previous sections, the types, procedures, settings, and themes of focus groups used in formative evaluation in multi-ethnic communities can be expected to differ from other communities. Questions about the meaning of health and prevention, normative communication patterns, empowerment and other predictors of community readiness, and perceptions of research can be used to develop focus group content. A National Heart, Lung, and Blood Institute (NHBLI) task force on research with minority groups recently concluded that subject recruitment procedures for focus groups and all phases of prevention research can be expected to involve multiple adaptations (National Heart, Lung, and Blood Institute, 1992). The adaptations include but are not limited to assessing the meaning of words on consent and procedural forms, and changing these accordingly; using cluster rather than random sampling; and promoting local publicity for recruitment. The same adaptations apply to the development of measures, intervention, and research designs. If health is perceived by the community as a slow, iterative growth process, then community organization and prevention program implementation may be expected to follow a similar iterative process. The concepts of time-limited, structured piloting and revision may require rethinking, rescheduling, and adaptation as part of the major research trial, traditionally conceptualized as summative evaluation.

SUMMARY

The general models described here are, for the most part, rational decision-making models built on culture-adaptable concepts of behavior change, most notably behavior modification concepts from social learning theory. Evidence is growing to support adaptations of these types of general models to multiethnic communities. However, in multiethnic communities with perceptions about drug abuse, prevention, and treatment that are radically different from rational theory—another concept from Western, white culture—some of these models may not hold. Researchers attempting to work in such communities are advised to conduct a thorough formative evaluation before determining whether any rational, deterministic, sequential models can be applied to prevention. If the formative evaluation yields findings that do not fit current theoretical and research schemata of drug abuse prevention, the researcher's subsequent role may be as an observer and documenter of a community process that may or may not develop into organizational models, and may or may not be generalizable to other communities.

References

Altman, D. G. (1986). A framework for evaluating community-based heart disease prevention programs. *Social Sciences and Medicine, 22,* 479-487.

Bachman, J. G., Johnston, L. D., & O'Malley, P. M. (1991). Explaining the recent decline in cocaine use among young adults: Further evidence that perceived risk and disapproval lead to reduced drug use. *Journal of Health and Social Behavior, 31,* 173-184.

Bandura, A. (1977). *Social learning theory.* Englewood Cliffs, NJ: Prentice Hall.

Baranowski, T. (1992). Interpersonal models for health behavior intervention with minority populations: Theoretical, methodologic, and pragmatic issues. In D. M. Becker, D. R. Hill, J. S. Jackson, D. M. Levin, F. A. Stillman, & S. M. Weiss (Eds.), *Health behavior research in minority populations: Access, design, and implementation* (NIH National Heart, Lung, and Blood Institute, NIH Publication No. 92-2965, pp. 112-121). Washington, DC: Government Printing Office.

Boruch, R. F., & Shadish, W. R. (1983). Design issues in community intervention research. In E. Seidman (Ed.), *Handbook of social intervention* (pp. 73-98). Beverly Hills, CA: Sage.

Botvin, G. J., Batson, J. H., Witts-Vitale, S., Bess, V., Baker, E., & Dusenbury, L. (1989). A psychosocial approach to smoking prevention for urban black youth. *Public Health Reports, 104,* 573-582.

Botvin, G. J., & Botvin, B. M. (1992). Adolescent tobacco, alcohol, and drug abuse: Prevention strategies, empirical findings, and assessment issues. *Journal of Developmental and Behavioral Pediatrics, 13,* 2990-3301.

Bracht, N. F. (Ed.). (1990). *Health promotion at the community level.* Newbury Park, CA: Sage.

Brown, C. (1984). *The art of coalition building: A guide for community health promotion.* New York: American Jewish Committee.

Caetano, R., & Medina-Mora, M. E. (1988). Acculturation and drinking among people of Mexican descent in Mexico and the U.S. *Journal of Studies on Alcohol, 49,* 462-471.

Chavis, D. M., & Wandersman, A. (1990). Sense of community in the urban environment: A catalyst for participation and community development. *American Journal of Community Psychology, 18,* 55-81.

Farquhar, J. W., Fortmann, S. P., & Maccoby, N. (1984). The Stanford Five-City Project: An overview. In J. D. Matarazzo, H. A. Herd, N. E. Miller, & S. M. Weiss (Eds.), *Behavioral health: A handbook of health enhancement and disease prevention* (pp. 1154-1165). New York: John Wiley.

Feighery, E., & Rogers, T. (1990). Building and maintaining effective coalitions. *How-to guides on community health promotion.* Palo Alto, CA: Stanford Center for Research in Disease Prevention, Health Promotion Resource Center.

Fighting Back. (1993, March 31). Annual Evaluation Meeting minutes. Proceedings of the "Fighting Back" Annual Evaluation Meeting, Technical Advisory Group, Robert Wood Johnson Foundation, Princeton, NJ.

Fisher, E. B., Auslander, W., Sussman, L., Owens, N., & Jackson-Thompson, J. (1992). Community organization and health promotion in minority neighborhoods. In D. M. Becker, D. R. Hill, J. S. Jackson, D. M. Levin, F. A. Stillman, & S. M. Weiss (Eds.), *Health behavior research in minority populations: Access, design, and implementation* (NIH National Heart, Lung, and Blood Institute, NIH Publication No. 92-2965, pp. 53-72). Washington, DC: Government Printing Office.

Florin, P., Chavis, P., Wandersman, A., & Rich, R. (in press). A systems approach to understanding and enhancing grassroots organizations: The block booster project. In R. Levin & R. Fitzgerald (Eds.), *Analysis of dynamic psychological systems.* New York: Plenum.

Florin, P., & Wandersman, A. (1990). An introduction to citizen participation, voluntary organi-
    zations, and community development: Insights for empowerment through research.
    American Journal of Community Psychology, 18, 41-53.
Freeman, L. (1978). Centrality in social networks: Conceptual clarification. *Social Networks, 1,*
    215-239.
Galaskiewicz, J. (1979). The structure of community organizational networks. *Social Forces,
    57,* 1346-1364.
Giachello, A. L. (1992). Reconciling the multiple scientific community needs. In D. M. Becker,
    D. R. Hill, J. S. Jackson, D. M. Levin, F. A. Stillman, & S. M. Weiss (Eds.), *Health
    behavior research in minority populations: Access, design, and implementation* (NIH
    National Heart, Lung, and Blood Institute, NIH Publication No. 92-2965, pp. 237-
    241). Washington, DC: Government Printing Office.
Goodman, R. M., & Steckler, A. (1990). A model for the institutionalization of health promotion
    programs. *Family and Community Health, 11*(4), 63-78.
Green, D. W., Kreuter, M, Deeds, S. G., & Partridge, K. B. (1980). *Health education planning:
    A diagnostic approach.* Palo Alto, CA: Mayfield.
Hansen, W. B. (1992). School-based substance abuse prevention: A review of the state of the art
    in curriculum, 1980-1990. *Health Education Research, 7,* 403-430.
Hawkins, J. V., Catalano, R. F., & Miller, J. Y. (1992). Risk and protective factors for alcohol
    and other drug problems in adolescents and early adulthood: Implications for sub-
    stance abuse prevention. *Psychological Bulletin, 112,* 64-105.
Javier, R. A. (1992). Design and implementation as a function of models: Critical assessment of
    models. In D. M. Becker, D. R. Hill, J. S. Jackson, D. M. Levin, F. A. Stillman, & S.
    M. Weiss (Eds.), *Health behavior research in minority populations: Access, design,
    and implementation* (NIH National Heart, Lung, and Blood Institute, NIH Publication
    No. 92-2965, pp. 141-144). Washington, DC: Government Printing Office.
Johnson, C. A., Pentz, M. A., Weber, M. D, Dwyer, J. H., MacKinnon, D. P., Flay, B. R., Baer,
    N. A., & Hansen, W. B. (1990). The relative effectiveness of comprehensive commu-
    nity programming for drug abuse prevention with risk and low risk adolescents.
    Journal of Consulting and Clinical Psychology, 58, 4047-4056.
Landrine, H., & Klonoff, E. A. (1992). Culture and health-related schemas: A review and
    proposal for interdisciplinary integration. *Health Psychology, 11,* 2667-2276.
Legge, C., & Sherlock, L. (1990-1991). Perception of alcohol use and misuse in three ethnic
    communities: Implications for prevention programming. *International Journal of the
    Addictions, 25,* 629-653.
National Heart, Lung, and Blood Institute. (1992). Recruitment of minority communities for
    health behavior research. In D. M. Becker, D. R. Hill, J. S. Jackson, D. M. Levin,
    F. A. Stillman, & S. M. Weiss (Eds.), *Health behavior research in minority populations:
    Access, design, and implementation* (NIH National Heart, Lung, and Blood Institute,
    NIH Publication No. 92-2965, pp. 94-103). Washington, DC: Government Printing
    Office.
Oetting, E. R., & Beauvais, F. (1991). Critical incidents: Failure in prevention. *International
    Journal of the Addictions, 26,* 797-820.
Pentz, M. A. (1986). Community organization and school liaisons: How to get programs started.
    Journal of School Health, 56, 382-388.
Pentz, M. A. (1989). A model public/private collaborative program for drug abuse prevention
    among adolescents: The Midwestern Prevention Project. In *Evaluating school-based
    prevention strategies: Alcohol, tobacco and other drugs* (pp. 31-35). San Diego:
    University of California-San Diego.

Pentz, M. A. (1993). Comparative effects of community-based drug abuse prevention. In J. S. Baer, G. A. Marlatt, & R. J. McMahon (Eds.), *Addictive behaviors across the lifespan: Prevention, treatment, and policy issues* (pp. 69-87). Newbury Park, CA: Sage.

Pentz, M. A. (1994). Target populations and interventions in prevention research: What is high risk? In B. Bukowski & Z. Amzel (Eds.), (pp. 75-94). Washington, DC: Government Printing Office.

Pentz, M. A. (in press-a). Alternative models of community prevention research. In P. Langton (Ed.). Washington, DC: U.S. Department of Health and Human Services.

Pentz, M. A. (in press-b). A comprehensive strategy to prevent the abuse of alcohol and other drugs: Theory and methods. In R. Coombs & D. Ziedonis (Eds.), *Handbook on drug abuse prevention.* Englewood Cliffs, NJ: Prentice Hall.

Pentz, M. A., Alexander, P., Cormack, C., & Light, J. (1990). Issues in the development and process of community-based alcohol and drug prevention: The Midwestern Prevention Project. In N. Giesbrecht, P. Consley, R. W. Denniston, L. Glicksman, H. Holder, A. Pederson, R. Room, & M. Shain (Eds.), *Research, action, and the community: Experiences in the prevention of alcohol and other problems* (OSAP Prevention Monograph No. 4, pp. 131-135). Washington, DC: U.S. Department of Health and Human Services.

Pentz, M. A., Cormack, C., Flay, B. R., Hansen, W. B., & Johnson, C. A. (1986). Balancing program and research integrity in community drug abuse prevention: Project STAR. *Journal of School Health, 56,* 389-393.

Pentz, M. A., Dwyer, J. H., MacKinnon, D. P., Flay, B. R., Hansen, W. B., Wang, E. Y. I., & Johnson, C. A. (1989). A multi-community trial for primary prevention of adolescent drug abuse: Effects on drug use prevalence. *Journal of the American Medical Association, 261,* 3259-3266.

Pentz, M. A., & Montgomery, S. B. (in press). Research-based community coalitions for drug abuse prevention: Guidelines for replication. *Health Education Research.*

Pentz, M. A., & Valente, T. (1993). Project STAR: A substance abuse prevention campaign in Kansas City. In T. E. Backer, E. Rogers, M. Rogers, & R. Denniston (Eds.), *Impact of organizations on mass media health behavior campaigns* (pp. 37-66). Newbury Park, CA: Sage.

Perkins, D. D., Florin, P., Rich, R. C., Wandersman, A., & Chavis, M. (1990). Participation in the social and physical environment of residential blocks: Crime and community context. *American Journal of Community Psychology, 18,* 83-115.

Perry, C. L., Klepp, K. I., & Shultz, J. M. (1988). Primary prevention of cardiovascular disease: Community-wide strategies for youth. *Journal of Consulting and Clinical Psychology, 56,* 358-364.

Prestby, J., & Wandersman, A. (1985). An empirical exploration of a framework of organizational viability: Maintaining block organizations. *Journal of Applied Behavioral Science, 2*(13), 287-305.

Puska, P., Tuomilehto, J., Nissinen, A., Salonen, J. T., Vartiainen, E., Pietinen, P., Koskela, K., & Korhonen, H. J. (1989). The North Karelia Project: 15 years of community-based prevention of coronary heart disease. *Annals of Medicine, 21,* 69-173.

Rothman, J. (1979). Three models of community organization practice, their mixing and phasing. In F. M. Cox et al. (Eds.), *Strategies of community organization: A book of readings* (3rd ed., pp. 25-45). Itasca, IL: F. E. Peacock.

Sarason, S. B. (1974). *The psychological sense of community: Prospects for a community psychology.* San Francisco: Jossey-Bass.

Schilling, R. F., Schinke S., Nichols S. E., & Botvin, G. J. (1989). Developing strategies for AIDS prevention research with black and Hispanic drug users. *Public Health Reports, 104,* 2-11.

Sussman, L. K. (1992). Critical assessment of models. In D. M. Becker, D. R. Hill, J. S. Jackson, D. M. Levin, F. A. Stillman, & S. M. Weiss (Eds.), *Health behavior research in minority populations: Access, design, and implementation* (NIH National Heart, Lung, and Blood Institute, NIH Publication No. 92-2965, pp. 145-148). Washington, DC: Government Printing Office.

Tobler, N. S. (1992). Drug prevention programs can work: Research findings. *Journal of Addictive Diseases, 11,* 1-28.

Valente, T. W., & Pentz, M. A. (1990, February). *Communication networks as predictors of perceived program efficacy.* Paper presented at the Sunbelt 10th International Social Network Conference, San Diego.

Wandersman, A., & Giamartino, G. A. (1980). Community and individual difference characteristics as influences on initial participation. *American Journal of Community Psychology, 8,* 217-228.

Wandersman, A., & Goodman, B. (1992, January). *Development of a community partnership.* Paper presented at the Third National Workshop for OSAP Community Partnership Grantees, Washington, DC.

Zimmerman, M. A., & Rappaport, J. (1988). Citizen participation, perceived control, and psychological empowerment. *American Journal of Community Psychology, 16,* 725-750.

Prevention in Community Settings

Steven Schinke
Kristin Cole

This chapter describes the needs for responsive interventions for youth at high risk of future drug use. The chapter begins by reviewing the background and nature of drug use among youth who are at high risk for using and encountering problems associated with drugs. Against that backdrop, we offer an approach to intervening with high-risk youth to prevent drug use and its attendant problems. The preventive intervention approach includes relevant theory and applicable principles and specific strategies. Finally, we summarize the strengths and limitations of the prevention approach offered to combat problems of drug use among high-risk youth.

Background

According to the National Institute on Drug Abuse (1985), America's youth are the largest consumers of illicit drugs in the industrialized nations of the world. Declines in drug consumption rates achieved prior to 1982 have since stabilized. Subsequently, the United States has witnessed an increase in Americans' use of cocaine, PCP, and opiates other than heroin. Nearly 80% of all young adult Americans have experimented with an illicit drug by age 25 years. In this country, the sale of illicit drugs generates between $27 and $110 billion dollars a year for organized crime (U.S. House Select Committee on Narcotics Abuse and Control, 1985).

Besides its direct adverse effects, drug abuse contributes to the violent lifestyles of young adults. Forty-two percent of males arrested for serious crime in New York City in 1985 tested positive for cocaine use (Wish, 1985); by 1988, the percentages had increased to 74% of male arrestees and 75% of female arrestees (National Institute of Justice, 1990). Substance abuse is also linked to fatal traffic accidents. Between 1984 and 1987 in New York City, 56% of all drivers killed in traffic accidents had detectable levels of alcohol, cocaine, or both at the time of their death (Marzuk et al., 1990). Substance use is also associated with health, school, and behavior problems (Jessor, 1987). Longitudinal data suggest that early substance use can lead to later, serious abuse (Yamaguchi & Kandel, 1984).

Past Approaches

Past research has shown that information alone is a necessary but insufficient influence on changing drug use and other refractory health-related behaviors (Bandura, 1990). Education programs designed to give young people drug information toward persuading them not to use drugs have often failed to produce desired effects (Snow, Gilchrist, & Schinke, 1985). Recent years, however, have witnessed considerable research demonstrating that skills-based prevention interventions offer a promising approach to drug abuse problems among youth (Botvin & Wills, 1985; Flay, 1985; Fraser & Kohlert, 1988). Especially promising are interventions that focus on enhancing personal and social skills using cognitive-behavioral problem-solving, decision-making, and communication elements (Botvin & Botvin, 1992; Pentz, 1983; Schinke & Gilchrist, 1984).

Despite the promise of skills interventions, community-based approaches to prevent drug abuse among youth at highest risk for habitual and damaging use patterns are still lacking (Fraser & Kohlert, 1988; Greenwald, Cullen, & McKenna, 1987; McKay, Murphy, McGuire, Rivinus, & Maisto, 1992; U.S. Department of Health and Human Services, 1985; Zigler, Taussig, & Black, 1992). Among the reasons for the limited testing of such approaches for community settings are research designs that favor studies with stable, compliant, homogeneous populations. School-based studies, the venue for most skills intervention research, are apt to overlook high-risk and ethnic/racial minority group youth. Investigations are further hampered by limited access to ethnic community institutions and the lack of viable collaborations between research groups and community agencies and institutions.

Comparative Findings

To shed empirical light on the need for targeted prevention services aimed at substance abuse problems among youth in community settings, data were recently analyzed from two samples of similarly aged adolescents. One sample was school based, and the other was drawn from community agency settings. Adolescents in the samples were aged 12 to 14 years and resided in the same neighborhood in New York City. All data were collected over the same time and employed the same items and scales. Care was taken to ensure that the same youths did not appear in both samples.

Youths in the school-based sample totaled 639 and were nearly evenly divided between females (49.8%) and males (50.2%). The ethnic/racial background of these youths was 48% African American, 36.8% Hispanic American, and 4.9% nonminority. The community sample of youths was 52.8% female, 69.4% African American, 13.9% Hispanic American, and 8.3% nonminority.

Figure 11.1 shows results from a questionnaire item on alcohol use rates among youths in the school-based and community-based samples. As seen in the table, more youths in the school sample than in the community sample indicated that they never or occasionally used alcohol. Youths in the community sample were more likely than youths in the school sample to report weekly or daily use of alcohol.

Further comparing the two groups of youths, Figure 11.2 shows the number of drinks consumed per alcohol use event by participants in the school and community samples. Not surprisingly, given the data in Figure 11.1, youths in the community sample were more likely than youths in the school sample to report drinking across the three types of use events: 1 to 3 drinks, 4 to 7 drinks, and 8 to 12 drinks. As for the never-drink category, youths in community sample reported lower rates than youths in the school sample, confirming findings shown in Figure 11.1.

Figure 11.3 shows similar differences between the two samples of youths on rates of marijuana use. Whereas youths in the school sample were more likely to report never having used marijuana, youths in the community sample reported higher rates of marijuana use, from 1 to 5 times a month and from 5 to 10 times a month. Across Figures 11.1, 11.2, and 11.3, a pattern emerges indicating higher substance abuse patterns among youths in the community setting sample when compared with youths in the school-based sample.

New Approaches to Prevention for Community Settings

Under the auspices of the Institute for Prevention Research at Cornell University Medical College, we are developing new approaches to prevent drug abuse among youth in community settings. Accordingly, the Institute for Prevention Research is attempting to overcome traditional impediments to drug abuse prevention research. By drawing nonschool samples from

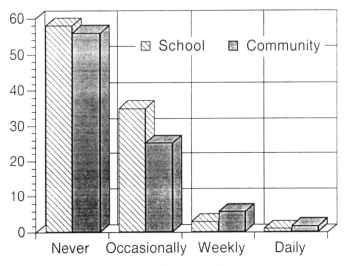

Figure 11.1. Comparison of School and Community Samples on Alcohol Use

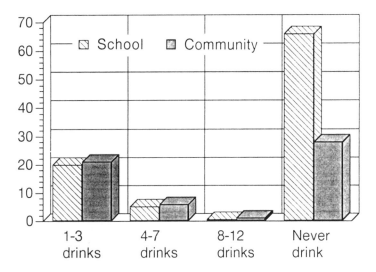

Figure 11.2. Comparison of School and Community Samples on Number of Drinks per Event

community-based agencies serving high-risk youth, the research will enhance efforts to recruit, involve, and retain adolescents who are sorely in
need of responsive preventive intervention services. The prevention approach under development is based on prior work on skills interventions.

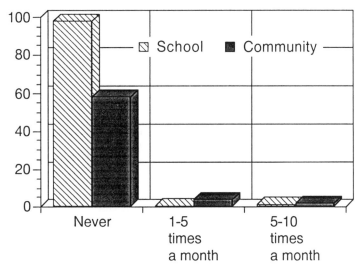

Figure 11.3. Comparison of School and Community Samples on Marijuana Use

SKILLS INTERVENTIONS

Derived from social learning theory (Bandura, 1977), skills interventions help adolescents prevent problems and promote health through problem solving, coping, and enhanced communication skills (Schinke & Gilchrist, 1985). Through the use of established principles that include modeling, role playing, coaching, feedback, reinforcement, and transfer training, skills-based approaches seek to promote the acquisition and enhancement of general, personal, and social competence skills to resist negative peer and familial influences and pressures to use drugs.

Skills-based interventions have been studied to prevent drug and related substance abuse among Native American youth and other at-risk populations (Bobo, Cvetkovich, Trimble, Gilchrist, & Schinke, 1988; Cvetkovich, Earle, Schinke, Gilchrist, & Trimble, 1987). Tests of skills interventions designed for Native American youth have revealed reductions in tobacco, alcohol, and drug use among subjects who received intervention relative to subjects who were placed randomly in minimal intervention, information-only, or test-only conditions (Gilchrist, Schinke, Trimble, & Cvetkovich, 1987; Moncher, Trimble, & Schinke, in press; Schinke, Moncher, Holden, Botvin, & Orlandi, 1989; Schinke, Orlandi, et al., 1988; Schinke, Schilling, Palleja, & Zayas, 1987). Involving African American and Hispanic youth, another series of studies has tested new ways to reach and intervene with youths at high risk for drug use (Forgey & Schinke, in press; Orlandi, 1992; Orlandi, Weston, & Epstein, 1992; Schinke, Moncher, Palleja, Zayas, & Schilling, 1988).

In other drug abuse prevention studies, theory-driven approaches were designed and tested to address information-processing factors among youth (Cvetkovich et al., 1987), help adolescents respond to media influences toward alcohol and other substance use (Orlandi, Lieberman, & Schinke, 1989), and respond to psychosocial variables in the lives of high-risk youth (Botvin, Schinke, & Orlandi, 1989; Moncher, Holden, & Schinke, 1991; Orlandi, Landers, Weston, & Haley, 1990; Resnicow, Orlandi, & Wynder, 1989). Because skills interventions in the present work are being applied to high-risk youth, an operational definition of these young people is in order.

HIGH-RISK YOUTH

Behavioral patterns associated with increased substance use—including tobacco, alcohol, and drug use—are more common among young people from households with incomes below the poverty line than among youth from less impoverished households (Dusenbury et al., 1992; Hechinger, 1992; Hiatt, Klatsky, & Armstrong, 1988; Walter et al., 1992). Consequently, for our purposes, youth at high risk for the adoption of drug use are defined as early adolescents aged 10 and 11 years from families with household incomes below the federal poverty line. The *federal poverty line* refers to annually indexed income levels published by the Bureau of the Census to estimate the number of Americans who live in poverty (Fisher, 1984).

In 1991, the poverty line for a family of four was $13,400. Thus, a family of four was deemed by the Bureau of the Census to live in poverty if its household income was at or below $13,400 ("Annual Update of the Federal Poverty Guidelines," 1991). Following guidelines from the Bureau of the Census on income criteria for families of various sizes, investigators can use ZIP code and census track data to identify catchment areas to recruit early adolescents who live in households with incomes below the poverty line.

As for the appropriate age cohort of high-risk youths for preventive intervention efforts, adolescents aged 10 and 11 years offer an ideal developmental period for targeting drug abuse prevention programs. From about age 10 through the middle teen years, youths separate from their parents, develop independence, establish self-identity, and acquire skills to function as adults. As youths move from childhood to adolescence, they experience a decline in parental influence accompanied by an increase in the influence of peers (Utech & Hoving, 1969). Increased reliance on peers weakens parental influence and facilitates deviance (Jessor, 1984; Urberg & Robbins, 1983). Early adolescence is thus a time to experiment with new patterns of behavior (Bailey, 1992).

Youths aged 10 and 11 years offer an efficient target for drug abuse prevention and health behavior risk reduction efforts. By age 10 years, youths control their own behavior and can implement prevention principles and skills. Still amenable to adult-directed activities, early adolescents nonetheless have large blocks of discretionary and unsupervised time in which to engage in risks associated with drug and other substance use. Old enough to understand outcome measurement items, early adolescents are young enough to adopt new lifestyle habits and avoid drug abuse problems altogether.

THEORY

Theories on the etiology of risk taking during adolescence have value for directing drug abuse prevention strategies. Rather than defining risk taking as pathological, early theorists viewed youthful deviance as resulting from socially induced pressures and normal developmental needs to achieve socially desirable goals (Cloward & Ohlin, 1960). Later, theorists perceived drug use and other risk taking among youth as a result of weak ties to conventional norms (Hirschi, 1969). Building on these tenets, subsequent theorists saw a pattern of risk taking as occurring when youths' conventional social bonds are neutralized through attenuating experiences (Elliot, Ageton, & Cantor, 1979). Recently, three theories have emerged to further explain risk taking in adolescence and to guide prevention strategies aimed at tobacco, alcohol, and drug use. These theories are social learning theory, problem behavior theory, and peer cluster theory.

According to *social learning theory,* people learn how to behave through a process of modeling and reinforcement (Bandura, 1977). Moreover, according to this theory, youths' perceptions that deviant behaviors are standard practice among their peers may promote deviance through the establishment of negative normative beliefs. Such perceptions may tell adolescents that deviant acts are socially acceptable and that these acts are necessary to be popular, grown up, and sophisticated. Perceived payoffs for deviance increase adolescents' susceptibility to peer pressure.

Problem behavior theory explains why youths engage in deviant acts (Jessor & Jessor, 1977). According to this theory, tobacco and alcohol use and unsafe sexual behavior result from an interaction of personal, physiological and genetic, and environmental factors (Jessor, Collins, & Jessor, 1972). The theory suggests that some adolescents find deviant acts functional because the acts help them achieve personal goals. For adolescents who are not doing well academically, deviancy may provide a way of achieving social status. Also according to problem behavior theory, youth are more vulnerable to peer pressure when they have few effective coping strategies, few skills to handle social situations, and anxiety about social situations. Although deviant behavior is difficult to prevent if it is functional for youths, that functionalism is vitiated when youths have positive ways of achieving their goals.

Peer cluster theory assumes that peer interactions largely determine risk-taking behavior (Oetting & Beauvais, 1986, 1987). Peer clusters include friends, dating dyads, family, classmates, sports teams, and clubs. According to theorists, peer clusters not only account for the presence and type of risk taking among adolescents, but also may help youths reduce pressures and influences toward deviance. The therapeutic use of peer clusters in an intervention context may therefore enhance the effects of efforts to reduce adolescents' risks of drug abuse.

These theoretical constructs have informed a preventive intervention approach responsive to high-risk youth in community settings, as described below.

SKILLS INTERVENTION

Delivered by community-level providers and by peer leaders, skills intervention for high-risk youth as developed by the Institute for Prevention Research includes elements on drug use facts, problem solving skills, coping, and communication skills.

Drug Use Factors

Drug use factors focus on avoidable risks associated with tobacco use, alcohol use, and other drug use. This element addresses personal and lifestyle decisions about each area of risk through vignettes. Incorporating cultural and social influences, the vignettes demonstrate how youths can reduce their drug use risks through small lifestyle changes (Dwyer, 1992). Via interactive exercises, youths follow the lives of fictional characters. Some vignettes begin with the characters' risk-taking behavior and end with subsequent problems, including drug addiction. Other vignettes depict characters who avoid high-risk behaviors and escape problems. For homework, youths gather facts about drug use risks and their reduction.

Problem-Solving Skills

Problem-solving skills teach students a five-step sequence for reducing the likelihood of drug use. Steps in the sequence are *Stop, Options, Decide, Act,* and *Self-Praise.* In the Stop step, youths pause and define drug-related problems and their role in solving them. In the second step, *Options,* youths consider alternatives to behavioral risks associated with drug use. In the *Decide* step, youths systematically choose the best solution from their options. Youths rank their options on costs, benefits, and feasibility. On the basis of these criteria, youths choose the most appropriate option for problem situations. Act, the fourth step, involves planning and rehearsal.

After planning thoughts, words, and gestures appropriate to the problems, youths practice how to handle personal choices. In the *Self-Praise* step, youths reward themselves for using problem solving. Skills intervention leads youths through exercises of increasing complexity to learn each problem-solving step. Initially, subjects interact in semistructured situations related to hypothetical behavioral risks. As intervention progresses, youths apply problem-solving steps to everyday situations.

Coping

Coping content teaches youths cognitive and behavioral strategies to adaptively handle stresses that may trigger drug use. Cognitive skills emphasize internal statements of self-praise and affirmation to help adolescents manage their behavior and reduce their drug risks. Behavioral coping skills teach youths to reward themselves overtly for successful prevention efforts. The intervention introduces coping skills through vignettes of high-risk adolescents who lowered their chances of substance abuse by engaging in healthy behavior. Homework that applies coping skills in everyday situations helps youths learn the skills.

Ccommunication Skills

Communication skills, also introduced through vignettes, show youths how other adolescents successfully interacted with peers and others to avoid interpersonal triggers for drug use. Youths learn communication skills to accomplish such different purposes as achieving an objective, maintaining a relationship, and gaining self-respect. In role-play situations, youths practice communication skills. For homework, youths observe interactions among peers. Homework assignments also ask youths to apply communication skills. Youths refine their communication skills first in routine situations, then in more challenging interactions.

PARENT INVOLVEMENT

Intended to strengthen youths' substance abuse risk reduction learning, parent intervention emphasizes positive interactions and relationships (Hawkins, Catalano, & Miller, 1992; Hawkins, Catalano, Morrison, et al., 1992). These exercises encourage parent-child communication, not solely around drugs and alcohol, but also around shared enjoyable activities. For example, materials in this component encourage parents to learn how members of their families express needs, concerns, and ideas. Parents, including other significant adults in youths' lives, accomplish that aim in part by identifying the special language, rituals, and habits they and other family members observe at home.

Although generalizations are hazardous in describing such a varied population as parents of high-risk youth, prior data suggested that these parents might be so occupied with providing for their households that they would have limited time for working with their children around drug prevention goals. Admittedly, many drug abuse prevention activities presume a commitment of parents that may not always be possible. But through the help of focus groups and consultants, a parent involvement component was developed to accommodate many parenting styles.

From past research with parent involvement interventions for high-risk youth, expectations were modest for the quantity and quality of parent participation in the prevention program. Although parent involvement levels have been as high as 83% (number of involved parents ÷ number of eligible parents) in a social competence enhancement study of early adolescents from families living in poverty (Moncher et al., 1991), involvement rates were also as low as 21% in a study of drug abuse prevention in public housing developments (Schinke, Orlandi, & Cole, 1992).

Due to the multiple risk factors addressed by this intervention and its relative intensity, we projected a parent involvement level of no less than 50%. That level represents our expectation of the number of parents who will complete 75% or more of all designated exercises with their children during the course of initial intervention and booster sessions. As detailed later, we are measuring levels of parental involvement and analyzing these levels relative to drug risk outcomes for early adolescents.

Illustrative of our methods for engaging parents in the intervention was having parents and youths read together a comic book story about a family situation. After going through the story, parents and youths identified family members in the plot, drug abuse risk, prevention behaviors dealt with during the story, and responsibilities of each depicted family member. Parents and children then discussed whether the story portrayed a family that behaved like their family.

Parent involvement also occurs through easily followed workbooks. Community providers who are delivering the intervention explain to youths how to employ the workbooks at home and serve as resources to parents and other family members in the application of workbook materials. Because the workbooks address a range of backgrounds, we designed them to maximize comprehension without highly developed literacy. We accomplished this objective by illustrating richly the workbooks with diagrams and cartoons.

To facilitate an understanding of the workbooks, we introduced a set of self-explanatory symbols to guide parents and youths through the material. These symbols orient parents and youths to the content, players, and exercises needed for each workbook section. By following the action of the material and noting the symbols involved, parents and youths can determine easily the requirements and processes of workbook content. Although the workbooks seek to increase parental involvement, youths direct most workbook activities with their parents and significant others. To ensure that workbooks contained thematically coherent content on drug abuse risk reduction intervention, we organized the content into three major categories: self-esteem, interpersonal skills, and decision making.

Self-Esteem

This content includes exercises for family members to enhance youths' feelings of self-worth. Exercises focus on ways for parents to build their children's knowledge and awareness of their own special role in the world. These exercises teach parents how they can instill in their child a sense of uniqueness and importance. For example, parents use worksheets that allow children to view themselves relative to milestones of their lives. Through structured exercises, children share feelings and perceptions of themselves and their worlds. In so doing, parents establish positive levels of intimacy with their children, and children experience the unconditional positive regard of their parents.

Exercises in the self-esteem unit enable parents and children to learn and apply material on substance abuse risk reduction, health promotion, future goals, and positive habits. Worksheets and exercises for these objectives provide children and parents with games to identify their own healthy habits, to describe current and future special skills, and to set life goals in several areas. As such, the self-esteem unit lays a solid, thematically consistent foundation of mutual understanding, knowledge, and trust for parents and children to build upon for the remaining substance abuse prevention materials.

Interpersonal Skills

Parents and youths also learn communication skills. Covering fundamentals of communication, this content raises parents' awareness of their current and desired communication levels; teaches parents new strategies for talking with and being understood by their children and other family members; and increases the likelihood that youths will learn effective modes of communication for interacting in a healthy manner with peers, adults, and siblings around substance abuse prevention and a variety of topics.

The content introduces parents and children to the diversity and specialness of those around them. In an illustrative exercise, parents learn how they can engage in family events in their neighborhoods and communities. As

they move through workbook materials, family members gain an appreciation for other people's lives, feelings, and motives. Consequently, children
learn to more effectively communicate their appreciation for others. Just as
important, role plays acquaint parents and children with the means for
learning new behaviors. Role plays allow children to practice in advance for
new and difficult situations related to drug use.

Decision Making

Incorporated into decision making are concepts of self-control, problem
solving, and values clarification. Our inclusion of these components into the
decision-making unit creates opportunities for parents to teach youths an
array of skills for reducing their drug risks and for promoting healthy
lifestyles. Exercises for decision making include problem-solving skills, as
covered by skills intervention. Besides problem-solving skills, decision-
making content helps parents direct children toward and away from influences on their behavior, depending on the nature of the influence. For
example, through exercises they complete with their parents, children learn
how to recognize when they are faced with unhealthy and risky situations.
With equal emphasis, the materials show parents ways to teach their children
how to take advantage of situations with positive potential.

Exercises in the parent component enable youths to identify helpful
adults in their environments to whom they can turn for assistance. By complet-
ing worksheets structured for engaging such assistance, youths learn who
can help them and what help those persons can lend when they confront situations that are beyond their abilities. As such, decision-making content in the
parent intervention materials covers information on the processes and substance of decision making relative to positive and negative circumstances.

COMMUNITY INVOLVEMENT

Concurrent with skills and parent components, community involvement
strategies extend drug prevention activities into high-risk youths' neighborhoods and everyday environments. That extension occurs as participants plan
and execute events that involve extended family members, neighborhood
residents, and community members. These events are community meetings,
poster-making exercises, and problem-solving contests. Community agency
staff and peer leaders who deliver skills intervention lead youths through
each component.

Community meetings take place at collaborating sites. Besides youths
and intervention providers, these meetings include youths' extended kinship
network members, community residents, and neighbors. Each study partici-

pant invites a minimum of three people and a maximum of six people to each meeting. Intervention delivery agents encourage youths to invite community leaders (e.g., local politicians, elected and government officials, and clergy), professionals, merchants and business representatives, and extended family members (including unrelated neighbors) to the meetings. Even so, youths can extend the invitations to anyone they choose, as long as the participants who attend the meetings are adults from the local community.

Through hand-delivered announcements, youths invite participants to community meetings. Invitations explain the purposes of community intervention and contain a calendar with meeting dates and times, a map to the meeting place, and meal, child care, and transportation provisions for attendees. Five days before each community meeting, all those who agreed to attend receive telephone reminders.

Intervention staff, peer leaders, and youths plan meetings for the early evening and serve supper, which is prepared by youths. Planning for meetings also involves youths in arranging for the provision of child care for community participants. After on-site staff explain the theme for each community meeting, youths develop and rehearse an agenda. Each meeting begins with introductions and supper. Next, intervention agents review the objectives for the meeting and for community involvement procedures. Youths then present skits, lead group discussions, and show audiovisual materials on drug prevention.

Presentations demonstrate what youths know about drug abuse risk reduction and how those in attendance can help youths avoid behavioral risks associated with drugs. After the presentations, youths and peer leaders answer questions. At the end of the meeting, youths thank participants for attending. Each participant receives a written summary of steps covered at the meeting to help youths avoid risky behaviors associated with drug use.

Interpersonal communication posters engage youths in designing, creating, and distributing throughout their neighborhoods and communities posters about preventing drug use. Posters remind community members that everyone is responsible for assisting youths in avoiding lifestyle behaviors associated with drugs. In their poster designs, youths incorporate landmarks, language, and symbols that have meaning for them. Youths exhibit the posters throughout their neighborhoods in stores, community centers, and other public places. Intervention agents and peer leaders visit each poster display, take photographs of the posters, and display the photographs at each community site.

A problem-solving contest begins with two planning sessions as youths review problem solving, as covered in skills intervention. Directed by on-site staff and peer leaders, youths divide into teams of three and four to plan the problem-solving contest. Each team receives a series of assignments related to a hypothetical youth who has encountered a problem related to drug risks. Next, team members apply problem-solving steps to plan how those hypothetical persons will resolve their problems and reduce their risks. The application of each step brings youths into contact with community members. Youths analyze and apply outside information they gather within a problem-solving format.

Concurrently, the contest exposes community members to intervention as youths collect information, conduct interviews, and draw on resources beyond the community site. Youths earn points for each piece of information they gather and for each community member with whom they interact relative to drug risks. For example, team members gain points for the options they generate via resources to resolve the hypothetical situation posed by another team. Teams receive additional points for enlisting the help of neighbors, community members, health and human services professionals, and civic leaders in their problem-solving efforts.

Discussion

Increasingly, prevention researchers are discovering that American youth from socioeconomic strata that have family household incomes below the federal poverty line are at high risk for encountering future and lifelong problems with drugs, including alcohol and tobacco. In response to that discovery, drug abuse preventive interventions must be developed expressly for such high-risk youth. Those interventions will wisely address developmental as well as parental and community factors that influence drug use among high-risk youth. Toward that end, we are working with the Institute for Prevention Research at Cornell University Medical College to design and test responsive interventions for high-risk youth.

The interventions include elements on drug use facts, problem solving, coping, and communication skills. Incorporating the community, family, and individual youths, the intervention seeks to build youths' self-esteem, interpersonal skills, and decision-making abilities. With enhanced self-esteem, skills to resist peer pressure, and their family's and community's support and involvement, study participants will hopefully avoid permanently the lifestyle and behaviors associated with drug abuse.

Admittedly, this prevention approach and its application has limitations. Involving participants' parents and their communities takes extraordinary time and effort. Many working parents simply do not have the time to participate in the activities that this intervention requires. Yet their involvement is critical to the successful outcome of the prevention project. Similarly, participants find recruiting community members formidable and occasionally disappointing; some community members promise to participate and then do not attend. Developing an intervention that is culturally relevant for every ethnic/racial minority group represented in the study population is also challenging.

Still, on balance, the skills intervention approach advocated here has much to recommend it for youth at high risk for problems associated with drug and other substance abuse. Additional research will refine and expand this prevention approach so that it ultimately reaches all of the high-risk youth who can benefit from aggressive efforts to prevent drug use and abuse.

References

Annual update of the federal poverty guidelines. (1991, February 20). *Federal Register,* pp. 6859-6861.

Bailey, S. L. (1992). Adolescents' multisubstance use patterns: The role of heavy alcohol and cigarette use. *American Journal of Public Health, 82,* 1220-1224.

Bandura, A. (1977). *Social learning theory.* Englewood Cliffs, NJ: Prentice Hall.

Bandura, A. (1990). Perceived self-efficacy in the exercise of control over AIDS infection. *Evaluation and Program Planning, 13,* 9-17.

Bobo, J. K., Cvetkovich, G. T., Trimble, J. E., Gilchrist, L. D., & Schinke, S. P. (1988). Cross-cultural service delivery to minority communities. *Journal of Community Psychology, 16,* 263-272.

Botvin, G. J., & Botvin, E. M. (1992). School-based and community-based prevention approaches. In J. H. Lowinson, P. Ruiz, & R. B. Millman (Eds.), *Substance abuse: A comprehensive textbook* (2nd ed., pp. 910-927). Baltimore: Williams & Wilkins.

Botvin, G. J., Schinke, S. P., & Orlandi, M. A. (1989). Psychosocial approaches to substance abuse prevention: Theoretical foundations and empirical findings. *Crisis, 10,* 62-77.

Botvin, G. J., & Wills, T. A. (1985). Personal and social skills training: Cognitive-behavioral approaches to substance abuse prevention. In C. Bell & R. Battjes (Eds.), *Prevention research: Deterring drug abuse among children and adolescents* (NIDA Research Monograph No. 63, pp. 8-49). Washington, DC: Government Printing Office.

Cloward, R., & Ohlin, L. (1960). *Delinquency and opportunity.* New York: Free Press.

Cvetkovich, G., Earle, T. C., Schinke, S. P., Gilchrist, L. D., & Trimble, J. E. (1987). Child and adolescent drug use: A judgment and information processing perspective to health-behavior interventions. *Journal of Drug Education, 17,* 295-313.

Dusenbury, L., Kerner, J. F., Baker, E., Botvin, G., James-Ortiz, S., & Zauber, A. (1992). Predictors of smoking prevalence among New York Latino youth. *American Journal of Public Health, 82,* 55-58.

Dwyer, J. T. (1992). Nutritional remedies: Reasonable and questionable. *Annals of Behavioral Medicine, 14,* 120-125.

Elliot, D., Ageton, S., & Canter, R. (1979). An integrated theoretical perspective on delinquent behavior. *Journal of Research in Crime and Delinquency, 16,* 3-27.

Fisher, G. M. (1984). The 1984 poverty income guidelines. *Social Security Bulletin, 47,* 24-27.

Flay, B. R. (1985). Psychosocial approaches to smoking prevention: A review of the findings. *Health Psychology, 4,* 449-488.

Forgey, M. A., & Schinke, S. P. (in press). Developing and testing preventive interventions for substance abuse among African American and Hispanic American urban youth. In R. Clayton (Ed.), *Prevention research: An international perspective*. Thousand Oaks, CA: Sage.

Fraser, M., & Kohlert, N. (1988). Substance abuse and public policy. *Social Service Review, 62*, 103-125.

Gilchrist, L. D., Schinke, S. P., Trimble, J. E., & Cvetkovich, G. T. (1987). Skills enhancement to prevent substance abuse among American Indian adolescents. *International Journal of the Addictions, 22*, 869-879.

Greenwald, P., Cullen, J. W., & McKenna, J. W. (1987). Cancer prevention and control: From research through applications. *Journal of the National Cancer Institute, 79*, 389-400.

Hawkins, J. D., Catalano, R. F., & Miller, J. Y. (1992). Risk and protective factors for alcohol and other drug problems in adolescence and early childhood: Implications for substance abuse prevention. *Psychological Bulletin, 112*, 103-115.

Hawkins, J. D., Catalano, R. F., Morrison, D. M., O'Donnell, J., Abbott, R. D., & Day, L. E. (1992). The Seattle Social Development Project: Effects of the first four years on protective factors and problem behaviors. In J. McCord & R. Tremblay (Eds.), *The prevention of antisocial behavior in children* (pp. 139-161). New York: Guilford.

Hechinger, F. M. (1992). *Fateful choices: Healthy youth for the 21st century*. New York: Carnegie Corporation.

Hiatt, R. A., Klatsky, A. L., & Armstrong, M. A. (1988). Alcohol consumption and the risk of breast cancer in a prepaid health plan. *Cancer Research, 48*, 2284-2287.

Hirschi, T. (1969). *Causes of delinquency*. Berkeley: University of California Press.

Jessor, R. (1984). Adolescent development and behavioral health. In J. D. Matarazzo, S. M. Weiss, J. A. Herd, N. E. Miller, & S. M. Weiss (Eds.), *Behavioral health* (pp. 69-90). New York: John Wiley.

Jessor, R. (1987). Problem behavior theory, psychosocial development, and adolescent problem drinking. *British Journal of Addiction, 82*, 331-342.

Jessor, R., Collins, M. I., & Jessor, S. L. (1972). On becoming a drinker. *Annual of the New York Academy of Sciences, 197*, 199-213.

Jessor, R., & Jessor, S. L. (1977). *Problem behavior and psychosocial development*. New York: Academic Press.

Marzuk, P. M., Tardiff, K., Leon, A. C., Stajic, M., Morgan, E. B., & Mann, J. J. (1990). Prevalence of recent cocaine use among motor vehicle fatalities in New York City. *Journal of the American Medical Association, 263*, 250-256.

McKay, J. R., Murphy, R. T., McGuire, J., Rivinus, T. R., & Maisto, S. A. (1992). Incarcerated adolescents' attributions for drug and alcohol use. *Addictive Behaviors, 17*, 227-235.

Moncher, M. S., Holden, G. W., & Schinke, S. P. (1991). Psychosocial correlates of substance abuse among youth: A review of current etiological constructs. *International Journal of the Addictions, 26*, 377-414.

Moncher, M. S., Trimble, J. E., & Schinke, S. P. (in press). Drug and alcohol abuse prevention among Native American youth. *Journal of Consulting and Clinical Psychology*.

National Institute of Justice. (1990, March). *1988 Drug use forecast and annual report*. Washington, DC: Research in Action.

National Institute on Drug Abuse. (1985). *Drug use among American high school students, college students, and other young adults*. Rockville, MD: Government Printing Office.

Oetting, E., & Beauvais, F. (1986). Peer cluster theory: Drugs and the adolescent. *Journal of Counseling and Development, 65*, 17-22.

Oetting, E., & Beauvais, F. (1987). Peer cluster theory, socialization characteristics and adolescent drug use: A path analysis. *Journal of Counseling Psychology, 34,* 205-213.

Orlandi, M. A. (1992). The challenge of evaluating community-based prevention programs: A cross-cultural perspective. In M. A. Orlandi, R. Weston, & L. Epstein (Eds.), *A guide for alcohol and other drug abuse prevention practitioners working with racial/ethnic communities* (pp.). Washington, DC: Office for Substance Abuse Prevention, Division of Community Prevention and Training.

Orlandi, M. A., Landers, C., Weston, R., & Haley, N. (1990). Diffusion of health promotion innovations. In K. Glanz, F. M. Lewis, & B. K. Rimer (Eds.), *Health behavior and health education: Theory, research and practice* (pp. 288-313). San Francisco: Jossey-Bass.

Orlandi, M. A., Lieberman, L. R., & Schinke, S. P. (1989). The effects of alcohol and tobacco advertising on adolescents. *Drugs and Society, 3,* 77-97.

Orlandi, M. A., Weston, R., & Epstein, L. (Eds.). (1992). *A guide for alcohol and other drug abuse prevention practitioners working with racial/ethnic communities.* Washington, DC: Office for Substance Abuse Pr‍‍‍on, Division of Community Prevention and Training.

Pentz, M. A. (1983). Prevention of adolescent substance abuse through social skills. In T. J. Glynn, C. G. Leukefeld, & J. P. Ludford (Eds.), *Preventing adolescent drug abuse: Intervention strategies* (NIDA Research Monograph No. 47, pp. 195-232). Washington, DC: Government Printing Office.

Resnicow, K. A., Orlandi, M. A., & Wynder, E. L. (1989). Toward an effective school health education policy: A call for legislative and educational reform. *Preventive Medicine, 18,* 1-9.

Schinke, S. P., & Gilchrist, L. D. (1984). *Life skills counseling with adolescents.* Baltimore, MD: University Park.

Schinke, S. P., & Gilchrist, L. D. (1985). Preventing substance abuse with children and adolescents. *Journal of Consulting and Clinical Psychology, 53,* 598-602.

Schinke, S. P., Moncher, M. S., Holden, G. W., Botvin, G. J., & Orlandi, M. A. (1989). American Indian youth and substance abuse. *Health Education Research, 4,* 137-144.

Schinke, S. P., Moncher, M. S., Palleja, J., Zayas, L. H., & Schilling, R. F. (1988). Hispanic youth, substance abuse, and stress: Implications for prevention research. *International Journal of the Addictions, 23,* 809-826.

Schinke, S. P., Orlandi, M. A., Botvin, G. J., Gilchrist, L. D., Trimble, J. E., & Locklear, V. S. (1988). Preventing substance abuse among American Indian adolescents: A bicultural competence skills approach. *Journal of Counseling Psychology, 35,* 87-90.

Schinke, S. P., Orlandi, M. A., & Cole, K. C. (1992). Boys and girls clubs in public housing developments: Prevention services for youth at risk. *Journal of Community Psychology, 28,* 118-128.

Schinke, S. P., Schilling, R. F., Palleja, J., & Zayas, L. H. (1987). Prevention research among ethnic racial minority group adolescents. *Behavior Therapist, 10,* 151-155.

Snow, W. H., Gilchrist, L. D., & Schinke, S. P. (1985). A critique of progress in adolescent smoking prevention. *Children and Youth Services Review, 7,* 1-9.

Urberg, K., & Robbins, R. (1983). *Adolescent invulnerability.* Unpublished manuscript, Wayne State University.

U.S. Department of Health and Human Services. (1985). *Report of the Secretary's Task Force on Black and Minority Health: Vol. 2. Crosscutting issues in minority health.* Washington, DC: Author.

U.S. House Select Committee on Narcotics Abuse and Control. (1985, January 3). *Annual report of the year, 1984.* H.R. 1199, 98th Cong., 2d Sess.

Utech, D., & Hoving, K. L. (1969). Parents and peers as competing influences in the decisions on children of differing ages. *Journal of Social Psychology, 78,* 267-274.

Walter, H. J., Vaughan, R. D., Gladis, M. M., Ragin, D. F., Kasen, S., & Cohall, A. T. (1992). Factors associated with AIDS risk behaviors among high school students in an AIDS epicenter. *American Journal of Public Health, 82,* 528-532.

Wish, E. (1985●●). *Drug use and crime arrestees in Manhattan.* Paper presented at the 47th annual scientific meeting of the Committee on Problems of Drug Dependency, Baltimore.

Yamaguchi, K., & Kandel, D. B. (1984). Patterns of drug use from adolescence to young adulthood: III. Predictors of progression. *American Journal of Public Health, 74,* 673-681.

Zigler, E., Taussig, C., & Black, K. (1992). Early childhood intervention. *American Psychologist, 47,* 997-1006.

Developing Interventions for Multiethnic Populations

A Case Study With Homeless Youth

Linda Dusenbury
Tracy Diaz

One of the initial steps in working with any group of people is to understand the social, economic, and cultural perspectives of that group. According to Orlandi (1992), *culture* refers to norms, values, and customs that are shared by a group of people. With multiethnic populations, a variety of racial and ethnic heritages and cultures are represented in a single setting. Our prevention efforts have taken place in schools, shelters for homeless families, community centers, and housing developments in and around New York City. In each of these settings, there are multiethnic populations. Although the population is primarily African American and Latino, both of these groups represent numerous cultural heritages. For example, African Americans in New York City may have cultural backgrounds that are urban, rural, southern, northeastern, or Caribbean. The four major Latino groups in New York City are Puerto Rican, Dominican, Ecuadorian, and Colombian. In our work in multicultural settings, it therefore has been necessary to design interventions that are sensitive to multiple cultures at the same time.

The purpose of this chapter is to describe a strategy we have used for identifying and developing feasible and appropriate drug abuse prevention approaches for multiethnic audiences. In order to illustrate the strategy to develop interventions for multiethnic communities, we describe our experience in shelters for homeless families, as well as the intervention model we developed for homeless youth.

Identifying Prevention
Strategies for Multiethnic Populations

We believe that an effective strategy for identifying prevention approaches for use in multiethnic communities must involve an active collaboration between drug abuse prevention researchers and representatives of the target community. Drug abuse prevention researchers provide expertise in three crucial conceptual areas: (a) They have important information about the causes of drug abuse; (b) they are aware of the history of drug abuse prevention approaches, and they know what types of prevention approaches are most likely to work; and (c) they have an understanding of the developmental stage at which substance use begins (typically early in adolescence) and how substance abuse develops.

However, what drug abuse prevention researchers may lack is an understanding of the multiethnic cultures in which they work. Although it may be possible for prevention researchers to increase their cultural competence in the communities in which they work by reading available literature as well as by interacting and collaborating with members of the target community, we believe that in order to design truly feasible and acceptable interventions, it is also necessary for them to enlist the active involvement of members or representatives of the community in developing drug abuse prevention programs. Representatives of the target community can make important contributions in three basic areas: (a) helping to determine the types of intervention strategies that are likely to be acceptable to the community, (b) providing drug abuse researchers with credibility in the community, and (c) helping to identify ways of communicating the benefits of participation in the intervention to the community.

The Community's Contribution

DETERMINING ACCEPTABLE
INTERVENTIONS AND PROVIDING CREDIBILITY

Helping to determine acceptable prevention interventions and providing credibility in the community can be achieved through the active involvement of community members in the prevention project. Our strategy, which has evolved over the course of the past 8 years in our work in schools, and over the past 5 years in shelters, involves a number of levels of community involvement. The first and perhaps most important level is participation of representatives of the community on the prevention team itself. We believe that it is crucial to have members of the target ethnic or racial group on the research staff in order to help shape research questions and intervention strategies. In addition, we have found that it is important to have members of the target ethnic or racial groups on the field staff. In our experience, field staff are instrumental in shaping recruitment strategies as well as intervention strategies and evaluation protocols. In addition, when field staff are integrated members of the prevention team, those who share an ethnic and/or racial heritage with members of the target community provide the prevention team with credibility in the target community.

A second level of involvement is participation of highly visible community leaders and public figures who endorse or otherwise actively support the prevention activities. These individuals might be local political figures who are identified as leaders by members of the target community. In New York City, we have found this level of involvement to be more complicated than one might expect initially. On the one hand, although simply gaining support in the form of endorsements is not terribly difficult, it can appear superficial and be less impressive to the community. On the other hand, enlisting the active support of highly visible leaders carries with it the risk of alienating others when political rivalries exist, as well as the risk of falling out of favor when the leader loses popularity. These risks become particularly treacherous in highly complex political communities such as those in New York City.

A third, related level of community involvement that avoids some of the risk of the previous level is based on identifying natural community leaders who are well known and well respected in the neighborhoods in which they live. These individuals might be presidents or active members of the PTA or might be actively involved in community boards. They are usually identified by members of the target community as highly credible. Although the risks of political rivalries are lessened at this level, they are not fully eliminated. Politics is a dangerous force at any level.

A fourth level of community involvement consists of the participation of employees at the intervention site in the prevention project. In school settings, for example, principals, assistant principals, and teachers might review intervention materials and recruitment strategies and provide feedback and suggestions. In community settings, site directors and their support staff, including recreation staff, might be asked to participate in the development and refinement of the prevention program. Because of their knowledge and experience working in the community, feedback from these individuals can be invaluable in designing successful prevention interventions for the target community.

A fifth level of community involvement involves soliciting input and feedback from members of the community who will be directly affected by the intervention. For our purposes, this level has included parents and children from participating prevention sites. Focus groups can be instrumental in achieving this level of involvement. Typically, we conduct focus groups with children or adolescents and parents separately in order to obtain qualitative information about the concerns and issues facing different groups in the community and feedback about the types of approaches most likely to be acceptable and appropriate in the community.

COMMUNICATING THE
BENEFITS OF PARTICIPATION

One of the critical functions an effective program must undertake is to clarify and communicate the benefits of the intervention to the community. This involves more than simply communicating directly with children or adolescents targeted by the intervention; it is equally important to communicate to the adults involved with the children whom we attempt to recruit for the program.

There are several groups of adults to be concerned with. In the context of school-based interventions, the primary adults are parents, teachers, and school principals. For example, principals review program materials and agree to school participation in the program, teachers buy in as program providers, and parents provide either active or passive consent for the participation of each child. One-by-one recruitment of parents may represent the most difficult and least aggregate of the researcher's tasks. Each victory may involve one or two or three children at most, yet each victory can prove elusive and difficult to achieve.

To deliver the prevention program in a homeless shelter or other non-school environment, we face another array of adults as gatekeepers: shelter staff (who include professionals and paraprofessionals), parents, and older children. As with any gatekeeper performing any expected or sanctioned official function, the task of getting that person on board often requires some deliberation about strategy. Often, a principal requirement is presenting an acceptable image and an acceptable explanation of tasks.

In general, multicultural professionals and parents are highly invested in the gatekeeping functions they perform. Parents, in particular, see themselves as protectors of their children, in environments where they believe the children often need to be protected from researchers. Multicultural communities, particularly African American communities, at times have been observed to show a high level of mistrust toward researchers, perhaps as a result of previous studies such as the Tuskegee Study (Jones & Battjes, 1985;

Thomas & Quinn, 1991), which began in Alabama in the 1930s. In the Tuskegee Study, treatment was deliberately withheld for over 30 years from African American men infected with syphilis (Dalton, 1989). Participants were not informed about the true nature of the study, nor were they ever educated about their disease or how to prevent transmission (Jones & Battjes, 1985; Thomas & Quinn, 1991). Thus, distrust on the part of individuals who see themselves as protectors of the children has had a long history and is firmly entrenched in the upbringing of many of the parents and involved adults who have a gatekeeping role. There are additional issues concerning mistrust, including distrust by aliens of questions or official documents, which may interfere with research efforts.

It is important in communications between researchers and gatekeepers to remain focused on winning explanations of the program, its components, and its reported and intended outcomes. Focusing on the benefits of the program represents an arena in which the program developers have clear information that parents and other gatekeepers are likely to be attracted to.

Prevention programs offer numerous benefits. For example, the competence enhancement approach to drug abuse prevention (described by Botvin, Chapter 9 of this volume) offers benefits in terms of personal skills training, social skills training, self-esteem enhancement, drug use prevention, and smoking prevention. Indeed, one of the important benefits to communicate, and repeat, to gatekeepers is the roster of specific skills that the prevention program will teach. These skills need to be defined, and the rationale for selecting each skill explained. The assumption that parents are aware of or skilled at the competencies that the program endeavors to teach children may be erroneous; it would be useful in communicating with parents and other gatekeepers to allow the possibility that there is also a potential benefit to parents of being exposed to the program components.

We have not found technical presentations about evaluation studies to be appropriate or effective in communicating the potential benefits to gatekeepers. However, effort does need to be made to find ways of communicating the potential effectiveness of the prevention program to those adults who have the power to grant permission for a child's participation in a project.

The need for communication between researchers and gatekeepers that is explicit and that provides important information reflects an exciting synergy of the research process. In the past, researchers and academics from the dominant culture were accustomed to a research process that involved only the project/program developers and the academic reviewers who commented on the papers resulting from the research. In multicultural communities, however, gatekeepers retain the power to permit or refuse participation in the project. Involving these gatekeepers in a partnership with the researcher can enhance the research itself.

What the Prevention Researcher Can Offer

The prevention researcher contributes three areas of expertise that are indispensable to designing effective prevention interventions: (a) expertise in drug abuse etiology, (b) expertise in drug abuse prevention, and (c) expertise about the developmental stage at which drug use begins, which is usually adolescence.

DRUG ABUSE ETIOLOGY

In order to prevent drug abuse, it is necessary first to understand the causes of the behavior (Botvin & Botvin, 1992). There is extensive literature in the general population regarding the correlates and predictors of substance abuse, which can generally be categorized as social factors, psychological characteristics, cognitive and attitudinal factors, and pharmacological factors (Blum & Richards, 1979; Jessor & Jessor, 1977; Jones & Battjes, 1985; Newcomb & Bentler, 1988). Of these, social influences appear to be the most powerful predictors of substance use. Social influences include attitudes and behaviors of parents, siblings, and friends (Barnes & Welte, 1986; Brown, Clasen, & Eicher, 1986; Kandel & Andrew, 1987). In terms of individual characteristics, substance use has been associated with low self-esteem, assertiveness, personal control, and self-sufficiency (Clarke, MacPherson, & Holmes, 1982; Dielman, Leech, Lorenger, & Horvath, 1984; Page, 1989), as well as increased anxiety, impulsivity, and rebelliousness (Jessor & Jessor, 1977; Jones & Battjes, 1985). Cognitive factors and attitudes also play a role: Not surprisingly, individuals with more positive attitudes toward drug use are more likely to use drugs compared with those with less positive attitudes. People who consider substance use "normal" and believe that most people use substances are more likely themselves to use substances (Chassin, Presson, Sherman, & Edwards, 1992). Although there is considerable variability in the pharmacology of different substances, commonly used substances are similar in that their effects are reinforcing and produce dependency. For the most commonly abused substances, including cigarettes, alcohol, and "recreational" drugs, tolerance quickly develops, resulting in increasing consumption and frequency of use. Culture exerts a powerful influence on health behaviors, establishing values and norms and determining whether and how a behavior will be reinforced (Kozol, 1988). For this reason it is preferable to have expertise in drug abuse etiology for the particular ethnic or racial groups in the target community. Unfortunately, information about drug abuse etiology in multiethnic communities is often limited. Moreover, there appears to be considerable variability across cultural groups in terms of predictors of substance use, though we have been impressed by the similarities of certain predictors across ethnic and racial groups, both in the literature generally and in our own studies (Botvin, Batson, et al., 1989; Botvin, Dusenbury, Baker, James-Ortiz, & Kerner, 1989). For example, one of the consistently most powerful predictors of smoking, alcohol, or other drug use is use of these substances by peers. This is true for white populations (Botvin & Botvin, 1992), African American populations (Botvin, Batson, et al., 1989), and Latino populations (Dusenbury et al., 1992). However, there are also differences between racial and ethnic groups, and understanding these differences may allow interventions to be tailored to more specifically address culturally relevant experiences in certain populations. For example, familial influences appear to predict substance use in Latino populations, and tailoring interventions to include family components may result in greater efficacy.

DRUG ABUSE PREVENTION

A second area of expertise that a drug abuse prevention researcher can offer to the community is knowledge about the field of drug abuse prevention, in terms of both theory and empirical studies. Historically, drug abuse prevention efforts can be grouped into five general approaches: (a) information dissemination approaches, including fear arousal and moralistic appeals; (b) affective education; (c) alternatives; (d) social influence approaches; and (e) broader competency enhancement that promotes the development of broader personal and social skills.

The goal of information dissemination is to increase knowledge about drugs and the dangers of drug use through the use of lectures, discussions, media presentations, displays, school assemblies, and so on. Many types of information dissemination attempt to dramatize the danger and arouse fear. An extensive literature evaluating information dissemination clearly shows that this approach alone does not work (Dorn & Thompson, 1976; Kinder, Pape, & Walfish, 1980; Schaps, Bartolo, Moskowitz, Palley, & Churgin, 1981; Swisher & Hoffman, 1975). Some studies have even suggested that information dissemination may be associated with increased experimentation, possibly because it stimulates curiosity (Swisher, Crawford, Goldstein, & Yura, 1971).

Affective education is designed to increase self-understanding and acceptance, and relies on activities relating to decision making, effective communication, and assertiveness. As with information dissemination, evaluation of affective education approaches has been disappointing. Although affective education approaches have occasionally affected correlates of substance use, they have not been shown to affect substance use behavior (Kearney & Hines, 1980; Kim, 1988).

Alternatives programs are designed to provide adolescents with alternatives to drug use and the activities that may lead to drug use. Alternatives programs have included a wide range of activities, including community service, entertainment, participation in vocational activities, academic tutoring, sports, hobbies, and Outward Bound. Although some alternatives activities (such as academic activities, involvement in religious activities, and participation in sports) have been shown to be related to nonsubstance use, others, such as entertainment and social activities, as well as participation in vocational activities, have been associated with increased substance use (Swisher & Hu, 1983). Activities that might be the most appropriate as alternatives may be less interesting, particularly to those at highest risk for using drugs. No evaluations of alternatives programs have been able to demonstrate an impact on substance use behavior (Schaps et al., 1981; Schaps, Moskowitz, Malvin, & Scheffer, 1986).

Social influence approaches and competence enhancement approaches have been based to varying degrees on communications theory (McGuire, 1964, 1968), social learning theory (Bandura, 1977), and adolescent problem behavior theory (Jessor & Jessor, 1977). These two approaches are related, yet distinct. The social influence approach was intended to affect the social influences promoting substance use. The pioneering work with this approach was conducted by Evans and his colleagues (Evans et al., 1978), who developed an intervention focusing on social influences related to cigarette smoking. The intervention was specifically designed to "inoculate" adolescents against pressures to smoke by correcting misperceptions concerning the prevalence of smoking as well as by teaching resistance skills. In evaluation, a number of variations on this approach have been shown to reduce smoking (Hurd et al., 1980; Orlandi, 1992), as well as alcohol and marijuana use (McAlister, Perry, Killen, Slinkard, & Maccoby, 1980), with program effects evident for up to 2 years after program completion (Luepker, Johnson, Murray, & Pechacek, 1983; McAlister et al., 1980; Telch, Killen, McAlister, Perry, & Maccoby, 1982).

The broader competence enhancement approach is designed to address the factors related to substance use more comprehensively (Botvin & Eng, 1982; Pentz, 1983). Specifically, the goal of this approach is to promote the development of important personal and social skills that heighten competence generally and to reduce motivation to smoke, drink, or use drugs. This approach emphasizes generic skills training and includes some combination of decision making and problem solving; cognitive skills for resisting social influences to use substances, including media influences to smoke or drink; skills for increasing self-control and promoting self-esteem; stress management skills and anxiety reduction techniques; general social skills; and assertiveness skills. A series of studies with this approach show its effectiveness at reducing smoking, drinking, and marijuana use (Botvin, Baker, Botvin, Filazzola, & Millman, 1984; Botvin, Baker, Filazzola, & Botvin, 1990; Botvin & Eng, 1980; Botvin, Eng, & Williams, 1980; Botvin, Renick, & Baker, 1983; Pentz, 1983; Schinke, 1984; Schinke & Blythe, 1981; Schinke & Gilchrist, 1983, 1984), with results evident up to 3 years.

EFFECTIVENESS OF
DRUG ABUSE PREVENTION

Although evaluation of information dissemination approaches, affective education, and alternatives programs have been disappointing, evaluation studies of the social influence approach and the competence enhancement approach clearly demonstrate the efficacy of these approaches to substance abuse prevention. In addition, in response to methodological criticisms of the social influence approach and the competence enhancement approach (Biglan & Ary, 1985; Botvin, 1986; Flay, 1985; Glasgow & McCaul, 1985; Schaps et al., 1981), prevention research has become progressively more rigorous. Indeed, the most recently published studies are impressive in terms of their size, scope, and methodological sophistication (Botvin, Baker, Dusenbury, Tortu, & Botvin, 1990; Pentz, Brannon, et al., 1989; Pentz, Dwyer, et al., 1989). The growing empirical evidence indicates quite clearly that the social influence and competence enhancement approaches *are* effective. However, even more persuasive than data from the most recently published evaluation studies, with all of their methodological sophistication, is the replicability and consistency of findings across studies and research groups.

Knowledge of the drug abuse prevention literature is essential to developing new interventions because many of the strategies that are intuitively appealing (e.g., information dissemination and fear arousal) and may be recommended or even actively promoted by members of the target community have not worked. For example, we have been urged to include scare tactics in our intervention approach in virtually every focus group we have ever conducted with teenagers or lay adults, as well as by numerous school personnel, in urban, rural, and suburban communities, regardless of SES or race. Of course, although community members will often suggest approaches that have not worked in the past, it is not necessary and in fact would be counterproductive to dismiss these suggestions in a heavy-handed or condescending way. To begin with, these suggestions are often made in the context of brainstorming, and a range of other more promising approaches (e.g., resistance skills training) may also be mentioned. An awareness of the drug prevention literature allows the prevention researcher to focus on promising suggestions and to tactfully ignore less promising approaches.

THE STAGE AT WHICH DRUG USE BEGINS

The drug abuse prevention researcher brings important information about the developmental stage at which substance use begins to the task of developing appropriate prevention interventions. Drug use has been observed to follow a predictable developmental progression (Hamburg, Braemer, & Jahnke, 1975; Kandel, 1978), beginning with experimentation and recreational use of cigarettes and alcohol, and proceeding only later to marijuana or, in the inner cities, cocaine or crack. Prior to use of marijuana, the risk of using other illicit substances appears low (Yamaguchi & Kandel, 1984). Use of opiates and hallucinogens usually appears late in the sequence. The drug abuse prevention researcher understands the importance of including cigarettes and alcohol as targets of prevention techniques because of their importance in the developmental sequence of substance use behavior.

Experimentation with cigarettes, alcohol, and other drugs and the early stages of drug abuse typically begin in adolescence (Millman & Botvin, 1983). Adolescence represents a critical stage in human development. In psychological terms, the general four major tasks of the adolescent period are (a) to adjust to the physical changes of puberty, (b) to become independent from parents, (c) to establish relationships with peers, and (d) to prepare for work. Though normal, these tasks are challenging and difficult (Mussen, Conger, & Kagan, 1979), and may lead to feelings of powerlessness, alienation, and rebellion. Adolescence is a time for practicing and preparing for new roles and tasks, and after age 10 the preadolescent begins experimenting with an array of new behaviors. Unfortunately, for many, regardless of culture or ethnic group, cigarettes, alcohol, and other drugs are perceived as a normal part of coming of age (Carnegie Corporation of New York, 1990).

The developmental stage of adolescence is associated with dramatic physical, social, and cognitive changes (Mussen et al., 1979) that can result in new stresses and anxieties and also may increase vulnerability to peer pressure. Puberty involves dramatic physical changes that may be disruptive to self-image and self-esteem. In addition, puberty is associated with an increasing interest in members of the opposite sex, altering the status of different members of the peer group. Socially, adolescence is marked by increased independence from parents and increased reliance on peers for validation and guidance (Utech & Hoving, 1969). Conformity to the peer group increases rapidly just before and in early adolescence, when it peaks and then gradually declines (Mussen et al., 1979). Acceptance by peers is crucially important to the adolescent, and rejection by peers can be devastating.

Because of cognitive development, there are also a number of ways in which adolescent thought changes (Ginsburg & Opper, 1978; U.S. Congress, 1991). Adolescents are able to think hypothetically and more flexibly than younger children. As a result, they are able to begin questioning rules that previously were taken for granted, and to consider or experience novel and alternative lifestyles (Mussen et al., 1979).

Thought becomes introspective during adolescence, but it remains relatively egocentric compared with adult thought. For example, adolescents have developed to the point that they understand that other people have lives independent of them and that other people have internal thoughts of their own. But adolescents have more difficulty separating their own thoughts from the thoughts of others, and they often assume that others are as preoccupied with their behavior as they themselves are. Their "imaginary audience" may help to explain the excruciating level of self-consciousness frequently observed in adolescence (Carnegie Corporation of New York, 1990; Elkind, 1978).

Thus, the issues of adolescence include an increasing reliance on peers, as well as increasing anxiety about social situations. As a result of cognitive changes, adolescents tend to be more interested in information pertaining to the "here and now" as opposed to the far-off future. By understanding the stage at which substance use begins and the defining characteristics and issues of that stage of development, the prevention researcher is able to design interventions that not only address the reasons people begin to experiment with drugs but also do so in a way that is meaningful and appealing to the target audience.

Developing Interventions
for Homeless Youth: A Case Study

Over the years, we have developed prevention interventions for use in multiethnic communities using the collaborative strategy outlined above. Below, we describe our experience developing an intervention for youth living in shelters for homeless families in New York City.

Families with young children are the fastest growing segment of the homeless population; of the newly homeless in the United States, 75% are families (Kozel, 1988). On average, these families have two children, and 90% are headed by women. One quarter of these families are white, three quarters Latino and African American. In New York City, between 5,000 and 6,000 families receive shelter each year (New York City Mayor's Office on Homelessness, 1993).

In 1988 we were invited by the New York Children's Health Project to develop a drug abuse prevention approach for use in shelters for homeless families in New York City. The New York Children's Health Project provides pediatric services to children living in the New York City shelter system, using mobile medical units staffed by pediatricians and nurses. Because the majority of residents living in the shelter system in New York City are African American and Latino, including Puerto Ricans and Dominicans, the prevention strategy we would develop needed to be appropriate for use in multiethnic communities.

The prevention program for use with homeless youth has continued to develop over the course of the past 5 years. The developmental phase covered the first 3 years. In the last 2 years, we have conducted a preliminary evaluation study in four shelters in New York City; this study was designed to assess the efficacy of the prevention approach we had developed, and data analysis is now underway. In the remainder of this chapter, we describe our work in shelters and the prevention model developed there. We conclude with a discussion of issues that have emerged during our work and that require further attention.

For 3 years, beginning in 1988, we worked in a large shelter for homeless families in New York City. A total of 214 families and 600 total residents lived in this shelter. The majority (89%) of families were headed by single women, and over 90% were African American or Latino. The average stay in the shelter ranged from 6 to 10 months. The developmental phase was implemented by a project director who was white and an on-site field coordinator who was black and Latino.

Because we had not worked with youth in shelters prior to that point, we began by developing relationships with administrators in the shelter. We asked the director of the center to identify staff most familiar with families and the issues they faced. He identified the director of family services, who became instrumental in helping to shape the prevention approach. We began with initial meetings with the director of family services and his staff in which we tried to become more informed about the issues families faced and the nature of the system set up to provide services to homeless families. We also asked staff members to identify "natural leaders" among both the parents and the young teenagers. With the assistance of the Department of Family Services, we set up two focus groups with adolescents ranging in age from 12 to 17. The focus groups were led by a psychologist, a research assistant, and an attractive moderator in her early 20s who was both black and Latino. The primary purpose of these focus groups was to understand what life was like for these young people. We discussed a range of issues in these focus groups, including experiences in school, experiences in the shelter, relationships with friends, plans for the future, thoughts about drug use, and sources of stress.

1. *Experiences in school.* Most of the adolescents we spoke with had transferred to a school near the shelter when their families were placed there.

The school they attended had a large number of homeless students and was suffering from numerous problems associated with overcrowding and transience. Homeless students were easily identifiable to other students as homeless because they came to school on a van from the shelter. The youth we spoke to felt ostracized and reported tension and fights with other students in the school.

2. *Experience in the shelters.* Most of the young adolescents we spoke to were not happy living in the shelter and did not consider the shelter "home." Life in the shelter was described as boring, with little to do besides hang out. Living in the shelter was to be temporary. Some adolescents also complained about the food and the rules in the shelter.

3. *Relationships with friends.* Because everyone in the shelter was to be there temporarily, most of the adolescents in the focus groups said that they were not terribly interested in making new friendships in the shelter. Instead, many of the adolescents went to great lengths to maintain friendships in their old neighborhoods, commuting for up to 2 hours on weekends to visit friends. It was not unusual for adolescents not to tell friends that they were living in a shelter for homeless families, but instead to say simply that they had moved.

4. *Plans for the future.* Like adolescents in most other settings, the adolescents in the focus groups planned to have rewarding careers in the future. Some wanted to be doctors, lawyers, athletes, and comedians.

5. *Thoughts about drug use.* All of the adolescents we spoke with were aware of drug use in and around the shelter. They had relatively fatalistic views of drug use, not believing it might be possible to prevent it.

6. *Sources of stress.* A number of sources of stress were identified in the focus groups. School represented a major source of stress in terms of academics, adjusting to a new school, and dealing with tensions at school between homeless youth and nonhomeless youth. Noise at the shelter was another source of stress and included shouting in the halls, loud music, and gunshots outside. Drug abuse, fights, shootings, and gang-related activities in the neighborhood also troubled the focus group participants. An additional burden to adolescents was increasing family responsibilities since moving to the shelter. As parents were dealing with the bureaucratically complex tasks of seeking public assistance and permanent housing, they often gave adolescents household responsibilities beyond their years. For example, adolescents might be expected to watch younger siblings, shop for groceries, and

do the laundry. In families in which there was a language barrier, adolescents might even serve as translator for the parent. In general, there seemed to be a frustration among youth that they had little or no control over things that happened to them now that they lived in the shelter.

On the basis of our focus groups with adolescents, we concluded that primary concerns for young people living in this shelter were feeling alienated from other adolescents, desiring affiliation with others and belonging to a group, desiring a sense of control over things that happened, and desiring experiences that would promote a sense of self-worth and self-esteem.

For purposes of intervention development, we also asked adolescents to discuss the kinds of things they might like to do as a group. Adolescents mentioned art projects, video productions, dance classes, sports, and writing projects such as newsletters.

We also conducted a series of focus groups with parents who were identified by shelter staff as "natural leaders." Understandably, parents tended to be focused on trying to find permanent housing, and the dominant issues in their lives revolved around dealing with this immediate crisis. However, parents were very interested in having additional services available for their children. As plans began to emerge for the prevention services, we also conducted numerous interviews and planning meetings with shelter staff, as well as follow-up meetings with adolescents to plan specific prevention program activities.

Substance use was conceptualized within the theoretical framework of social learning theory (Bandura, 1977) and problem behavior theory (Jessor & Jessor, 1977), and a primary objective of our work was to promote in adolescents the development of important personal and social skills as well as to foster self-esteem. (A more detailed description of the competence enhancement approach to drug abuse prevention can be found in Chapter 9 of this volume.) On the basis of our developmental work with adolescents, parents, and shelter staff, we had three additional objectives. First, we wanted to design a prevention program that would promote a sense of affiliation with and acceptance by a positive peer group. Second, we wanted the prevention program to promote a sense of group efficacy. Finally, we wanted to promote a perception among adolescents that there are positive alternatives to drug use.

PROGRAM STRUCTURE

The shelter we were working in had a preexisting structure for delivering recreational and educational services to youth. Specifically, adolescents were divided into two groups: "teens," who were 14 years old or older, and "juniors," who included children and young adolescents up to age 13. Our initial target age for the prevention program was 11 to 13. However, we found it very difficult to exclude younger children or older adolescents who had limited activities available to them and were eager to participate in the program activities we organized. Therefore, initially we created two prevention programs: one for older adolescents (the "teens") and one for younger adolescents and children (the "juniors"). As one would expect given their maturity, teens were more focused and reflective, whereas the attention span of the juniors was much shorter.

THE PREVENTION PROGRAM

In follow-up meetings with teens and juniors, and with the endorsement of the shelter's administration, we proposed creating groups for adolescents. In order to create a sense of group identity and experiences adolescents could use to derive a sense of self-worth, as well as to promote the perception that there are ways besides drug use to achieve personal goals, we felt it was critically important that adolescents have ownership of the group. Therefore, adolescents selected their own group name. In order to create a sense of organization and a sense that individual roles within the group were meaningful and important, an effort was made to define roles for everyone. For example, if the adolescents were working on a newsletter, everyone in the group had a role (e.g., editor, art director, science editor, advice columnist). With younger children, roles might involve serving as a helper during art activities (e.g., passing out paper) or as a model during skill demonstrations.

Over the 5 years we have worked in the shelters, the prevention program has revolved around a number of activities the adolescents chose: publishing a biweekly newsletter, dance productions, art projects, and video productions. These activities gave the group an appealing purpose for existing and helped to attract participants. These activities were important in and of themselves then, in terms of promoting a sense of group identity and affiliation, a sense of group efficacy, and the perception that there are positive alternatives to drug use. However, from the standpoint of prevention, these activities served primarily as a vehicle for skills training. Specifically, within the context of group activities, core components of the competence enhancement approach to substance abuse prevention were presented. These are described below.

Self-Image and Goal Setting. The concepts of self-image and goal setting provided a means of organizing and structuring the groups. The group picked as a goal something they wanted to work toward and achieve (e.g., write a newsletter or create a wall mural). The goal was broken down into short-term, weekly goals (e.g., create a concept for the mural, draw sketches, choose final sketch, learn painting techniques, outline mural, paint mural).

Progress toward meeting these weekly goals was discussed in weekly group meetings, and the final product was publicly displayed. In art projects, adolescents created self-portraits and then discussed them in terms of self-image and self-esteem.

Decision Making and Problem Solving. To help adolescents develop good problem-solving skills, an effective decision-making formula was presented to the group. The formula was then applied to group situations in which decisions had to be made.

Coping With Anxiety. To teach effective ways of coping with anxiety, the concepts of stress and anxiety were discussed during group meetings, and relaxation techniques were demonstrated and practiced. For example, at the beginning of many group meetings the adolescents practiced one or more of the relaxation techniques (e.g., positive visualization, deep breathing, muscle relaxation, mental rehearsal). Also, when anxiety-producing situations were mentioned in discussions, the concept of anxiety was discussed, and ways of coping were reviewed and practiced.

Communication, Social, and Assertiveness Skills. During group inter-actions, principles of effective communication and social interaction were discussed and put into practice. Where appropriate, assertiveness techniques were also covered. For example, in planning for the group projects, the adolescents sometimes needed to involve other people at the shelter or in the community. To prepare to ask someone for help on a project, adolescents practiced in role plays of how to approach the individual and how the conversation might go. These role plays allowed discussion, demonstration, and practice of communication skills such as eye contact and body language, as well as social skills (e.g., how to start a conversation, how to keep it going, and how to end it smoothly) and assertive skills (e.g. how to express your feelings, how to stand up for your rights, how to say no when you want to). Thus, at every opportunity during group interactions, competence enhance-ment concepts were applied and reinforced.

THE PREVENTION PROGRAM PROVIDER

A critical element of the prevention program developed for use in shelters was the prevention program provider. The provider must be able to effectively lead group discussions. The provider also needs to be able to teach new skills, which involves demonstrating skills and creating opportunities for practice and generalization of skills through coaching and reinforcement.

Because of the integration of the program activities (e.g., art, newsletters) with competence enhancement components (e.g., self-image and goal setting, decision making, communication skills), the program provider is responsible for synthesizing the intervention components with the activities. Finally, the provider must effectively provide reinforcement as well as elicit reinforcement from other members of the group.

In order to fulfill all of these functions, the program provider must be fluent in competence enhancement training. He or she must be able to recognize opportunities to apply skills training into various activities. We have found that it also makes the program more meaningful to adolescents if providers are themselves talented in the activity the group is focusing on; for this reason we have involved artists and dancers as providers.

For practical reasons, we have found that it is helpful if the provider is familiar with the shelter system. Providers who are not familiar with the shelter system may have a greater tendency to become frustrated with the shelter system bureaucracy and run a greater risk of burnout.

In terms of recruiting adolescents and maintaining a high level of participation, we have found that the providers should be attractive role models. Adolescents must identify with and look up to the provider if they are to join the prevention program or attend regularly. For this reason, we have found that the best providers are relatively young (in their 20s) and appear to be "down" or "cool" to adolescents, yet are professional and appropriate to shelter administrators.

The importance of the program provider cannot be too heavily underscored. In practical reality, the presentation of the program, the consistent representation of the program, and the appeal of the program to children are fully dependent on the program provider. To the extent possible, providers are recruited to be cultural and professional/occupational models for the children as well.

Conclusion

The challenges to effectively implementing prevention programs in multicultural settings are numerous. For example, we have found that intervention delivery in shelters and other nonschool settings (e.g., community centers and housing developments) is beset with problems related to recruitment, retention, and variable attendance. Further, because the program is delivered in the "home" environment rather than in school or some other formal setting, we find that there are many distractions and competing demands on the children we are trying to recruit. In terms of program evaluations, there are obstacles to obtaining parental and organizational consent. This limits our ability to collect data from enough participants to test the program's efficacy by more customary research methods.

As program developers, we must address these barriers, and the first step is to understand their source. For example, we have identified competing demands and distractions as barriers to consistent attendance in program activities. However, these competing demands and distractions may reflect different underlying issues. On the one hand, distractions may be the result of the influence of the drug culture or other deviant subcultures. Our job as program providers, in this instance, is to pull out all the stops to impress upon the adolescents (or their gatekeepers) that the options presented by the program can be more fulfilling than the competing distraction.

On the other hand, competing demands for the participant's time may have to do with the family demands placed on adolescents in these settings. Often, these demands have to do with caring for siblings, preparing meals, or otherwise standing in for the parent. In this case, our job as program providers might be to help the family meet its needs. We might, for example, provide baby-sitting services for younger siblings at the time that program activities are taking place.

As we learn which efforts yield the best results in overcoming barriers to implementation and evaluation, these efforts can be refined and used consistently, and those that have not worked well can be retired. Agility and openness may well be the key to success in working with multiethnic communities.

References

Bandura, A. (1977). *Social learning theory.* Englewood Cliffs, NJ: Prentice Hall.

Barnes, G. M., & Welte, J. W. (1986). Patterns and predictors of alcohol use among 7-12th grade students in New York State. *Journal of Studies on Alcohol, 47,* 53-62.

Biglan, A., & Ary, D. V. (1985). Current methodological issues in research on smoking prevention. In C. Bell & R. Battjes (Eds.), *Prevention research: Deterring drug abuse among children and adolescents* (NIDA Research Monograph No. 63, pp. 170-195). Washington, DC: Government Printing Office.

Blum, R., & Richards, L. (1979). Youthful drug use. In R. I. Dupont, A. Goldstein, & J. O'Donnell (Eds.), *Handbook on drug abuse* (pp. 257-267). Washington, DC: Government Printing Office.

Botvin, G. J. (1986). Substance abuse prevention research: Recent developments and future directions. *Journal of School Health, 56,* 369-386.

Botvin, G. J., Baker, E., Botvin, E. M., Filazzola, A. D., & Millman, R. B. (1984). Alcohol abuse prevention through the development of personal and social competence: A pilot study. *Journal of Studies on Alcohol, 45,* 550-552.

Botvin, G. J., Baker, E., Dusenbury, L., Tortu, S., & Botvin, E. M. (1990). Preventing adolescent drug abuse through a multimodal cognitive-behavioral approach: Results of a three-year study. *Journal of Consulting and Clinical Psychology, 58,* 437-446.

Botvin, G. J., Baker, E., Filazzola, A., & Botvin, E. M. (1990). A cognitive-behavioral approach to substance abuse prevention: A one-year follow-up. *Addictive Behaviors, 15,* 47-63.

Botvin, G. J., Batson, H., Witts-Vitale, S., Bess, V., Baker, E., & Dusenbury, L. (1989). A psychosocial approach to smoking prevention for urban black youth. *Public Health Reports, 104,* 573-582.

Botvin, G. J., & Botvin, E. (1992). Drug abuse prevention strategies. *Developmental and Behavioral Pediatrics, 13,* 290-301.

Botvin, G. J., Dusenbury, L., Baker, E., James-Ortiz, S., & Kerner, J. (1989). A skills training approach to smoking prevention among Hispanic youth. *Journal of Behavioral Medicine, 12,* 279-296.

Botvin, G. J., & Eng, A. (1980). A comprehensive school-based smoking prevention program. *Journal of School Health, 50,* 209-213.

Botvin, G. J., & Eng, A. (1982). The efficacy of a multicomponent approach to the prevention of cigarette smoking. *Preventive Medicine, 11,* 199-211.

Botvin, G. J., Eng, A., & Williams, C. L. (1980). Preventing the onset of cigarette smoking through life skills training. *Preventive Medicine, 9,* 135-143.

Botvin, G. J., Renick, N., & Baker, E. (1983). The effects of scheduling format and booster sessions on a broad-spectrum psychosocial approach to smoking prevention. *Journal of Behavioral Medicine, 6,* 359-379.

Brown, B., Clasen, D., & Eicher, S. (1986). Perceptions of peer pressure, peer conformity dispositions, and self-reported behavior among adolescents. *Developmental Psychology, 22,* 521-530.

Carnegie Corporation of New York. (1990). Adolescence: Path to a productive life or a diminished future? *Carnegie Quarterly, 35,* 1-13.

Chassin, L., Presson, C. C., Sherman, S. J., & Edwards, D. A. (1992). The natural history of cigarette smoking and young adult social roles. *Journal of Health and Social Behavior, 33,* 328-347.

Clarke, J. G., MacPherson, B. V., & Holmes, D. R. (1982). Cigarette smoking and external focus of control among adolescents. *Journal of Health and Social Behavior, 23,* 253-259.

Dalton, H. L. (1989). AIDS in blackface. *Daedalus, 118,* 205-227.

Dielman, T. E., Leech, S. L., Lorenger, A. T., & Horvath, W. J. (1984). Health locus of control and self-esteem as related to adolescent health behavior and intentions. *Adolescence, 19,* 935-950.

Dorn, N., & Thompson, A. (1976). Evaluation of drug education in the longer term is not an optional extra. *Community Health, 7,* 154-161.

Dusenbury, L., Kerner, J. F., Baker, E., Botvin, G. J., James-Ortiz, S., & Zauber, A. (1992). Predictors of smoking prevalence among New York Latino youth. *American Journal of Public Health, 82,* 55-58.

Elkind, D. (1978). Understanding the young adolescent. *Adolescence, 8,* 127-134.

Evans, R. I., Rozelle, R. M., Mittlemark, M. B., Hansen, W. B., Bane, A. L., & Havis, J. (1978). Deterring the onset of smoking in children: Knowledge of immediate physiological effects and coping with peer pressure, media pressure, and parent modeling. *Journal of Applied Social Psychology, 8,* 126-135.

Flay, B. R. (1985). Psychosocial approaches to smoking prevention: A review of findings. *Health Psychology, 4,* 449-488.

Ginsburg, H., & Opper, S. (1978). *Piaget's theory of intellectual development.* Englewood Cliffs, NJ: Prentice Hall.

Glasgow, R. E., & McCaul, K. D. (1985). Life skills training programs for smoking prevention: Critique and directions for future research. In C. Bell & R. Battjes (Eds.), *Prevention research: Deterring drug abuse among children and adolescents* (NIDA Research Monograph No. 63, pp. 50-66). Washington, DC: Government Printing Office.

Hamburg, B. A., Braemer, H. C., & Jahnke, W. A. (1975). Hierarchy of drug use in adolescence: Behavioral and attitudinal correlates of substantial drug use. *American Journal of Psychiatry, 132,* 1155-1167.

Hurd, P., Johnson, C. A., Pechacek, T., Bast, C. P., Jacobs, D., & Luepker, R. (1980). Prevention of cigarette smoking in 7th grade students. *Journal of Behavioral Medicine, 3,* 15-28.

Jessor, R., & Jessor, S. L. (1977). *Problem behavior and psychosocial development: A longitudinal study of youth.* New York: Academic Press.

Jones, C. L., & Battjes, R. J. (Eds.). (1985). *Etiology of drug abuse: Implications for prevention* (NIDA Research Monograph No. 56). Washington, DC: Government Printing Office.

Kandel, D. B. (1978). Convergences in prospective longitudinal surveys of drug use in normal populations. In D. B. Kandel (Ed.), *Longitudinal research on drug use: Empirical findings and methodological issues* (pp. 3-38). Washington, DC: Hemisphere.

Kandel, D. B., & Andrew, K. (1987). Processes of adolescent socialization by parents and peers. *International Journal of the Addictions, 22,* 319-342.

Kearney, A. L., & Hines, M. H. (1980). Evaluation of the effectiveness of a drug prevention education program. *Journal of Drug Education, 10,* 127-134.

Kim, S. (1988). A short- and long-term evaluation of "Here's Looking at You." II. *Journal of Drug Education, 18,* 235-242.

Kinder, B. N., Pape, N. E., & Walfish, S. (1980). Drug and alcohol education programs: A review of outcome studies. *International Journal of the Addictions, 15,* 1035-1054.

Kozol, J. (1988). *Rachel and her children: Homeless families in America in America.* Boston: Ballantine.

Luepker, R. V., Johnson, C. A., Murray, D. M., & Pechacek, T. F. (1983). Prevention of cigarette smoking: Three year follow-up of educational programs for youth. *Journal of Behavioral Medicine, 6,* 53-61.

McAlister, A., Perry, C. L., Killen, J., Slinkard, L. A., & Maccoby, N. (1980). Pilot study of smoking, alcohol, and drug abuse prevention. *American Journal of Public Health, 70,* 719-721.

McGuire, W. J. (1964). Inducing resistance to persuasion: Some contemporary approaches. In L. Berkowitz (Ed.), *Advances in experimental social psychology* (pp. 192-227). New York: Academic Press.

McGuire, W. J. (1968). The nature of attitudes and attitude change. In G. Lindzey & E. Aronson (Eds.), *Handbook of social psychology* (pp. 136-314). Reading, MA: Addison-Wesley.

Millman, R. B., & Botvin, G. J. (1983). Substance use, abuse, and dependence. In M. D. Levine, W. B. Carey, A. C. Crocker, & R. T. Gross (Eds.), *Developmental-behavioral pediatrics* (pp. 683-708). Philadelphia: W. B. Saunders.

Mussen, P. H., Conger, J. J., & Kagan, J. (1979). *Child development and personality* (5th ed.). New York: Harper & Row.

New York City Mayor's Office on Homelessness. (1993, March). *New York City revised and updated plan for housing and assisting homeless single adults and families.* Unpublished manuscript.

Newcomb, M. D., & Bentler, P. M. (1988). *Consequences of adolescent drug use: Impact on the lives of young adults.* Newbury Park: Sage.

Orlandi, M. A. (1992). The challenge of evaluating community based prevention programs: A cross cultural perspective. In M. A. Orlandi, R. Weston, & L. G. Epstein (Eds.),

Cultural competence for evaluators: A guide for alcohol and other drug abuse prevention practitioners working with ethnic/racial communities (OSAP Cultural Competence Series 1, U.S. DHHS No. ADM 92-1884). Washington, DC: Government Printing Office.

Page, P. M. (1989). Shyness as a risk factor for adolescent substance use. *Journal of School Health, 59,* 432-435.

Pentz, M. A. (1983). Prevention of adolescent substance abuse through social skill development. In T. J. Glynn, C. G. Leukefeld, & J. B. Ludford (Eds.), *Preventing adolescent drug abuse: Intervention strategies* (NIDA Research Monograph No. 47, pp. 195-232). Washington, DC: Government Printing Office.

Pentz, M. A., Brannon, B. R., Charlin, V. L., Barrett, E. J., MacKinnon, D. P., & Flay, B. R. (1989). The power of policy: The relationship of smoking policy to adolescent smoking. *American Journal of Public Health, 79,* 857-862.

Pentz, M. A., Dwyer, J. H., MacKinnon, D. P., Flay, B. R., Hansen, W. B., Wang, E. Y., & Johnson, C. A. (1989). A multicommunity trial for primary prevention of adolescent drug abuse: Effects on drug prevalence. *Journal of American Medical Association, 261,* 3259-3266.

Price, J. H., Desmond, S. M., & Smith, D. (1991). A preliminary investigation of inner city adolescents' perceptions of guns. *Journal of School Health, 61,* 255-259.

Schaps, E., Bartolo, R. D., Moskowitz, J., Palley, C. S., & Churgin, S. (1981). A review of 127 drug abuse prevention program evaluations. *Journal of Drug Issues, 11,* 17-43.

Schaps, E., Moskowitz, J. M., Malvin, J. H., & Scheffer, G. H. (1986). Evaluation of seven school-based prevention programs: A final report on the Napa Project. *International Journal of the Addictions, 21,* 1081-1112.

Schinke, S. P. (1984). Preventing teenage pregnancy. In M. Hersen, R. M. Eisler, & P. M. Miller (Eds.), *Progress in behavior modification* (16th ed., pp. 31-63). New York: Academic Press.

Schinke, S. P., & Blythe, B. J. (1981). Cognitive-behavioral prevention of children's smoking. *Child Behavior Therapy, 3,* 25-42.

Schinke, S. P., & Gilchrist, L. D. (1983). Primary prevention of tobacco smoking. *Journal of School Health, 53,* 416-419.

Schinke, S. P., & Gilchrist, L. D. (1984). Preventing cigarette smoking with youth. *Journal of Primary Prevention, 5,* 48-56.

Swisher, J. D., Crawford, J. L., Goldstein, R., & Yura, M. (1971). Drug education: Pushing or preventing? *Peabody Journal of Education, 49,* 68-75.

Swisher, J. D., & Hoffman, A. (1975). Information: The irrelevant variable in drug education. In B. W. Corder, R. A. Smith, & J. D. Swisher (Eds.), *Drug abuse prevention: Perspectives and approaches for educators* (pp. 49-62). Dubuque, IA: William C. Brown.

Swisher, J. D., & Hu, T. W. (1983). Alternatives to drug abuse: Some are and some are not. In T. J. Glynn, C. G. Leukefeld, & J. P. Ludford (Eds.), *Preventing adolescent drug abuse: Intervention strategies* (NIDA Research Monograph No. 47, pp. 141-153). Washington, DC: Government Printing Office.

Telch, M. J., Killen, J. D., McAlister, A. L., Perry, C. L., & Maccoby, N. (1982). Long-term follow-up of a pilot project on smoking prevention with adolescents. *Journal of Behavioral Medicine, 5,* 1-8.

Thomas, S. B., & Quinn, S. C. (1991). Public health then and now. The Tuskegee Syphilis Study, 1932 to 1972: Implications for HIV education and AIDS risk education programs in the Black community. *American Journal of Public Health, 81,* 1498-150.

U.S. Congress Office of Technology Assessment. (1991). Aids and other sexually transmitted diseases: Prevention and services. In *Adolescent health: Vol. 2. Background and the effectiveness of selected prevention and treatment services* (pp. II 257-II 263). Washington, DC: Government Printing Office.

Utech, D., & Hoving, K. L. (1969). Parents and peers as competing influences in the decisions on children of differing ages. *Journal of Social Psychology, 78,* 267-274.

Yamaguchi, K., & Kandel, D. B. (1984). Patterns of drug use from adolescence to young adulthood: III. Predictors of progression. *American Journal of Public Health, 74,* 673-681.

Strengthening Families to Prevent Drug Use in Multiethnic Youth

Karol L. Kumpfer
Rose Alvarado

Strengthening the ability of families to raise successful, nonviolent, and non-drug-using children is a critical social goal. Failure to deal with this issue will result in a lower quality of life and make the United States less competitive in the 21st century. The family is the social unit primarily responsible for child-rearing functions. When families fail to fulfill this responsibility, the entire society suffers. Families are responsible for providing physical necessities, emotional support, learning opportunities, and moral guidance, and for building self-esteem and resilience. *Family* or *parents* are defined to be whoever fulfills the caretaking role for a child, including nontraditional family arrangements that could include adoptive, foster, or institutional care.

This chapter reviews etiological research on family risk and protective factors that influence youth's uses of alcohol, tobacco, or other drugs (ATOD). It emphasizes, in particular, known risk or protective factors for ethnic youth. Resiliency processes are covered as well as internal protective family dynamics. The chapter ends with a review of family interventions effective in reducing improper ATOD use and increasing protective resiliency processes in ethnic youth and families. Suggestions are offered for making family programs more culturally relevant to ethnic youth and their families.

Family Influence on
Youth Alcohol and Drug Use

To design effective, family-focused prevention programs requires familiarity with research on family influences on youth's ATOD use. Although researchers have focused for several decades on peer influences almost to the exclusion of family influences, there are convincing arguments for also including family as a focus for prevention efforts in multicomponent programs (Kandel, 1980; Kumpfer, 1990a; Penning & Barnes, 1982). Although peer influences are consistently found to be the final pathway to ATOD use or abuse, recent research supports family processes as mediators of association with drug-using and deviant peers (Conger & Rueter, in press; Elliott, in press; Kumpfer & Turner, 1990-1991; Patterson, Reid, & Dishion, 1992). Several longitudinal studies (Brook & Brook, 1992) following preadolescents into the drug-using teenage years find that although peer factors become more important between preadolescence and adolescence, parental factors do not seem to lose their importance. Coombs, Paulson, and Richardson (1991) reported that parental influence was, in fact, found more important than peer influence in youth's reasons for nonuse for both Anglo and Hispanic 9- to 17-year-olds. A 24-state survey conducted by the Parents' Resource Institute for Drug Education (PRIDE) revealed that most ATOD-using youth use drugs in their homes, in the homes of their friends, and in cars—not in or around schools. Hence, it appears that we have more of a "home drug problem" than a "school drug problem"—one that could be improved with increased family monitoring and attention to availability of alcohol and drugs at home.

Despite this research evidence, most substance abuse prevention programs continue to bypass "the use of the family as a major target audience or targeted delivery system for alcohol and drug messages" (Stern, 1992, p. 4). In order to increase effectiveness, ATOD prevention researchers working with high-risk ethnic populations in large-scale school-based prevention programs (Botvin, Baker, Dusenbury, Tortu, & Botvin, 1990; Hawkins, Catalano, Morrison, et al., 1992; Rohrbach et al., in press) have sought in recent years to involve parents in multicomponent prevention programs. Because these family involvement efforts are so recent, outcome data are scant. Consistent evidence of effectiveness comes from parent or family skills-training programs dealing with other youth problems such as conduct disorders and aggression (McMahon, 1987) or delinquency (Lipsey, 1992).

RESEARCH EVIDENCE FOR A
BIOPSYCHOSOCIAL FAMILY INFLUENCE MODEL

For centuries it has been recognized that substance abuse runs in families. Unfortunately, the impact of family biological and environmental influences has only recently been researched. As more studies are conducted, the prevention field will have a better picture of the pervasive influence of families on alcohol and drug use by youth. More research is needed to better understand these complex parent/child transactional influences. For instance, family environment can serve as a protective or a risk factor depending on the developmental level and temperament of the child and on family processes. An example is parental discipline style, which should change with increased cognitive and social development of the child.

Empirical evidence supporting the strong influence of families on ATOD use comes from many different research areas, namely (a) epidemiological data, (b) etiological studies, (c) empirically tested ATOD theories, (d) empirical studies of family protective and risk factors, and (e) the success of family-focused treatments or prevention efforts. Each is discussed below.

Epidemiological Survey Studies

Large-sample surveys, such as the Epidemiological Catchment Area Studies (Robins, 1980), have found that alcohol and drug abuse occurs with a higher probability in certain families, along with antisocial personality and Briquet's syndrome (psychosomatic disorders primarily found in women). As noted by Bush and Iannotti, (1985), these large-sample surveys have been successful in identifying key family risk factors (such as nonintact families), but less successful in identifying the more complex family processes that would make a youth more vulnerable to become chemically dependent. Longitudinal studies with carefully chosen family process measures that are analyzed using structural equation modeling and eventually neural computation or neural network analysis (Buscema, 1993) could be helpful in identifying these critical family processes.

Etiological Research Studies

Biological and genetic vulnerabilities have been implicated in a number of twin studies (Kaij, 1960; Pickens & Svikis, 1986), adoption studies (Bohman, Sigvardsson, & Cloninger, 1981; Cloninger, Bohman, & Sigvardsson, 1981), and children of alcoholics (COA) studies (Schuckit, 1983, 1985). These studies have found that even children of alcoholic parents who are raised by nonalcoholic adoptive parents have a two to nine times' greater risk of alcoholism, depending on whether the biological parent was a Type I or Type II alcoholic (Cloninger et al., 1981). It is important to remember, however, that genetic vulnerability research has been conducted primarily with Northern Europeans (Kumpfer, 1987, 1990a). Hence, it is not possible to say whether other ethnic groups have similar genetic vulnerabilities, except possibly Native Americans.

Research suggests that increased vulnerability to this "family disease" or syndrome has both biological and environmental causes. Youth with inherited biological risk factors such as hyperactivity, depression, irritability, autonomic hyperactivity, or alcohol and drug tolerance (for a more complete review, see Kumpfer, 1987) often live with parents who have the same risk factors. Such parents model the use of alcohol and other drugs as ways to cope with stress often generated by poor life skills. Hence, youth with biological vulnerabilities may live in the worst possible family environments.

Many genetic/environment interactive family processes could increase a youth's risk for drug use. For instance, ATOD-abusing parents are often depressed. Depression decreases the caretaker's parenting ability (Forehand, Lautenschlager, Faust, & Graziano, 1986; Patterson, 1982). Normal, active children's behaviors irritate them excessively. In ATOD-using parents, biochemical imbalances exacerbate this irritability and could lead to child abuse and neglect (Kumpfer & Bayes, 1995).

Etiological ATOD Use Models

With the development of more sophisticated statistical analysis procedures capable of testing many variables simultaneously, a number of etiological models have been empirically tested. Kumpfer and associates have used structural equation modeling (LISREL) to confirm a model of risk and protective factors for adolescent ATOD use, called the social ecology model, in a general population sample (Kumpfer & Turner, 1990-1991) and in a Hispanic youth sample (Kumpfer, Alvarado, Turner, & Griffin, 1993). The results replicate other empirically tested models (Dielman, Shope, & Butchart, 1989; Newcomb & Bentler, 1986; Newcomb, Maddahian, & Bentler, 1986; Swaim, Oetting, Edwards, & Beauvais, 1989) that have found peer influence to be the final pathway to use, but have also found a significant impact of family processes on later empirically verified ATOD use mediators. Specifically, the social ecology model included the impact of family climate and school climate on the youth's self-esteem, school bonding, and eventual choice of peers. Although the impact of family was indirect within the primarily white sample, a more recent study of Hispanic youth found a direct pathway between family relations and youth ATOD use. A study by Schinke et al. (1992) with

Hispanic, African American, and white youth found that low maternal education (a marker of complex family risk processes) is a significant precursor of a youth's failure in school. According to the social ecology model, this school failure could result in decreased school bonding and choice of antisocial and drug-using peers.

If parents are unable to fulfill their parenting roles because of mental dysfunctions (e.g., substance abuse, depression, anxiety disorders, narcissism), separation from the child (either voluntary or imposed), family conflict, or inability to discipline or supervise the child effectively, the child has a higher risk of developing a host of problems. If a close bond is not developed with the parents, the child may never identify with the parents, develop the capacity for intimacy, or trust others. Major theories of substance abuse, such as the social development model (Hawkins & Weiss, 1985), point to the importance of the social bond with the family in normal development.

ETHNIC FAMILY RISK FACTORS

Research on family risk and protective factors and processes is necessary to design needs assessments and effective prevention programs. The probability of a child's developing problems increases rapidly as the number of family problems or risk factors increases (Rutter, 1987, 1990). Children and youth generally are able to withstand the stress of one or two family problems in their lives; however, when they are continually bombarded by family problems, their probability of becoming an ATOD user increases (Bry, McKeon, & Pandina, 1982; Newcomb & Bentler, 1986; Newcomb, Maddahian et al., 1986).

Unfortunately, family risk factors often tend to cluster together in high-risk, ethnic families. Children of poverty must contend with multiple problems— among them, parental absence because of working parents, or fathers who are absent because they are incarcerated or otherwise cannot provide financial support to the family. Federal and state regulations encourage fathers of poor families to leave their family so that the mother and children can qualify for medical and social assistance. Other family problems that stem from poverty include irritable and depressed parents or caretakers, lack of money for social or educational opportunities, and, in extreme cases, homelessness, combined with lack of food, clothing, and medical care. Parent-child conflict over meager resources such as money can lead to parent hostility and adolescent antisocial behavior and depression (Conger, Ge, Elder, Lorenz, & Simons, in press). Raising a child is a difficult task, and fathers are useful as agents of socialization (Phares & Compas, 1992). Lack of support from fathers and extended family or community members reduces opportunities for successful socialization of the child.

Changes in public assistance regulations and increased discriminatory imprisonment have reduced the numbers of fathers in ethnic families and doubled the child poverty rate from 1960 to 1979. In 1991, 21.8% of all U.S. children were living in poverty, which represents a 24% increase from 1980. In 1991, female-headed families living in poverty represented half of all poor families. Of the 11.7 million female-headed families, 36% were poor compared to only 23% in 1959 (U.S. Bureau of the Census, 1991). Over half of the children living in poverty are members of ethnic minorities. It is important to note that children from families with higher income and occupational status do engage in nonchronic delinquency and occasional alcohol use and marijuana experimentation (Simcha-Fagan, Gersten, & Langner, 1986). Hawkins, Lishner, Jenson, and Catalano (1987) pointed out, however, that "persistent serious crime and the regular use of illicit drugs appear more prevalent among those raised in conditions of extreme social and economic deprivation" (p. 92).

In an extensive review of family research, Loeber and Stouthammer-Loeber (1986) found that unsatisfactory socialization factors (i.e., lack of supervision, parental rejection of the child and child rejection of the parent, and lack of parent/child involvement) were the strongest predictors of delinquency in *longitudinal* studies. Parental dysfunction, such as criminality or poor marital relations, was a mid-level predictor, and parental health and absence were weak predictors. However, in concurrent *comparative* studies, the strongest correlates of problem behaviors in children and youth are the child's rejection of the parents and the parent's rejection of the child. The importance of effective parental discipline was higher in these studies than the longitudinal studies. The effect of these risk factors appears to be the same for boys and girls.

From this and other reviews (including Hawkins, Catalano, & Miller, 1992; Kumpfer, 1987; Wright & Wright, 1992), as well as other primary sources, a list of family correlates of ATOD use can be assembled:

- *Parental and sibling drug use,* including the impact of parental ATOD use (Smart & Fejer, 1972) and modeling (Brook, Gordon, Whiteman, & Cohen, 1986; Hansen et al., 1987; Kandel, 1980), youth's perceptions of parent's drug use (Newcomb et al., 1986), parental permissiveness of youth ATOD use (Barnes & Welte, 1986; Kandel & Andrews, 1987), reduced effective child management, and sibling drug use (Brook, Whiteman, Gordon, & Brook, 1988; Needle et al., 1986) on youth's choice to associate with drug-using peers (Conger & Rueter, in press; Estrada, Rabow, & Watts, 1982)

- *Poor socialization practices,* including parents' ATOD norms (Kline, Canter, & Robins, 1987), disagreement between peer and parent norms (Barnes & Windle, 1987), modeling of antisocial values and behaviors (Kandel &

Andrews, 1987), failure to disapprove of youth's ATOD use (Dielman, Shope, Leech, & Butchart, 1989; Grube & Morgan, 1986), failure to promote positive moral development, and neglect in teaching life, social, and academic skills to the child

- *Poor supervision of the child,* including failure to monitor the child's activities (Baumrind, 1985; Loeber & Stouthammer-Loeber, 1986), neglect, latchkey conditions (Richardson et al., 1989), sibling supervision (Steinmetz & Straus, 1974), and too few adults to care for the number of children

- *Poor discipline skills,* including lax, inconsistent, or harsh discipline (Barnes, 1990; Baumrind, 1985; Jones & Houts, 1990), high levels of negative reinforcement (love withdrawal, yelling, physical punishment) (Barnes & Windle, 1987), parental conflict over child-rearing practices (Vicary & Lerner, 1986), failure to set clear rules with consequences for ATOD use (Kandel & Andrews, 1987), parental expectations unrealistic for the developmental level of the child (which can create a failure syndrome and low self-efficacy) (Kumpfer & DeMarsh, 1986; Reilly, 1992), and excessive, unrealistic demands or harsh physical punishment (Cohen & Brook, 1987; Conger & Rueter, in press)

- *Poor parent/child relationships,* including rejection of the child by the parents or of the parents by the child (Brook, Brook, Gordon, Whiteman, & Cohen, 1990), low parental attachment (Baumrind, 1985), cold and unsupportive maternal behavior (Shedler & Block, 1990), lack of involvement and time together (Kumpfer & DeMarsh, 1986) and maladaptive parent/child interactions (Kumpfer & Turner, 1990-1991)

- *Excessive family conflict, marital discord, and domestic violence,* which are associated with increased verbal, physical, or sexual abuse (Kumpfer & Bayes, in press; Kumpfer & DeMarsh, 1986) and can lead to poor conflict resolution or anger management skills (Sowder & Burt, 1978a, 1978b), coercive family processes (Patterson, 1982; Patterson et al., 1992), youth violence, association with antisocial peers (Kumpfer & Turner, 1990-1991), and illicit drug use (Simcha-Fagan et al., 1986)

- *Family chaos and stress,* often because of poor family management skills, inadequate life skills, or poverty, resulting in fewer consistent family routine and rituals (Wolin, Bennett, & Noonan, 1979) and inappropriate role modeling and socialization (Patterson, DeBaryshe, & Ramsey, 1989)

- *Poor parental mental health,* including depression and irritability that cause negative views of the child's behaviors, parent hostility to child, and harsh discipline (Conger & Rueter, in press)

- *Family social isolation* and lack of community support resources (Wahler, Leske, & Rogers, 1979)

- *Differential family acculturation* and role reversal or loss of parental control over adolescents by parents who are less acculturated than their children (Delgado, 1990; Szapocznik et al., 1986).

RECIPROCAL PARENT/CHILD PROCESSES

Youths' temperament, personality, and behaviors also affect their parent's behaviors toward them. Brook, Whiteman, Gordon, Brook, and Cohen (1990) created a developmental theoretical framework called the *family interactional theory* that applies transactional theory of dynamic reciprocal interactions within families to risk and protective processes for ATOD abuse. For example, parentally disapproved behaviors, specifically regular use of drugs (marijuana), have been found to negatively affect parent/child relations over time (Brook, Gordon, Brook, & Brook, 1989). These researchers also reported that many protective processes for ATOD use are family mediated, including (a) strong parent/youth attachment, (b) adolescent conventionality, (c) positive maternal characteristics, and (d) marital harmony.

Additional research is needed to better understand reciprocal parent/child processes and their impact on drug use. As discussed by Coie et al. (1993), studies of family prevention intervention programs could be useful in better understanding family process mechanisms by varying person-environment causal mechanisms and testing the impact on youth.

RESILIENCY AND
PROTECTIVE FAMILY FACTORS

Because all youth cannot be spared high-risk families and environments, research increasingly supports the importance of understanding the mediating role of protective factors and processes, in addition to the current emphasis on risk factors. Protective factors may directly reduce ATOD use or buffer risk factors (Brook, Nomura, & Cohen, 1989; Newcomb, 1991). Knowledge of protective family processes that develop resilient youth should be the foundation for family intervention planning and development. Garmezy and associates (Garmezy, 1985; Masten & Garmezy, 1985) studied stress-resistant, "invulnerable," or resilient children and found that supportive family environments lead to competent, motivated, and successful youth.

Rutter (1987, 1990) concluded that protective mechanisms operate at key junctures in the lives of youth and that they must be given special attention. Resilient children and youth are better able to deal with stressors in their lives because they have coping skills to minimize negative impacts and focus on maintaining their self-esteem and gaining access to opportunities. The process of developing resiliency in youth by teaching them skills for dealing with challenges and life traumas has been explored by Richardson and his associates (Richardson, Neiger, Jensen, & Kumpfer, 1990). Below is a list of family protective factors and processes discussed in the resiliency research literature.

One Caring Adult

Positive interpersonal relationships with one caring parent or adult are a major protective factor for drug use (Minty, 1988; Rutter, 1987; Werner, 1986). Most often, the one caring parent is the mother; hence, maternal characteristics become critical. Researchers (Franz, McClelland, & Weinberger, 1991; Lytton, 1990; McCord, 1991) have found that competent mothers who are affectionate, self-confident, and nonpunitive and who have leadership skills produce children less likely to become delinquent or drug users. Brook, Nomura, and Cohen (1989) reported that a mutual attachment in the mother-adolescent relationship serves as a mitigating protective factor in reducing the impact of early childhood risk factors for drug use. Family support and flexibility in later years are protective processes reported by Santisteban, Szapocznik, and Rio (1993).

Attachment and Identification (Bonding)

Most integrated, etiological theories of adolescent drug use stress the importance of family, school, and community bonding (Hawkins & Weiss, 1985). This ability to "bond" is highly correlated with positive outcomes according to many empirical studies of ATOD use (Kumpfer & Turner, 1990-1991) and delinquency (Thornberry, 1987). The ability of the child to develop a close, trusting relationship with someone else may be the actual resiliency factor. However, in the absence of an opportunity to form a close attachment to a positive, caring parent, attachments with other caring adults (e.g., grandparent, relative, older sibling, adoptive or foster parent, teacher, "adopted surrogate parent," or friend's parent) can provide the needed bond with "one caring adult." The extended family support often present in traditional ethnic families increases the likelihood of cultivating that "one caring adult." Some youth have been found to exercise self-agency (Bandura, 1989) by escaping rejecting, violent, or chaotic homes and finding more positive family (Wolin & Wolin, 1993) or institutional settings. Strong parent/child bonds with parents who are still abusing drugs may promote youths' drug use (Foshee & Bauman, 1992). Avoidance of drug use (Wolin & Wolin, 1993) and delinquency (Mulvey & LaRosa, 1986) in such cases may depend on youths' ability to create for themselves a more positive "family" life. Children in unhealthy families are less likely to become drug users or delinquent if they have social support from a close relationship with a sibling or teen sport coaches and teammates (Kruttschmitt, Ward, & Sheble, 1987).

Purpose in Life

Having a dream, engaging in long-range planning, and being able to delay gratification have also been shown to be important in resilient youth. In a longitudinal study of institutionally reared women, Rutter and Quinton (1984) found that women with the most successful life adjustments and marriages were those who exercised "planning" in their life choices (e.g., marriage partner, job, pregnancies). Women who planned had better marriages to less deviant husbands, had much more positive school experiences, and had significantly lower teenage pregnancy rates (19% vs. 48%). It appears that the ability to develop long-range goals or a "dream" is critical in protecting youth from potentially disastrous life decisions. In a study of resiliency, Neiger (1991) found that having purpose in life was the most significant resiliency factor in successful life adjustment for college students, followed by problem solving and self-esteem.

Teaching Multicultural Competencies

Parents and other family members play an important role in teaching youth cognitive and behavioral competencies through guided participation in culturally sanctioned activities (Rogoff, 1990). Because American youth are likely to be in multicultural settings, family members should also support development of their children's flexibility to move smoothly between cultural contexts. Youth with multicultural competencies have been reported by Oetting and Beauvais (1990) to be more resistant to the use of drugs. Families can help a child by teaching positive coping skills for stressors rather than the use of alcohol, tobacco, or other drugs. Laosa (in press) is studying "stress-resistant" children of Hispanic immigrants and has found that the role of modeling in the extended family is critical to how the children learn to deal with stress.

Strong Extended Family
and Friend Support Structures

Strong extended families provide additional role models and support for high-risk children (Becerra, 1988). However, to be protective against ATOD use, the extended family support system must contain members who do not condone the excessive use of alcohol or any drug use. A characteristic of resilient youth is that they "adaptively distance" themselves from ATOD-abusing family members (Berlin, Davis, & Orenstein, 1988).

Support in Critical Decision Making

In addition, families can help youth make good decisions that will influence their life for some time, such as educational or vocational training, job selection, choice of a mate, and social groups to join. Longitudinal studies by Rutter and others have found that making positive choices at such critical life junctures can have a major impact on future problems (Rutter & Quinton, 1984). A supportive family with years of accumulated wisdom from elder members can help youth make good decisions. In addition, supportive families are likely to discuss family values and attitudes about the world, including alcohol and drug use. They also can help youth to learn to delay gratification and develop dreams about what they want to be and do someday. Without a vision for themselves or a dream for the future, youth are more prone to make unwise choices that would jeopardize their chances for success.

Parent's ATOD Rules and Standards

Parents' disapproval of children's ATOD use and setting a clear standard for nonuse are significant protective factors against use (McIntyre, White, & Yoast, 1990). Twelve-year-olds whose parents allowed them to drink at home when 10 or 11 years old have been found by Dielman, Shope, Leech, and Butchart (1989) to use alcohol more in unsupervised settings than youth whose parents did not allow them to drink at home.

Required Helpfulness and Opportunities
for Meaningful Family Involvement

Children who contribute valued and meaningful services to their families are more likely to become resilient to drug use (Werner, 1986). Involving youth in family activities and duties such as assigned chores, care of siblings and elders, help with siblings' homework, or help with a family business develops increased competencies and self-esteem (Kumpfer, 1990b). Benard (1990), in a review of ATOD resilience research, concluded that "when children are given responsibilities, the message is clearly communicated that they are worthy and capable of being contributing members of the family" (p. 9). Typically, children in other cultures are given meaningful family duties, such as carrying wood and water, gathering and preparing food, household chores, gardening, and animal and child care, as early as age 3 (Kurth-Schai, 1988). Through child-adult processes of guided participation (Rogoff, 1990), these children learn life skills to successfully complete these responsibilities.

High Parental or Family
Expectations for Child's Performance

According to Benard (1990), high expectations by parents, school personnel, and community members for youth are a major protective factor.
Youth whose parents have developed in them the attitude that they have what
they need to be successful were found by Mills (1990) to be less likely to use
alcohol or other drugs. Expectations, however, should be within appropriate
developmental levels, or the child may develop a "failure syndrome," noted
by Kumpfer and DeMarsh (1986) in children of addicted parents who had
developmentally inappropriate expectations.

Other Protective Factors or Processes

Additional protective family influences include (a) cohesive, supportive,
nonconflictual families (Moos & Billing, 1982); (b) providing the right degree
of hazard in life experiences so that youth have opportunities to develop
coping skills and self-confidence (Rutter, 1987); (c) maintaining family routines
and rituals (Wolin et al., 1979); (d) support with academic, social, and life
skills development; (e) promoting positive normative and moral development (Damon, 1988) through family religious involvement (Estrada, Rabow,
& Watts, 1982) and family values education; and (f) help in selecting positive
friends and activities.

CULTURE, ETHNICITY, AND DRUG USE

Ethnicity per se has not been found to be an inherent risk factor for drug
use in youth except when genetic vulnerabilities are prevalent, as occurs in
some Northern Europeans (Vaillant, 1983) and Native Americans. Some researchers have suggested that cultural norms such as *machismo* or *marian-
isma* may influence use by Hispanic youth based on gender (Austin &
Gilbert, 1989; Oetting & Beauvais, 1990). Others have suggested that youth
who have increased pride in their cultural heritage, cultural bonding, and
cultural identification are less likely to use drugs (Cardenas, 1992). Researchers
(Kumpfer, Alvarado, et al., 1993) have had difficulties confirming the impact
of cultural pride, identification, and bonding on ATOD use or mediators even
when using multiple standardized measures. One exception is that multicul-
turally competent youth who maintain their traditional culture as well as
learning other cultural competencies are less likely to use alcohol or other
drugs (Oetting & Beauvais, 1990).

Ethnic researchers (De La Rosa, 1988; Rodriguez, 1988) suggest that
the use of alcohol and drugs in ethnic groups in the United States may be

less related to ethnicity than to demographic and structural factors influencing families. Jones and DeMaree (1975), in their research on ethnic, high-risk families, concluded that social and environmental conditions such as poverty, prejudice, unemployment, frequent family moves, low educational level, and community crime levels are intricately interrelated with family functioning. These structural factors, often beyond the control of family members, contribute to family disruption, overcrowding, stress, and depression, leading to parent-child conflict and hostility (Christensen & Margolin, 1988; Conger et al., in press).

Reviews concur that the final pathway for influence of family factors on substance abuse is the way that the family functions, rather than external demographic variables. According to Zill (1993), "It is important to look at the realities of how families are actually functioning, rather than labeling some types of families as inevitably bad and others as invariably good"; for instance, "Many single parents do manage to provide stable, secure, stimulating and supportive homes for their youngsters" (p. 22).

Review of Family Intervention Programs

The previous review highlighted the need for family-level interventions to enlist the family's support in creating an enduring family environment that is conducive to ATOD prevention. As noted by Kazdin (1993), prevention programs with early and broad impact, such as parenting and family programs, are critically important.

On the basis of reviews of effectiveness from controlled studies, a number of prevention researchers strongly support family- focused prevention interventions as a necessary component of any comprehensive prevention plan for delinquency (Fraser, Hawkins, & Howard, 1988; Loeber & Stouthammer-Loeber, 1986; McMahon, 1987) and substance abuse (Kaufman, 1986; Kaufman & Borders, 1988; Kaufman & Kaufman, 1979; Stanton & Todd, 1982). Rose, Battjes, and Leukefeld (1984) stressed the importance of considering family-focused skills-training approaches to ATOD prevention.

Despite repeated reminders to the field about the usefulness of involving parents in ATOD prevention initiatives, historically, family and environmental change approaches to prevention have been the underfunded Cinderellas of drug abuse prevention (Kumpfer, 1990a). Although family environment change technology exists in the form of many different types of family and parenting approaches to prevent youth problems, unfortunately, few have been specifically designed and evaluated for drug use prevention. Rohrbach et al. (in press) stated: "Despite the evidence that parental modeling of drug use, attitudes toward drug use, and parenting practices are significant risk factors for adolescent drug use, to date most drug abuse prevention programs have paid little attention to involving parents and other family members in the education process."

Most drug use prevention programs work only with high-risk or general population youth, rather than the whole family. Kazdin (1993) commended the substance abuse prevention field for the development of effective, school-based skill-training programs (Botvin et al., 1990). Nevertheless, what is needed now is a focus on family skills training to complement these youth skills-training programs. Adoption of family interventions are growing in popularity, particularly with agencies dealing with ethnic families. Program planners need not feel that they have to choose between youth skills-training or family programs because some family skills-training programs include children's skills-training curricula but add parenting and family relationship and resiliency-building sessions.

Family-focused approaches have been tried with youth who are already initiating use (Santisteban et al., 1993; Szapocznik et al., 1988; Szapocznik & Kurtines, et al., 1989) and with drug-abusing parents in treatment (Catalano, Haggerty, & Gainey, in press; DeMarsh & Kumpfer, 1986; Kumpfer, 1993) or not in treatment (Kumpfer, 1990c). However, little has been done until recently to involve large numbers of parents of nonusing youth in family-focused prevention programs. School-based tobacco prevention programs have for many years involved parents in homework assignments with reasonable success. Flay et al. (1987) found that 94% of the students reported that their parents participated in the homework assignments and, more important, that parent involvement may have influenced program success. Perry, Pirie, Holder, Halper, and Dudovitz (1990) found that 70% of parents reported that their adolescents had brought home a parent/adolescent smoking prevention program.

Recently, school-based alcohol and drug prevention specialists have begun including parent involvement activities as adjuncts to the school programs the students attend. For example, the large-scale Midwestern Prevention Program tested the impact of adding various parent involvement activities, such as parent/child homework assignments, family skills training, family friendship circles, parent participation in community drug prevention meetings, and committee or advisory council work (Rohrbach, Hansen, & Pentz, 1992). When Rohrbach and associates (Rohrbach, in press) directly requested parents to complete a parent survey reporting their involvement in any of these activities, they found that 66% of parents returning the parent survey reported helping their children participate in the I-STAR curriculum with the homework assignments, 23% reported participating in the two-session family skills-training program and prevention meetings, 9% reported being on the parent committee, and 7% reported being on the I-STAR Community

Advisory Council. In addition, parent involvement was associated with reduced student alcohol and tobacco use at an 18-month follow-up. Undoubtedly, one of the primary disincentives for ATOD prevention specialists using parent- and family-strengthening approaches is the perceived need to involve all parents. Even when stipends for participation are offered, researchers (Grady, Gersick, & Boratynski, 1985) often report only being able to recruit about one third of the eligible parents. Rather than considering this a failure, prevention specialists should consider this a success.

Kumpfer and associates (DeMarsh & Kumpfer, 1986; Kumpfer, 1992) have reviewed a number of family-focused prevention programs that can be used for substance abuse prevention. Traditionally, when considering family-focused prevention, ATOD specialists considered only parent education and, if abuse was present, family therapy. However, there are many more family approaches being used today to reduce a wide range of youth problems.

Family-focused prevention has been promoted primarily by specialists trained in family systems theory, family therapy, and behavioral/skills therapy. Psychotherapy has always stressed the importance of family interventions. Coleman and Stanton (1978) wrote that "it is an understatement to say that family approaches to psychotherapy have increased in popularity and breadth during recent years" (p. 479). Family systems theory and family therapy techniques for substance abuse treatment are increasingly being taught in training programs for therapists. Recommendations for making these family interventions more culturally adapted for ethnic families were proposed by Kaufman and Borders (1988).

The increased success of treatment when the family is involved is widely acknowledged by therapists and documented in the research literature (Gurman & Kniskern, 1978; Stanton & Todd, 1982). Most therapists are acutely aware of the damage that family members can do to a client's therapeutic progress if they are not supportive of the treatment goals or are unaware of their impact on the client. Obvious and subtle forms of sabotage occur as family members attempt to redevelop the former family balance and dynamic.

MODELS OF FAMILY
INTERVENTION PROGRAMS

Only the most popular and promising family intervention strategies (shown in Table 13.1) are reviewed here. One major distinction is between strategies that involve the parents or caretakers only, called *parenting approaches,* and strategies that involve the parents with at least the target child, often called *family approaches.* Some basic variants of each of these two major approaches are discussed below, including several model programs.

A national search by Kumpfer (1992) for the Office of Juvenile Justice and Delinquency Prevention (OJJDP) of over 500 family programs to determine the best methods for strengthening families to prevent delinquency and drug use yielded 25 major intervention strategies (as well as many variations or combinations). A wide diversity of family programs exist because family needs and cultures vary and programs must be tailored to meet those values and needs. As shown in Table 13.1, major factors to consider when selecting the most appropriate family program are the target child's age and the level of identified family dysfunction.

At the top left are the earliest interventions possible, such as family or parent education in schools before young people even become parents. Family education can begin as early as elementary school in order to prepare youth for future family responsibilities. At the other extreme (bottom right) are programs for families in crisis who have a youth on probation for drug use or criminal involvement.

Parenting Approaches

The major parenting approaches defined and described below include parent education, behavioral parent training, Adlerian parent training, parent support groups, in-home parent education or parent aid, and parent involvement in youth groups. Some programs are difficult to categorize in this taxonomy and may involve several approaches.

Parent Education Programs. Parent education programs are distinguished from parent training programs because education programs generally involve fewer sessions and do not have the parents practice skills in groups or do assigned homework. Parent education programs can range from a single motivational lecture to a series of lectures that may involve experiential exercises and self-ratings. Topics include a wide range of ideas on how to improve youth behavior and values.

If tailored for drug abuse prevention, these programs also include information about the risks of alcohol and drug use, early warning signs of use, other behavioral or family risk factors, the family disease concept, and ways to talk with children about alcohol and drug abuse. Stern (1992) strongly recommended that family-focused prevention programs include two messages: (a) a high-risk-factor message, "Using alcohol and other drugs can cause you to have serious health problems," and (b) a protective factor message, "The stronger you are and the more love, attention, and care you give your own family relationships, the stronger the resiliency factors you are building in your child" (p. 5).

TABLE 13.1 Matrix of Program Types by Age of Child and Severity of Family or Child Problems

AGE	GENERAL POPULATION FAMILY PROGRAMS	HIGH-RISK FAMILY PROGRAMS	IN-CRISIS FAMILY PROGRAMS
Pre-parent	• High school parent education • Parent/teen sex education • Teen pregnancy prevention peer education	• Pre-parenting • High school pre-parenting • Pregnancy prevention/sex education	• Pre-parenting education for foster care youth • Pre-parenting for delinquents in custody
Prenatal	• Infant parenting and health care • Parent education	• Prenatal substance abuse prevention program • Infant mortality case management	• Teen pregnancy case managing • Pregnant teen school • Pregnant teen residency
Infancy/ toddler	• Parent education (TV, video) • Parent support	• In-home parent education (PHS nurse, social worker) • Parent aide • Case work • Family services • Parent support	• Protective services • Nurturing program for child abuse/neglect • Foster parents • Teen parent support services • Young parents' school
Childhood	• Parent education • School-based home;/school achievement programs • Media-based prevention	• Preschool parent training • School and treatment agency • Parent training • Parent aid • Family skills training • Surrogate parent training • Parent involvement	• Family services • Family skills training • Foster parent training • Protective services • Family preservation • Family reunification • Family treatment • Residential shelter • Day treatment • Parent aid • Parent training
Preteen/ Adolescent	• Parent education • Family education • Family meetings and activities • Sex education	• Family communication and relationship enhancement • Parent support groups • Family volunteers • Parent involvement in youth group • Surrogate parent training • Parent/school/treatment - truancy • Juvenile diversion/gang prevention • Parent education • Parent skills training • Drop-out education prevention	• Family therapy • Family services • Parent or family support • Protective services • Family preservation • Intense probation • Teaching family model • Day treatment/alternative school • Foster parent program • Residential treatment

Stern (1992) recommended reaching large numbers of parents with basic ATOD information. Parent outreach can be conducted in many different ways to educate hard-to-reach families (Kumpfer, 1991). For example, high-risk families may not have time to attend parenting classes, but most watch television. Many low-income, ethnic families learn more effectively by having visual images and examples of appropriate parenting skills. Studies confirm that nondrug users (Flay & Sobel, 1983) and drug users (Jason,

1990) both use mass media as their most important source of information about drugs. Kumpfer, Gopelrud, and Alvarado (1994) recommended the use of television shows with viewer participation in game shows to demonstrate learning of parenting principles. Some parenting programs are available on audiotape or videotape to be reviewed at home (Webster-Stratton, 1987). Magazines often carry feature or serial articles on improving parenting and family relations. Some businesses offer parenting classes during lunch hours (an excellent way to attract fathers).

Popular antidrug programs such as the Parents' Resource Institute for Drug Education (PRIDE) and the National Federation for Drug Free Youth include parent education components about such topics as teaching parents how to talk to their children about alcohol or drugs (as does the National Council on Alcoholism's "Talking With Your Kids About Alcohol," developed by the Prevention Research Institute).

Behavioral Parent Skills-Training Programs. There are many types of behavioral parent training programs, but most are variants of the parenting model developed by Patterson and associates at the Oregon Social Learning Center. Patterson's book *Families: Applications of Social Learning to Family Life* (1975) explains this type of parent training, which teaches parents how to discipline more effectively and control both overt and covert conduct disorders. Examples of parent training for drug abuse prevention include statewide evaluation of parent training conducted by Klein and Swisher (1983) and the two-parent training programs used in the Seattle Social Development Project with ethnic parents: (a) Catch 'Em Being Good, a seven-session, discipline-focused curriculum for first and second graders, and (b) How to Help Your Child Succeed in School, a four- session curriculum aimed to improve parent-child communication and academic support (Hawkins, Catalano, Morrison, et al., 1992). Although effect sizes were small, a 4-year follow-up found significant differences in family management, communication, bonding, and involvement reported by intervention students compared to comparison students. Many other studies have documented effectiveness of parent skills training in reducing noncompliance and behavior problems that precede drug use (McMahon, 1987).

Adlerian Parenting Programs. These programs are based on clinical psychology principles of improving family relationships, communication, and disciplining using natural and logical consequences to improve the child's self-concept and dignity. They work better with preteens and adolescents than do the traditional behavior programs. Examples include Dinkmeyer and McKay's (1976) Systematic Training for Effective Parenting (STEP) program, Gordon's (1970) Parent Effectiveness Training (PET) program, and Glenn's (1984) Developing Capable Young People program.

Parent Support Groups. These groups are generally grassroots organizations of parents who provide support and education for members. Examples include the National Federation of Parents for Drug Free Youth, Toughlove, PRIDE, Mothers at Home, Mothers of Pre-Schoolers (MOPS), and Families in Action. These national organizations provide parenting and alcohol and drug education materials. Their local chapters often offer parent support groups. Some of these groups, like Toughlove, provide temporary respite care for parents with ATOD-abusing adolescents. Some organizations, like STRAIT, provide residential treatment for drug-using youth, followed by several months of living with other parents in the support group. Evaluations suggest a positive impact on family relations and parental control of youth's activities, but little impact on youths' drug use. Results were inconclusive, however, due to weaknesses in the research design (Klitzner, Gruenewald, & Bamberger, 1990).

Parent Aid or In-Home Parent Education. Because of the difficulty of attending family programs due to barriers such as child care and transportation, in-home prevention programs are worth considering with ethnic families. Minnesota Early Learning Designs (MELD) is an example of an in-home program successful in attracting low-education, low-income ethnic mothers of infants and toddlers. Because these programs can be very costly if staffed by professionals, paraprofessionals and trained volunteers are sometimes used.

Parent Involvement in Youth Groups. As mentioned earlier, this approach is currently being advocated as an adjunct to community or school-based skills-training programs (Rohrbach et al., in press). The least demanding on parents is to participate in homework assignments with their children at home. Most parent involvement programs for ethnic parents gradually involve distrustful parents in the children's groups by asking them to bring food or help with recreational activities. Eventually, they may participate in parenting skills through observing teachers or trainers work with the children. For example, City Lights in Washington, D.C., gradually gains the trust and interest of inner-city, low-income, African American parents by calling them to notify them about their child's achievements in their youth activities program. Eventually, with increased contact, parents occasionally are willing to volunteer to help with the youth activities or join a parenting group. In San Antonio, Rodriguez-Andrew's Los Niños Project includes three levels of parent involvement in the children's groups, ranging from no involvement to helping with food and materials, and, finally, to helping with the children's activities.

Headstart and preschool programs have for some time informally taught parenting skills by involving parents in preschool activities. The positive results of the Perry Preschool Project may be mainly due to this direct modeling of appropriate ways to discipline, support, and help children. The parents learn by watching the teachers and by working with their own child.

Family Prevention Approaches

Several major family interventions have been used to help prevent delinquency, substance abuse, and other teen problems. These include family education programs, family skills-training programs, family therapy, family services, and in-home family crisis services or family preservation programs. Each intervention type is discussed below.

Family Education Programs. These programs provide the family with lectures or educational sessions on family values, responsibility to society and others, family communications, alcohol and drug use, relationship enhancement techniques, and other family-strengthening strategies. This approach has been used as either a single session or a series of lectures or experiential sessions conducted in schools, churches, community centers, juvenile courts, youth rehabilitation centers, adolescent group homes, alcohol and drug treatment centers, and public agencies. Workbooks help families to conduct family discussions at home.

Family Skills-Training Programs. These programs are often called *behavioral family therapy* (if trained therapists work with individual families) or *behavioral family training* (if multifamily groups are used), and include separate structured skills-training groups for the parents and the children in the first hour using "guided participant modeling" by trainers (Rosenthal & Bandura, 1978). In the last hour, the family is brought together to practice learned skills and participate in fun family activities. The Nurturing Program (Bavolek, Comstock, & McLaughlin, 1983), Families and Schools Together, the Strengthening Families Program (SFP) (Kumpfer, DeMarsh, & Child, 1989), Focus on Families (Catalano et al., in press), and Family Effectiveness Training (Szapocznik, Santisteban, Rio, Perez-Vidal, & Kurtines, 1989) have all been used for drug use prevention. The Nurturing Program and the Strengthening Families Program (SFP) are being tested in 10 Center for Substance Abuse Prevention (CSAP, 1993) sites with ethnic youth.

SFP was developed after a research project funded by the National Institute on Drug Abuse (NIDA) demonstrated that combining parent and youth skills training with family skills training was more effective in decreasing risk factors than either parent training or child training only (DeMarsh & Kumpfer, 1986). The program is an intensive (14-week) parenting and youth skills-training program specifically for drug abuse prevention with 6- to 12-year-old children of drug- or alcohol-abusing parents. SFP has been modified to be culturally relevant, and has been found effective in decreasing child and family behavioral and emotional precursors of drug use for rural and urban African American families (the Safehaven Program; Kumpfer, Bridges, & Williams, 1993), Hispanic families, and Asian and Pacific Islander families. Strengthening Families Program II (Molgaard & Kumpfer, 1994) is a 7-week adaptation of SFP for sixth-grade rural youth and low-income parents. This school-based family program, complete with videotapes, is currently being evaluated by Iowa State University (Spoth & Redmond, in press) in a massive large-scale dissemination trial in Iowa funded by the National Institute of Mental Health. In addition, these researchers are evaluating the efficacy of the Hawkins and Catalano's Preparing for the Drug-Free Years Program. This five-session parent program (one session includes the youth) includes videotapes and works well for statewide dissemination through schools and community agencies. Focus groups have been conducted to tailor the program for high-risk and ethnic families. Catalano and associates (in press) are currently testing the effectiveness of a 33-session, parent and child skills-training program, called Focus on Families, for methadone maintenance patients that also includes in-home case management and starts with a 5-hour family retreat. The children attend 12 parent sessions to practice developmentally appropriate skills with their parents.

Family Therapy Programs. These family intervention approaches depend on the discretion of the individual therapist to determine the appropriate application and timing of specific techniques and exercises. Kaufman and Borders (1988) recommended adapting family therapies of adolescent substance use to the individual family culture on the basis of an understanding that different types of substance abuse may be present in different ethnic groups and a knowledge of family patterns and values in the cultural group. Examples include structural family therapy (Minuchin, 1974; Szapocznik et al., 1988; Szapocznik, Kurtines, et al., 1989), functional family therapy (Alexander & Parsons, 1973, 1982), strategic family therapy (Haley, 1963), and structural-strategic family therapy (Stanton & Todd, 1982). Szapocznik and associates (Szapocznik, Kurtines, et al., 1989) reported that family therapy was effective in reducing Hispanic adolescent drug use. The Institute for Human Resource Development (IHRD) in Utah demonstrated effectiveness in improving family risk factors through adapting Szapocznik's family therapy program for in-home family support with high-risk Hispanic families (Courtney, 1983).

Family Services Models. This is the traditional family services model in which a large number of needed services are brokered by a caseworker or a case manager. High-risk families often need more than family therapy or skills training. Rather, they often have immediate basic needs, such as food, clothing, medical care, and housing. Only after these emergency needs are met can the family begin to consider parenting and family enhancement program involvement.

In-Home Family Case Management. Increasingly becoming a popular drug abuse prevention approach with high-risk ethnic families, in-home case management involves five primary functions: assessment, planning, advocacy, service linkage or referrals, and monitoring (Haggerty, Wells, Jenson, Catalano, & Hawkins, 1989). Recently, this traditional model has been expanded for ethnic families to include outreach, in-home counseling and support, empowerment and family skills training, and family relationship development (Chamberlin & Rapp, 1991). Applications of locally tailored family support and case management programs have been found effective in improving ATOD risk and protective factors in both Hispanic families (Courtney, 1983) and Asian/Pacific Islander families (Cheng, Kumpfer, & Sasagawa, 1994). Two critical elements in success include case managers' modeling of critical family skills and support in accessing tangible hard services (Fraser & Haapala, 1987/1988).

Family Preservation Programs. Designed for families in crisis, this approach involves in-home crisis services to prevent child outplacement. Homebuilders, the prototype program, was developed in Washington by Haapala and Kinney (1979). This model has been so successful in reducing youth placement in state custody that it is currently being replicated in many states. In this model, a team of highly trained family services workers arrive at the family's home and provide whatever intensive, short-term, in-home services are needed.

SUMMARY OF FAMILY INTERVENTION EFFECTIVENESS

Because most parenting and family skills-training programs often target young children, few follow-up studies have been funded to determine the ultimate impact on adolescent ATOD use. Most parenting programs can demonstrate immediate reductions in precursors of negative child behaviors, such as depression, conduct disorders, poor family management, intentions to use tobacco and alcohol (Bry, 1983; DeMarsh & Kumpfer, 1986), and school achievement and delinquency in preadolescents (Fraser et al., 1988; Patterson, Chamberlain, & Reid, 1982). In a 3-year follow-up study, Tremblay et al. (1990) reported that parent training combined with child social skills training for kindergarten boys reduced school adjustment problems and delayed the onset of delinquency. Grady et al. (1985) found that parent training focusing on preparing to deal with teenage substance abuse increased communication and decision-making skills. DeMarsh and Kumpfer (1986) found that parent-child relationships improved only when the program involved working with the whole family part of the time as compared to parent training or child skills training only. Spoth and Redmond (in press) reported that family skills-training effectiveness was enhanced significantly by parent readiness to change, program involvement, and parent-child affective bond, and pretest levels of protective parent behavior. Overall, family-focused interventions have been shown to be superior to child-only interventions (McMahon, 1987).

The evaluations of family programs differ in quality, and some have not been replicated by other researchers with other populations. Taken as a whole, however, these evaluations indicate the strength of family-focused approaches. Lipsey (1992), in an extensive meta-analysis of prevention programs for delinquency, found that family counseling approaches were more effective with high-risk youths than with adjudicated delinquents, who were possibly more alienated from their parents. In addition, the meta-analysis results suggested that skills-oriented approaches had the largest effect size with high-risk youths. These data support the author's observations that family skills training appears to be the most promising family-focused approach to prevention. The target child, along with the rest of the family, participates in structured activities designed to modify interaction patterns. This strategy is desirable for high-risk families, in which the therapist should monitor the changes in the parents and child interaction patterns throughout the training process. Many variations of family skills training have been developed and can be tailored to the specific needs of the family.

CULTURAL ISSUES
IN FAMILY PROGRAMS

Although programs that increase family strength are advocated by most prevention researchers working with ethnic families (Oetting, Beauvais, & Edwards, 1988), until recently most parenting and family programs have not been culturally adapted (Kumpfer, 1991). Generally, prevention programs are developed and evaluated for effectiveness with a broad general population before being adapted for special populations. In the last few years, parenting and family training programs have begun to be revised to be more culturally sensitive and appropriate. Recommendations for making family-focused programs more effective for each ethnic group are discussed below.

It is critical that these recommendations be viewed in the context of generalizations regarding the various ethnic groups. There are wide ranges of heterogeneity in each group attributable to factors such as geographic and regional differences, language (ranging from monolingual in the language of the country of origin to monolingual in English) as well as a wide range of dialects, educational levels, degrees of acculturation, socioeconomic status, gender differences, family migration patterns, generational differences, and variations in ethnic subgroups. It is imperative that prevention specialists be sensitized to this diversity while recognizing that generalizations used out of context can perpetuate stereotypes. A pronounced example of this is that there are 300 American Indian tribes in the United States alone, all with unique backgrounds and experiences (Tafoya, 1990). Despite this diversity, there are factors within each ethnic group that seem to provide some common bonds and some guidelines or direction for developing culturally appropriate prevention and treatment programs.

Kazdin (1993) recommended deriving culturally relevant principles to guide program modifications, rather than developing separate models for each diverse ethnic group. However, most ethnic groups want parenting and family programs to be as much "theirs" as possible, including video and graphic material that includes only their ethnic families. Ho (1992) asserted that "it is clear that therapy with ethnic minority children requires an organized, culturally sensitive, theoretical framework, from which different treatment modalities can be applied to meet the specific needs of individual ethnic . . . children and youth" (p. 182). Working toward these goals would be extremely useful to the fields of prevention and therapy.

Native American Families

May (1992) offered guidelines for designing prevention programs for American Indians, including focusing on the specific tribal culture and empowering the participants. Fleming (1992) reminded program developers to consider level of acculturation, degree of identity, residential status, language preferences, and lifestyle preference. In addition, Edwards and Edwards (1990) advocated including culturally appropriate methods and materials in parenting and family programs for Native Americans as well as cultural enrichment and cultural identification components. After pointing out that "American Indians have traditionally been very supportive of imme-diate, extended, and clan family members" (p. 298), they recommended (a) involving as many family, clan, or tribal members in the planning and possibly the intervention; (b) identifying and working through nondrinking family members; (c) helping families access needed resources; (d) holding out "hope" to the family; (e) dealing with behaviors and not feelings, which are difficult for Native Americans to express; (f) explaining role modeling principles; and (g) including direct parent/child communications practice concerning children's use or nonuse of alcohol. The youth skills-training components of the family program should include (a) cultural competencies and cultural pride, (b) problem-solving skills, (c) academic skills, (d) leadership skills, (e) alternative activities to ATOD use, and (f) recreational or physical education.

Several Native American parenting programs have been developed, such as Positive Indian Parenting: Honoring Our Children by Honoring Our Traditions, originated by the Northwest Indian Child Welfare Institute, and the 14-week parenting program of the Lac Du Flambois tribe (CSAP, 1993). The CSAP-funded Soaring Eagles program in Minneapolis includes a youth group with regular family activities and an annual summer family retreat at a nearby Indian reservation (Edwards & Edwards, 1990).

African American Families

Nobles, Goddard, Cavil, and George (1987) believed that an erosion of black family cultural orientation and values is one possible explanation for the increase in substance abuse in the African American community. According to Oyemade and Washington (1990), "Few [prevention programs] have focused on the family and often those are aimed at, or at least more accessible to the middle class community. . . . Any serious effort toward prevention must take into account the family and other societal predictors of later drug use" (p. 279). They further suggested that family prevention programs need to address (a) differences in child-rearing practices (e.g., black parents tend to be strict and direct with discipline); (b) religious orientation (blacks tend to use religion as a means to improve their ability to cope with the stressors of life); (c) the varying orientations of blacks of different social classes; and (d) the disproportionate numbers of black males who become involved in substance abuse. The Safehaven Program in Detroit for drug-abusing black fathers in recovery had a secondary goal of reuniting fathers with their children (Kumpfer, Bridges, & Williams, 1993).

Recently researchers such as Boyd-Franklin (1990) have embraced theories that highlight the strengths of the African American family and discarded the "deficit" theories once used to guide research. In her book on black families in therapy, Boyd-Franklin (1989) recommended that the treatment of black families focus on five key strengths: (a) the bond of the extended family, (b) the adaptability of the family roles, (c) the strong religious ethic, (d) the integral belief in the value of education and the work ethic, and (e) the ability to develop and use effective coping skills in the face of economic hardship. Her therapeutic multisystem approach for use with black families does not focus necessarily on drug abuse prevention, but does provide valuable information addressing intervention with African American families. Alvy, Fuentes, Harrison, and Rosen (1980), at the Center for the

Improvement of Child Caring (CICC) in Ventura, California, have developed a "Confident Parenting" program for African American parents. Kumpfer et al. (1989) have developed a parent training program for African American, low-SES, substance-abusing parents as part of their Strengthening Families Program. This program was effectively implemented in Selma, Alabama, for drug-abusing mothers and their 6- to 12-year-old children.

Latino Families

In a recent work on substance abuse and Hispanics, Cervantes (1993) stressed the "importance of fostering quality family relationships with any prevention effort" (p. 102). He stated, "Given the strong value placed on family relationships in many Hispanic communities, drug abuse prevention must consider the nuances of cultural factors and culturally specific stressors as these impact family functioning" (p. 102), including (a) the involvement of extended family and friends, (b) the role folk healers may play in some families' lives, (c) religion, and (d) merchant and social clubs. Language preference and degree of acculturation are other major variables (Delgado & Rodriguez-Andrew, 1990). Booth, Castro, and Anglin (1990) also recommended designing programs that recognize the wide range of the national origins of Hispanics, gender differences, social class, and urban and rural differences.

Understanding the acculturation process is critical in working with Latino populations. Szapocznik and his associates at the University of Miami have worked extensively with Cuban families to develop innovative prevention and treatment programs that address intergenerational conflict and substance abuse associated with acculturative stress and family disorganization. They have developed and evaluated several family interventions for Hispanic families, namely structural family therapy for youth already using (Szapocznik, Kurtines, Santisteban, & Rio, 1990; Santisteban et al., 1993), a family skills-training program called Family Effectiveness Training for Hispanic families of high-risk preadolescents (Szapocznik et al., 1989), and a Bicultural Effectiveness Training Program (Szapocznik et al., 1986) that focuses on the acculturation conflict.

Caetano (1992) provided a review of prevention programs that are designed for Latino families and are culturally sensitive. Additional examples of family skills-training interventions for drug abuse prevention include (a) the Hispanic Family Intervention Program (Cervantes, 1993), focusing on coping skill enhancement, academic achievement skill training, and drug education; (b) the Strengthening Hispanic Families Program in Denver; (c) Prime Time, of House Next Door, in Deland, Florida, which also includes in-home family sessions for youth ages 10 to 15 and their families; (d)

Padres, a parent involvement program for Latino children and adolescents in Corpus Christi, Texas; and (e) the CODA Program in Downey, California.

Asian and Pacific Islander Families

According to Kim, McLeod, and Shantzis (1992), "Most Asian prevention agencies consider the family-oriented strategy to be one of the most important" (p. 227). As with other ethnic groups, extended family networks have been cited as a protective factor for substance abuse.

The diverse Asian population includes more than 60 separate groups, many with very different cultures. Hence, cultural relevance is a complicated issue. Chao (1992) recommended that program developers working with Southeast Asian families understand the unique cultures of Vietnamese, Laotian, Lao Lu, Cambodian, H'Mong, Chinese-Vietnamese, and Chinese-Cambodian, and other Asian groups.

When working with immigrant families, one must consider (a) level of acculturation (traditional, transitional, bicultural, or "Americanized" family), (b) family migration and relocation history, (c) degree of trauma and loss associated with war situations (i.e., loss of family, friends, material goods, community support), (d) differences in rates of acculturation of family members, (e) family work and financial stress (i.e., many parents may be forced to take jobs that have lower status than in their home country), and (f) language barriers (Lee, 1990). An ecological approach, recommended by Ho (1992), considers "the child's reality, culture, biculturalism, family tradition and structure, degree of acculturation, language, and help-seeking behavior" (p. 183).

Program materials should also be appropriate to the reading and conceptual level of the population being served. This is one area that requires close scrutiny because many low-income ethnic families have very low reading and educational levels. In some situations, the individual may not be literate in his or her native tongue or English. If materials are too difficult to read or understand, program effectiveness is diminished.

IMPROVING FAMILY PROGRAM EFFECTIVENESS WITH ETHNIC FAMILIES

In addition to cultural relevance, a number of program design and implementation issues can make the difference between success and failure of family intervention programs with ethnic families, including the following:

1. *Provide programs of sufficient intensity.* The more needy the family, the more time required to develop trust, determine the family's needs, and

provide or locate support services (CSAP, 1993). At least 30 to 40 contact hours are needed for a positive and lasting impact (Kazdin, 1987), particularly if participants are missing sessions or having difficulty implementing skills taught at home (Kumpfer & DeMarsh, 1986).

2. *Match the program to the family's needs.* Tailoring the intervention based on an accurate assessment of typical problems of local ethnic families or individual families is critical to success, as shown in L'Abate's (1977) Family Enrichment Program.

3. *Time programs for developmental appropriateness.* The program content must match the primary issues found in the target youth and families.

4. *Screen for parental dysfunction.* Parents with excessive depression and mental health problems that could reduce program effectiveness or cause group disruption should be referred for treatment. Dumas (1986) found a composite index of maternal and paternal psychopathology, family violence, and SES disadvantage to be most predictive of outcomes in parent training. Low scores on standardized assessments are not necessarily predictive of less program success. Kumpfer (1990c) found that southern African American mothers with lower Global Assessment Scores (GAS) benefited as much as those with higher GAS scores.

5. *Pay sufficient attention to recruitment and retention.* Typically only about 25% of parents targeted participate in intensive 12- to 14-session family interventions (Kazdin, 1987; Spoth & Redmond, in press); therefore, recruitment through community outreach, incentives, and reducing barriers to participation is critical. Hawkins, Catalano, Morrison, et al. (1992) found that 43% of targeted parents attended at least one session of their 3- to 5-session parent training classes as part of the Seattle Social Development Project. Ways to reduce barriers include (a) providing transportation, a safe convenient and nonstigmatizing place for the program, and child care; (b) increasing a sense of ownership and cultural relevance by using indigenous leaders and involving parents in modifications; (c) holding discussions on possible barriers to attendance; and (d) extending personal invitations and contacting members who miss sessions. Kumpfer and DeMarsh (1988) developed an assessment of barriers (including unstated fears of loss of children to protective services) with possible strategies to overcome these barriers.

6. *Provide other needed services.* High-risk ethnic families often need comprehensive family services to reduce poverty stress and increase support

networks. Volunteer family sponsorship programs involving matched-SES, successful parents from the same neighborhood, church, or social group have been effective in supporting other family needs and skills training; unfortunately, little research exists on this very natural or traditional type of family intervention.

7. *Review program materials for cultural relevance.* Few culturally appropriate program materials (videos, films, evaluation instruments) are available. Ethnic families want parenting programs developed specifically for their type of families and their issues.

8. *Measure and disseminate program effectiveness.* Because so little research exists on the effectiveness of family programs for the prevention of drug abuse, program providers should be encouraged to measure and publish the program's effectiveness. Research is particularly needed on the newly emerging, culturally relevant parenting and family programs. Follow-up studies are also needed to track the longer term effectiveness of promising programs. Funding from the beginning of the program should be earmarked for the follow-up evaluation.

SUMMARY

Family interventions should be a critical part of any comprehensive drug prevention program with ethnic youth. Ethnic families will often demand to be involved because they consider themselves "family." The multitude of promising family programs reviewed should demonstrate that *there is no one best family strategy for the prevention of drug use.* Instead, family interventions should be tailored to the cultural needs of the families, ages of the children, level of dysfunction of the family, and primary parenting and family needs. One key factor in effectiveness is the fit between the family's needs and the content and duration of the intervention. Other major factors in program success include implementation issues, such as program fidelity, successful recruitment and retention strategies, and follow-up.

Kazdin (1987) suggested that we not think in terms of "single-shot" family inoculation programs. Ethnic families with long-term, multiple problems are not likely to benefit from weak-dose, single-shot family programs. They need coordinated and long-term help, including ongoing support and booster sessions with coordinated family services. Such intensive, comprehensive programs are likely to be most successful in helping families raise non-drug-using youth.

Note

1. Kumpfer and DeMarsh (1986) summarized many of the suggestions for ways to recruit and maintain high-risk and low-SES families into family programs. A more complete review of possible reasons for recruitment and attrition problems and tips on how to decrease this problem were presented by Kumpfer and DeMarsh (1988) to the Second National Office of Substance Abuse Prevention (OSAP) Learning Community Conference in Washington, D.C. An article by Kumpfer (1991) is included in the new monograph edited by D. Pines, *Parent Training Is Prevention: Preventing Alcohol and Other Drug Problems Among Youth in the Family.*

References

Alexander, J. F., & Parsons, B. V. (1973). Short-term behavioral intervention with delinquent families: Impact on family process and recidivism. *Journal of Abnormal Psychology, 81,* 219-225.

Alexander, J. F., & Parsons, B. V. (1982). *Functional family therapy.* Monterey, CA: Brooks/Cole.

Alvy, K. T., Fuentes, E. G., Harrison, D. S., & Rosen, L. D. (1980). *The Culturally-Adapted Parent Training Project: Original grant proposal and first progress report.* Studio City, CA: Center for the Improvement of Child Caring.

Austin, G. A., & Gilbert, M. J. (1989). Substance abuse among Latino youth. *Prevention Research Update, 3,* 1-26.

Bandura, A. (1989). Human agency in social cognitive theory. *American Psychologist, 44,* 1175-1184.

Barnes, G. M. (1990). Impact of the family on adolescent drinking patterns. In R. L. Collins, K. E. Leonard, & J. S. Searles (Eds.), *Alcohol and the family: Research and clinical perspectives* (pp. 137-161). New York: Guilford.

Barnes, G. M., & Welte, J. W. (1986). Patterns and predictors of alcohol use among 7-12th grade students in New York State. *Journal of Studies on Alcohol, 47,* 53-62.

Barnes, G., & Windle, M. (1987). Family factors in adolescent alcohol and drug abuse. *Pediatrician, 14,* 13-18.

Baumrind, D. (1985). Familial antecedents of adolescent drug use: A developmental perspective. In C. L. Jones & R. J. Battjes (Eds.), *Etiology of drug abuse: Implications for prevention* (NIDA Research Monograph No. 56, pp. 13-44). Washington, DC: Government Printing Office.

Bavolek, S. J., Comstock, C. M., & McLaughlin, J. A. (1983). *The nurturing program: A validated approach to reducing functional family interactions* (Final report, Grant No. 1R01MH34862). Rockville, MD: National Institute of Mental Health.

Becerra, R. M. (1988). The Mexican American family. In C. F. H. Mindel, R. W. Habestein, & R. Wright (Eds.), *Ethnic families in America: Patterns and variations* (3rd ed., pp. •••). New York: Elsevier.

Benard, B. (1990). *Fostering resilience in kids: Protective factors in family, school, and community.* San Francisco: Western Center for Drug-Free Schools and Communities.

Berlin, R., Davis, R. B., & Orenstein, A. (1988). Adaptive and reactive distancing among adolescents from alcoholic families. *Adolescence, 23,* 577-584.

Bohman, M., Sigvardsson, S., & Cloninger, R. (1981). Maternal inheritance of alcohol abuse: Cross-fostering analysis of adopted women. *Archives of General Psychiatry, 38,* 965-969.

Booth, M. W., Castro, F. G., & Anglin, M. D. (1990). What do we know about Hispanic substance abuse? A review of the literature. In R. Glick & J. Moore (Eds.), *Drugs in Hispanic communities* (pp. 21-43). New Brunswick, NJ: Rutgers University Press.

Botvin, G. J., Baker, E., Dusenbury, L., Tortu, S., & Botvin, E. M. (1990). Preventing adolescent drug use through a multimodal cognitive-behavioral approach: Results of a 3-year study. *Journal of Consulting and Clinical Psychology, 58,* 437-446.

Boyd-Franklin, N. (1989). *Black families in therapy: A multisystems approach.* New York: Guilford.

Boyd-Franklin, N. (1990). Five key factors in the treatment of Black families. In G. W. Saba, B. M. Karrer, & K. V. Hardy (Eds.), *Minorities and family therapy* (pp. 53-69). New York: Haworth.

Brook, D. W., & Brook, J. S. (1992). Family processes associated with alcohol and drug use and abuse. In E. Kaufman & P. Kaufman (Eds.), *Family therapy of drug and alcohol abuse* (pp. 15-33). Boston: Allyn & Bacon.

Brook, J. S., Brook, D. W., Gordon, A. S., Whiteman, M., & Cohen, P. (1990). The psychological etiology of adolescent drug use: A family interactional approach. *Genetic, Social, and General Monographs, 116,* 111-267.

Brook, J. S., Gordon, A. S., Brook, A., & Brook, D. W. (1989). The consequences of marijuana use on intrapersonal and interpersonal functioning in black and white adolescents. *Genetic, Social, and General Psychology Monographs, 115,* 351-369.

Brook, J. S., Gordon, A. S., Whiteman, M., & Cohen, P. (1986). Some models and mechanisms for explaining the impact of maternal and adolescent characteristics on adolescent stage of drug use. *Developmental Psychology, 22,* 460-467.

Brook, J. S., Nomura, C., & Cohen, P. (1989). Prenatal, perinatal, and early childhood risk factors and drug involvement in adolescence. *Genetic, Social, and General Psychology Monographs, 115,* 123-145.

Brook, J. S., Whiteman, M., Gordon, A. S., & Brook, D. W. (1988). The role of older brothers in younger brothers' drug use viewed in the context of parent and peer influences. *Journal of Genetic Psychology, 151,* 59-75.

Bry, B. H. (1983). Empirical foundations of family-based approaches to adolescent substance abuse. In T. J. Glynn, C. G. Leukefeld, & J. P. Ludford (Eds.), *Preventing adolescent drug abuse: Intervention strategies* (NIDA Research Monograph No. 47, pp. 154-171). Washington, DC: Government Printing Office.

Bry, B. H., McKeon, P., & Pandina, R. (1982). Extent of drug use as a function of number of risk factors. *Journal of Abnormal Psychology, 91,* 273-279.

Buscema, M. (1993). *Squashing theory: An evaluation and prediction model for complex systems: Drug-addiction behavior* (Italian Presidency of the Council of Minister, Department of Social Affairs, Trans.). Rome: Semeion Research Center of Sciences of Communication.

Bush, P. J., & Iannotti, R. (1985). The development of children's health orientations and behaviors: Lessons for substance use prevention. In C. C. Jones & R. J. Battjes (Eds.), *Etiology of drug abuse* (NIDA Research Monograph No. 56, pp. 45-74). Rockville, MD: National Institute on Drug Abuse.

Caetano, R. (1992, May). *The prevention of alcohol-related problems among U.S. Hispanics: A review.* Paper presented at the National Institute on Alcohol Abuse and Alcoholism, Working Group on Alcohol Prevention Research in Ethnic Minority Communities, Washington, DC.

Cardenas, P. (1992). *Culture and cultural competency youth focused prevention and intervention: A manuscript for program planners and service providers.* Unpublished manuscript submitted to the Colorado Division of Substance Abuse.

Catalano, R. F., Haggerty, K. P., & Gainey, R. R. (in press). Prevention approaches in methadone treatment settings: Children of drug abuse treatment clients. In W. J. Bukoski & Z. Amsel (Eds.), *Drug abuse prevention: Sourcebook on strategies and research.* Westport, CT: Greenwood.

Center for Substance Abuse Prevention (CSAP). (1993). *Signs of effectiveness in preventing alcohol and other drug problems* (Contract No. ADM-SA-88-005). Rockville, MD: U.S. Department of Health and Human Services.

Cervantes, R. C. (1993). The Hispanic family intervention program: An empirical approach to substance abuse prevention. In R. S. Mayers, B. L. Kail, & T. D. Watts (Eds.), *Hispanic substance abuse* (pp. 157-173). Springfield, IL: Charles C Thomas.

Chamberlin, R., & Rapp, C. A. (1991). A decade of case management: A methodological review of outcome research. *Community Mental Health Journal, 27,* 171-187.

Chao, C. M. (1992). The inner heart: Therapy with Southeast Asian families. In L. A. Vargas & J. D. Koss-Chioino (Eds.), *Working with culture: Psychotherapeutic interventions with ethnic minority children and adolescents* (pp. 157-181). San Francisco: Jossey-Bass.

Cheng, S., Kumpfer, K. L., & Sasagawa, M. (1994). *Third year evaluation report on the Prevention Through Intervention (PTI) program* (report completed for the Asian Association of Utah). Salt Lake City: University of Utah.

Christensen, A., & Margolin, G. (1988). Conflict and alliance in distressed and non-distressed families. In R. A. Hinde & J. Stevenson-Hinde (Eds.), *Relationships within families: Mutual influences* (pp. 263-282). Oxford, UK: Clarendon.

Cloninger, R., Bohman, M., & Sigvardsson, S. (1981). Inheritance of alcohol abuse: Cross-fostering analysis of adult men. *Archives of General Psychiatry, 38,* 861-868.

Cohen, P., & Brook, J. (1987). Family factors related to the persistence of psychopathology in childhood and adolescence. *Psychiatry, 50,* 332-345.

Coie, J. D., Watt, N. F., West, S. G., Hawkins, J. D., Asarnow, J. R., Markman, H. J., Ramey, S. L., Shure, M. B., & Long, B. (1993). The science of prevention: A conceptual framework and some directions for a national research program. *American Psychologist, 48,* 1013-1022.

Coleman, S. B., & Stanton, M. D. (1978). An index for measuring agency involvement in family therapy. *Family Process, 17,* 479-483.

Conger, R. D., Ge, X., Elder, G. H., Lorenz, F. O., & Simons, R. L. (in press). Economic stress, coercive family process, and developmental problems of adolescents. *Child Development.*

Conger, R. D., & Rueter, M. A. (in press). Siblings, parents, and peers: A longitudinal study of social influences in adolescent risk for alcohol use and abuse. In G. Brody (Ed.), *Sibling relationships: Their causes and consequences.* Norwood, NJ: Ablex.

Coombs, R. H., Paulson, M. J., & Richardson, M. A. (1991). Peer vs. parental influence in substance use among Hispanic and Anglo children and adolescents. *Journal of Youth and Adolescence, 20,* 73-88.

Courtney, R. J. (1983). *Evaluation of an in-home family intervention with Hispanic families.* Unpublished report, Institute for Human Resource Development (now Centro de la Familia), Salt Lake City, UT.

Damon, W. (1988). *The moral child: Nurturing children's natural moral growth.* New York: Free Press.

De La Rosa, M. (1988). Natural support systems of Puerto Ricans: A key dimension for wellbeing. *Health and Social Work, 15,* 181-190.

Delgado, M. (1990). Hispanic adolescents and substance abuse: Implications for research treatment and prevention. In A. R. Stiffman & L. E. Davis (Eds.), *Ethnic issues in adolescent mental health* (pp. 303-320). Newbury Park, CA: Sage.

Delgado, M., & Rodriguez-Andrew, S. (1990). *Alcohol and other drug use among Hispanic youth* (OSAP Technical Report-4, DHHS Publication No. ADM 90-1726). Washington, DC: Government Printing Office.

DeMarsh, J. P., & Kumpfer, K. L. (1986). Family-oriented interventions for the prevention of chemical dependency in children and adolescents. In S. Griswold-Ezekoye, K. L. Kumpfer, & W. Bukoski (Eds.), *Childhood and chemical abuse: Prevention and intervention* (pp. 49-91). New York: Haworth.

Dielman, T. E., Shope, J. T., & Butchart, A. T. (1989). A covariance structure model test of antecedents of adolescent alcohol misuse and a prevention effort. *Journal of Drug Education, 19,* 337-361.

Dielman, T. E., Shope, J. T., Leech, S. L., & Butchart, A. T. (1989). Differential effectiveness of an elementary school-based alcohol misuse prevention program by type of prior drinking experience. *Journal of School Health, 59,* 255-263.

Dinkmeyer, D., & McKay, G. D. (1976). *Systematic training for effective parenting.* Circle Pines, MN: American Guidance.

Dumas, J. E. (1986). Parental perception and treatment outcome in families of aggressive children: A causal model. *Behavior Therapy, 17,* 420-432.

Edwards, D., & Edwards, M. E. (1990). American Indian adolescents: Combating problems of substance use and abuse through a community model. In A. R. Stiffman & L. E. Davis (Eds.), *Ethnic issues in adolescent mental health* (pp. 285-302). Newbury Park, CA: Sage.

Elliott, D. S. (in press). Health enhancing and health compromising lifestyles. In S. G. Millstein, A. C. Petersen, & E. O. Nightingale (Eds.), *Promoting the health of adolescents: New directions for the twenty-first century.* New York: Oxford University Press.

Estrada, A., Rabow, J., & Watts, R. (1982). Alcohol use among Hispanic adolescents: A preliminary report. *Hispanic Journal of Behavioral Sciences, 4,* 339-351.

Flay, B. R., Hansen, W. B., Johnson, C. A., Collins, L. M., Dent, C. W., Dwyer, K. M., Grossman, L., Hockstein, G., Rauch, J., Sobel, J., Sobol, D. F., Sussman, S., & Ulene, A. (1987). Implementation effectiveness trial of a social influences smoking prevention program using schools and television. *Health Education Research, 2,* 385-400.

Flay, B. R., & Sobel, J. L. (1983). The role of mass media for preventing adolescent substance abuse. In T. J. Glynn, C. G. Leukefeld, & J. P. Ludford (Eds.), *Preventing adolescent drug abuse: Intervention strategies* (NIDA Research Monograph No. 47, pp. 5-35). Washington, DC: Government Printing Office.

Fleming, C. (1992). American Indians and Alaska natives: Changing societies past and present. In M. A. Orlandi (Ed.), *Cultural competence for evaluators: A guide for alcohol and other drug abuse prevention practitioners working with ethnic/racial communities* (OSAP Cultural Competence Series I, DHHS Publication No. ADM 92-1884, pp. 147-171). Washington, DC: Government Printing Office.

Forehand, R., Lautenschlager, G. J., Faust, J., & Graziano, W. G. (1986). Parent perceptions and parent-child interactions in clinic-referred children: A preliminary investigation of the effects of maternal depressive moods. *Behavior Research and Therapy, 24,* 73-75.

Foshee, V., & Bauman, K. E. (1992). Parental and peer characteristics as modifiers of the bond-behavior relationship: An elaboration of control theory. *Journal of Health and Social Behavior, 33,* 66-76.

Franz, C., McClelland, D., & Weinberger, J. (1991). Childhood antecedents of conventional social accomplishment in midlife adults: A 36-year prospective study. *Journal of Personality and Social Psychology, 60,* 1-10.

Fraser, M., & Haapala, D. (1987/1988). Home-based family treatment: A quantitative-qualitative assessment. *Journal of Applied Social Sciences, 12,* 1-22.

Fraser, M. W., Hawkins, J. D., & Howard, M. O. (1986). Parent training for delinquency prevention: A review. *Child and Youth Services, 11,* 93-125.

Garmezy, N. (1985). Stress resistant children: The search for protective factors. In J. Stevenson (Ed.), *Recent research in developmental psychopathology* (pp. 213-233). Oxford, UK: Pergamon.

Glenn, H. S. (1984, June). *Developing capable young people.* Paper presented at the 33rd annual conference of the University of Utah School on Alcoholism and Other Drug Dependencies, Salt Lake City.

Gordon, T. (1970). *Parent effectiveness training.* New York: P. H. Wyden.

Grady, K., Gersick, K. E., & Boratynski, M. (1985). Preparing parents for teenagers: A step in the prevention of adolescent substance abuse. *Family Relations, 34,* 541-549.

Grube, J. W., & Morgan, M. (1986). *Smoking, drinking, and other drug use among Dublin post-primary school pupils.* Dublin: Economic and Social Research Institute.

Gurman, A. S., & Kniskern, D. P. (1978). Research on marital and family therapy: Progress, perspective and prospect. In S. L. Garfield & L. E. Bergin (Eds.), *Handbook of psychotherapy and behavior change: An empirical analysis* (2nd ed., pp. 817-902). New York: John Wiley.

Haapala, D. A., & Kinney, J. M. (1979). Homebuilders approach to the training of in-home therapists. In S. Maybanks & M. Bryce (Eds.), *Home-based services for children and families* (pp. 248-252). Springfield, IL: Charles C Thomas.

Haggerty, K., Wells, E. A., Jenson, J., Catalano, R. F., & Hawkins, J. D. (1989). Delinquents and drug use: A model program for community reintegration. *Adolescence, 24,* 439-456.

Haley, J. (1963). *Strategies of psychotherapy.* New York: Grune & Stratton.

Hansen, W. B., Graham, J. W., Sobel, J. L., Shelton, D. R., Flay, B. R., & Johnson, C. A. (1987). The consistency of peer and parent influences on tobacco, alcohol, and marijuana use among young adolescents. *Journal of Behavioral Medicine, 10,* 559-579.

Hawkins, J. D., Catalano, R. F., & Miller, J. Y. (1992). Risk and protective factors for alcohol and other drug problems in adolescence and early adulthood: Implications for substance abuse prevention. *Psychological Bulletin, 112,* 64-105.

Hawkins, J. D., Catalano, R. F., Morrison, D. M., O'Donnell, J., Abbott, R. D., & Day, L. E. (1992). The Seattle Social Development Project: Effects of the first four years on protective factors and problem behaviors. In J. McCord & R. Tremblay (Eds.), *The prevention of antisocial behavior in children* (pp. 139-161). New York: Guilford.

Hawkins, J. D., Lishner, D. M., Jenson, J. M., & Catalano, R. F. (1987). Delinquents and drugs: What the evidence suggests about prevention and treatment programming. In B. S. Brown & A. R. Mills (Eds.), *Youth at high risk for substance abuse* (DHHS Publication No. ADM 87-1537, pp. 82-132). Washington, DC: Government Printing Office.

Hawkins, J. D., & Weiss, J. G. (1985). The social development model: An integrated approach to delinquency prevention. *Journal of Primary Prevention, 6,* 73-97.

Ho, M. K. (1992). Differential application of treatment modalities with Asian American youth. In L. A. Vargas & J. D. Koss-Chioino (Eds.), *Working with culture: Psychotherapeutic interventions with ethnic minority children and adolescents* (pp. 182-203). San Francisco: Jossey-Bass.

Jason, L. (1990). A multimedia-based approach to increasing communication and the level of AIDS knowledge within families. *Journal of Community Psychology, 18,* 361-373.

Jones, A. P., & DeMaree, R. G. (1975). Family disruption, social indices, and problem behavior: A preliminary study. *Journal of Marriage and the Family, 37,* 497-504.

Jones, D. C., & Houts, R. (1990). Parental drinking, parent-child communication, and social skills in young adults. *Journal of Studies on Alcohol, 53,* 48-56.

Kaij, L. (1960). *Studies on the etiology and sequels of abuse of alcohol.* Lund, Sweden: University of Lund, Department of Psychiatry.

Kandel, D. B. (1980). Drug and drinking behavior among youth. *Annual Review of Sociology, 6,* 235-285.

Kandel, D. B., & Andrews, K. (1987). Processes of adolescent socialization by parents and peers. *International Journal of the Addictions, 22,* 319-342.

Kaufman, E. (1986). A contemporary approach to the family treatment of substance abuse disorders. *American Journal of Drug and Alcohol Abuse, 12,* 119-211.

Kaufman, E., & Borders, L. (1988). Ethnic family differences in adolescent substance use. *Journal of Chemical Dependency Treatment, 1,* 99-121.

Kaufman, E., & Kaufman, P. N. (1979). Multiple family therapy with drug abusers. In E. Kaufman & P. Kaufman (Eds.), *Family therapy of drug and alcohol abuse* (pp. 81-94). New York: Gardner.

Kazdin, A. E. (1987). Treatment of antisocial behavior in children: Current status and future directions. *Psychological Bulletin, 102,* 187-203.

Kazdin, A. E. (1993). Adolescent mental health: Prevention and treatment programs. *American Psychologist, 48,* 127-140.

Kim, S., McLeod, J. H., & Shantzis, C. (1992). Cultural competence for evaluators working with Asian-American communities: Some practical considerations. In M. A. Orlandi (Ed.), *Cultural competence for evaluators: A guide for alcohol and other drug abuse prevention practitioners working with ethnic/racial communities* (OSAP Cultural Competence Series I, DHHS Publication No. ADM 92-1884, pp. 203-260). Washington, DC: Government Printing Office.

Klein, M. A., & Swisher, J. D. (1983). A statewide evaluation of a communication and parenting skills program. *Journal of Drug Education, 13,* 73-82.

Kline, R. B., Canter, W. A., & Robins, A. (1987). Parameters of teenage alcohol use: A path analytic conceptual model. *Journal of Consulting and Clinical Psychology, 55,* 521-528.

Klitzner, M., Gruenewald, P. J., & Bamberger, E. (1990). The assessment of parent-led prevention programs: *Journal of Drug Education, 13,* 73-82.

Kruttschmitt, C., Ward, D., & Sheble, J. A. (1987) Abuse-resistant youth: Some factors that may inhibit violent criminal behavior. *Social Forces, 66,* 501-519.

Kumpfer, K. L. (1987). Special populations: Etiology and prevention of vulnerability to chemical dependency in children of substance abusers. In B. Brown & A. Mills (Eds.), *Youth at high risk for substance abuse* (pp. 1-71). Rockville, MD: Office for Substance Abuse Prevention.

Kumpfer, K. L. (1990a). Environmental and family-focused prevention: The Cinderellas of prevention want to go to the ball, too. In K. H. Rey, C. L. Faegre, & P. Lowery (Eds.), *Prevention research findings: 1988* (OSAP Prevention Monograph-3, DHHS Publication No. ADM-89-1615, pp. 194-220). Washington, DC: Government Printing Office.

Kumpfer, K. L. (1990b). *Resiliency and AOD use prevention in high risk youth.* Unpublished manuscript submitted to the Center for Substance Abuse Prevention, Department of Health Education, University of Utah, Salt Lake City.

Kumpfer, K. L. (1990c, March). *YCOSA Black Parenting Project: Second year evaluation report.* Unpublished manuscript submitted to the Alabama Department of Mental Health and Mental Retardation.

Kumpfer, K. L. (1991). How to get hard to reach parents involved in parenting programs. In D. Pines (Ed.), *Parent training is prevention: Preventing alcohol and other drug problems among youth in the family* (DHHS Publication No. ADM 91-1715, pp. 87-95). Washington, DC: Government Printing Office.

Kumpfer, K. L. (1993). *Strengthening America's families: Promising parenting and family strategies for delinquency prevention. A user's guide.* Washington, DC: U.S. Department of Justice, Office of Juvenile Programs.

Kumpfer, K. L. (1993, June). *Safe Haven African American Parenting Project: Second year evaluation report.* Unpublished manuscript submitted to City of Detroit Health Department, Health Behavior Laboratory, Department of Health Education, University of Utah, Salt Lake City.

Kumpfer, K., Alvarado, R., Turner, C., & Griffin, E. (1993, February). *A preliminary predictive model of alcohol and other drug use for Hispanic adolescents.* Paper presented at the Center for Substance Abuse Prevention's 1993 National/International Prevention Conference, "New Dimensions in Prevention: Sharing Today, Shaping Tomorrow," Washington, DC.

Kumpfer, K. L., & Bayes, J. (1995). Child abuse and alcohol, tobacco and other drug abuse: Causality, coincidence or controversy? In J. H. Jaffe (Ed.), *The encyclopedia of drugs and alcohol.* New York: Macmillan.

Kumpfer, K. L., Bridges, S., & Williams, K. (1993, October). *The Safehaven Program: Strengthening African-American families.* Unpublished manuscript submitted to the Detroit City Health Department by the Department of Health Education, University of Utah, Salt Lake City.

Kumpfer, K. L., & DeMarsh, J. P. (1986). Family environmental and genetic influences on children's future chemical dependency. In S. Griswold-Ezekoye, K. L. Kumpfer, & W. Bukoski (Eds.), *Childhood and chemical abuse: Prevention and intervention* (pp. 49-91). New York: Haworth.

Kumpfer, K. L., & DeMarsh, J. P. (1988, December). *Recruitment and attrition issues.* Paper presented at the Office for Substance Abuse Prevention Conference, San Antonio, TX.

Kumpfer, K. L., DeMarsh, J. P., & Child, W. (1989). *Strengthening Families Program: Children's skills training curriculum manual (prevention services to children of substance-abusing parents).* Salt Lake City: Department of Health, Alcohol and Drug Research Center.

Kumpfer, K. L., Gopelrud, E., & Alvarado, R. (1994). Assessing individual risks and resiliencies. In N. Miller (Ed.), *Principles of addiction medicine.* Chicago: University of Chicago Press.

Kumpfer, K. L., & Turner, C. W. (1990-91). The social ecology model of adolescent substance abuse: Implications for prevention. *International Journal of the Addictions, 25,* 435-463.

Kurth-Schai, R. (1988). The roles of youth in society: A reconceptualization. *Educational Forum, 52,* 131-132.

L'Abate, L. (1977). *Enrichment: Structured interventions with couples, families and groups.* Washington, DC: University Press of America.

Laosa, L. M. (in press). Psychosocial stress, coping and development of Hispanic immigrant children. In F. C. Serafica, A. I. Schuevel, R. K. Russel, P. D. Isaac, & L. Myers (Eds.), *Mental health of ethnic minorities.* New York: Praeger.

Lee, E. (1990). Assessment and treatment of Chinese-American immigrant families. In G. W. Saba, B. M. Karrer, & K. V. Hardy (Eds.), *Minorities and family therapy* (pp. 99-122). New York: Haworth.

Lipsey, M. W. (1992). Juvenile delinquency treatment: A meta-analytic inquiry into the variability of effects. In T. D. Cook, H. Cooper, D. S. Cordray, H. Hartmann, L. V. Hedges, R. J. Light, T. A. Louis, & F. Mosteller (Eds.), *Meta-analysis for explanation* (pp. 83-127). New York: Russell Sage.

Loeber, R., & Stouthammer-Loeber, M. (1986). Family factors as correlates and predictors of juvenile conduct problems and delinquency. In N. Morris & M. Tonry (Eds.), *Crime and justice: An annual review of research* (pp. 29-149). Chicago: University of Chicago Press.

Lytton, H. (1990) Child and parent effects in boys' conduct disorder: A reinterpretation. *Developmental Psychology, 26,* 683-697.

Masten, A. S., & Garmezy, N. (1985). Risk, vulnerability, and protective factors in developmental psychopathology. In B. B. Lahey & A. E. Kazdin (Eds.), *Advances in clinical child psychology* (Vol. 8, pp. 1-51). New York: Plenum.

May, P. A. (1992, May). *The prevention of alcohol and other substance abuse among American Indians: A review and analysis of the literature.* Paper presented at the National Institute on Alcohol Abuse and Alcoholism, Working Group on Alcohol Prevention Research in Ethnic Minority Communities, Washington, DC.

McCord, J. (1991). Family relationships, juvenile delinquency, and adult criminality. *Criminology, 29,* 397-418.

McIntyre, K., White, D., & Yoast, R. (1990). *Resilience among high risk youth.* Madison: Wisconsin Clearinghouse.

McMahon, R. J. (1987). Some current issues in the behavioral assessment of conduct disordered children and their families. *Behavioral Assessment, 9,* 235-252.

Mills, R. (1990, June). *Substance abuse, dropout and delinquency prevention: The Modello-Homestead Gardens Early Intervention Project.* Paper presented at the Ninth Annual Conference of Psychology of Mind, St. Petersburg, FL.

Minty, B. (1988). Public care or distorted family relationships: The antecedents of violent crime. *Howard Journal, 27,* 172-187.

Minuchin, S. (1974). *Families and family therapy.* Cambridge, MA: Harvard University Press.

Molgaard, V., & Kumpfer, K. L. (1994). *Strengthening Families Program II.* Ames: Iowa State University, Social and Behavioral Research Center for Rural Health.

Moos, R. H., & Billing, A. G. (1982). Children of alcoholics during the recovery process: Alcoholic and matched-control families. *Active Behaviors, 7,* 155-163.

Mulvey, E. P., & LaRosa, Jr., J. F. (1986). Delinquency cessation and adolescent development: Preliminary data. *American Journal of Orthopsychiatry, 56,* 212-224.

Needle, R., McCubbin, H., Wilson, M., Reineck, R., Lazar, A., & Mederer, H. (1986). Interpersonal influences in adolescent drug use—the role of older siblings, parents, and peers. *International Journal of the Addictions, 21,* 739-766.

Neiger, B. (1991). *Resilient reintegration: Use of structural equations modeling.* Unpublished doctoral dissertation, University of Utah, Salt Lake City.

Newcomb, M. D. (1991). Understanding the multidimensional nature of drug use and abuse: The role of consumption, risk factors, and protective factors. In M. D. Glantz & R. Pickens (Eds.), *Vulnerability to drug abuse* (pp. 255-297). Washington, DC: American Psychological Association.

Newcomb, M. D., & Bentler, P. M. (1986). Substance use and ethnicity: Differential impact of peer and adult models. *Journal of Psychology, 120,* 83-95.

Newcomb, M. D., Maddahian, E., & Bentler, P. M. (1986). Risk factors for drug use among adolescents: Concurrent and longitudinal analyses. *American Journal of Public Health, 76,* 525-531.

Nobles, W., Goddard, L. L., Cavil, W. E., & George, P. Y. (1987). *In the culture of drugs in the black community*••• (pp. 10-36). Oakland, CA: Black Family Institute.

Oetting, E. R., & Beauvais, F. (1990). Adolescent drug use: Findings of national and local surveys. *Journal of Consulting and Clinical Psychology, 58,* 385-394.

Oetting, E. R., Beauvais, F., & Edwards, R. W. (1988). Alcohol and Indian youth: Social and psychological correlates and prevention. *Journal of Drug Issues, 18,* 87-101.

Oyemade, U., & Washington, V. (1990). The role of family factors in the primary prevention of substance abuse among high risk black youth. In A. R. Stiffman & L. E. Davis (Eds.), *Ethnic issues in adolescent mental health* (pp. 267-284). Newbury Park, CA: Sage.

Patterson, G. R. (1975). *Families: Applications of social learning to family life* (Rev. ed.). Champaign, IL: Research Press.

Patterson, G. R. (1982). *A social learning approach: Coercive family process* (Vol. 3). Eugene, OR: Castalia.

Patterson, G. R., Chamberlain, P., & Reid, J. B. (1982). A comparative evaluation of a parent training program. *Behavior Therapy, 13,* 638-650.

Patterson, G. R., DeBaryshe, B. D., & Ramsey, E. (1989). A developmental perspective on antisocial behavior. *American Psychologist, 44,* 329-335.

Patterson, G. R., Reid, J. B., & Dishion, T. J. (1992). *Antisocial boys.* Eugene, OR: Castalia.

Penning, M., & Barnes, G. E. (1982). Adolescent marijuana use: A review. *International Journal of the Addictions, 17,* 749-791.

Perry, C. L., Pirie, P., Holder, W., Halper, A., & Dudovitz, B. (1990). Parent involvement in cigarette smoking prevention: Two pilot evaluations of the "Unpuffables Program." *Journal of School Health, 60,* 443-447.

Phares, V., & Compas, B. (1992). The role of fathers in child and adolescent psychopathology: Make room for daddy. *Psychological Bulletin, 111,* 387-412.

Pickens, R., & Svikis, D. (1986). Use of the twin method in the study of vulnerability to drug abuse. In M. C. Braude & H. M. Chau (Eds.), *Genetic and biological markers in drug abuse and alcoholism* (NIDA Research Monograph No. 66, pp. •••). Washington, DC: Government Printing Office.

Reilly, D. M. (1992). Drug-abusing families: Intrafamilial dynamics and brief triphasic treatment. In E. Kaufman & P. Kaufman (Eds.), *Family therapy of drug and alcohol abuse* (pp. 105-119). Boston: Allyn & Bacon.

Richardson, G. E., Neiger, B. L., Jensen, S., & Kumpfer, K. L. (1990). The resiliency model. *Health Education, 21,* 33-39.

Richardson, J., Dwyer, K., McGuigan, K., Hansen, W. B., Dent, C., Johnson, C. A., Sussman, S. Y., Brannon, B., & Flay, B. (1989). Substance use among eighth-grade students who take care of themselves after school. *Pediatrics, 84,* 556-566.

Robins, L. N. (1980). The natural history of drug abuse. *Acta Psychiatrica Scandinavica, 62*(Suppl. 284), 7-20.

Rodriguez, O. (1988, March). *A conceptual approach to Hispanic adolescent drug use.* Paper presented at the meeting of the Society for Research on Adolescence, Alexandria, VA.

Rogoff, B. (1990). *Apprenticeship in thinking: Cognitive development in social context.* New York: Oxford University Press.

Rohrbach, L. A., Hansen, W. B., & Pentz, M. A. (1992, November). *Strategies for involving parents in drug abuse prevention: Results from the Midwest Prevention Program.* Paper presented at the annual meeting of the American Public Health Association, Washington, DC.

Rohrbach, L. A., Hodgson, C. S., Broder, B. I., Montgomery, S. B., Flay, B. R., Hansen, W. B., & Pentz, M. A. (in press). Parental participation in drug abuse prevention: Results from the Midwestern Prevention Project. *Journal of Research on Adolescence.*

Rose, M., Battjes, R., & Leukefeld, C. (1984). *Family life skills training for drug abuse prevention* (DHHS Pub. No. ADM 84-1340). Washington, DC: Government Printing Office.

Rosenthal, T., & Bandura, A. (1978). Psychological modeling: Theory and practice. In S. Garfield & A. E. Bergin (Eds.), *Handbook of psychotherapy and behavior change: An empirical analysis* (pp. 621-658). New York: John Wiley.

Rutter, M. (1987). Continuities and discontinuities from infancy. In J. Rolf, A. S. Masten, D. Cicchetti, K. H. Neuchterlein, & S. Weintraub (Eds.), *Risk and protective factors in the development of psychopathology* (pp. 181-214). New York: Cambridge University Press.

Rutter, M. (1990). Psychosocial resilience and protective mechanisms. *American Orthopsychiatric Association, 316-331.*

Rutter, M., & Quinton, D. (1984). Long-term follow-up of women institutionalized in childhood: Factors promoting good functioning in adult life. *Journal of Developmental Psychology, 18,* 225-234.

Santisteban, D. A., Szapocznik, J., & Rio, A. T. (1993). Family therapy for Hispanic substance abusing youth: An empirical approach to substance abuse prevention. In R. S. Mayers, B. L. Kail, & T. D. Watts (Eds.), *Hispanic substance abuse* (pp. 157-173). Springfield, IL: Charles C Thomas.

Schinke, S., Orlandi, M., Vaccaro, D., Espinoza, R., McAlister, A., & Botvin, G. (1992). Substance use among Hispanic and non-Hispanic adolescents. *Addictive Behaviors, 17,* 117-124.

Schuckit, M. (1983). A prospective study of genetic markers in alcoholism. In I. Hanin & E. Usden (Eds.), *Biological markers in psychiatry and neurology* (pp. •••). Oxford, UK: Pergamon.

Schuckit, M. A. (1985). Ethanol induced changes in body sway in men at high alcoholism risk. *Archives of General Psychiatry, 42,* 375-379.

Shedler, J., & Block, J. (1990). Adolescent drug use and psychological health: A longitudinal inquiry. *American Psychologist, 45,* 612-630.

Simcha-Fagan, O., Gersten, J. C., & Langner, T. (1986). Early precursors and concurrent correlates of items of illicit drug use in adolescence. *Journal of Drug Issues, 60,* 7-28.

Smart, R. G., & Fejer, D. (1972). Drug use among adolescents and their parents: Closing the generation gap in mood modification. *Journal of Abnormal Psychology, 79,* 153-160.

Sowder, B., & Burt, M. (1978a, November). *Children of addicts: A population in need of coordinated comprehensive mental health services.* Paper presented at the American Association of Psychiatric Services for Children, Atlanta.

Sowder, B., & Burt, M. (1978b). *Children of addicts and non-addicts: A comparative investigation in five urban sites.* Bethesda, MD: Gurt Associates.

Spoth, R., & Redmond, C. (in press). Study of participation barriers in family-focused prevention. Research issues and preliminary results. *International Journal of Community Health Education.*

Stanton, M. D., & Todd, T. (1982). Principles and techniques for getting "Resistant" families into treatment. In M. D. Stanton & T. Todd (Eds.), *The family therapy of drug abuse and addiction* (pp. •••). New York: Guilford.

Steinmetz, S. K., & Straus, M. H. (1974). *Violence in the family.* New York: Dodd, Mead.

Stern, A. (1992). *A review of the research on family influences on alcohol and other drug-taking behavior: Implications for prevention programming.* Paper prepared for the Southwest Regional Center for Drug-Free Schools and Communities.

Swaim, R. C., Oetting, E. R., Edwards, R. W., & Beauvais, F. (1989). Links from emotional distress to adolescent drug use: A path model. *Journal of Consulting and Clinical Psychology, 57,* 227-231.

Szapocznik, J., & Kurtines, W. M. (1989). *Breakthroughs in family therapy with drug-abusing and problem youth.* New York: Springer.

Szapocznik, J., Kurtines, W., Santisteban, D. A., & Rio, A. T. (1990). The interplay of advances among theory, research and application in treatment interventions aimed at behavior problem children and adolescents. *Journal of Consulting and Clinical Psychology, 58,* 696-703.

Szapocznik, J., Perez-Vidal, A., Brickman, A. L., Foote, F., Santisteban, D., Hervis, O, & Kurtines, W. (1988). Engaging adolescent drug abusers and their families into treatment: A strategic structural systems approach. *Journal of Consulting and Clinical Psychology, 56,* 552-557.

Szapocznik, J., Santisteban, D., Rio, A., Perez-Vidal, A., & Kurtines, W. M. (1989). Family effectiveness training: An intervention to prevent drug abuse and problem behaviors in Hispanic adolescents. *Hispanic Journal of Behavioral Sciences, 11,* 4-27.

Szapocznik, J., Santisteban, D., Rio, A., Perez-Vidal, A., Kurtines, W. M., & Hervis, O. (1986). Bicultural effectiveness training (BET): An intervention modality for families experiencing intergenerational/intercultural conflict. *Hispanic Journal of Behavioral Sciences, 6,* 303-330.

Tafoya, T. (1990). Circles and cedar: Native Americans and family therapy. In G. W. Saba, B. M. Karrer, & K. V. Hardy (Eds.), *Minorities and family therapy* (pp. 71-98). New York: Haworth.

Thornberry, T. P. (1987). Toward an interactional theory of delinquency. *Criminology, 25,* 863-891.

Tremblay, R. E., McCord, J., Boileau, H., LeBlanc, M., Gagnon, C., Charlebois, P., & Larivee, S. (1990, November). *The Montreal prevention experiment: School adjustment and self-reported delinquency after three years of follow-up.* Paper presented at the 42nd annual meeting of the American Society of Criminology, Baltimore.

U.S. Bureau of the Census. (1991). *Money income and poverty status in the United States, 1989* (Current Population Reports P-60, No. 168, p. 104). Washington, DC: Government Printing Office.

Vaillant, G. E. (1983). *The natural history of alcoholism.* Cambridge, MA: Harvard University Press.

Vicary, J., & Lerner, J. (1986). Parental attributes and adolescent drug use. *Journal of Adolescence, 9,* 115-122.

Wahler, R., Leske, G., & Rogers, E. (1979). The insular family: A deviance support system for oppositional children. In L. S. Hamerlynck (Ed.), *Behavioral systems for the developmentally disabled: Vol. 1. School and family environments* (pp.). New York: Brunner/Mazel.

Webster-Stratton, C. (Producer). (1987). *The parents and children series* [Videotape]. Eugene, OR: Castalia.

Werner, E. E. (1986). Resilient offspring of alcoholics: A longitudinal study from birth to age 18. *Journal of Studies on Alcoholism, 47,* 34-40.

Wolin, S. J., Bennett, L. A., & Noonan, D. L. (1979). Family rituals and the recurrence of alcoholism over generations. *American Journal of Psychiatry, 136,* 589-593.

Wolin, S. J., & Wolin, S. (1993). *The resilient self: How survivors of troubled families rise above adversity.* New York: Villard.

Wright, K. N., & Wright, K. E. (1992). *Family life and delinquency and crime: A policy-maker's guide to the literature.* Unpublished manuscript, Office of Juvenile Justice and Delinquency Prevention, Washington, DC.

Zill, N. (1993). The changing realities of family life. *Aspen Institute Quarterly, 5,* 27-51.

14

Substance Abuse
Prevention Involving Asian/
Pacific Islander American Communities

Sehwan Kim
Shirley D. Coletti
Charles Williams
Nancy A. Hepler

The purpose of this chapter is to present some of the important cultural issues one must address when developing and implementing community-based alcohol, tobacco, and other drug (ATOD) abuse prevention programs involving Asian/Pacific Islander American (for short, Asian American) groups or communities. As such, this chapter is concerned with large-scale community-based prevention programs rather than with issues pertaining to ATOD addiction treatment. Specifically, its emphasis is on generating culturally relevant intervention strategies that are applicable to Asian American communities. From the outset, it must be noted that the ultimate goal of all prevention research is not only to describe the outcome/impact of a particular approach, but also to obtain information for further refinement of the intervention approach. Within the dual context of evaluative judgment and program refinement, cultural competence of program developers and evaluators is viewed as the capacity to acknowledge the importance of cultural uniqueness and the associated cultural specificities that either hinder or promote the ATOD usage of a population under investigation. Cultural competence is also the capacity of prevention researchers and practitioners to function effectively with the population involved in a particular prevention project.

In determining the cultural specificities that affect the outcome of a community-based prevention evaluation project, one must emphasize that no social scientific evaluation research operates in a vacuum (i.e., in a manner that is context-free). Further, no such research is atheoretical; it is always based on some theoretical orientation or set of intuitive assumptions, not only about the particular prevention program itself, but also about the population it seeks to serve.

All prevention research must therefore be based on a firm understanding of the workings of a multitude of factors that determine the program outcome. These factors include the demographic and socioeconomic characteristics of the target populations served; the ATOD usage pattern of Asian Americans; the theoretical frameworks on which prevention programs rest; cultural specificities, values, and aspirations that affect both the implementation of the program and its outcome; the risk factors associated with the ATOD abuse; and the rationale behind the selection of various prevention strategies being implemented with Asian American youth.

Demographic Configuration of Asian Americans

The term *Asian /Pacific Islander* comprises over 60 separate racial and ethnic groups and subgroups. They are very heterogeneous, differing in their histories, languages, dialects, religions, cultures, immigration and generation histories experienced in the United States, socioeconomic statuses (SES), places of birth (percentage foreign born vs. born in the United States), nationalities, and so on (Criddle & Mam, 1987; Sue, 1987).

In general, there are vast differences in the degree to which they are acculturated and assimilated (Kitano & Daniels, 1988) into the white Anglo-American mainstream culture. At one extreme are unassimilated Asian Americans living in their own "cultural islands"—Chinatowns, Koreatowns, Japantowns, or Vietnamtowns—insulated from the surrounding white culture. They often have their own newspapers, radio and TV stations, churches, and shopping places where English is hardly spoken. At the other extreme, one can observe second- and third-plus-generation Asians whose values and thought processes are indistinguishable from those of the white culture.

Many Chinese and Japanese families have been in the United States for three generations or more. The vast majority of Vietnamese, Koreans, Asian Indians, and Filipinos in the United States were born overseas. Hawaiians, Samoans, Japanese, and Guamanians, however, were largely born in the United States. Also, there is a great deal of variation in the degree to which particular communities maintain their cohesiveness in terms of traditional customs, values, languages, and ethnic organizations (Austin, Prendergast, & Lee, 1989).

Accordingly, it does not make much sense to combine Asian Americans together unless one is presenting others' data as originally reported. The tendency to group such diverse nationalities into a single Asian American category confuses the already lamentable state of research on this topic (Yu, & Liu, 1987).

Asian Americans have changed the demographic landscape of the United States during the past two decades. Census figures document the staggering growth of this population from 1.7 million in 1970 to nearly 7.8 million by 1991. Table 14.1 shows that there were nearly 7.3 million Asian Americans living in the United States as of 1990—a number similar to the total population of the state of New Jersey. This constitutes nearly 3% of the U.S. population. During the 1980s, Asian Americans were the fastest growing group among all the ethnic groups identified by the U.S. Census Bureau. Between 1980 and 1990, the rate of increase observed was about 95% for Asians as compared to 53% for Hispanics, 13.2% for blacks, and 6% for whites (U.S. Bureau of the Census, 1993). The U.S. population in 1990 was just below 249 million. It is estimated that the Asian/Pacific Islander population in the United States will be nearing 10 million by 1995, or just below 4% of the U.S. population. Of these 10 million Asian/Pacific Islanders, 2 million or 20% are expected to be aged 5 through 17.

Table 14.2 shows educational attainment of Asian Americans in comparison to other ethnic groups in the United States for the year 1991. The Asian American group has the largest (39.1%) proportion of the college educated—a proportion significantly higher than that observed for the United States as a whole (21.4%). Educational attainment of Pacific Islanders is significantly lower than that of other Asian American groups.

As shown in Table 14.3, the median household income of Asian Americans ($42,661) observed for 1991-1992 is far above the national average ($35,939). (It should be noted, however, that the Asian household income is often based on multiple incomes rather than a single income source.) The same income for Pacific Islanders only is significantly below the national average, and the proportion of Pacific Islanders living below the poverty level as defined by the U.S. Census Bureau is above the proportion observed for the national population as a whole (U.S. Bureau of the Census, 1993). As might be expected, the proportion of married couples among Asian Americans (79.1%) is somewhat higher than the national average (78.1%).

The demographic and socioeconomic information provided thus far will soon be outdated. In recent years, Southeast Asian refugees, Filipinos, and Koreans have been the fastest growing Asian groups. According to the 1990 U.S. census (U.S. Bureau of the Census, 1993), Chinese (1,645,472), Filipinos (1,406,770), and Japanese (847,562) constituted the largest groups among all Asian and Pacific Islander groups identified. By the year 2000, it is estimated that Filipinos will be the largest group, followed by the Chinese,

TABLE 14.1 Resident U.S. Population by Ethnicity (in Millions), 1980-1990

	1980	1990	% Change, 1980-1990
White	188.4	199.7	+6.0%
	(83.1%)	(80.3%)	
Black	26.5	30.0	+13.2%
	(11.7%)	(12.2%)	
Asian/Pacific Is.	3.7	7.3	+94.6%
	(1.6%)	(2.9%)	
Amer. Indian & Alaskan	1.4	2.0	+37.9%
	(0.6%)	(0.8%)	
Hispanic[a]	14.6	22.4	+53.0%
	(6.4%)	(9.0%)	
U.S. population	226.5	248.7	+9.8%
	(100.0%)	(100.0%)	

SOURCE: U.S. Bureau of Census, 1993, p. 18.
a. Hispanic persons may be of any race. Thus, the sum of the ethnic groups constitutes more than the total U.S. population.

TABLE 14.2 Educational Attainment by Ethnic Population Aged 25 Years or Older: 1991

	4+ Years of High School	4+ Years of College	Rank Order
U.S. population	79.4	21.4	3
White	79.9	22.1	2
Black	66.7	11.5	4
Asian & Pacific Is.	81.8	39.1	1
Hispanic	51.3	9.7	5

SOURCE: U.S. Bureau of the Census, 1993.

TABLE 14.3 Other SES Characteristics of the U.S. Population by Ethnicity, 1991-1992

	% Unemployed	% Married Couples	Median Income	% Below Poverty Level
U.S population	7.4 (3)	78.1 (3)	$35,939 (3)	n/a
White	6.5 (4)	82.3 (1)	37,783 (2)	11.3
Black	14.1 (1)	47.1 (5)	21,548 (5)	32.7
Hispanic	9.9 (2)	69.3 (4)	23,431 (4)	28.1
Asian/Pacific Is.	6.3 (5)	79.1 (2)	42,661 (1)	13.8

SOURCE: U.S. Bureau of the Census, 1993.
NOTE: Values in the parentheses refer to rank orders column-wise.

Vietnamese, Koreans, Asian Indians, and Japanese. Thus, in the near future, there will be significant changes in socioeconomic, demographic, and ethnic profiles of Asian groups. Such changes will undoubtedly bring about certain changes in ATOD usage patterns of Asian communities in the United States.

ATOD Incidence and Prevalence Rates

Most of the information pertaining to alcohol, tobacco, and other drug (ATOD) use among Asian Americans comes from isolated, ad hoc, nonrandom, snowball (referral) surveys (local, community, or campus based) or statewide surveys conducted either by individual researchers or, in some cases, by state agencies. There are no prevalence data pertaining to the Asian American population at the national level. Most of the available survey data are on the use of alcohol and tobacco. The three major national surveys—the National Institute on Drug Abuse (NIDA) National Household Survey, the NIDA National Adolescent School Health Survey, and the National High School Seniors Survey—do not report data on Asian American groups. Prior to 1991, NIDA National Household Surveys excluded Alaska and Hawaii from the survey sample frames altogether.

On the basis of limited survey data generated by independent researchers and the states of Hawaii (Murakami, 1989) and California (Skager, Fisher, & Maddahian, 1986; Skager, Frith, & Maddahian, 1989), one may find a somewhat more stable pattern of ATOD use among Asian groups than among whites. However, there are significant regional and ethnic differences according to country of origin, SES, place of birth, age, family structure, marital status, generation and immigration history, and so on.

ADULTS

The most conspicuous finding concerning alcohol and other drug use among Asian Americans is that it is lower than for non-Asian individuals in general, with the exception of cigarette use (Iiyama, Nishi, & Johnson, 1976; Johnson, Nagoshi, Ahern, Wilson, & Yuen, 1987; McLaughlin, Raymond, Murakami, & Goebert, 1987; Sue & Morishima, 1982; Sue, Zane, & Ito, 1979; Trimble, Padilla, & Bell, 1987; Tucker, 1985). Most researchers consistently report that Asian groups have lower levels of alcohol use when compared to other ethnic groups, with the exception of native Hawaiians, whose alcohol use appears to be comparable to that of whites (Le Marchand, Kolonel, & Yoshizawa, 1989). Asians have perhaps the lowest alcohol prevalence rate of any major ethnic group in the United States, male or female. Asian females consume alcohol far less frequently than white females. As is true of all other

TABLE 14.4 Past Month Cigarette Use Among Ethnic Groups, for Males

Ethnicity	Source	Observation Year	Prevalence Rate (%)
White	NIDA, 1991	1990	30
Black	NIDA, 1991	1990	29
Hispanic	NIDA, 1991	1990	26
Vietnamese in California	CDC, 1992		
	U.S. DHHS, 1990	1989-1991	35-65
Chinese in California	CDC, 1992	1989-1991	28
Laotians in Chicago	Levin et al., 1988	1988	72
Laotians in California	U.S. DHHS, 1990	1988	92
Cambodians in California	U.S. DHHS, 1990	1988	71

ethnic groups, Asian males are more likely to drink and to drink heavily than Asian females, and the gender gap in drinking behavior may be larger in the Asian group than in any other major ethnic group in the United States.

Within Asian American groups, only native Hawaiians drink alcohol at levels similar to those of whites. According to surveys conducted by Hawaii's Department of Health (Hawaii Department of Health, 1979; Murakami, 1989), native Hawaiians had a higher prevalence rate than Filipinos, Japanese, or Chinese. There is some indication that the alcohol use among Asian Americans is increasing. Japanese Americans generally rank after whites and, in Hawaii, after native Hawaiians. In this context, it is interesting to note that Hawaiian residents of Chinese and Japanese ancestry had lower mean levels of alcohol use if they were born in Asia than if they were born in Hawaii (Johnson et al., 1987). On the other hand, Hawaiian residents of Caucasian ancestry had lower mean levels of alcohol use if they were born in Hawaii than if they were born on the mainland. These differences held up even after controlling for the age of subjects (Johnson & Nagoshi, 1990).

Outside of Hawaii, there is considerable variation in drinking patterns among different Asian groups, although it is generally believed that Japanese Americans drink the most, followed by Korean Americans and Chinese Americans (Chi, Lubben, & Kitano, 1989). In terms of heavy drinking, however, Koreans seem to be at a similar level to that found among Japanese Americans. Heavy drinking is typified in business entertainment and after work in drinking establishments such as bars and nightclubs in New York, Chicago, Los Angeles, and in Hawaii, especially among foreign-born Korean and Japanese Americans.

As shown in Table 14.4, cigarette use among Asian groups, however, is much higher than in other ethnic groups in the United States. Among California immigrants, for example, smoking rates among men are 72% to 92% for

Laotians, 71% for Cambodians, and 65% for Vietnamese (U.S. Department of Health and Human Services, 1990), compared with 30% for the overall American white male population. Some of the main factors contributing to higher smoking practice among Asian immigrant men are (a) earlier exposure to higher nicotine and tar contents of Asian brands of cigarettes as compared to American brands, (b) wide social acceptability and use of cigarettes in their countries of origin, (c) the cultural practice of offering cigarettes to guests, and (d) a significant degree of cultural insulation and isolation from mainstream white American culture.

YOUTH

Among the young, data indicate that ATOD use is not as extensive within any Asian group as within the mainstream population or within most other ethnic groups. Most surveys indicate that ATOD use by Asian youths is the lowest among all major ethnic groups found in the United States, with the possible exception of African American youths (Bachman et al., 1991; Wallace & Bachman, 1991). Table 14.5 shows findings from a national survey of high school seniors, Monitoring the Future, conducted from the University of Michigan (Bachman, Wallace, O'Malley, Johnson, & Kurth, 1990). On the basis of combined data during 1985-1989, the highest annual prevalence rate is observed among Native Americans. This is followed by rates for whites, Mexican Americans, Puerto Ricans/Latin Americans, Asian Americans, and, last of all, African Americans.

Similarly, a longitudinal survey of drug use among students in Los Angeles in 1976, 1979, and 1980 reported that white students had the highest rates of use, followed by Hispanics, Asians, and, last of all, blacks (Maddahian, Newcomb, & Bentler, 1986). In recent years, however, drug use among Asian American students has been increasing at an alarming rate. According to a survey of students in Mecklenburg County, North Carolina, there was a significant increase in drug use among Asian students during 1986-1989, even though there was a general decline in student drug use in all other ethnic groups identified during the same time period (Kim & Shantzis, 1989). In this study, the highest ATOD use was found among Chicanos/ Mexican Americans, followed by Puerto Ricans/Latin Americans, American Indians, whites, Asian Americans, and African Americans.

As far as casual alcohol use is concerned, Asian youths drink less than most of the major ethnic groups found in the United States. Similarly, the proportion of fifth-grade students who initiate substance use is observed to be smaller among Asians than among other major ethnic groups in the United States (Gillmore et al., 1990). However, when it comes to heavy drinking (defined as drinking at least once a week and drinking large amounts of

TABLE 14.5 Annual Prevalence of 13 Types of Drugs by Ethnicity, 1985-1989, High School Seniors Only

	White	Black	Percentage Who Used During Last 12 Months			
			Puerto Rican/ Mexican American	Latin American	Asian American	Native American
Marijuana/hashish	38.04	23.54	31.50	25.84	18.39	42.99
Inhalants	6.95	2.38	5.13	3.97	4.03	7.01
Hallucinogens	6.60	1.19	4.00	4.25	2.61	9.50
LSD	5.40	0.75	3.35	2.22	2.21	7.50
Cocaine	10.56	4.18	11.06	11.81	5.75	14.85
Heroin	0.49	0.54	0.64	0.79	0.30	1.25
Other opiates	5.88	1.52	2.64	2.28	2.62	6.55
Stimulants	14.17	3.78	10.68	6.93	6.28	18.19
Sedatives	4.84	1.65	3.67	3.58	3.01	7.61
Barbiturates	4.09	1.46	3.23	3.23	2.46	6.70
Methaqualone	1.93	0.57	0.84	1.38	1.21	3.51
Tranquilizers	5.85	1.54	2.34	3.61	2.52	7.79
Alcohol	88.45	74.89	77.89	78.86	68.43	81.65
Mean Index	14.87	9.08	12.07	11.44	9.22	16.55
Rank order	2	6	3	4	5	1

SOURCE: Bachman et al., 1990.

alcohol at a typical occasion), Asian youths seem to assume one of the highest ranks, which may be quite comparable to that of white youths. Asian groups that appear at the highest risk for developing ATOD abuse and those who actually abuse ATOD have seldom been studied or have not been separately identified in previous research. The absence of studies involving these youths seems to have contributed to the traditional underreporting of the prevalence rates involving Asian American youths.

Explaining ATOD Use Among
Asian Americans: Theories and Conjectures

No valid evaluation research operates in a context-free environment, and no evaluation task remains atheoretical. Atheoretical evaluation can say that a given prevention project succeeded or failed but cannot say why. It is empirical rather than scientific in its approach; as such, it cannot contribute much to the task of refining the program. It is precisely for this reason that prevention evaluators have to emphasize clarification of the theoretical underpinnings of a prevention project before embarking on an evaluation task. In the absence of knowledge concerning the inner workings of the major factors that contribute to ATOD-using behavior of a particular Asian community, one cannot either come up with an appropriate prevention program or delineate a set of relevant dependent variables with which to assess the program with any degree of sensitivity, objectivity, and realism.

As we attempt to explain the ATOD-using behavior of Asian Americans, we are faced with a multitude of theories, conjectures, hypotheses, correlates, and/or risk factors often cited in the ATOD research involving Asians (Messolonghites, 1979). Their ATOD-using behavior is influenced by a multitude of factors over and beyond those often cited for whites. Risk factors often cited for whites include low religiosity, low self-confidence, low self-esteem, boredom, perception of incohesive family relationships, stress, negative peer pressure, sensation seeking, excessive rebelliousness, lack of value attachment to school, poor student-teacher relationships, and negative social attitudes, to name a few (Cooper, 1983; Hawkins, Lishner, & Catalano, 1985; Hawkins & Weiss, 1985; Jessor, Chase, & Donovan, 1980; Jones & Battjes, 1985; Kandel, 1982; Kaplan, 1980; Kaplan, Martin, & Johnson, 1986; Kim, 1981; Kim & Newman, 1982; Maddahian, Newcomb, & Bentler, 1988; Murray & Perry, 1985). To these factors, which are cross-culturally shared, we now must add a host of other cultural and situational variables pertinent to Asian groups: the content of cultural values, traditions, attitudes, and beliefs; the degree to which one is socialized to the native culture; the degree to which one is acculturated to the dominant values of the host culture; acculturation processes leading to cultural conflict, including conflict across a generation gap; family conflicts; role conflicts; alienation and identify conflict; racism; and a host of other situational risk factors dictated by immigration history and the economic stress, especially among immigrant families.

In general, theoretical approaches to ATOD use among Asian Americans can be grouped in three categories: (a) cultural content, (b) cultural interaction, and (c) assumed risk factors. What follows is a presentation of some of the major hypotheses that have been generated on Asian Americans' ATOD use, grouped according to these three approaches, although much of the material is based on alcohol studies.

CULTURAL CONTENT APPROACH

This approach is based on the idea that cultural backgrounds and norms governing ATOD-using styles in various cultures differ. For example, it is often noted that mainstream white American culture values assertiveness, individual achievement, individualism, and spontaneity, whereas Chinese, Korean, and Japanese cultures value responsibility to others, interdependence, restraint, moderation, and group achievement. Alcohol use is thus presumed to be more congruent with white culture than with Eastern traditions (Kua, 1987; Sue, 1987).

Asian drinking is also thought to be more social than solitary, occurring in prescribed settings (usually with food) to enhance social interaction rather than as a method of escapism, and occurring within the context of moderate drinking norms. Asian women are expected to drink little or no alcohol. To be more precise, it is obviously true that descriptions of cultural backgrounds and drinking styles in various Asian groups differ in detail. This may account for some of the variations in the ATOD usage pattern of numerous Asian groups that have been observed. But it is also true that drinking attitudes and customs of the various Asian American cultures are similar in their encouragement of moderation, and that no Asian American culture advocates or encourages excessive alcohol use. This may account for a significantly lower prevalence rate of alcohol use among Asian American groups as compared to whites. Likewise, many studies, perhaps starting with Ullman (1958), make the argument that uncertainties and mixed messages in the culture about alcohol use produce ambivalent feelings about drinking within individuals and that these feelings increase the probability of problems once an individual begins to drink (Peele, 1987; Room, 1976).

Certain values are to some extent shared by many cultures. But even when two cultures share a value, they may place different degrees of emphasis on it. For example, there generally seems to be a higher degree of emphasis placed upon educational values among Asian Americans than among some

TABLE 14.6 California Statewide Dropout Rates for Grades 10-12, by Ethnic Group, Classes of 1986, 1991, and 1992 (in percentages)

	1986	1991	1992
Asian American	16.3	10.4	9.2
Filipino American	19.8	10.5	10.2
White	20.2	12.0	10.8
Pacific Islander American	22.8	18.6	16.0
Native American	25.6	18.9	19.2
Hispanic American	35.1	27.2	24.6
Black	35.7	29.4	26.4

SOURCE: California Department of Education, 1993.

other ethnic groups in the United States. Many Asian parents hope for fulfillment in their own lives through the success of their children. Japanese, Korean, and Chinese parents instill in their children very early the idea that parental acceptance is contingent upon their educational performance. Low performance by the child will elicit not only parental disapproval and criticism, but also disappointment and sometimes shame among one's relatives as well. High educational performance by other Asians is often given special recognition in the respective communities. This may partially explain why many Asian children are doing well in school and why their dropout rates are so low compared to those of other ethnic groups (see Table 14.6), although environmental factors other than culture also seem to have a significant impact on overall student performance.

With highly critical parents, however, Asian youth not only may get involved with drugs, but also may want to move away from their cultural identity, especially if their educational performance falls short of parental expectations. Some Asian American youths are under great pressure to succeed because of the "model minority" stereotype and the high expectations for achievement imposed upon them by their parents. Furthermore, many Asian parents, especially Korean, Japanese, Chinese, and Vietnamese, believe that one can only survive in the larger mainstream society through excellence in education and educational attainment. Asian American youths who experience a gap between what is expected of them and what they have actually achieved may suffer from high levels of emotional stress, specifically a fear of failure that they may try to relieve through ATOD use (Sekiya, 1989).

By far, the cultural approach to understanding drinking is the most widely shared view involving Asian American drinking. However, it has its limitations in that it fails to account for vast differences in the drinking behavior of many Asian subgroups. Accordingly, any attempt to explain drinking on the basis of culture alone is bound to be inadequate.

CULTURAL INTERACTION APPROACHES

Cultural interaction approaches attempt to explain Asian American ATOD-using behavior on the basis of the different processes through which different individuals in a minority culture adapt to the larger mainstream American culture. There are three leading approaches: (a) acculturation theory, (b) orthogonal cultural identification theory, and (c) cultural conflict approaches.

Acculturation theory is based on the assumption that cultural transition occurs along a single continuum, such that an increasing identification with the mainstream American culture implies diminishing identification with the minority culture. On the other hand, orthogonal cultural identification theory assumes that there are numerous dimensions of cultural identification (multiple continua) and that increasing identification with the white culture does not imply diminishing identification with the minority culture. Finally, cultural conflict approaches are based on the assumption that the ATOD-using behavior of Asian Americans is influenced by clashes of cultural values during the processes of adjustment to the dominant white culture.

Acculturation Theory

Acculturation theory describes the response of a minority culture to a larger dominant culture within which it is situated. *Acculturation* is defined as the cultural modification of an individual, group, or people through prolonged and continuous interaction involving intercultural exchange and borrowing from different cultures. Within the dominant white American culture, cultural transition occurs along a single continuum, whereby an increasing identification with the white culture is associated with diminishing cultural identification with the native culture. Accordingly, acculturation theory attempts to explain substance-using behavior of Asian Americans in terms of their associated cultural transition, which is assumed to be unidirectional: a transition from a minority culture to the dominant culture. Much of this theory is tested on the basis of the alcohol-using behavior of Asian Americans.

According to this theory, Asians who are recent immigrants should drink in a manner similar to the drinking pattern in their home country. As Asians become more acculturated into the dominant culture, their alcohol-using behavior should be more like that of white Americans. Following this line of reasoning, then, drinking patterns of the first, second, third generations, and so on should progressively become more similar to those of white Americans. This is so because the dominant American culture contains more lenient attitudes toward alcohol consumption, including the possibility of alcohol abuse (Chi et al., 1989; Kitano, Hatanaka, Yeung, & Sue, 1985; Sue et al., 1979; Yuen & Johnson, 1986).

However, others have challenged the acculturation theory by noting that the degree of acculturation is not a significant predictor of drinking by Asian American college students (Akutsu, Sue, Zane, & Nakamura, 1989). They have operationalized the concept of acculturation in terms of the Contrasting Values Survey (Connor, 1977), which is based on an absolute benchmark definition of acculturation (i.e., Eastern cultural values vs. Western cultural values) rather than a relativistic (moving target) definition of acculturation to dominant American culture (i.e., a definition based on ever-changing cultural values pertaining to a particular group within the mainstream white culture). Research by Kitano, Chi, Law, Lubben, and Rhee (1988) and Kitano and Chi (1985) also refutes the explanatory capability of the acculturation theory by noting numerous other mediating variables that lie in between the logical chain of acculturation itself on the one hand and actual drinking behavior on the other: community and family cohesion, receptivity by the dominant community, life experience, and so on.

One study reports assimilation (especially acculturation with marital or mixed parentage) into the white culture as having an important incremental influence on level of alcohol use in that individuals of mixed Asian-Caucasian ancestry had a mean alcohol consumption level that was very similar to that of the Caucasian group and considerably higher than that of the Asian groups (Wilson, McClearn, & Johnson, 1978). This study, which was based in Hawaii, also controlled for socioeconomic variables (i.e., social class and gender).

Orthogonal Cultural Identification (OCI) Theory

The main theme of OCI theory (Oetting & Beauvais, 1990) is that a person's cultural identification is not placed along a single continuum. Rather, there are numerous dimensions of cultural identification, and these dimensions or identifications are independent of each other (i.e., increasing identification with one culture does not require decreasing identification with another). Thus, one's identification with Asian culture does not entail loss or decreasing level of identification with the white American culture.

According to Oetting and Beauvais (1990), higher cultural identification is related to positive psychosocial characteristics. Thus, strongly bicultural youth have the highest self-esteem and the strongest socialization links, whereas anomic youth (having a low level of identification with both cultures, native and host) are expected to show the lowest self-esteem and the weakest links to family and school, two major socialization systems. Again, as applied to Asian American youths, Asian and mainstream American cultural identifications are expected to coexist and function as essentially equivalent sources of personal/social strength. Therefore, youths with strong bicultural identification are expected to have the lowest ATOD use because they simply have a greater adaptability than those who have weaker bicultural identification and feelings of anomie.

My own field research involving Asian Americans, based on the focus group method, suggests that ATOD is more prevalent among the U.S. born and the culturally marginal than among those who are bicultural. That is, U.S.-born Asian Americans who are not brought up in and socialized to an Asian culture are considered by the majority of the native born and native reared to be outsiders. As such, they are often referred to, not only by Asians but also by their white peers, as "bananas," meaning that they are "white" inside but "yellow" outside. Accordingly, they are not fully recognized as part of either group to which they want to belong, so that they are likely to experience anomie.

The implication for prevention, according to OCI theory, is to teach U.S.-born Asian Americans the cultural norms of the native culture or cultures that they want to know. Such is the strategy of many minority-oriented prevention programs that are based on a cultural enrichment model.

Cultural Conflict Approaches

Generation Gap Leading to Family Conflict. The problems of early immigrants and first-plus generations usually are not language or basic survival needs, but problems related to conflict between their parents' culture and the dominant culture. Specifically, Asian youths need to cope with the conflicting demands of the dominant culture to be more "Americanized" and the expectations, and sometimes demands, of their parents to be more like them. Although the processes and effects of acculturation are complex, it is safe to state that young people generally learn and adapt to the new environment at a faster rate than their parents. In such a context, the type of parenting skills used by Asian parents may often prove to be ineffective and/or inappropriate in the eyes of their children. This gap in acculturation between parents and children (i.e., a generation gap) has the potential to contribute to identity crises and/or family instability. The latter further contributes to children's perception of incohesive family relationships, typified by such statements as "My parents and I don't understand each other," "My parents don't know what they are talking about," or "My parents and I can't communicate with each other." Parental responses are typified by statements such as "This is our way" or "This is what we do in our culture."

Youth: Peer Group Pressure. Due to cultural conflicts, many Asian youths separate themselves from their families and create their own support networks with their peers. Many second-and third-generation Asian American youth do not want to be identified as "Asian" because of the association with newly arrived immigrants and refugees. Many American-born youths carry negative views of newcomers, whether because they learn such views from their elders or because they feel threatened by the rapid transformation and the new "foreignness" of their neighborhoods. Sensing this hostility, immigrant youths may further isolate themselves, ratcheting up the level of their mistrust. For either group, the tumultuous new environment does not leave much room for an appreciative understanding of each other.

New immigrant youths also lose respect for their parents and begin to identify more with peer clusters. An extreme example of peer involvement is the Asian youth gangs whose delinquent behaviors are on the rise in some of the major metropolitan areas of the country. The mainstream media are beginning to pay more attention to Asian youth gangs and their crimes of extortion, violence involving firearms, auto theft, gambling, drug use, drug trafficking, and wars with rival gangs. Often these gangs are made up of youths who have dropped out of school and been forced out of their homes and who are now living on the streets.

Asian Women: Role Conflict. Asian women drink far less than Caucasian women. However, there seems to be an increasing rate of cigarette, alcohol, and tranquilizer abuse among Asian women. One factor that cuts across Asian subcultural lines is rapidly changing attitudes on the part of Asian women about their traditional roles and functions. Traditionally, the Asian woman is supposed to be a demure, docile, passive, and humble person who is reluctant to express herself. Her self-worth is measured by her marriage to a "good" husband, and her femininity in terms of the accommodating role she assumes with family members while being subservient to her husband.

However, this traditional characterization of accommodating Asian women is being eroded and challenged by the dominant culture, which places a high value on individualism, independence, and self-worth (Arakaki & Antonis, 1978; Namkung, 1972) and by Asian women's desire to develop their own uniqueness (Arakaki & Antonis, 1978). Their traditional role is also challenged by sheer economic factors, which force both the husband and wife to work while the wife is expected to assume added responsibilities of attending to household chores and cooking for the family. Many Asian husbands are trained to consider housework far more demeaning to perform than white husbands would.

Alienation and Identity Conflict. Due to their small size, lack of political power, skin color, passivity, and prejudicial perceptions of Asians held by the majority population, many Asian youths and adults do not feel a part of the mainstream society. In particular, many Asian Americans of lower SES face the threat of discrimination, racism, and even violence in their daily lives. One is reminded of the Stockton school yard massacre of Southeast Asian children by a mentally ill gunman who hated Asians; cross burning on the lawns of Filipino families in Daly City; and Korean merchants challenged by African Americans in New York (Goodstein, 1990), Chicago, Los Angeles, San Francisco, and Washington, D.C. These are vivid examples of the threat of prejudice and racism. Due to a multitude of social forces over which they do not have much control, Asian Americans feel alienated and experience identity conflict. These feelings are often accompanied by loneliness, absence of a sense of belonging, helplessness, powerlessness, low self-esteem, and, for some, loss of a sense of life's meaning—all of which are frequently cited as factors contributing to ATOD abuse cross-culturally.

RISK FACTORS APPROACHES

In addition to the numerous risk factors already cited as common to both Asian and non-Asian youths, Asian youths and adults experience personal, family, and social problems caused by their immigration status, economic stress, racism, and discrimination.

Feelings of Personal Failure

For many adult immigrants, the greatest stress lies in the overwhelming priority that must be placed on basic survival needs. This leaves little room for emotional support, attention, time and skill to discipline children, and building of social skills. Consequently, many immigrants experience defeats in personal competency shortly after their settlement. The attention given to basic survival needs and adjustment demands continue to erode individual life and family life just at the time when they are needed the most. For example, educated immigrants are often underemployed: That is, there is a drastic difference in the social status of the jobs they held in their country of origin and the jobs they now hold in host country.

Family Role Reversals

In families in which the parents do not speak English, children who do speak English may be forced to accept certain adult responsibilities, such as the responsibility of acting as spokesperson for the family. This is a clear role reversal for the father, who traditionally is the main source of authority in the family. Youth may lose respect for their elders because the elders are unable to assume the traditional authoritative roles or provide financial support to the family. The discrepancy between one's capability (or the "respectable" job held in the country of origin) and what one now does for living in the host country (perhaps a "demeaning" job as interpreted by one's child) can mean a loss of control over the well-being of the child. The impact of these discrepancies on the family can be depression, alienation, anomie, family conflicts, and the abuse of alcohol and other drugs.

Economic Stress

Many recent immigrant Asian families are unable to support themselves financially due to lack of job skills, low English proficiency, and relatively large family sizes. Southeast Asian refugees are three to four times more likely to be on public assistance than African Americans or Hispanic Americans. Although Filipino Americans show low unemployment, they are often in nonprofessional, service-oriented job markets that are subject to poor pay, frequent layoffs, lack of job advancement opportunities, and differentiated work schedules. Compared to other Asian immigrants, Korean Americans are the most likely to be self-employed. This means long hours and hard work with limited financial return.

Many recent immigrant Asian families are supporting not only their immediate family but extended family members in their native countries. These mutual assistance "family obligations" put additional economic pressure on the family. The economic stress limits parents' involvement in their children's lives. Due to long working hours and low wages, many children are unsupervised and live in marginal conditions.

Economic stress can be transmitted to youth in many ways. Asian youth are often obligated to work in the family business without compensation and have limited social lives. Furthermore, they may be ostracized by peers for not being able to afford to dress in trendy fashions and not having spending money to participate in "normal" youth activities. Particularly for the recently arrived refugee and immigrant population, the following have been cited frequently as common problems: low English literacy or illiteracy; learning style incompatible with Western teaching style; lack of experience in the learning situation; absence of health insurance for many self-employed who operate "mom and pop" (small) shops; very little knowledge of the cultural norms of the majority population; transportation difficulties such as no funds to own a car, and lack of skills or appropriate knowledge about driving or traveling by bus or by other means. Some researchers have therefore placed refugees and recent immigrants at a higher risk of ATOD abuse resulting from these economic stresses than other Asian groups (Zane & Sasao, 1990).

Prevention Strategies

From a logical and an ideal viewpoint, prevention strategies (or prevention models) should have been developed after a theory or theories on the etiology of ATOD abuse involving Asian American groups were advanced. In the development of prevention strategies for Asians, however, there has been a lack of communication between theorists and program developers/ practitioners.

Consequently, many community-based prevention strategies (or prevention models) for Asian communities have been devised based on conjectures and intuitions, and sometimes as a response to the specific needs of Asian communities and their youth. Significantly, many of these prevention strategies have been developed independently of the theoretical advances involving Asian Americans and their ATOD use. Some of these strategies have been implemented without any real knowledge of whether they contribute to the deterrence of ATOD use in Asian American communities. Prevention practitioners frequently place more emphasis on the personality styles of fieldworkers and their level of commitment than on a particular theoretical orientation.

Since the early 1970s, a few community-based prevention programs came into being in Los Angeles, New York, San Francisco, and Hawaii and the Pacific Islands. These were based on differing theoretical assumptions, conjectures, urgency, and client needs reflecting various common and unique characteristics of their client base. Essentially, developments in Asian community-based prevention strategies have relied on the following eight prevention models: (a) case management model, (b) family-oriented model, (c) information deficit model, (d) empowerment model, (e) cultural enrichment model, (f) mutual support model, (g) vocational training model, and (h) alternatives/recreational model.

In what follows, an effort is made to describe these prevention models and, whenever possible, establish a conceptual link between these models and the theories enumerated in the previous section. No claim is made that these classes of prevention models are mutually exclusive and that they together constitute a totality of all the prevention strategies available to date. It is hoped that others may add to or branch out from the list created here.

CASE MANAGEMENT MODEL

The case management model is based on the assumption that no prevention or intervention services can be successful unless the basic needs of the minority clients are addressed (Cross, Bazron, Dennis, & Isaacs, 1989), especially for recent refugees and immigrants. These Asian families usually present a variety of needs, both economic and emotional, and ranging from mundane to specialized—for example, applying for a driver's license, learning to use public transportation, getting job training, opening a checking account, and accessing health care. Many minority children, youth, and their families expect formal helpers to be able to deal with a variety of problems.

Due to the depth and breadth of the problems of many of these Asians, the service philosophy based on case management with networking has become the essential part of the prevention services rendered to many Asian minority groups. Here, networking involves referring clients not only to formal social service agencies but also to other informal support networks such as churches, schools, associations, self-help groups, and business and industry. As one of the mainstay prevention strategies for many Asian refugees and immigrants, the case management model is either implicitly or explicitly founded on recognition of the high risk of economic stresses, as well as on cultural conflict theories.

Case management is more than simple referral service. In order to establish a rapport with the family, one needs to use a native speaker as facilitator or case manager. This role may include speaking for and with both child and parent to representatives from other organizations, such as schools, mental health clinics, juvenile courts, and recreational programs. The goal is to persuade other people to join a collaborative effort to design, develop, and sustain a system of care for the child and his or her family. Case management, therefore, is seen as an opportunity to teach self-advocacy, to assess the strengths of the client, and to learn about the client's natural support network, such as friends, relatives, neighbors, and church ministers. For prevention projects that use this model, the evaluation system must be ready to gauge the degree to which community-based prevention programs are ready to accommodate these and other basic needs that may be taken for granted among the mainstream service agencies. The prevention programs targeted for this type of refugee/immigrant population need to have services that are suited to them. The evaluation projects need to reflect upon these services as their concomitant dependent variables.

FAMILY-ORIENTED MODEL

Most Asian prevention agencies consider the family-oriented strategy as one of the most important components of prevention. This strategy is based on the traditional Asian cultural content, which puts the family's needs above individual needs. Many researchers have emphasized Asian family cohesiveness and stability (e.g., lower divorce rate) as one of the major deterrents to and protective forces against youthful problem behaviors and involvement with ATOD. In fact, many Asian ATOD abuse prevention agencies treat family strengths as one of the most important deterrents to substance use as well as other antisocial and self-defeating behaviors. Traditionally, the Asian family unit is the pillar of strength and stability for all its members and plays a critical role in the ongoing development and support of the child even into adulthood. Furthermore, familial decision making and control usually include extended family members such as grandparents and other significant relatives. Children are taught to be obedient to elders and to put family's needs above individual needs.

Therefore, Asian families and extended kinship networks have often been cited as an important protective factor against many mental health problems (Hsu, 1973). Johnson and Nagoshi (1990) also suggested that the existence of extended families among Asian Americans serves as a factor leading to reduced alcohol consumption.

Similarly, we are aware that ATOD abuse among Asian Americans is underreported due to denial of the problem by Asian families and extreme resistance on their part to outside interventions, especially from non-Asian social service agencies. Reflecting upon this cultural content, the family-oriented approach emphasizes the importance of including family members in all its prevention, intervention, and treatment programs.

INFORMATION DEFICIT MODEL

The essence of this model is to treat the limited skills and competencies of Asian groups and their adjustment problems—both social and family—as skills and information deficits rather than as cultural or ethnic weaknesses. According to this model, the prevention facilitator is expected to project him or herself as a provider of information, facilitating an opportunity for the immigrants/refugees to learn. The program facilitator is expected to provide helpful services and not to assume a role as a "fixer" who will enter their lives to change them or fix them up. Prevention agencies are expected to present themselves as information providers or as providers of opportunities to learn. This model emphasizes Asian respect for education while downplaying "opportunity to change."

With regard to drug-specific information, many American-born Asians tend to subscribe to a more inclusive definition of *drugs* that includes alcohol and cigarettes. Foreign-born Asians, on the other hand, are more likely to subscribe to a more restricted definition of *drugs* that excludes alcohol and cigarettes. Zane and Sasao (1990) found similar results involving Japanese Americans. This may have important prevention implications for Asian Americans whose parents were not born in the host country. Due to this misconception, prevention strategies are devised to increase knowledge about drugs, including education on alcoholism and drug abuse, to lessen the stigma attached to seeking professional help among Asian Americans.

EMPOWERMENT MODEL

This model was originally developed in African American communities during the late 1960s and early 1970s. It is in part based on the alienation and hopelessness syndrome as a potential cause of ATOD abuse. The empowerment model directs its emphasis away from "hand-downs" and "hand-outs" (from the privileged to the deprived) and toward an indigenous grass-roots movement seeking self-determination and self-sufficiency in a setting of cultural pluralism (Asian American Community Mental Health Training Center, 1981; Blum, 1979). Such an empowerment process is built around the notion of strengthening the members of the indigenous group chosen as the target population. Prevention strategies based on this model therefore seek to know not only the needs (or problems) of the community (i.e., needs assessment) but, more important, the assets available to the community (i.e., assets assessment). As such, one of the essential components of this model is a detailed assets analysis of the targeted community and the resources of the people in it. The basic idea is to connect these assets to action plans that enhance the common interest and/or common good of the community. The empowerment process therefore acknowledges the challenge of assisting a grassroots effort through mobilizing rather than leading, organizing rather than controlling, and responding rather than enforcing.

Operationally, one of the criteria for the measurement of program success can be the degree to which the indigenous actors participate in the empowerment process (i.e., organized movement by the indigenous group toward community self-determination and self-sufficiency). For those community-based prevention programs based on this model, one may include the following as the potential indicators of program success: number of people in the target population holding decision-making positions in the governing body of that minority group, and number of community-initiated projects launched, such as self-help groups, forums, supportive services organizations, task forces, special interest groups, fraternal or school associations, and sporting activities.

CULTURAL ENRICHMENT MODEL

During the discussion of cultural interaction approaches, it was noted that all immigrants go through the process of adapting to dominant American cultural values. During this cultural interactive process, however, some lose their Asian cultural identity (as suggested by acculturation theory), whereas others maintain it (as implied through orthogonal cultural identification theory). Many community-based prevention programs are built around the notion that ATOD use is less frequent among individuals with either bicultural or monocultural identification than among those who are anomic. Programs based on cultural enrichment model are either implicitly or explicitly related to the major theoretical proposition advanced by the orthogonal cultural identification theory: Identification with either the minority or the majority culture is a source of both personal and social strength.

A major consideration in evaluating the success or failure of a prevention project based on this model should then be its influence in shaping and enhancing subculturally valued cultural characteristics within the project group (e.g., respect for the elderly, the practice of culturally unique ceremonial activities). Also, the cultural norms for what is acceptable drinking behavior and what is not within Asian cultures are fairly clear.

MUTUAL SUPPORT MODEL

This model is to a large extent based on the risk factor approach. Its central strategy is the formation of Asian groups to share information about experiences that may be helpful in the process of adapting to the larger pluralistic society. Group members discuss their common problems and solutions to problems that they have encountered concerning cultural conflict, life adjustment, family conflict, child rearing, and so on. In recent years, many prevention and treatment professionals have realized the value of getting their clients together with others who have similar problems. Through mutual help and support, the participants in these group meetings discover additional or alternative ways of coping with both normal and unusual crises in their lives. By talking with others about their difficulties and the ways they are trying to overcome them, participants find both comfort and enlightenment (Silverman, 1980). It is also believed that the sharing of similar types of problems in a mutually supportive setting instills a sense of normality and stability, so that individuals do not panic or make crisis-oriented, hasty decisions that may be disruptive to their families and themselves.

VOCATIONAL TRAINING MODEL

This model is founded on the assumption that young people without gainful employment or underemployment hardly make connection to the future and that they fail to learn the delayed rewards associated with hard work and perseverance. Thus, the intent of this model is to make clients more employable through vocational training ranging from basic skills development such as literacy programs to more technical occupational training. Gainful employment is equated not only with increased self-esteem but also with enhanced feelings of purpose in life.

ALTERNATIVES/
RECREATIONAL MODEL

This model is based on the assumption that ATOD use and abuse are behaviors that develop in the absence of interesting alternatives and/or due to boredom, and that providing such alternatives will effectively prevent ATOD abuse and other self-destructive or maladaptive behavior. It is often assumed that organized sports or recreational activities enhance discipline and teamwork, and improve self-esteem of the participants.

Understanding Cultural Nuances
Relevant to Preventive Interventions

Different cultures have different nuances, and even the same words, gestures, symbols, and behavior may connote different meanings, with plenty of room for uncertainty, misconceptions, and misinterpretations. Many times, we have the tendency to argue that "we are all alike when it comes right down to it." But in fact, we both are and are not alike at the same time. (For and example of an evaluation instrument that may be inappropriate for Asians, as well as those from other cultures, see Figure 14.1.)

Listed below are some Asian cultural differences that may have implications for the outcome of intervention and evaluation processes. Researchers who are not aware of the cultural behavior of Asian youth could easily interpret each of these differences as weakness, resistance, or family dysfunction. Adaptation to the usual assessment process involves learning what is "normal" in the context of Asian cultures.

- To many Asian Americans who are not acculturated to the mainstream American culture, idioms, metaphors, and labels commonly used in the white American culture, such as *feeling blue, low,* or *down in the dumps,* do not have the same currency.

- In many Asian groups, children are taught to express their remorse about a misdeed by not looking at the adult who is correcting them. In some Asian cultures, the very act of looking straight into the eyes in situations such as this is considered a sign of disrespect. In fact, direct eye contact is often avoided in formal conversation even among adults.

- A limp hand in the act of shaking hands by a person from some Asian subculture may well mean humility and respect. White mainstream male culture often judges a person's character by the firmness of the hand grip (Cross et al., 1989).

- In many Asian cultures, silent patience is thought to be a virtue in life. In organizational settings, any formal or informal complaint directed toward the higher level of that organization is therefore refrained from and delayed as long as possible until the time that the Asian employee thinks "it has gone too far." The very act of silent patience also inhibits open communication, especially around issues involving grievances. This frequently results in the silent expectation that the person responsible for the situation will remedy

```
                    PARTICIPANT DAILY EVALUATION SHEET

TODAY'S AM SESSION WAS

1               2               3               4               5

BOMB            TURKEY          SO-SO           THUMBS-UP       STAR
```

TODAY'S PM SESSION WAS

```
1               2               3               4               5

BOMB            TURKEY          SO-SO           THUMBS-UP       STAR
```

I really like_____

_____

_____

I wish we would_____

_____

_____

I'd like to know more about_____

_____

_____

I'm eager to address_____

_____

Figure 14.1. Example of a Culturally Inappropriate Evaluation Instrument

it through his or her own soul searching and self-awareness. If, in fact, an employee registers a formal complaint directed to the management of an organization in which he or she works, the conflict resolution is not likely to be a "routine" process. The employee may by this point have high emotional feelings charged and bottled up to an almost unbearable level, and such feelings may easily result in behavior that could be interpreted as "unacceptable" by the mainstream American culture, leaving no room to improve the situation or come to a resolution acceptable to both the management and the employee.

- The demonstration of one's importance in social interactions, and associated symbols or connotations of "I" or "self-assertion," are interpreted by some Asian cultures as signs of immaturity and lack of social skill. Especially among Koreans, it is in fact social etiquette to talk down about oneself and one's family members.

- In Korean and Japanese languages, usage of the responses "yes" and "no" is fundamentally different from American usage. Assume that Charlie missed school yesterday. If one asks Charlie in English, "You didn't go to school yesterday, did you?" the correct answer by Charlie is "no." In both Korean and Japanese, however, the correct response is "yes," because Charlie is confirming what the questioner assumed. Thus, the answer in Korean and Japanese is responding to the assumption of the person asking the question as interpreted by the listener. The questioner assumed Charlie did not go to school; the questioner assumed correctly; therefore, the answer is "yes." If, on the other hand, someone asks Charlie in Korean or Japanese, "You went to school yesterday, didn't you?" the correct answer in this case is "no" because the person asking the question assumed incorrectly. In English, the answer is based on the assessment, on the part of the person being questioned, as to what he or she did or did not do, irrespective of the particular assumption from which the question was asked. In Chinese, the choice of "yes" or "no" is identical to that of English usage.

- Some Asian groups express politeness through maintaining an agreeable demeanor in a helping encounter. This may be mistaken for acceptance and for rapport when in fact the Asian youth may have little or no understanding of what is expected (Ho, 1976).

- Failure to address the male first in some cases will seriously restrict what can be accomplished. In traditional Asian families, failure to engage elders—especially elder males as the primary access to the rest of the family—will inhibit the effectiveness of the professional in the cross-cultural intervention process (Ho, 1976).

- To many Asian groups, physical contact (e.g., handshake, hugging, or facial contact in greetings) between opposite genders is often interpreted as a sexual advance or overture.

- Many Asian groups, especially peoples who have been subjected to a history of slavery and political oppression, show little emotion (e.g., do not smile or laugh much) and are not likely to be expressive about their own feelings and desires. For example, strangers in general neither exchange smiles nor greet one another, even in close encounters. This does not mean that they are unfriendly or disrespectful to one another.

- For some Asian groups, especially recent immigrants, it is somewhat uncomfortable to say "Thank you" or "You are welcome" as responses to such compliments as "You look nice today," or "I love your hairstyle," or "Thank you very much for helping me." To some, these typical American responses are somewhat awkward, although not unacceptable, because they are interpreted as a sort of acquiescence to self-affirmation. The usual response of these groups is a mild denial such as "Oh, it's a cheap old dress I bought a long time ago," a slight gesture of denial accompanied by turning one's head away from the complimenter (especially to compliments such as "You look nice today"), or acts of avoidance such as keeping silent or making an awkward facial expression. These social interactive behaviors, it must be noted, do not signify lack of appreciation. This type of communication style is embedded in the traditional culture, which deemphasizes the self and individualism while emphasizing humility in social interactions.

- In most Asian cultures, stretching one's legs on a table even in informal settings is thought to be not only impolite and unacceptable, but also highly disrespectful to others. In American mainstream culture, this act may be considered impolite and unacceptable, but not to the same degree as in Asian American groups.

- Bringing children to formal and informal social engagements is thought to be acceptable, to a large degree, among many Asian groups.

- The Arabic number four is associated with death in Korean, Japanese, and Chinese cultures.

- Despite social, moral, and legal sanctions against spouse abuse in Korea and Japan, wife abuse among Koreans and Japanese is far more common than what has been estimated in the mainstream American culture. Such an act, therefore, may not be interpreted as "abnormal" at the intensity level of the American cultural norm.

- For some Asian societies, offering of cigarettes to guests is considered to be social etiquette and a sign of hospitality, although this practice may be changing due to "Westernization."

- For many Asian societies, there are stricter social guidelines concerning the consumption of alcohol and cigarettes. For example, there are significant family sanctions against young people who either smoke or drink in front of elders.

- Anthropological fieldwork with native Hawaiian children has revealed that peer assistance is very important in children's daily activities, learning occurs most often in "child-constructed" contexts, and children are seldom individually directed and monitored by adults.

- In some Asian communities, as in some Latino and Native American groups, the concept of time is diffused, lax, and less formal. Accordingly, the formal appointment may be a foreign concept. Unless such a scheduled appointment is followed through by a personal phone call, the appointment may not be realized. Among indigent Asian groups, work hours, spiritual practices, or family obligations may conflict with scheduled appointments.

- Many Asian groups strongly believe that parents have the right as well as the responsibility to inflict physical punishment on a child when he or she misbehaves. Such a practice is far more common in Asian groups than in mainstream American culture.

- For many Asians, exchange of small gifts is embedded in social interactions. Such exchange plays a very important social function that may be described as a sort of social lubrication (i.e., "It makes things go smoothly"). Thus, it is very helpful to share materially helpful household items (not money) when making home visits.

These are some of the major cultural factors that may have direct consequences on the effectiveness of preventive interventions as well as evaluation. It must be noted that all cultural variables are in flux and that many of the values and behavioral modes of Asians listed above are going through gradual change, especially among the young. Accordingly, caution is warranted; these cultural factors may not apply to every case. Moreover, there is always the danger that any of the statements listed above may promote stereotypical attributions involving Asian Americans.

SUMMARY AND
FUTURE DIRECTIONS

Examination of ATOD prevention approaches for Asians makes clear that there is a lack of theory and basic research for guiding the development of reliable and effective prevention programs. In the process of increasing the knowledge base for prevention programs involving Asians, the first task must be the redefinition and more detailed specification of the ethnic diversities and immigration backgrounds embedded in the traditionally used, all-encompassing classification of *Asian American/Pacific Islanders*. Asian and Pacific Islander communities include Asian Indian, Cambodian, Chinese, Filipino, Guamanian, Hawaiian, Japanese, Korean, Laotian, Samoan, Thai, Vietnamese, Melanesian, Micronesian, and Polynesian. All Asian Americans are not alike in their pattern of ATOD use or in the attributes that appear to be predictive of substance use. Different factors predict differential ATOD use among the Asian groups (McLaughlin et al., 1987). Recent immigrants and refugees are more likely to handle problems within their own community, whereas those who have become more acculturated or assimilated into the mainstream American society are probably more comfortable using available public services.

Another issue is the assumption that ATOD use is most prevalent among individuals alienated from their Asian culture and that enhanced identification with the native culture increases the resiliency or a "protective" factor, which, in turn, reduces the probability for ATOD use. This type of assumption is certainly consistent with the orthogonal cultural identification theory developed by Oetting and Beauvais (1990) and with the prevention strategy based on the cultural enrichment model. However, there has not been any empirical study of ATOD-using behavior comparing monocultural, bicultural, and alienated Asian Americans. Furthermore, these variations in cultural identification (i.e., monocultural, bicultural, or alienated) may well be confounded with socioeconomic differences, other demographic differences, and cultural content differences, not to mention the many possible interactions among these variables. In the absence of such basic research involving Asian groups, it is somewhat difficult to establish a firm foundation on which the refinement of future prevention strategies can be carried out. Absence of a scientifically validated theory or a set of related theories means difficulty in delineating the appropriate outcome variables, especially those instrumental outcome variables to be used in the evaluation tasks.

Acculturation/assimilation is one of the most important domains of individual differences within Asian groups. As such, there needs to be a greater dialogue along conceptual as well as operational domains if the prevention field is to advance toward the goals of ATOD prevention involving Asian American groups and communities.

In prevention projects involving Asian youth, it has also proven to be particularly difficult to motivate the participants. Accordingly, special emphasis should be placed on collecting social, demographic, and lifestyle characteristics of those who participate and those who do not. Such information will be an invaluable asset toward the refinement and the overall success of the program implemented.

In family-oriented prevention approaches, there also is a considerable degree of confusion. As we have examined, the family system is viewed as both a protective factor against substance abuse and a source of stress. Asian families and extended kinship networks have often been cited as an important protective factor against many mental health problems (Hsu, 1973), although others have noted that Asian families can become a significant source of stress for the individual, as evidenced by intergenerational and family role conflicts (Lee, 1982).

Given this, we need to elaborate more about the environmental and family conditions under which these manifestations are observed (e.g., generation, nationality, immigration history, U.S. born or foreign born, SES conditions, interracial or intraracial marriage, degree of acculturation, and so on). In the absence of such elaboration, it is very likely that researchers who promote family-oriented prevention models that have failed to produce an enhanced perception of family cohesiveness among participants will never know why their models continue to fail and how to resolve this quandary.

Clearly, more research is needed to increase our understanding of the causes of ATOD use among various Asian American groups and effective prevention approaches. Careful consideration of the material contained in this chapter, along with other material throughout this book, should provide important information concerning these populations and facilitate the development of more effective prevention approaches.

References

Akutsu, P. D., Sue, S., Zane, N. W. S., & Nakamura, C. Y. (1989). Ethnic differences in alcohol consumption among Asians and Caucasians in the U.S.: An investigation of cultural and physiological factors. *Journal of Studies on Alcohol, 50,* 261-267.

Arakaki, A. A., & Antonis, S. (1978). Asian/Pacific Island women and substance abuse. In D. E. Smith, S. M. Anderson, M. Buxton, N. Gottlieb, W. Harvey, & T. Chung (Eds.), *A multicultural view of drug abuse* (pp. 604-607). Cambridge, UK: Schenkman.

Asian American Community Mental Health Training Center. (1981). *Bridging cultures: Southeast Asian refugees in America.* Los Angeles: Author.

Austin, G. A., Prendergast, M. L., & Lee, H. (1989). Substance abuse among Asian American youth. *Prevention Research Update, 5,* 1-13.

Bachman, J. G., Wallace, J. M., O'Malley, P. M., Johnston, L. D., & Kurth, C. L. (1990). *Drug use among black, white, Hispanic, Native American, and Asian American high school seniors (1976-1989): Prevalence, trends, and correlates* (Monitoring the Future Occasional Paper No. 130). Ann Arbor, MI: Institute for Social Research.

Bachman, J. G., Wallace, J. M., O'Malley, P. M., Johnston, L. D., Kurth, C. L., & Neighbors, H. W. (1991). Racial/ethnic differences in smoking, drinking, and illicit drug use among American high school seniors, 1976-89. *American Journal of Public Health, 81,* 372-377.

Blum, M. D. (1979). Service to immigrants in a multicultural society. In J. E. Huddleston (Ed.), *The social welfare forum* (pp.). New York: Columbia University Press.

California Department of Education. (1993). *California school dropout picture continues to improve* (News Release REL#93-27). Sacramento, CA: Author.

Center for Disease Control. (1992). Cigarette smoking among Chinese, Vietnamese and Hispanics, 1989-1991. *Morbidity and Mortality Weekly Report, 41,* 362-367.

Chi, I., Lubben, J. E., & Kitano, H. H. L. (1989). Difference in drinking behavior among three Asian-American groups. *Journal of Studies on Alcohol, 50,* 15-23.

Connor, J. W. (1977). *Tradition and change in three generations of Japanese Americans.* Chicago: Nelson-Hall.

Cooper, S. E. (1983). Surveys on studies on alcoholism. *International Journal of the Addictions, 18,* 971-985.

Criddle, J. D., & Mam, T. B. (1987). *To destroy you is no loss: The odyssey of a Cambodian family.* New York: Doubleday.

Cross, T. L., Bazron, B. J., Dennis, K. W., & Isaacs, M. R. (1989). *Toward a culturally competent system of care.* Washington, DC: Georgetown University Child Development Center,

Gillmore, M. R., Catalano, R. F., Morrison, D. M., Wells, E. A., Iritani, B., & Hawkins, J. D. (1990). Racial difference in acceptability and availability of drugs and early initiation of substance use. *American Journal of Drug and Alcohol Abuse, 16,* 185-206.

Goodstein, L. (1990, May 15). Embattled Korean grocers wait out racially charged boycott. *Washington Post,* p. A3.

Hawaii Department of Health. (1979). *Hawaii state substance abuse survey.* Honolulu: Author.

Hawkins, D. J., Lishner, D. M., & Catalano, R. F. (1985). Childhood predictors of adolescent substance abuse. In C. L. Jones & R. J. Battjes (Eds.), *Etiology of drug abuse:*

Implications for prevention (NIDA Research Monograph No. 56, pp. 75-126). Washington, DC: Government Printing Office.

Hawkins, J. D., & Weiss, G. J. (1985). The social development model: An integrated approach to delinquency prevention. *Journal of Primary Prevention, 6,* 73-97.

Ho, M. K. (1976). Social work with Asian Americans. *Social Casework, 57,* 195-200.

Hsu, F. L. K. (1973). Kinship is the key. *Center Magazine, 6,* 4-14.

Iiyama, P., Nishi, S., & Johnson, B. (1976). *Drug use and abuse among U.S. minorities.* New York: Praeger.

Jessor, R., Chase, J. A., & Donovan, J. E. (1980). Psychosocial correlates of marijuana use and problem drinking in a national sample of adolescents. *American Journal of Public Health, 70,* 604-613.

Johnson, R. C., & Nagoshi, C. T. (1990). Asians, Asian-American and alcohol. *Journal of Psychoactive Drugs, 22,* 45-52.

Johnson, R. C., Nagoshi, C. T., Ahern, F. M., Wilson, J. R., & Yuen, S. H. L. (1987). Cultural factors as explanations for ethnic group differences in alcohol use in Hawaii. *Journal of Psychoactive Drugs, 19,* 67-75.

Jones, C. L., & Battjes, R. J. (Eds.). (1985). *Etiology of drug abuse: Implications for prevention* (NIDA Research Monograph No. 56). Washington, DC: Government Printing Office.

Kaplan, H. B. (1980). Self-esteem and self-derogation theory of drug abuse. In D. J. Letterieri, K. Sayers, & H. W. Pearson (Eds.), *Theories of drug abuse* (NIDA Research Monograph No. 30, pp. 128-131). Rockville, MD: National Institute on Drug Abuse.

Kaplan, H. B., Martin, S. S., & Johnson, R. J. (1986). Self-rejection and the explanation of deviance: Specification of the structural among latent constructs. *American Journal of Sociology, 92,* 384-411.

Kandel, D. (1982). Epidemiological and psychological perspectives on adolescent drug use. *Journal of the American Academy of Child Psychiatry, 21,* 328-347.

Kim, S. (1981). Student attitudinal inventory for program outcome evaluation of adolescent drug abuse. *Journal of Primary Prevention, 2,* 91-100.

Kim, S., & Newman, S. H. (1982). Synthetic-dynamic theory of drug abuse: A revisit with empirical data. *International Journal of the Addictions, 17,* 913-923.

Kim, S., & Shantzis, C. (1989). *Drug use by students in Mecklenburg County, North Carolina: Main finding.* Tampa, FL: DER Publications.

Kitano, H. H. L., & Chi, I. (1985). Asian Americans and alcohol: The Chinese, Japanese, Koreans, and Filipinos in Los Angeles. In D. Spiegler, D. Tate, S. Aitken, & C. Christian (Eds.), *Alcohol use among U.S. ethnic minorities* (NIAAA Research Monograph No. 18, pp. 373-382). Rockville, MD: National Institute on Alcohol Abuse and Alcoholism.

Kitano, H. H. L., Chi, I., Law, C. K., Lubben, J., & Rhee, S. (1988). Alcohol consumption of Japanese in Japan, Hawaii, and California. In L. H. Towle & T. C. Harford (Eds.), *Cultural influences and drinking patterns: A focus on Hispanic and Japanese populations* (NIAAA Research Monograph No. 19, pp. 99-133). Washington, DC: Government Printing Office.

Kitano, H. H. L., & Daniels, R., (1988). *Asian Americans: Emerging minorities.* Englewood Cliffs, NJ: Prentice Hall.

Kitano, H. H. L., Hatanaka, H., Yeung, W. T., & Sue, S. (1985). Japanese American drinking patterns. In L. A. Bennett & G. M. Ames (Eds.), *The American experience with alcohol: Contrasting cultural perspective* (pp. 335-357). New York: Plenum.

Kua, K. E. (1987). Drinking in Chinese culture: Old stereotypes re-examined. *British Journal of Addiction, 82,* 224-225.

Le Marchand, L., Kolonel, L. N., & Yoshizawa, C. N. (1989). Alcohol consumption patterns among five major ethnic groups in Hawaii. In D. Spiegler, D. Tate, S. Aitken, &

C. Christian (Eds.), *Alcohol use among U.S. ethnic minorities* (NIAAA Research Monograph No. 18, pp. 355-371). Rockville, MD: National Institute on Alcohol Abuse and Alcoholism.

Lee, E. (1982). A social systems approach to assessment and treatment for Chinese American families. In M. McGoldrick, J. K. Pearce, & J. Giordano (Eds.), *Ethnicity and family therapy* (pp. 527-551). New York: Guilford.

Levin, B., Nachampassack, S., Xiong, R. (1988). Cigarette smoking and the Laotian refugee. *Migration World, 16*(4/5), 12-19.

Maddahian, E., Newcomb, M. D., & Bentler, P. M. (1986). Adolescents' substance use: Impact of ethnicity, income, and availability. *Advances in Alcohol and Substance Abuse, 5,* 63-78.

Maddahian, E., Newcomb, M. D., & Bentler, P. M. (1988). Risk factors for substance abuse: Ethnic differences among adolescents. *Journal of Substance Abuse, 1,* 11-23.

McLaughlin, D. G., Raymond, J. S., Murakami, S. R., & Goebert, D. (1987). Drug use among Asian Americans in Hawaii. *Journal of Psychoactive Drugs, 19,* 85-94.

Messolonghites, L. (1979)., *Multicultural perspectives on drug abuse and its prevention: A resource book* (DHEW Publication No. ADM 78-671, pp. 8-12). Rockville, MD: National Institute on Drug Abuse.

Murakami, S. R. (1989). An epidemiological survey of alcohol, drug, and mental health problems in Hawaii. In D. Spiegler, D. Tate, S. Aitken, & C. Christian (Eds.), *Alcohol use among U.S. ethnic minorities* (NIAAA Research Monograph No. 18, pp. 343-353). Rockville, MD: National Institute on Alcohol Abuse and Alcoholism.

Murray, D. M., & Perry, C. L. (1985). The prevention of adolescent drug abuse: Implications from etiological, developmental, behavioral, and environmental models. In C. L. Jones & R. J. Battjes (Eds.), *Etiology of drug abuse: Implications for prevention* (NIDA Research Monograph No. 56, pp. 236-256). Washington, DC: Government Printing Office.

Namkung, P. S. (1972, December). *Asian American drug addiction: The quiet problem.* Paper presented at the National Conference on Drug Abuse, Washington, DC.

National Institute on Drug Abuse. (1991). *National Household Survey on Drug Abuse: Population estimates 1990.* Washington, DC: Government Printing Office.

Oetting, E. R., & Beauvais, F. (1990). Orthogonal cultural identification theory: The cultural identification of minority adolescents. *International Journal of the Addictions, 25,* 655-685.

Peele, S. (1987). The limitation of control-of-supply models for explaining and preventing alcoholism and drug addiction. *Journal of Studies on Alcohol, 48,* 61-77.

Room, R. (1976). Ambivalence as a sociological explanation: The case of cultural explanation of alcohol problems. *American Sociological Review, 41,* 1047-1065.

Sekiya, C. (1989, Spring). Asian youth and drug usage: When "just say no" becomes "just say yes." *Rice Paper* (Asian American Drug Abuse Program, Los Angeles), pp. 1-2.

Silverman, P. R. (1980). *Mutual help groups: Organization and development.* Beverly Hills, CA: Sage.

Skager, R., Fisher, D. G., & Maddahian, E. (1986). A statewide survey of drug use among California students in grades 7, 9, and 11. Sacramento, CA: Office of the Attorney General, Crime Prevention Center.

Skager, R., Frith, S. L., & Maddahian, E. (1989). *Biennial Survey of California students in grades 7, 9 and 11: Winter 1987-1988.* Sacramento, CA: Office of the Attorney General, Crime Prevention Center.

Sue, D. (1987). Use and abuse of alcohol by Asian Americans. *Journal of Psychoactive Drugs, 19,* 57-66.

Sue, S., & Morishima, J. K. (1982). *The mental health of Asian Americans.* San Francisco: Jossey-Bass.

Sue, S., Zane, N., & Ito, J. (1979). Alcohol drinking patterns among Asian and Caucasian Americans. *Journal of Cross-Cultural Psychology, 10,* 41-56.

Trimble, J. E., Padilla, A., & Bell, C. S. (Eds.). (1987). *Drug abuse among ethnic minorities* (DHHS Publication No. ADM 87-1474). Rockville, MD: National Institute on Drug Abuse.

Tucker, M. B. (1985). U.S. ethnic minorities and drug use: An assessment of the science and practice. *International Journal of the Addictions, 20,* 1021-1047.

Ullman, A. D. (1958). Sociocultural backgrounds of alcoholism. *Annals of the American Academy of Political and Social Sciences, 3,* 48-54.

U.S. Bureau of the Census. (1990). *Statistical abstract of the U.S. 1990.* Washington, DC: Government Printing Office.

U.S. Bureau of the Census. (1993). *Statistical abstract of the U.S. 1993.* Washington, DC: Government Printing Office.

U.S. Department of Health and Human Services. (1990). *Healthy people 2000: National health promotion and disease prevention objectives* (Conference ed.). Washington, DC: Government Printing Office.

Wallace, J. M., & Bachman, J. G. (1991). Explaining racial/ethnic differences in adolescent drug use: The impact of background and lifestyle. *Social Problems, 38,* 333-357.

Wilson, J. R., McClearn, G. E., & Johnson, R. C. (1978). Ethnic variations in use and effects of alcohol. *Drug and Alcohol Dependence, 3,* 147-151.

Yu, E. S. H., & Liu, W. T. (1987). Alcohol use and abuse among Chinese Americans: Epidemiologic data. *Alcohol Health and Research World, 11,* 14-17.

Yuen, S. H. L., & Johnson, R. C. (1986). *Mother-daughter comparisons in reported alcohol use.* Unpublished manuscript, University of Hawaii, Behavioral Biology Laboratory.

Zane, N., & Sasao, T., (1990). *Research on drug abuse among Asian Pacific Americans.* Unpublished manuscript, University of California, Santa Barbara.

Name Index

Subject Index

About the Editors

Gilbert J. Botvin received his Ph.D. from Columbia University in 1977 with training in both developmental and clinical psychology. After graduate school, he spent 3 years at the American Health Foundation, first as a staff psychologist and later as Director of Child Health Behavior Research. He is currently a Professor of Psychology at Cornell University Medical College with a joint appointment in the Department of Public Health and the Department of Psychiatry. He is also the Director of Cornell's Institute for Prevention Research and Director of the New York Hospital-Cornell Medical Center Smoking Cessation Service, where he has been involved in the treatment of addictive behavior. He has conducted research in child and adolescent development, adolescent health behavior, and behavioral approaches to chronic disease risk reduction, and is internationally known for his groundbreaking work in tobacco, alcohol, and drug abuse prevention. He has authored or coauthored over 100 scientific papers and chapters, and presented over 100 papers at national and international conferences. He has served as a consultant to a number of state and federal agencies in the United States, including the National Cancer Institute and the National Institute on Drug Abuse.

Mario A. Orlandi, Ph.D., M.P.H. is Chief, Division of Health Promotion Research at the American Health Foundation in New York City. In this position for more than 12 years, he has developed and evaluated a wide variety of health promotion innovations for all age groups and for settings ranging from schools and work sites to entire communities. In recent years, his research has focused on the study of cultural competence as a tool for maximizing program efficacy and for accelerating cost-effective dissemination. He serves as an advisor to various local, state, and federal health agencies, and he is active in a number of ongoing international multicultural studies including projects in Italy, Japan, and South Africa. He is a contributing editor of a number of peer-reviewed professional journals and is Series Editor of the Center for Substance Abuse Prevention (CSAP) Cultural Competence Monograph Series.

Steven Schinke, Ph.D., received his doctoral degree in social welfare from the University of Wisconsin at Madison in 1975. Subsequently, he served on the faculty of the University of Washington School of Social Work, in Seattle. He joined the faculty at Columbia University in 1986 and is currently a Professor in the School of Social Work. In that capacity, he teaches research methods courses to doctoral students. His research interests center on prevention training, with a special focus on substance abuse and minority culture adolescents. Currently, he is Principal Investigator of research studies to develop and test preventive intervention among high-risk youth. He currently serves as a consulting editor to *Addictive Behaviors, Behavioral Medicine Abstracts, Children and Youth Services Review, Journal of Adolescent Research, Journal of Family Violence, Journal of Social Service Research,* and *Research on Social Work Practice.* He has published over 170 articles on preventive interventions and skills training for adolescents.

About the Contributors

Rose Alvarado, Ph.D., is a Research Associate for the Department of Health Education at the University of Utah. Her current work entails coordinating an extensive evaluation for a Hispanic youth substance abuse prevention program. Her academic training includes a B.A. and master's degree in psychology, with an emphasis on research design and cross-cultural psychology. Her doctoral work was in the area of instructional psychology with a focus on program development and evaluation. Her work history includes extensive experience developing and coordinating social service programs in the community, including substance abuse prevention programs. Her experience has been in direct service areas such as program coordination for a substance abuse prevention program in a local school district, instruction of parenting classes, coordination of a family literacy program, and direction of job training programs. She has a particular interest in and knowledge of the Latino community and at-risk populations. She has provided extensive volunteer service to the community in a variety of capacities. She is a member of the Utah State Health Options Commission and the U.S. Civil Rights Advisory Council and is Director of the Utah Hispanic Women's Leadership Institute.

Jerald G. Bachman completed a Ph.D. in psychology at the University of Pennsylvania in 1962. Since then he has been a Program Director and Research Scientist at the University of Michigan's Institute for Social Research. He was Principal Investigator of the Youth in Transition project, and is now a Principal Investigator (along with Lloyd Johnston) of the Monitoring the

Future project. He has authored or coauthored more than 170 scientific publications. His recent work deals with drug use and other topics involving youth and young adults.

Kristin Cole, M.S., received her masters degree in social work from Columbia University. She is an Associate Research Scholar at Columbia University School of Social Work. In that capacity, she currently is involved in a National Cancer Institute study to reduce cancer risks among Native American youth in the Northeast, as well as a National Institute on Alcohol Abuse and Alcoholism (NIAAA) study to prevent alcohol abuse among Native American youth. She has contributed papers on services to families of high-risk youth, prevention services to high-risk youth, and methodological issues in conducting prevention research in ethnic/racial communities.

Shirley D. Coletti, President, Operation PAR, Inc., was the driving force behind the founding of Operation PAR. Her efforts and personal commitment have helped to develop the agency from a grass-roots organization to a large comprehensive substance abuse treatment program. Among her many honors and accomplishments are her presidential appointment to the United States Senate Caucus on International Narcotics Control and her appointment by the U.S. Health and Human Services Secretary Bowen to the National Institute of Drug Abuse (NIDA) Advisory Council. She chairs the National Education Committee of the All Babies Count, Inc. and is a member of the Child Welfare League of America Chemical Dependency Program Advisory Committee. She has served as a U.S. delegate to international drug abuse conferences on three continents and as a long-time advisor to state and national leaders regarding substance abuse issues and concerns.

R. Lorraine Collins, Ph.D., is currently a Senior Research Scientist at the Research Institute on Addictions in Buffalo, New York, and an Adjunct Research Associate Professor, Department of Psychology, State University of New York at Buffalo. She received her B.A. in psychology from McGill University and her doctorate in clinical psychology from Rutgers University. She conducted postdoctoral research in the Department of Psychology, University of Washington, and was a member of the faculty of the Department of Psychology, State University of New York at Stony Brook. Her research interests include cognitive and behavioral approaches to the conceptualization and treatment of addictive behaviors as well as ethnicity and women's issues as they relate to substance use and abuse. She has conducted research on various topics in the areas of alcohol use and smoking, and has received funding from both the National Institute on Drug Abuse (NIDA) and the National Institute on Alcohol Abuse and Alcoholism (NIAAA). She is currently a member of NIDA's National Advisory Council on Drug Abuse. Prior to that, she served as a member of NIDA's Drug Abuse Epidemiology and Prevention Research Initial Review Group (1989-1993). She is active in various professional organizations, including the Association for Advancement of Behavior Therapy and the American Psychological Association. Along with publication of numerous journal articles, she is co-editor (with K. E. Leonard and J. S. Searles) of a book entitled *Alcohol and the Family: Research and Clinical Perspectives.*

Tracy Diaz, M.A., is a Senior Project Coordinator at the Institute for Prevention Research. She has been responsible for coordinating federally funded large-scale alcohol and drug abuse prevention interventions in schools, as well as small developmental projects in housing developments, community centers, and homeless shelters, for over 5 years. She received her M.A. in general psychology from Hunter College and is currently enrolled in Columbia University's doctoral program in developmental psychology. Her research interests include women's health and development and family/child health and development, as well as tobacco, alcohol, and drug abuse prevention. She has coauthored over 14 journal articles and has conducted drug prevention training workshops and presentations nationally.

Linda Dusenbury completed her doctorate in social-developmental psychology at the University of Vermont in 1984, and spent a postdoctoral year in clinical psychology at Indiana University. She is currently an Associate Professor of Psychology in the Department of Public Health and the Department of Psychiatry at Cornell Medial College. Since the beginning of her career, her research has focused on prevention and health promotion. Her current research focuses on substance abuse prevention and competence promotion with adolescents. She has worked extensively in New York City schools, and she recently trained over 200 New York City public school teachers, guidance counselors, and administrators in substance abuse prevention techniques. As part of the Institute for Prevention Research, she also directs prevention projects for homeless youth.

María Félix-Ortiz, Ph.D., is an Assistant Professor in the Department of Psychology at University of Southren California, where she conducts research and community service. She recently finished a clinical psychology fellowship at the University of California, San Francisco, during which she conducted research and provided clinical services at Substance Abuse Services, Department of Psychiatry, at San Francisco General Hospital. She has worked clinically with a variety of populations, including HIV-infected, psychiatrically ill substance abusers and gang-affiliated Latino youth. Her research interests include the etiology and prevention of drug use and abuse, especially among Latino youth, and the development of client-led support groups as adjuncts to structured addiction treatment. She retains an interest in combining community service and research. She was named a Ford Predoctoral Fellow (1987-1991) and was given the Joseph A. Gengerelli Award for Most Distinguished Dissertation in the UCLA Department of Psychology in 1993. Her recent publications appear in the *Hispanic Journal of Behavioral Sciences* and *Journal of Personality and Social Psychology*.

Mindy Thompson Fullilove, M.D., is a graduate of Bryn Mawr College and Columbia University College of Physicians and Surgeons. She did her psychiatric residency at New York Hospital-Westchester Division and Montefiore Hospital. She is currently Associate Professor of Clinical Psychiatry and Public Health at Columbia University and Co-Director, with her husband, Dr. Robert Fullilove, of the Community Research Group at the New York State Psychiatric Institute. Before joining the faculty at Columbia, she served as Director of Multi-cultural Inquiry and Research on AIDS (MIRA), at the University of California, San Francisco and the Bayview Hunters Point Foundation. In February 1994 she was named by the Clinton administration to the Federal Task Force on AIDS Drug Development, whose mandate is to identify new approaches to help speed the search for new drugs to combat HIV/AIDS. Her recent publications have examined the role of traumatic experiences in the lives of women crack users and methods for conducting research in minority communities.

Robert E. Fullilove, Ed.D., is currently Associate Dean for Community and Minority Affairs at Columbia University's School of Public Health. He is also an Assistant Professor of Clinical Public Health and the Co-Director of the Community Research Group at the New York State Psychiatric Institute. He received his B.A. from Colgate University (1986), his M.S. from Syracuse University (1972), and his Ed.D. from Columbia University (1984). Prior to his joining the Faculty of Medicine at Columbia, he was Assistant Director of Multicultural Inquiry and Research on AIDS (MIRA), a minority research team at the University of California, San Francisco, and the Bayview Hunters Point Foundation, which was headed by his wife, Dr. Mindy Fullilove. The Fulliloves have made numerous presentations on HIV disease among people of color and have published extensively. Their research encompasses a wide range of topics, including crack cocaine use and sexually transmitted disease in the AIDS era; trauma-related disorders and their impact on sexual risk taking; and science, mathematics, and medical education for African Americans and other students of color.

Nancy A. Hepler is a Research Associate Professor in the Department of Anthropology at The University of Memphis. She is the Director of the Tennessee Alcohol and Drug Prevention Outcome Longitudinal Evaluation (TADPOLE) and Associate Director of the Tennessee Outcomes for Alcohol and Drug Services (TOADS), which evaluate the outcomes of state-funded alcohol and drug prevention and treatment programs in Tennessee. She is also Co-Project Director of the Supported Intensive System of Treatment, Empowerment and Recovery (SISTER), a nationally renowned treatment program for addicted African-American women who live in public housing. She serves on internal review groups for both the Center for Substance Abuse Treatment and the Center for Substance Abuse Prevention. As a consultant, she has provided assistance in the design and implementation of evaluations to state agencies and to local programs in many states.

Lloyd D. Johnston is Program Director and Research Scientist at the University of Michigan's Institute for Social Research. He is a social psychologist by training, and since 1975 has been a Principal Investigator of Monitoring the Future, the ongoing national surveys of drug use among American secondary school students, college students, and young adults. He is the author of more than 20 books and monographs and over 60 chapters and articles in the field of substance abuse. He has served on the National Advisory Council on Drug Abuse (1982-1986), chaired its Subcommittee on Prevention (1983-1986), consulted for many national and international organizations and foreign governments, and written and lectured extensively in the area of substance abuse. He was the recipient of the national "Pacesetter Award" in research (1982) from the National Institute on Drug Abuse and the co-recipient of the first University of Michigan Senior Research Scientist Award (1987). In 1987 he received a presidential appointment as conferee to the White House Conference for a Drug-Free America. More recently, he served on the National Commission for Drug-Free Schools. He is currently a member of the Resource Group for Goal 6 of the National Education Goals and Chair of the Technical Planning Group for Goal 6.

Denise B. Kandel is Professor of Public Health in Psychiatry at the College of Physicians and Surgeons of Columbia University, and Chief of the Epidemiology of Substance Abuse at the New York State Psychiatric Institute. Born in Paris, France, she received her Ph.D. in sociology from Columbia University. Her major research interests are in the epidemiology, natural history, risk factors, and consequences of drug use, the developmental pathways of various risk behaviors in adolescence, and the epidemiology of child psychiatric disorders. She has been following a cohort for close to 20 years from adolescence to adulthood. Currently, she is studying changing patterns of drug use as individuals age, the impact of drug use on family functioning, and the intergenerational transmission of drug use and other problem behaviors. Recent publications include "From Beer to Crack: Developmental Patterns of Involvement in Drugs," coauthored with K. Yamaguchi, in the *American Journal of Public Health,* 1993, and "Maternal Smoking During Pregnancy and Smoking by Adolescent Daughters," in the *American Journal of Public Health,* 1994.

Sehwan Kim holds a Ph.D. in public policy, with a specialty in behavioral research methods, from the University of Maryland. He is currently Director of Research and Evaluation at Operation PAR, Inc. and a member of the editorial board of the *Journal of Drug Education.* He has published extensively in the area of community-based and school-based drug abuse prevention program evaluation. During 1982-1987, he was appointed as member of the Initial Review Group of the National Institute of Drug Abuse. Currently, he serves as a professional advisory member/evaluation consultant to numerous organizations including, Quest International, State of Tennessee Prevention and Early Intervention Project (TADPOLE), Institute for Prevention Research at Cornell Medical Center, and the Pacific Institute for Research and Evaluation. He also serves as an Initial Review Group member for the Center for Substance Abuse Prevention at the U.S. Department of Health and Human Services. His main research interests are innovative evaluation designs, cultural competency in program evaluation, benefit-cost analysis of community and school based communities/populations, and prevention program development involving positive youth development and empowerment. He has also served on a number of standing grant and contract review committees of the National Institute on Alcohol Abuse and Alcoholism, the National Institute on Drug Abuse, and the Substance Abuse and Mental Health Services Administration.

Karol L. Kumpfer is a psychologist with over 20 years' experience in alcohol and drug abuse treatment and prevention research. She is currently Associate Professor of Health Education at the University of Utah, where she has conducted federally funded research for the National Institute on Drug Abuse, the National Institute on Alcohol Abuse and Alcoholism, the National Institute for Mental Health, the Office of Substance Abuse Prevention, the Department of Energy, FIPSE, and the Office of Juvenile Justice and Delinquency Prevention on family, school, and community approaches to drug prevention. A frequent conference speaker, she has coauthored a book on prevention entitled *Childhood and Chemical Abuse: Prevention and Intervention* (Ezekoye, Kumpfer, & Bukoski, 1986), as well as journal articles and monographs, including *The Strengthening Families Program* (Kumpfer, DeMarsh, & Child, 1989). She is involved in the Strengthening Families

Program, a national search for the best family programs in the country for the Office of Juvenile Justice and Delinquency Prevention, and in research on its applications to different high-risk families and youth. She is an evaluation specialist who was Co-Principal Investigator on the Center for Substance Abuse Prevention (CSAP) National Evaluation of the High Risk Youth Demonstration Program and consultant on the Pregnant and Post Partum Drug Abusing Women and Infant Grantee Program. She is currently evaluator for several CSAP High-Risk Youth and Community Youth Activity Program grants. She has coauthored a book *Measurement in Prevention* (Kumpfer, Shur, Ross, Bunnell, Librett, & Milward, 1993) on measurement instruments for prevention program evaluators.

Michael D. Newcomb, Ph.D., is Professor of Counseling Psychology and Chairperson of the Division of Counseling Psychology at the University of Southern California. He is also Research Psychologist and Co-Director of the Substance Abuse Research Center in the Psychology Department at the University of California, Los Angeles (UCLA). He received his Ph.D. in clinical psychology from UCLA and is a licensed clinical psychologist in the state of California. He is fellow in several divisions of the American Psychological Association and also in the American Psychological Society. He is Principal Investigator on several grants from the National Institute on Drug Abuse. He has published more than 150 papers and chapters and has written three books: two on drug problems—*Consequences of Adolescent Drug Use*, coauthored with P. M. Bentler (Sage), and *Drug Use in the Workplace* and a third on sexual abuse and development of women: *Sexual Abuse and Consensual Sex: Women's Developmental Patterns and Outcomes*, coauthored with G. E. Wyatt & M. H. Riederlie (Sage). He has served on several journal editorial boards, including the *Journal of Personality and Social Psychology, Archives of Sexual Behavior, Journal of Addictive Diseases*, and *Journal of Child and Adolescent Substance Abuse*. His research interests include the etiology and consequences of adolescent drug abuse; structural equation psychology; attitudes and affect related to nuclear war; and cohabitation, marriage, and divorce. He has served on several national review and advisory committees for the National Institute of Mental Health, the Office of Substance Abuse Prevention, and various research centers.

Patrick M. O'Malley is Program Director and Research Scientist in the Survey Research Center, Institute for Social Research, University of Michigan. He received his Ph.D. in psychology from the University of Michigan in 1975 and has been associated with the Monitoring the Future project since then. He has over 100 publications, most dealing with alcohol, tobacco, and illicit drug use, and related attitudes and beliefs. His research interests include causes and consequences of drug use, social epidemiology of drug use, and longitudinal survey data analysis.

Mary Ann Pentz is Associate Professor of Preventive Medicine at the University of Southern California, and directs community prevention research activities in USC's Institute of Health Promotion and Disease Prevention Research. She received her Ph.D. in clinical and school psychology at Syracuse University, and her B.A. in psychology from Hamilton College. Her research has focused almost exclusively on adolescent development and disease prevention. Specific areas of interest include adolescent stress and drug abuse prevention, the contribution of program implementer or of change agent factors and setting factors to intervention effects, and the development of research methods appropriate to large-scale prevention research trials. For almost a decade, she has evaluated the effects of school and multicomponent community program, on adolescent and parent tobacco, alcohol, and other drug use; and on community leader's behavior regarding studies that contributed to the formulation of a U.S. Senate bill intended as the basis of a new U.S. Anti-Drug Abuse Act. Most recently, she is concentrating her efforts on developing the field of prevention policy research. In addition to her faculty responsibilities, she chairs the National Institute on Drug Abuse Epidemiology and Prevention Studies section and serves on evaluation advisory boards for the Robert Wood Johnson Foundation's "Fighting Back" community drug prevention initiatives and the Office of Substance Abuse Prevention's Community Partnership grant. She is also developing a collaborative international trial, through NIDA's INVEST program, that will involve evaluating community leader communication and organization strategies for drug abuse prevention in 10 cities in the United States and Italy.

Orlando Rodriguez received his Ph.D. in sociology from Columbia University. He is Director of Fordham University's Hispanic Research Center and Professor at the University's Department of Sociology/ Anthropology. His research interests are in the areas of the etiology of problem behaviors among minority adolescents and mental health services issues relevant to Hispanics. Among his latest publications are "Integrating Mainstream and Subcultural Explanations of Drug Use Among Puerto Rican Youth," which appeared in a recent National Institute on Drug Abuse monograph, and "The Societal and Organizational Contexts of Culturally Sensitive Mental Health Services: Findings From an Evaluation of Bilingual/Bicultural Psychiatric Programs," which appeared in the *Journal of Mental Health Administration*.

Joseph E. Trimble, Ph.D. from the University of Oklahoma in 1969. He is a Professor of Psychology at Western Washington University, where he has been a faculty member since 1978. He also currently serves as a Center Scholar at the Tri-Ethnic Center for Prevention Research at Colorado State University. Throughout his 25-year career, he has focused his efforts on promoting psychological and sociocultural research with indigenous ethnic populations, especially American Indians and Alaska Natives. For the past 12 years, he has been working on drug abuse prevention research models for American Indian youth. Currently, he is collaborating on a series of studies concerning the etiology of drug abuse among American Indian youth, and the relationship between acculturative status and ethnic self-identification on drug use behavior. He has held offices in the International Association for Cross-Cultural Psychology and the American Psychological Association; he holds Fellow status in both organizations. In 1994 he received a Lifetime Distinguished Career Award from the American Psychological Associations' Division 45 for his research and dedication to cross-cultural and ethnic psychology. He has presented over 200 papers, invited addresses, and invited lectures at professional meetings, and has generated over 125 publications on cross-cultural topics in psychology. He also is the recipient of two awards from Western Washington University—the Outstanding Teacher-Scholar Award in 1985 and the Excellence in Teaching Award in 1987.

John M. Wallace, Jr., is a National Science Foundation Postdoctoral Scholar and a Research Investigator on the Monitoring the Future project at the University of Michigan's Institute for Social Research. He received his Ph.D. in sociology from the University of Michigan in 1991. His current research focuses on racial and ethnic differences in drug use, drug use among African American youth, the disproportionate availability of licit and illicit drugs in poor African American communities, and the role of religion in the prevention of adolescent problem behaviors. He has recently accepted a position as Assistant Professor at the University of Michigan's School of Social Work.

Charles Williams Jr., is Associate Professor in the Department of Anthropology at The University of Memphis. He received his Ph.D. from the University of Illinois. He has directed or been involved in research related to community health, mental health, the homeless, religion, mutual aid societies and economic development, and alcoholism. Currently, he is in the 6th year of a study sponsored by the Tennessee Department of Health, Bureau of Alcohol and Drug Abuse Services to do follow-up research with alcohol and drug clients 6 months after being released from state-supported treatment facilities throughout the state of Tennessee.